Disability and Social Theory

Disability and Social Theory

New Developments and Directions

Edited by

Dan Goodley
University of Sheffield, UK

Bill Hughes
Glasgow Caledonian University, UK

and

Lennard Davis
University of Illinois at Chicago, USA

First published 2012 by
PALGRAVE MACMILLAN

Palgrave Macmillan in the UK is an imprint of Macmillan Publishers Limited,
registered in England, company number 785998, of Houndmills, Basingstoke,
Hampshire RG21 6XS.

Palgrave Macmillan in the US is a division of St Martin's Press LLC,
175 Fifth Avenue, New York, NY 10010.

Palgrave Macmillan is the global academic imprint of the above companies
and has companies and representatives throughout the world.

Palgrave® and Macmillan® are registered trademarks in the United States,
the United Kingdom, Europe and other countries.

ISBN 978-1-349-31823-0   ISBN 978-1-137-02300-1 (eBook)
DOI 10.1057/9781137023001

This book is printed on paper suitable for recycling and made from fully
managed and sustained forest sources. Logging, pulping and manufacturing
processes are expected to conform to the environmental regulations of the
country of origin.

A catalogue record for this book is available from the British Library.

Library of Congress Cataloging-in-Publication Data
Disability and social theory : new developments and directions /
edited by Dan Goodley, Bill Hughes, Lennard Davis.
pages cm

1. People with disabilities.   2. Discrimination against people with disabilities.
3. Disabilities.   I. Goodley, Dan, 1972–   II. Hughes, Bill, 1956–   III. Davis,
Lennard J., 1949–
HV1568.D5638 2012
305.9'0801—dc23   2012012580

10   9   8   7   6   5   4   3   2   1
21 20 19 18 17 16 15 14 13 12

Transferred to Digital Printing in 2013

The editors would like to dedicate this book to the memory of the disability activist and pioneering theorist Vic Finkelstein (1938–2011). While he may have disagreed with some of the arguments in this text we are confident that he would have supported the need for debate in understanding and challenging the conditions of disablism

Table of Contents

Notes on Contributors

Theo Blackmore is the Strategic Liaison Manager for Disability Cornwall, the only pan-impairment disabled peoples' organisation in Cornwall, UK. Theo is interested in understanding inclusion, exclusion and disability, and his doctoral thesis at Exeter University – 'Half My Friends Don't See Me as Disabled: What Can Field, Capital and Habitus Reveal about Disability, Inclusion And Exclusion' – explored this. Theo occasionally lectures in disability studies at Cornwall College, and set up the Cornwall Disability Research Network to investigate issues for disabled people living in rural areas.

Rosi Braidotti is Distinguished Professor in the Humanities and Director of the Centre for the Humanities at Utrecht University, the Netherlands. Her work is strikingly significant in the areas of feminist philosophy, epistemology, post-structuralism and psychoanalysis. Her books include: *Nomadic Subjects: Embodiment and Sexual Difference in Contemporary Feminist Theory* (Columbia Univ. Press, 1994).

Fiona Kumari Campbell is Associate Professor and Deputy Head of School (Learning and Teaching Scholarship) Griffith Law School, Australia. She was Convenor, Disability Studies concentration, School of Human Services and Social Work Griffith University. Fiona has written on issues related to disability – philosophy, law, and technology. Following the successful publication of her book *Contours of Ableism* (Palgrave Macmillan, 2009), she is working on two books: *The Unveiling of (Dis)ability: Essays on Silence, Voice and Imprints* and *Crippin' the Law: Jurisprudential Narratives of Impairment*.

Tsitsi Chataika is a postdoctoral research fellow at Stellenbosch University, South Africa. Her research aims to explore possible pathways of including disabled people in the national development agenda. She is also interested in ways of building communities of trust between the Global South and the Global North researchers and how development partners can build communities of trust. She has published in the area including disability and development, and inclusive education.

Lennard Davis is Distinguished Professor of English, Disability and Human Development, and Medical Education at the University of Illinois at Chicago, US. His work in disability studies has focused on issues around identity, normality and theory. His most recent books include *Obsession: A History* (University of Chicago Press, 2008) and *Go Ask Your Father* (Random House, 2009).

Carolyn Frohmader is the Executive Director of Women With Disabilities Australia (WWDA). Under Frohmader's leadership, WWDA has received a number of prestigious awards for its groundbreaking work including the National Human Rights Award. Carolyn has a master's degree from Flinders University where she won the inaugural Michael Crotty Award for an outstanding contribution in Primary Health Care. In 2009, in recognition of her human rights work, she was inducted into the Tasmanian Women's Honour Roll, joining her late mother Wendy, who was posthumously inducted into the Roll in 2008 for services to education.

Anita Ghai is Associate Professor, Department of Psychology, Jesus and Mary College, University of Delhi, India and a disability activist in the areas of education, health, sexuality and gender. Currently she is Teenmurti Fellow at Nehru Memorial Museum Library and President of the Indian Association for Women's Studies. She is on the editorial board of *Disability and Society, Disability Studies Quarterly* and *Scandinavian Journal of Disability.* Her second book was *(Dis) Embodied Form: Issues of Disabled Women* (Haranand Publications, 2003).

Dan Goodley is Professor of Disability Studies and Education at the University of Sheffield, UK. His research and teaching aim to shake up dominant myths in psychology as well as contribute, in some small way, to the development of critical disability studies theories that understand and eradicate disablism. His recent publications include *Disability Studies: An Interdisciplinary Introduction* (Sage, 2011).

Shaun Grech is Research Associate at the Research Institute for Health and Social Change (RIHSC), Manchester Metropolitan University (MMU), UK. His interdisciplinary research focuses on disability, poverty and international development. Other areas of interest include post/neo-colonial approaches to the study of disability across cultures, decolonising research methodologies and the application of critical disability studies to the majority world. He has published in well-established journals, contributed to edited collections, and is co-editor of *Inclusive Communities: A Reader* (Sense Publishers, 2012). Shaun also established and organises the annual international conference series 'Disability and the Majority World', currently hosted at MMU. E-mail: S.Grech@mmu.ac.uk.

Mark Haydon-Laurelut is a lecturer in Psychology at the University of Portsmouth, UK and is a practising Systemic Psychotherapist. His work aims at challenging disablement in the lives of people with intellectual disabilities through teaching, research and systemic practice.

Stephen Lee Hodgkins is Director of Disability LIB, London, UK, an informal network of disabled peoples' organisations which challenges disablism, promotes inclusion and embraces diversity. Stephen has interests in the inclusion movement, community activism and disabled people's politics and culture. He lectures in critical psychology and disability studies at the University of Northampton where he recently completed a Ph.D. titled 'Discoursing Disability: The Personal and Political Positioning of Disabled

People', an abridged version of which was published in *Disabilities: Insights From Across Fields and Around the World* (Praeger, 2009).

Bill Hughes is Professor of Sociology and the Dean of the School of Law and Social Sciences at Glasgow Caledonian University, Scotland, and is a sociologist 'to trade'. His research interests include disability and impairment, social theory and the body. He is co-author of *The Body, Culture and Society: An Introduction* (Open University Press, 2000). He has published in the journals *Sociology* and *Body and Society* and is a regular contributor to and a member of the Editorial Board of *Disability and Society*.

Rebecca Lawthom is Associate Professor in Community Practice at Manchester Metropolitan University, UK. Her research and teaching focus on the connections of feminist and community psychologies with a particular interest in issues of marginalisation and discrimination. Her recent publications include *Critical Community Psychology: Critical Action and Social Change* (BPSTextbooks, 2011, with Mark Burton, Paul Duckett and Asiya Siddiquee).

Rebecca Mallett is Senior Lecturer in Disability Studies and allied to the Cultural, Communication and Computing Research Institute (C_3RI) at Sheffield Hallam University, UK. Her main areas of research include 'disability' in popular culture, the constitution and regulation of interpretative strategies within cultural disability studies and, more recently, the commodification of impairment.

Eimir McGrath is a psychotherapist and a dance practitioner, working with children and adults with physical and intellectual disabilities. She is also a trainer, lecturer and workshop facilitator, specialising in play therapy and disability. Her interest in dance as a means of integration came about through her work in education, where dance often provided a common ground in bringing diverse groups together. McGrath is completing a doctorate in dance and disability research at London Metropolitan University, England.

Helen Meekosha is Associate Professor in the School of Social Work, University of New South Wales, Sydney, Australia. Her research interests cross boundaries of race, ethnicity, disability and gender, and she has recently become interested in developing theories of disability that include those who live in the Global South or the majority world. In 1996 she was instrumental in establishing The Social Relations of Disability Research Network, a group of Australian interdisciplinary scholars, which resulted in the establishment of the Disability Studies and Research Centre at UNSW in 2008. She has been active in the disability movement for nearly 30 years and has been closely involved with Women With Disabilities Australia, both as President and as a Board member since its inception.

Rod Michalko teaches disability studies at the Ontario Institute for Studies in Education (OISE), University of Toronto. His current research centres on disability studies' conception of disability and its subsequent requirement of non-disability. He has written four books, including *The Difference that Disability Makes* (Temple, 2002) and most recently co-edited with Tanya Titchkosky, *Rethinking Normalcy: A Disability Studies Reader* (2009).

Karl Nunkoosing is Principal Lecturer at the Department of Psychology, University of Portsmouth, UK. He teaches the social construction of disability, qualitative methods and critical discourse analysis and the 'dark stuff'. His research includes the experiences of fathers of disabled sons and daughters, discourse of intellectual disability and the academic attainments of black and ethnic minority students in higher education. He is also interested in stories and narratives, gender, culture and in the serious business of playfulness.

James Overboe is Associate Professor in Sociology at Wilfrid Laurier University. His research affirms life expressed, particularly aspects associated with a pre-individual or impersonal registry especially within the context of disability studies. Recent publications include 'Affirming an Impersonal Life: A Different Register for Disability Studies', in 'Deleuze, Disability, and Difference', Special Issue of *Journal of Literary and Cultural Disability Studies* (2009).

Donna Reeve is Honorary Research Fellow with the Centre for Disability Research (CeDR) and Applied Social Science at Lancaster University. Her research and writing interrogates the phenomenon of psycho-emotional disablism and attempts to unpack the interconnections between disablism, impairment, identity and culture.

Griet Roets is a postdoctoral researcher affiliated to the FWO and based at the Department of Social Welfare Studies, Ghent University, Belgium. Her doctorate is in educational sciences. Her research interests are critical disability studies, poverty, gender, critical social work, and narrative and ethnographic research.

Katherine Runswick-Cole is Research Fellow in Disability Studies and Psychology at Manchester Metropolitan University, UK. Her research and publications focus on disability, childhood and family from a critical disability studies perspective. She has just finished working on an Economic and Social Research Council funded project titled 'Does Every Child Matter Post-Blair? The Interconnections of Disabled Childhoods'.

Tanya Titchkosky is Associate Professor of an interpretive sociological ilk at the Ontario Institute for Studies in Education (OISE) of the University of Toronto, Canada. Her current research examines conceptions of the (anti)human that are underscored, yet overlooked, by various institutionalized attempts to address disability and other social differences. Her most recent books include, *The Question of Access: Disability, Space, Meaning* (UTP, 2011) and *Rethinking Normalcy: A Disability Studies Reader* (2009) co-edited with Rod Michalko.

1
Introducing Disability and Social Theory

Dan Goodley, Bill Hughes and Lennard Davis

Introduction

Theorising disability lies at the heart of many recent social scientific engagements with the body, subjectivity, culture and society. Disability studies have developed across, through and with disciplines of the social sciences and humanities. The extent to which disability illuminates and puts into practice social theory and, moreover, the potential of social theory to add to our understandings of disability are key themes of this book. This text aims to further examine social theory and disability as resources for thought, action and activism.

Social theories of disability have been around for decades, with more critical approaches emerging around 40 years ago. The awareness of disability theory continues to lag behind that of other transformative arenas such as feminism, queer theory and postcolonialism. To some degree, disability theory has not had the sweep and global interest of these other areas due to the stigma that disability still carries, despite years of legislation and struggle. It still is not fashionable to be disabled. As a consequence, disability politics have been virtually ignored not only by dominant institutions of society but also by other politicised arenas. The disabled people's movement, while now global in scale and reach, continues to push for some of the most basic rights to education, life and health. At the time of writing, *The United Nations's Convention on the Rights of Persons with Disabilities* is still being ratified (or not) by some nations of the world. Disability studies continue to be slighted in many university courses and disability theory is often absent from readers on social theory. Our aim, as editors of this book, was to invite contributors from a broad range of social sciences and ask them to inject their chosen theoretical perspectives into disability studies. This is not to say that there have not already been many exciting theoretical developments throughout the history of disability studies. Many of our heroines and heroes in disability studies have long pushed for social theories that respond to the ambitions of disabled people and understand and challenge the conditions of disablism.

That said, at times, some scholars who were responsible for the early writings in disability studies have questioned the relevance and application of recent theoretical work (e.g. Oliver, 2009). Their concerns appear to centre on the dangers seemingly inherent in theoretical work, namely, obfuscation, over-abstraction and 'extravagant flights of academic fancy' (Barnes and Mercer, 2003: 83). Such criticisms of contemporary theory ignore the fact that even the early writings of disability studies necessarily drew upon theoretical ideas to enhance their potency. In Britain, for example, neo-Marxist theories were key to the development of the materialist social model of disability. Those of us who have had the pleasure of reading Marx and Engels will recall the challenges and, at times, difficulties of deciphering the key tenets of their arguments. The hard work was worth it, though, when we were able to view the analytical possibilities of employing such theories to probe the conditions of disablement (e.g. Oliver, 1990). It therefore seems contradictory for some of these scholars to reject the style of contemporary theoretical work (even if they are ideologically opposed to it) when it was precisely the use of their own preferred elliptical and even cryptic social theories that allowed them to develop understandings of the material, political and historical foundations of the exclusion of disabled people that, consequently, gave birth to the arena of disability studies.

We should, therefore, not be afraid of the inherent tendency of theory to challenge our thinking through complex and difficult prose. Instead, our concern should be whether or not social theory *enhances* our understandings of disability, culture and society. We should demand theory to provide us with ideas, concepts and resources that can be used in scholarly, professional, political and personal capacities. We should allow ourselves to be courted by theory, perhaps seduced, though ever mindful of the political origins of many people's engagement with disability studies in the first place. Disability studies have developed in some national contexts in ways that appear to be more inviting to the deployment of theory. Both Thomas (2007) and Goodley (2011a) have argued that, in comparison with British disability studies, North American, Canadian, Australian and Nordic disability studies boast a more interdisciplinary and theory-friendly approach to the study of disability. The editors of this collection have aimed to capture a number of theoretical interventions that are committed to the politics of disability in the hope that theory and praxis can be seen as interrelated. We know that social theory can change everyday norms, social policies, institutional arrangements, professional acts, family practices and personal values, because when social theory works at its best it demands us to reconsider the assumptions, discourses and taken-for-granted ideologies that undergird the exclusion of some people and the accentuation of the social roles of others. Perhaps, following Braidotti (2003), social theory allows us to identify and then deconstruct the tendency of contemporary society to uphold the life-worlds of 'the same' over those of 'many others'.

Disability studies, particularly in Britain, have tended to occupy a strong disciplinary base in sociology and social policy, often, though not exclusively, with a focus on materialist, neo-Marxist and structuralist perspectives (Barnes, Barton and Oliver, 2002; Barnes and Mercer, 2003). However, recent texts have deliberately blurred disciplinary walls and national boundaries in order to assess the material, cultural and psychological features of living as a disabled person in an exclusionary society (Hales, 1996; Albrecht, Seelman and Bury, 2003; Swain et al., 2004; Swain, French and Cameron, 2003; Shakespeare, 2006). Increasingly there has been work on the intersections of disability with other identity categories and multiple locations of marginalisation and resistance associated with feminism, critical race, queer and class analyses (Morris, 1996; Thomas, 1999; Davis, 1997; Kristiansen and Traustadóttir, 2004; Ghai, 2006; Sherry, 2004, 2007; Linton, 2005). There is no doubt that disability studies are branching out in many different exciting theoretical directions encompassing, for examples, post-structuralism (Corker and French, 1999; Corker and Shakespeare, 2002; Tremain, 2005), psychoanalysis (Olkin, 1999; Marks, 1999; Goodley, 2011b), medical sociology (Thomas, 2007) and critical psychology (Watermeyer et al., 2006; Goodley, 2011a). North American and Canadian disability studies have merged disciplines, with social scientists forming close alliances with the humanities (Snyder, Brueggemann and Garland-Thomson, 2002; Devlieger, Rusch and Pfeiffer, 2003; Michalko, 2002; Titchkosky, 2003; Snyder and Mitchell, 2006). It is important to acknowledge that debates about inclusive education have been heightened through an engagement with disability discourse (Gabel, 2005; Danforth and Gabel, 2007; Barton and Armstrong, 2007). Dominant ideas from powerful disciplines such as physiotherapy and psychology have been destabilised through importing a disability studies agenda (Swain and French, 1999; Goodley and Lawthom, 2005). Indeed, the intersectional character of disability is one of a number of reasons why we conceptualise the contemporary state of the field as *critical* disability studies. Critical disability studies start with disability but never end with it: disability is *the* space from which to think through a host of political, theoretical and practical issues that are relevant to all (Goodley, 2011a). The emergence of a critical approach to the analysis of disability may be put down to a number of developments in the 'noughties' (Meekosha and Shuttleworth, 2009). Perhaps, most significantly, critical disability studies is characterised by what Thomas (2007) defines as the *trans-disciplinary potential* to break down boundaries between disciplines, to speak across national and regional borders and to take the responsibilities of *social* theory seriously to reinvigorate disability studies critically. Such boundary-breaking allows different disciplines to speak to and with one another through theoretical language around disability. In effect, disability studies works best when it forms bridges between disciplines. As Shakespeare (2010) argues, disability studies will lose its radical potential to subvert, disrupt and deconstruct were it to collapse into a discipline in its own right.

This book aims to provide a sustained and coherent analysis of critical disability studies in relation to a host of disciplines and emerging theories, including perspectives from psychology, psychoanalysis, education, social and critical pedagogy, community work, sociology, philosophy, geography, critical race, development and women's studies. The contributors to this book each come with their own passionate interests in social theory. Behind all of their contributions is a shared opposition to the conditions of disablism and ableism that continue to marginalise disabled people from the everyday realities of social life. This book draws on a host of social theory and associated concepts and claims. We have supplemented the application of theory that you will find in each chapter with a glossary at the end of the book that draws out and summaries key concepts.

Theory should do some things in the social world: enhance our awareness of inequality and, wherever possible, permit new ways of thinking affirmatively about disability. Theory can shift our focus away from the perceived pathologies of disabled people on to the deficiencies of a disabling society and an abliest culture. We agree with Margrit Shildrick when she argues that 'it is crucial that non-disabled people need to interrogate their own cultural psycho-social location as non-disabled' (Shildrick, 2009: 9). A strong theme of this text, then, is to explore theoretical ideas and concepts that may be used by disabled people and 'the non-disabled' in order for both groups to interrogate and subvert conditions of exclusion. Disability is therefore not a stigmatising embodiment of an individual but a social portal that leads to an investigation of exclusionary practices in society at large.

This book builds on previous efforts that have brought together disparate theoretical writings with the shared aim of theorising disability (Barton, 2001; Corker and Shakespeare, 2002; Davis, 2002, 2006b; Barnes and Mercer, 2003; Swain et al., 2004). Following Meekosha and Shuttleworth (2009) and Shildrick (2009) this text contributes to the development of critical disability studies theory (Davis, 2006a; McRuer, 2003) where disability links together other identities as a moment of reflection that Davis (2002, 2006b) calls *dismodernism,* and impairment and disability are interrogated as phenomena enacted at the levels of the psyche, culture and society. Critical disability studies recognise the complexity of disability's intersections with poverty, gender, age, ethnicity, sexuality and national location. In the current climate of economic downturn and recession we clearly need sophisticated social theories that allow us to make sense of – and challenge – complex conditions of oppression and marginalisation.

Summarising the book

Part I of the book, 'Cultures', considers the cultural imaginaries and semiotic constructions that exist around disability. These chapters share the aim of reconceptualising disabled bodies-and-minds as social sites of power, language, discourse and action. Disability is not only culturally mediated but is constituted through culture. Hence, cultures of modernity gave rise to versions of disability and ability through which the contemporary position of disability is ontologically felt and epistemologically rooted. In addition, if we accept that we are living in an era characterised by the postmodernisation of life itself (Hardt and Negri, 2000), then what possibilities for resistance and change are permitted for cultural members? Does the disparate nature of knowledge and discourse allow disabled people to challenge grand narratives of science and progress that originally marked them as lacking, deficient, repugnant and uncivilised? This part of the book also considers the kinds of cultures that we might analyse. These include cultures of disablism; cultures premised on the myth of ableism; disability cultures that have emerged through the agitations of disabled people as alternatives to disablism and ableism. We are also encouraged to consider the ways in which these varying cultures are reliant upon one another. Disability culture is a necessary response to disablism. Disablism emerges as a consequence of the prominence of ableist worldviews. Cultures also infect one another. Questions are raised about the extent to which disability culture is hijacked by, for example, nation states whose constitutions are based upon a host of disablist ideas. Disability culture might, perhaps unknowingly, appropriate some of the standards of ableism – such as autonomy, control, independence – that lead to the exclusion of some disabled people who are unable to match up to these ableist ideals.

In Chapter 2, Bill Hughes draws on the work of Norbert Elias to propose that the treatment of disabled people in the modern period is a barbaric sideshow in the long march of the 'civilising process'. The 'personality structure' of non-disability in modernity transforms its own ontological precariousness into aversion for and disposal of disability. The negative response to biological and intellectual difference in modernity is strongly influenced by the tendency embedded in the 'civilising process' to incrementally deride the value of physical and intellectual difference and promote a sanitised norm of human behaviour and appearance. The social policy response to disability in the modern period cannot be separated from the emotional aversion to impairment characteristic of non-disabled hegemony. Hughes utilises Elias's concepts of *psychogenesis* and *sociogenesis* to explain that the story of disability in modernity is one that develops towards the social and ontological invalidation of disabled people's lives.

Chapter 3, by Rebecca Mallett and Katherine Runswick Cole, addresses autism as a cultural phenomenon through which they aim to understand better the ways in which 'impairment' is packaged and consumed within academia. In this chapter they are interested in approaching autism *critically*. They seek to understand the cultural contexts in which autism is made present and think through the associated implications. By positioning academia as part of contemporary consumer culture, they borrow from Marxist-inspired theories to conceptualise the processes by which seemingly the most enigmatic of conditions have become produced, traded and consumed within the social sciences. They discuss the role of 'desire' and use the concept of commodity fetishism to explore what we buy (into) when autism is purchased. Through this theorising, they end by arguing that the persistent presence of autism as a largely unproblematised entity within contexts such as academia, and within the study of disability in particular, works to jeopardise the emancipation of disabled people.

In Chapter 4, Shaun Grech moves the analysis of culture up a notch, by examining the global reach of disability studies. This chapter is inspired by post-structuralism as well as Latin American writings on coloniality and neocolonialism to explore and discuss critically some of the gaps left wide open in attempting to articulate a critical debate around disability in the 'majority world'. The chapter takes on the call to decolonise the methodologies of disability studies in order to constitute a new theoretical space: critical global disability studies. While pre-empting some of the debates that are explored in Part IV of the book, Grech draws attention to the nuanced ways in which disability and disablism emerge in specific Global South contexts. His analysis considers the varying ways in which disability is defined across and within cultures; the dangers of homogenising the disability experience as one ultimately of oppression; the recognition of hybrid spaces and lives that emerge in poor countries in responses to coloniality; the very 'real' effects of impairment and bodies of pain and the importance of faith and religion in some cultural locations. The chapter warns against a critical disability studies that remains located in, and then is exported from, a Western European and North American register.

In Chapter 5, Theo Blackmore and Stephen Lee Hodgkins use ideas from Michel Foucault and Pierre Bourdieu to explore the rise of the British disabled people's movement, the development of disabled people's organisations (DPOs) and, as they suggest, their recent colonisation by government and service agendas. Such an analysis is crucial if we are to theorise disability culture in what might be seen as a post-new social movement period of history. They ask: to what extent have the radical discourses of disability politics become part of everyday currency and discourse in welfare, educational and community settings? Writing as activists and members of DPOs they consider the ways in which disability politics at risk of moving from the radicalisation of new social movements to new forms of organisation that are more in tune with governmental and professionalised concerns. Through employing notions of power and resistance (from Foucault) and capital, field and habitus (adapted from Bourdieu), they identify opportunities and challenges for DPOs. These are critically considered in terms of the implications for the project of impairment-management, inclusion and the preservation of the cultures of disabled bodies, minds and identities.

In Part II of the book, 'Bodies', we develop further recent analyses that have challenged a previous tendency for somatophobia (fear of body) in disability studies writings. Our analysis of bodies considers their place in the world. As Margrit Shildrick (2009: 2) puts it: living in the disabled body lays bare the psycho-social imaginary that sustains modernist understandings of what it is to be a subject. Disabled bodies are often viewed as disrupting what it means to be a natural/ normal body. The body has always occupied a platform of debate in disability studies. For some, disability studies have failed to engage with the realities of impairment (Shakespeare, 2006). For others, disability studies has not gone far enough in recognising the cultural formations of impairment (Tremain, 2005). While other scholars have inserted the physicality of the brain and body into a dynamic relational model of individual and society (Traustadóttir, 2004), in this part of the book the body emerges as a complex site for the (re)constitution of culture, technology, performance and of life itself. Never simply biological, nor a cultural entity, the body raises more questions than it answers.

Chapter 6 permits Donna Reeve to revisit Donna Haraway's *A Cyborg Manifesto* and to ask: what can the cyborg offer disability studies? Opinions in disability studies are currently divided; some argue that cyborg theory cannot offer solutions for the material disadvantage faced by disabled people in society, others see the cyborg as providing a way of understanding the lack of a fixed boundary between disabled and non-disabled people. As well as presenting these debates, the chapter also considers other ways of using cyborg theory to make sense of the lived experience of impaired people who have intimate relationships with technology, for example, people with prosthetics, implants or who use assistive devices such as wheelchairs. After presenting a summary of Haraway's key work, Reeve looks at the *lived experience* of impaired cyborgs and then briefly touches on *cultural* representations of disability and cyborgs within science fiction. Finally, she discusses the notion of the iCrip – a term she has coined to represent new ways of being which are (non)disabled and (ab)normal.

In Chapter 7, Jim Overboe locates and examines the impaired body in the 'inhuman register'. He notes that since the 1960s, with the advent of identity politics, marginalised groups stake out their claim of legitimacy under the rubric of citizenship. Disability activism and by extension disability studies has followed feminism, queer movements and racialised people in adopting this method of social change. Yet, he suggests, this model of self-actualised individuals within a group membership with its reliance upon liberalism to some degree disavows impairments that coexist with the disabled identity. Overboe is interested in reclaiming the 'vivacity of our impairments' while being mindful of the dangers of the seductive lure of liberalism that denigrates those with impairments. Drawing on the theoretical works of Gilles Deleuze, Felix Guattari and Giorgio Agamben allows us, he argues, to shift our thinking away from the personal registry associated with humanism (and liberalism) to the impersonal registry associated with the inhuman (which affirms impairment). Through an analysis of pain, crippled life and the scandal of impairment, he argues that these impersonal singularities of impairment can affirm impairment because they break in, thieve, steal away and cause havoc in the normative human register and, ultimately, express life in productive ways. The point of this chapter is to illumine how impersonal singularities of the inhuman actually affirm impairments and thus lead to a fuller life expressed.

In Chapter 8, Tanya Titchkosky and Rod Michalko question the 'facticity' of the 'problem-of-disability'. They make use of a phenomenology-based disability studies approach in order to conceive of the oft-used, over-deterministic and under-theorised frame 'disability is a problem in need of a solution' as itself a solution to some implicit problem. Drawing on the work of theorists such Edmund Husserl and Maurice Merleau-Ponty permits them to ask, what sort of a problem do contemporary times need disability to be? And, what is the meaning of human embodiment that grounds the unquestioned status of disability as a problem? They further draw out these issues by conducting an exploration of how the phenomenon of disability-as-problem composes university life while teasing out how the language of the problem reflects the educational world views that arise through the lived bodies that we are. They note that disability may participate in normalcy, but it can never be normal let alone be valuable, enjoyable or necessary. In the doing of this phenomenological form of description, they offer a reflection regarding what a phenomenological approach does in order to do what it does and to say what it says and then show this at work in the university milieu. The phenomenological subjectivity is exposed as a possible space to think between disability and ability.

In Chapter 9 Eimir McGrath examines the disabled dancing body. Firstly, she considers the place of the disabled body in relation to Western theatre dance and the 'legitimate' dancing body. Secondly, the disruption of this understanding of a legitimate dancing body is examined, by tracing the changes that took place during the twentieth century which eventually facilitated the inclusion of differently abled bodies within professional dance. Thirdly, she argues that when the disabled dancing body is viewed through the lens of contemporary attachment theory, then this allows us to view dance as part of a process that facilities change. This approach, she suggests, allows us to view dancers of differing corporealities as bringing about a state of empathic attunement, where the humanity of the dancer is foremost and corporeal difference becomes merely an element of that dancer's embodied presence.

In Part III of the book, 'Subjectivities', we consider in more detail the psychological, psychical and ontological questions of disability. Appropriating Shildrick (2009: 89) one of the tasks of critical disability studies is to retrace the constitution of the normative subject and to reclaim other modes of being and/or becoming. There will be obvious overlap in this part with others – for example 'Cultures' and 'Bodies' – because any discussion of subjectivity cannot be divorced from wider sociocultural and political factors nor issues of embodiment. In this part of the book we stay with a broad notion of subjectivity to consider how the 'inner self' might be understood as a relational product (that is a constructionist phenomenon) rather than a simplified individualised entity held in the heads of people (as advocated by the constructivist tradition) (Corcoran, 2009). As Shildrick (2009: 33) has noted, disability is not so much strange as all too familiar. We (whoever 'we' are) already know disabled bodies because they come to embody psychical fantasies of dependency/nurture that are part of the collective unconscious of the body politic. Disability, therefore, speaks of a 'trans-historical ontological anxiety operating at a psychic level' (Shildrick, 2009: 52): 'it is as though each one knows, but cannot acknowledge, that the disabled other is a difference within, rather than external to, the self' (Shildrick, 2009: 58). Disability is a particular enunciation of specific identifications, and revealing the assumptions behind how we take notice of the appearance of embodiment through our reading and writing thus allows us to grapple with the meaning of disability (Titchkosky, 2009: 34). This part of the book deals with the ontology of disablism and disability: the subjective be/comings and goings that emerge around disability.

Chapter 10, by Griet Roets and Rosi Braidotti, sets out a version of disability studies as a project of affirmative politics. While their focus is fundamentally directed on the ways in which we do and can view subjectivity as it relates to disability. Their focus is on the lives of people with the label of intellectual disabilities (and their work as self-advocates) whom they represent as affirmative activists that challenge a dominant view of impairment-as-disability as mourning and melancholia. Inspired by Deleuze and Guattari they draw on their approach of nomadology in order to explore (i) notions of ontology and epistemology as they relate to disability, (ii) an expansion of our understanding of subjectivity as both embodied and non-dualistic, and (iii) a methodology that involves another way of forming subjectivity as transversal connections or assemblages with multiple others which makes our praxis nomadic.

Chapter 11, by Dan Goodley, aims to account for the subjectivities of the 'non-disabled' through the theories of the French psychoanalyst Jacques Lacan and the account of one of Britain's most famous disability activists Paul Hunt. Goodley argues that the non-disabled or ableist individual and collective unconscious produce precarious subjectivities which inevitably lead to a relationship of disavowal with disability. Using Lacan's phases of real, imaginary and symbolic, it is suggested that the non-disabled psyche becomes haunted but also fascinated by the fragmented nature of disability and the non-disabled failure to match up to ableist ideals of autonomy and mastery. Faced with such realities, a disablist subjectivity finds fault and fascination with disability. The lessons from Lacan are further illuminated through the work of Paul Hunt's classic 1966 text *A Critical Condition* which might be read as a politicised and psychoanalytic reading of disabling culture.

In Chapter 12, Karl Nunkoosing and Mark Haydon-Laurelut draw upon insights from Erving Goffman and Michel Foucault to make sense of some aspects of the lives of men and women with intellectual disabilities who live in residential group homes. They demonstrate how the contemporary group home is still engaged in the same project of the total institution that Goffman wrote about in the 1960s despite more recent changes in its composition. The subjectivities of both the staff and the intellectually disabled men and women they support are constructed in the production-consumption of these discourses and associated 'technologies'; people have to learn and be taught how to be intellectually disabled and how to be a worker in services for people with intellectual disabilities. By analysing the referrals written by group home workers, it is demonstrated that the subject of the referral is constructed as mentally suspect or bad, his/her reasoning is doubtful or that he or she is in need of surveillance-therapy-treatment.

In Chapter 13, Fiona Kumari Campbell stalks ableism through an analysis of the ways in which dis/abled bodies and minds – their subjectivities – are culturally and often quite literally fused together. She defines ableism as a network of beliefs, processes and practices that produces a particular kind of self and body (the corporeal standard) that is projected as the perfect, species-typical and therefore essential and fully human. Disability then is cast as a subjectively diminished state of being human. Ableism denotes the meaning of a healthy body, a normal mind, how quickly we should think and the kinds of emotions that are okay to express. She notes that we all live and breathe ableist logic, our bodies and minds daily become aesthetic sculptures for the projection of how we wish to be known in our attempt to exercise competency, sexiness, wholeness and an atomistic existence. It is harder to find the language and space to examine the implications of a failure to meet the standard or any ambivalence we might have about the grounds of the perfectibility project. First, she outlines an approach to expressing ableism (its theoretical features and character), and second, provides an example of how ableism works globally in the knowledge production of disability. Finally, she discusses the possibility of disabled people turning their backs on emulating abledness as a strategy for ontological and theoretical disengagement.

Part IV of the book, 'Communities', asks questions about the place of critical disability studies theory. Disability emerges in different ways in particular institutional, national and supranational spaces (Lawthom, 2010). *The United Nations's Convention on the Rights of Persons with Disabilities* and the World Health Organisation's (2001) *International Classification of Functioning, Disability and Health* are just two examples of the supranational location of disability that seeks to speak of disability across nations, cultures and economies. While these developments are crucial, questions are also raised about the potential for universal conceptions writing over more localised experiences and dynamics of disability. Furthermore, as Stone (1999), Gabel and Danforth (2008) and Meekosha (2008) have demonstrated, there are real dangers of erasing the accounts of disability emerging in poor, Global South nations if disability studies theory is written from the rich metropolises of the Global North. With these critical ideas in mind we consider the community location of disability.

Rebecca Lawthom (with Tsitsi Chataika) tackles a theorisation of community head on in Chapter 14. The theoretical framework of communities of practice developed by Jean Lave and Etienne Wenger is outlined. This approach, which has been largely ignored by disability studies, is considered in terms of its historical origins and its contemporary usage. Next this approach is considered alongside the work of a British organisation Breakthrough UK Ltd (run largely by and for disabled people) that aims to promote the independent living and employment opportunities of disabled people. Identity ownership and contestation has been a key issue for the disabled people's movement and for those who stand inside and outside it. Unpacking how disabled people may come to understand and situate their own identity and that of others is key to this identity project and the development of inclusive communities.

Chapter 15, by Tsitsi Chataika, provides a postcolonial critique of disability studies research of the Global North. Her chapter unpacks the political struggle in the disability, development and postcolonial discourses. The struggle, she suggests, is about challenging oppression, voicelessness, stereotyping, undermining, neocolonisation, postcolonisation, 'them and us' and bridging the gap between Global North (rich income, traditionally known as 'developed' countries) and Global South (low income so termed 'developing' countries) spaces in the disability and development research agenda. She seeks to bring together debates around disability and development and how they intertwine with postcolonialism. The intention of the chapter is to create a platform that is accessible to the usually marginalised Global South research communities by enabling them to make use of indigenous knowledge and building communities of trust with Global North comrades in ways that enrich a critical postcolonial disability studies research agenda.

Chapter 16 is written by Anita Ghai in the context of India. She begins by exploring the relationship between disability and karma which, she suggests, permits a sense of desolation and hope to be entertained together. This hybridisation of disability discourses is taken further in her analysis of gender and disability in the postcolonial context. She argues that an assimilation of postcolonial thinking into the critical disability studies enriches our understandings. Briefly, she examines the social framing and ideological work of disabled characters in a recent film *Black*. Using this film she underscores the dialectic between coloniser (read 'able subject') and colonised (read 'disabled subject'). Although cinema resists simple 'answers' to the question of how gender intersects with disability in the postcolonial world, films also offer stimulating instances of the transgressive potential of 'different' bodies.

In Chapter 17, Carolyn Fromader and Helen Meekosha argue that a precondition of women with disabilities achieving equalities experienced by their non-disabled peers is recognition and respect by wider society. Lack of recognition constitutes a form of harm. Following the work of Axel Honneth, they suggest that denial of recognition is a form of disrespect that can be injurious to women with disabilities, particularly in relation to their positive understandings of themselves. Mindful of the tensions that exist in relation to the lack of recognition of disabled women from the Global South, they demonstrate how disabled women experience all forms of disrespect in their daily lives by examining three issues: violence, sterilisation and the denial and shame attached to their perceived inability to parent. Using their own organisation, Women with Disabilities Australia (WWDA), as a case study, they look at the challenges and successes over the past two decades that have confronted the organisation and its members in trying to bring about change for women with disabilities. The lives and experiences of women with disabilities have been hidden from history and we are only just emerging as political actors in the struggle for human rights.

Our final chapter, Chapter 18, makes a case for the celebration of social theory and its contribution to the development of critical disability studies. In bringing together the contributors represented in this text our ambition was always to energise our thinking around the complexities of disability. We therefore hope that the ensuing critical disability studies analyses demonstrate the ways in which theory can bring to life this complexity in ways that further enable us all to challenge the often contradictory and always moving conditions of disablism.

References

Albrecht, G., Seelman, K. and Bury, M. (2003). *Handbook of Disability Studies*. New York: Sage.

Barnes, C., Barton, L. and Oliver, M. (eds) (2002). *Disability Studies Today*. Cambridge: Polity Press.

Barnes, C. and Mercer, G. (2003). *Disability: Key Concepts*. Cambridge: Polity Press.

Barton, L. (2001). *Disability, Politics and the Struggle for Change*. London: David Fulton.

Barton, L. and Armstrong, F. (eds) (2007). *Policy, Experience and Change: Cross-Cultural Reflections on Inclusive Education*. London: Springer.

Braidotti, R. (2003). 'Becoming Woman: Or Sexual Difference Revisited'. *Theory, Culture & Society*, 20 (3), 43–64.

Corcoran, T. (2009). 'Smiling at the Sky: Ontology's Hypnotic Lure'. Paper presented to Critical Community and Disability Studies Research Group Seminar Series, 3 February, in Manchester Metropolitan University, UK.

Corker, M. and French, S. (1999). *Disability Discourse*. Buckingham/Philadelphia: Open University Press.

Corker, M. and Shakespeare, T. (2002). *Disability/Postmodernity: Embodying Disability Theory*. London/New York: Continuum.

Danforth, S. and Gabel, S. (2007). *Vital Questions Facing Disability Studies in Education*. New York: Peter Lang Publishers.

Davis, L. J. (1997). *The Disability Studies Reader*. London: Routledge.

Davis, L. J. (2002). *Bending over Backwards: Disability, Dismodernism and Other Difficult Positions*. New York: New York University Press.

Davis, L.J. (ed.) (2006a). *The Disability Studies Reader* (second edition). New York: Routledge.

Davis, L. J. (2006b). 'The End of Identity Politics and the Beginning of Dismodernism: On Disability as an Unstable Category'. In L. Davis (ed). *The Disability Studies Reader* (second edition) (pp. 231–42). New York: Routledge.

Devlieger, P., Rusch, F. and Pfeiffer, D. (2003). *Rethinking Disability: The Emergence of New Definitions, Concepts and Communities*. Antwerpen/Apeldoorn: Garant.

Gabel, S. (2005). *Disability Studies in Education: Readings in Theory and Method*. New York: Peter Lang Publishers.

Gabel, S. and Danforth, S. (eds) (2008). *Disability and the International Politics of Education*. New York: Peter Lang Publishers.

Ghai, A. (2006). *(Dis)embodied Form: Issues of Disabled Women*. Delhi: Shakti Books.

Goodley, D. (2011a). *Disability Studies: An Interdisciplinary Introduction*. London: Sage.

Goodley, D. (2011b). 'Social Psychoanalytic Disability Studies'. *Disability & Society, 26* (6), 715–28.

Goodley, D. and Lawthom, R. (eds) (2005). *Disability and Psychology: Critical Introductions and Reflections*. London: Palgrave Macmillan.

Hales, G. (ed.) (1996). *Beyond Disability: Towards an Enabling Society*. London: Sage.

Hardt, M. and Negri, A. (2000). *Empire*. Cambridge, MA: Harvard University Press.

Kristiansen, K. and Traustadóttir, R. (eds) (2004). *Gender and Disability Research in the Nordic Countries*. Lund: Studentlitteratur.

Lawthom, R. (2010). 'The Space Between Disability Studies and Psychology: A Place for Community Psychology?' Keynote presentation to 'The Space Between: Disability In and Out of the Counselling Room' conference, University of Toronto, 8 October 2010.

Linton, S. (2005). *My Body Politic: A Memoir*. Michigan: University of Michigan Press.

Marks, D. (1999). *Disability: Controversial Debates and Psychosocial Perspectives*. London: Routledge.

McRuer, R. (2003). 'As Good as It Gets: Queer Theory and Critical Disability'. *GLQ: A Journal of Lesbian and Gay Studies, 9* (1–2), 79–105.

Meekosha, H. (2008). 'Contextualizing Disability: Developing Southern Theory'. Keynote presentation, Disability Studies Association 4th conference, Lancaster, 2–4 September 2008.

Meekosha, H. and Shuttleworth, R. (2009). 'What's So "Critical" about Critical Disability Studies?' *Australian Journal of Human Rights, 15* (1), 47–76.

Michalko, R. (2002). *The Difference That Disability Makes*. Philadelphia: Temple University Press.

Morris, J. (ed.) (1996). *Encounters with Strangers: Feminism and Disability*. London: The Women's Press.

Olkin, R. (1999). *What Psychotherapists Should Know about Disability*. New York: Guilford Press.

Oliver, M. (1990). *The Politics of Disablement*. Basingstoke: Palgrave Macmillan.
Oliver, M. (2009). *Understanding Disability: From Theory to Practice* (second edition). London: Macmillan.
Shakespeare, T. (2006). *Disability Rights and Wrongs*. London: Routledge.
Shakespeare, T. (2010). 'Practical Applications of British Disability Studies'. Paper presented at the British Disability Studies Symposium, University of Tokyo, 30 October 2011.
Sherry, M. (2004). 'Overlaps and Contradictions between Queer Theory and Disability Studies'. *Disability & Society*, 19 (7), 769–83.
Sherry, M. (2007). '(Post) Colonising Disability'. Special issue of *Wagadu, Journal of Transnational Women's and Gender Studies*, Volume 4, Summer, 10–22.
Shildrick, M. (2009). *Dangerous Discourses of Disability, Subjectivity and Sexuality*. London: Palgrave Macmillan.
Snyder, S. L., Brueggemann, B. J. and Garland-Thomson, R. (2002). *Disability Studies: Enabling the Humanities*. New York: The Modern Language Association of America.
Snyder, S. L. and Mitchell, D. T. (2006). *Cultural Locations of Disability*. Chicago/London: University of Chicago Press.
Stone, E. (ed.) (1999). *Disability and Development: Learning from Action and Research on Disability in the Majority World*. Leeds: The Disability Press, http://www.leeds.ac.uk/disability-studies/archiveuk/stone/intro.pdf, accessed 4 May 2008.
Swain, J., Barnes, C., French, S. and Thomas, C. (eds) (2004). *Disabling Barriers – Enabling Environments* (second edition). London: Sage.
Swain, J. and French, S. (1999). *Therapy & Learning Difficulties: Advocacy*. Butterworth-Heinemann.
Swain, J., French, S. and Cameron, C. (2003). *Controversial Issues in a Disabling Society*. Buckingham: Open University Press.
Thomas, C. (1999). *Female Forms: Experiencing and Understanding Disability*. Buckingham: Open University Press.
Thomas, C. (2007) *Sociologies of Disability and Illness: Contested Ideas in Disability Studies and Medical Sociology*. Basingstoke: Palgrave Macmillan.
Titchkosky, T. (2003). *Disability, Self and Society*. Toronto: University of Toronto Press.
Titchkosky, T. (2009). *Reading and Writing Disability Differently*. Toronto: University of Toronto Press.
Traustadóttir, R. (2004). 'Disability Studies: A Nordic Perspective'. Keynote lecture, British Disability Studies Association conference, Lancaster, 26–28 July 2004.
Tremain, S. (ed.) (2005). *Foucault and the Government of Disability*. Ann Arbor: University of Michigan Press.
Watermeyer, B., Swartz, L., Lorenzo, T., Schneider, M. and Priestley, M. (eds) (2006). *Disability and Social Change: A South African Agenda*. Cape Town: HSRC Press.
World Health Organisation (2001). *International Classification of Functioning, Disability and Health*. Geneva: World Health Organisation.

Part I
Cultures

Part I:
Cultu

2
Civilising Modernity and the Ontological Invalidation of Disabled People

Bill Hughes

Introduction

Elimination and/or correction have been the primary social response to disabled people in modernity. The primary form of experience (of disability), during the same period, has been one of invalidation. Invalidation carries a 'dual meaning' as both 'confinement through incapacity' and 'deficit of credibility' (Hughes, 2000: 558). This (latter and more crucial) claim is based on the view that in the non-disabled imaginary disability is an 'ontological deficit' – a reduction of *'leib'* to *'korpor'*, human to animal, subjectivity to flesh, identity to excessive corporeal presence. It is this deficit of credibility that provides the spurious rationale for the disposal of disabled bodies by means of elimination (*inter alia* extermination or segregation) or correction (*inter alia* sterilisation or rehabilitation). These are the social practices that have been used to erase both the psychological aversion and the problematic social difference that disability has come to represent.

In this chapter, I will argue – using Norbert Elias as a touchstone – that the treatment of disabled people in the modern period is a barbaric sideshow in the long march of the 'civilising process' (Elias, 2000). The 'personality structure' ableism (see Kumari Campbell (2001) and in this volume) in modernity transforms its own ontological precariousness into aversion for and disposal of disability. The negative response to biological and intellectual difference in modernity is strongly influenced by the tendency embedded in the 'civilising process' to incrementally deride the value of physical and intellectual difference and promote a sanitised norm of human behaviour and appearance (Elias, 2000). The social and social policy response to disability in the modern period cannot be separated from the emotional aversion to impairment characteristic of non-disabled hegemony. I will utilise Elias's concepts of *psychogenesis* and *sociogenesis*[1] to explain that the story of disability in modernity is one that develops towards the social and ontological invalidation of disabled people's lives.

The *sociogenisis* of disability is, in practice, twofold: it can be 'anthropoemic' or 'anthropophagic'. The first refers to social processes that root-out and eliminate people: if error and imperfection are the anti-heroes of modernity, then one might expect to find examples in which the desire for truth and purity is exercised through the root and branch elimination of those who offend against this moral universe. Locking disabled people into a 'zone of exception' (Agamben, 2004) in which they are subjected to the eugenic gaze and categorised as inhuman or sub-human is one strategy for dealing with disability (Reave, 2008). 'The real solution to heresy' suggested George Canguilhem in his discussion of the normal and the pathological (1991: 280) 'is extirpation', meaning to destroy totally or exterminate. In modernity medical ideas and practices have been a fertile source of radical solutions to impairment. Medical solutions also embrace anthropophagic strategies. They deal in the correction and rehabilitation of 'abnormal bodies'. Cure/rehabilitation stands at the heart of the medical doctrine of salvation (soteriology) and it is a prospect often held up to disabled people by optimists who fetishise scientific progress and promote biological solutions to impairment.

Both strategies – to kill or to cure – transmit the same core cultural message: disabled people represent 'what not to be' and are, therefore, ontologically invalid or 'uncivilised'. Social responses to impairment, in modernity, are underpinned by the processes that constitute the psychogenisis of disability. These include the emotional aversions and intolerances of impairment that derive from the civilising process. The ontological invalidation that disabled people experience in their everyday encounters is mediated primarily by the emotion of disgust (with fear and pity in tow). At an existential level the presence of the disabled body is unsettling for non-disabled people who are often in denial about their own vulnerability. This is the psychological and emotional component of what disability scholars call ableism. The standard resolution to this 'problem' of non-disability in modernity has been to have the object of discomfort – the disabled person – removed or corrected. The sociogenesis of anthropoemic and anthropophagic strategies for dealing with impairment are rooted in the emotional dispositions of non-disabled people as they develop their civilised protocols for behaviour and bodily comportment.

In what follows, I will focus on the ways in which the 'civilising process' invalidates impairment and demonstrate how opportunities to escape this ontological dead-end usually require the erasure of disabled identity. In the first section that follows I will give some examples of the way in which one can read disability as a product of the civilising process. In the section, thereafter, I will examine the psychogenesis of disability relating it to the disgust response to impairment and to the development of ableism, the complex of processes that exclude disabled people from the 'psychic habitus' (Elias, 2000: 367) of modernity. In the remaining two sections, I will examine the sociogenesis of disability in modernity by focusing on the two major 'civilising', social responses to impairment, namely elimination and correction.

Disability and the civilising process

The gods of Olympus showered heavenly mockery on deformity while those with earthly authority condoned infanticide for children born with impairments. The disabled *pharmakos* or scapegoat provided the communities of Antiquity with the opportunity to project their transgressions onto those who – by virtue of their physical or intellectual difference – existed on the margins of the *polis*. Such cultures of exclusion took new forms in the Christian Middle Ages. The Lord of the Old Testament feared that anomalous bodies might 'profane his sanctuaries'. Flesh and sin became so inextricably bound that any waywardness of the former became a sign of the latter. Disability was positioned as a moral and ontological pollutant.

Modernity brings a new set of challenges to the place of disabled people in the world. As cultures of superstition give way to the age of reason and rapid social change rips through the stasis of the long established courtly tradition, a cultural process marked by the march of 'civilisation' introduces new manners and technologies that slowly re-adjust Western self-consciousness, making anew, simultaneously, its personality, its emotional values and its organisational structures (Elias, 2000).

Yet the refinement of morals and manners that marks the civilising process is not without barbaric consequences. Civility segregates, creates social distance between those who embody refinement and those who do not, creating a new binary of bodies and minds and a new 'tyranny of normalcy' (Davis, 1995) predicated on the articulation of disgust for physical and mental 'inappropriateness'. As the quotidian demand for bodily delicacy and emotional refinement advanced, so too did the 'threshold of repugnance' (Elias, 2000: 98–9, 414–21) and so too did intolerance of impairment. 'A characteristic', wrote Elias (2000: 103), 'of the whole process that we call civilization is this movement of segregation, this hiding "behind the scenes" of what has become distasteful'. The deepening of emotional control and new stricter demands around bodily comportment reduces the social distance between social classes but creates an underclass of outsiders, a new stratum of marginal men and women who were beyond the pale of polite communion. In civilising modernity, the cultures of exclusion that taint disabled people's lives begin with pronouncements on etiquette that condemn the 'animalic' element of humanity and proceed to the construction of stark, institutional spaces, camps of confinement and death. These become places of internment for disabled people.

As civilising modernity plods along, it creates a new model of 'cultural' citizenship and, simultaneously, a framework for conduct that clarifies those who are eligible to embrace this cherished status. To do what is fitting, to be fit and to be fit to do what is fitting with respect to the intricacies and intimacies of social interaction is, increasingly, tailored and constrained. The detail of appropriate conduct and emotional control is developed at the quotidian level of everyday behaviour. Contempt and reserve is directed towards those who do not appear to represent the embodiment of the civilised citizen. The unfit fail the test of fitness for citizenship. Disabled people fail it every day, in the moralised environment where judgement of conduct takes place.

Elias (2000: 159) notes that 'The trend of the civilising movement towards the stronger and stronger and more complete "intimization" of all bodily functions, towards their enclosure in particular enclaves, to put them "behind closed doors", has diverse consequences'. However, what these consequences might be for disabled people remains a mystery. Although Elias recognises that the civilising process is a charter for segregation, he pays scant attention to what life is like behind the doors that have been closed. He describes the production of a secret world, an escalation of taboo and the acquisition of techniques of emotional and physical self-control that are developed to expiate disgust, shame and embarrassment. But what of those who live in the shadows of this secret world, forced by the intolerances of civility, to live behind its veil of righteousness? What of those who hide who and what they are because the dead weight of accumulated social convention will not let them be? What is life like for those who have been socially invalidated by the ever advancing 'threshold of repugnance'? Elias does not tell their story. However, he gives some clues about how it might be told. The rest of this section gives examples of the ways in which the civilising process configures disability.

As the idea of citizenship developed in modernity – particularly in the quotidian spaces of everyday conduct – disability played a crucial role. Garland-Thomson (1997: 42) argues that modern American citizenship is constructed on the fabled idea of self-governing individualism which implies a particular kind of body, one that is 'a stable, neutral instrument of the individual will'. The ideal citizen of the thrusting mid-nineteenth century Republic – drawn in fine detail for example in Ralph Waldo Emerson's work, particularly his portrait of Henry Thoreau (1862) – possesses the physical and intellectual capital that is conspicuously absent in the 'cripple' and the 'idiot'. The distinction between the normal body and its broken counterpart is sharpened and naturalised by both literary representations – for example the disabled and non-disabled characters in *Uncle Tom's Cabin* – and by certain cultural and social practices that draw the line between the dead world of the Rabelaisian grotesque and new civilised (yet as Elias points out, mythical and theoretically naive) world of *homo clausus*. Crucial among these cultural practices was the nineteenth-century 'freak show' which is based on the 'cardinal principle of enfreakment', that is, the abrogation of 'the freak's potential humanity' (Garland-Thomson, 1997: 44). The emotion of disgust – repugnance is Elias' preferred term – mediates the freak show. Not only does the emotion of disgust embody a 'curious enticement' but it also embodies 'a certain low evaluation of its object, a feeling of superiority' (Kolnai, 2004: 42–4). The 'show', of course, simultaneously serves the parallel 'positive' purposes of confirming the spectator's normalcy and humanity: manifest, most compellingly in the difference between the civilised spectators and the baroque creatures on display.

The freak shows and the 'lunatic exhibitions', common in early modern Germany, England and France in which asylum 'inmates were shown as caged monsters to a paying populace' (Winzer, 1997: 100), highlighted the difference between citizen/audience and exhibit/monster and consequently pushed the status of disability towards the animal. It is however, precisely, the drives of the body and the lowly impulses of nature that the civilising processes seek to subvert. Disability finds itself pushed away from the norms of conduct by the tide of civility, a tide that pushes 'the more animalic human activities ... behind the scenes of people's communal and social life' and colonises these activities, indeed, invests our 'whole instinctual and affective life' with 'feelings of shame' (Elias, 2000: 365).

Medicine as it grew in power and prestige, during the nineteenth century, replaced this carnival of normalisation and dehumanisation with a science of much the same, introducing new categories, such as pathology and abnormality, to sustain the ontological boundaries that kept disabled and non-disabled people compartmentalised. The architecture of modern Western citizenship is defined against the background of the ruin of disability, the broken timber of humanity that become candidates for the spaces of exclusions, those whose rights were spelt out in a declaration of dependency that was never written down.

Ableism and disgust: Psychogenesis and disability

The stratifying binary of disability/non-disability and the antagonism of the latter towards the former is mediated and maintained, principally, by the emotion of disgust. Disgust is the bile carried in a discursive complex that Campbell (2008: 153) calls 'ableism': 'a network of beliefs, processes and practices that produces a particular kind of self and body (the corporeal standard) that is projected as perfect, species-typical and therefore essential and fully human'. The body produced by ableism is equivalent to what Kristeva (1982: 71) calls the 'clean and proper body'. It is the body of the 'normate', the name that Rosemarie Garland-Thomson (1997) gives to the body that thinks of itself as invulnerable and definitive. It is the hygienic, aspirational body of civilising modernity. It is cast from the increasingly stringent norms and rules about emotional behaviour and bodily display that mark mundane social relations in the *lebenswelt* (lifeworld).

This curious non-disabled body/self has no empirical existence *per se*. On the contrary, the body of ableism is a normative construct, an invulnerable ideal of being manifest in the imaginary of 'modernist ontology, epistemology and ethics' as something 'secure, distinct, closed and autonomous' (Shildrick, 2002: 51). It embraces 'human perfectibility as a normative physical or psychological standard' and involves 'a curious disavowal of variation and mortality' (Kaplan, 2000: 303). It is what we are supposed to aspire to, to learn to be but can never become. It has no grounding in the material world. It is a 'body schema, a psychic construction of wholeness that ... belies its own precariousness and vulnerability' (Shildrick, 2002: 79). It is a 'body divorced from time and space; a thoroughly artificial affair' (Mitchell and Snyder, 2000: 7), the epitome of civilisation, closed off from any connection with the animal side of humanity and from the ways in which our bodily nature wallows in its carnal improprieties. It is a body aghast at the messiness of existence.

Disability is the opposite of this ideal body, its 'inverse reflection' (Deutsch and Nussbaum, 2000: 13). The disabled body is or has the propensity to be unruly. In the kingdom of the 'clean and proper body', disability is the epitome of 'what not to be'. As a consequence the disabled body can be easily excluded from the mainstream 'psychic habitus' (Elias, 2000: 167). The 'clean and proper' – a normative body of delicacy, refinement and self-discipline – has powerful social consequences most manifest in its normalising dynamics. It is the standard of judgement against which disabled bodies are invalidated and transformed into repellent objects. It is the emblem of purity that by comparison creates existential unease. It apportions the shame and repugnance that underwrite the civilising process (Elias, 2000: 114–19, 414–21).

Through ableism, modernity has been able to structure disability as uncivilised, outside or on the margins of humanity. One of the great books of the science of natural history published under the title *Systema Naturae* by Linnaeus in 1735 distinguishes between *homo sapiens* and *homo monstrosus*. In this classification impairment – at its extreme and highly visible end – is excluded from the human family. The distinction is, in itself, an act of violence and invalidation, an object lesson in transforming difference and 'defect' into the abominable. The distinction mobilises the aversive emotions of fear and disgust. Ableism is a cruel teacher. It embodies violence at many levels: 'epistemic, psychic, ontological and physical' (Campbell, 2008: 159). It is at its most bellicose when it is mediated by disgust: a mediation invoked mostly in the social fabrication of taboo and most compellingly in a context when the human/animal boundary is under threat.

Ableism rests on the effort to eliminate from awareness, chaos, abjection, animality and death: all that civilisation seeks to repress. It encourages us to live in the false hope that we will not suffer and die, to adopt a perspective of invulnerability, to confuse morality with beauty and to see death, pain and disability as the repulsive woes of mortality rather than as the existential basis for community and communication. Kolnai (2004: 74) reminds us that, 'in its full intention, it is death ... that announces itself to us in the phenomenon of disgust'. Disability, in modernity, has been produced in the ontological household of the abject, as the antithesis of communication and community, in a place that we might on occasion peer into only to 'choke' on the unsavoury sights that greet us. Disability is put out, put away, hidden, segregated or transformed into its opposite, covered up by whatever medical or aesthetic techniques are available to achieve this end. Any opportunity that disability might have to take its place at the heart of communication and community is thwarted by the ablest sensibilities that push it back down among the disgusting, the sick, the dead and the dying. In fact, as Elias (2000) suggested, the making of 'civilised' community and communication in modernity proceeds by exclusion and interdiction, by cutting out and hiding away whatever causes or might come to inspire *angar* (choking) or *anguista* (tightness).

It is important to understand ableist disgust as an emotion that attests to the failure of non-disabled people to fully recognise their own vulnerabilities and imperfections particularly as these relate to their mortal selves and to the death and decay that is the fate of all. Although it appears as an aversion to 'the other', it is a form of self-aversion or a means by which we hide from the bodily basis of our own humanity (Nussbaum, 2004). Indeed, disgust begins close to home and is derived from our discomfort with our own bodily functions, our oozy, sticky 'leaky selves' (Shildrick, 1997; Kolnai, 2004), the fact that we cannot contain ourselves within our own boundaries and the shame and embarrassment that the 'civilising process' brings to bear upon us if our leakiness is exposed to others. Because modernity is a charter for anal retentiveness, we cannot forgive ourselves for our physical impurities. We hold ourselves ransom to the myth of the 'clean and proper' body; the perfect body of ableist culture is a myth that we use to screen ourselves from the visceral realities of our own lives. The ableist body 'helps' non-disabled people cope with their fears about their own corporeal vulnerability. It does so by invoking its opposite, the disabled body, a foreign entity that is anomalous, chaotic and disgusting. Modern history helps to make this object of disgust more tangible. Civilising processes clarify stigma and make biological differences into socio-moral categories. Disgust provokes the civilising sensibilities. It warns them of the presence of possible contaminants (Miller, 1997). Consequently, psychological and social distance between disability and non-disability expands. Disgust in 'it's thought-content' is 'typically unreasonable, embodying magical ideas of contamination, and impossible aspirations to purity, immortality, and non-animality, that are just not in line with human life as we know it' (Nussbaum, 2004: 12). Disgust is an emotion that has a central role in our everyday relationships with our bodies, our patterns of social interaction and – most pressingly from the perspective of this chapter – in processes of social exclusion. Disgust is the emotional fuel of ableism.

The threat posed by ourselves to ourselves (and projected onto others), the threat of our 'bodiliness' and the shame and anxiety associated with it is a product of ableism, of the 'tyranny of perfection'. Ableism makes the world alien to disabled bodies and, at the same time, produces impairment as an invalidating experience. It is manifest in our cultural inclination towards normalcy by way of correction, towards homogeneity by way of disparagement of difference. What this means for disabled people is that they are 'expected to reject their own bodies' and 'adjust to the carnal norms of non-disabled people' (Paterson and Hughes, 1999: 608). The 'corporeality of the disabled body' is, according to Campbell (2008: 157), 'constantly in a state of deferral' awaiting the affective response that will demean it or the travails of sociogenesis that will either do away with it or 'make it better'.

Sociogenesis and the elimination of disability

Disabled people have to make a significant effort to establish their human worth. This effort is a struggle against the civilising process and its tendency to marginalise disability at an ontological level. This can be exemplified by the case of intellectual disability. Stainton (2008: 486) argues that 'the basic association of reason, personhood and human value has been at the heart of the exclusion and oppression of people with intellectual disabilities throughout western history'. The hypostatisation of reason traps disabled people in the cusp of the human–non-human/animal divide which is, according to Giorgio Agamben (2004), the fundamental division that underpins the very possibility of politics. The world of man is 'open to formation' intentional and free. By contrast, the animal is 'poor in the world', captivated by dependency on its instinctual armoury (Heiddeger, 1995). 'The animal', according to Heiddeger (1993: 230), 'is separated from man by an abyss'. The history of the exclusion of disability is (explicable through) the history of the human effort to efface its own animality, to close the door to the brute in its own breast, to disavow its unreflexive self, to expel messy nature from its core. The psychologist Paul Rozin argues that the things that disgust us deeply do so because they remind us of our animal origins (see, for example, Rozin and Fallon, 1987). Elias reminds us (2000: 365) that the civilising process is a struggle against the 'more animalic human activities', against those, for example, who are attributed with wounded reasoning.

In the early modern period, disability registered most strongly at the cultural level as corporeal excess, defect and monstrosity (Deutsch and Nussbaum, 2000). 'Freaks of nature' began to shed supernatural explanation and became objects of study for secular medical science. Teratology – the science of monsters and a matter of much philosophical and theological speculation during the early modern period – became, by the end of the nineteenth century, a sub-discipline of embryology (Park and Daston, 1981). Fiedler (1978: 24) argued that the 'freak ... challenges the conventional boundaries between male and female, sexed and sexless, animal and human'. On this view, encounters with spectacular forms of physical difference are emotionally powerful because they challenge the 'normal', stable view of embodied self. Putting emotional, physical and social distance between one's self and the cause of this kind of visceral identity shock can be achieved by an act of reclassification that dehumanises the aberrant body. Medieval ideas that linked monstrosity to, for example, copulation with animals began to decline in the wake of the rise of scientific explanations that 'proclaimed the biological fraternity of men and "monsters"'. However, 'the surveillance and policing of humans with congenital anomalies made them "less than human"' (Snigurowicz, 2004: 174). Indeed the Eugenics movement of the late Victorian and Edwardian period came hard on the heels of the 'discovery' of so-called objective, scientific and medical explanations for disability. Today, debates about selective abortion, pre-natal screening, euthanasia and physician-assisted death are intimately linked with sentiments that question disabled people's right to life (see, for example, Preistley, 2003: 35–60 and 166–88). It is not difficult to demonstrate a eugenic sensibility at the heart of the new genetics.

When people have their identity reduced to something less than human, to the animal in humanity, to objects of hatred and disgust like the Jews in Nazi Germany or disabled people during the Edwardian craze for Eugenics, or – to use Agamben's example – the prisoners in Guantanamo bay, they become reduced to 'bare life', become candidates for exclusion, torture, enslavement, extermination and genocide. In this liminal social space – what Agamben (2004: 79) calls 'a zone of exception' – that is the repulsive borderland between the animal and the human, the possibilities for cruelty are, as history has taught, all too imaginable. This 'zone of exception' may be (relatively) 'benign' as in the case of people with achondroplasia who were sometimes kept as pets by Roman Patricians (Garland-Thomson, 1995: 47) but it can be and has been transformed – under the Third Reich – into a slaughterhouse. Physical disability has been defined as a 'disruption in the field of the observer' (Davis, 2000: 56). Historically, there have been times when the observer has decided to clear the field.

From the perspective of non-disability, disability signals the presence of impairment, unreason, sickness, monstrosity, abjection and death, all the 'repulsive' embodied characteristics that civilisation refuses, point blank, to celebrate and seeks, desperately to disavow. Disability invokes too much of the natural and the animal in man to sit comfortably in a culture that has been intent on keeping an 'abyss' between them. The issue of distinction and categorical clarity is at the heart of Mary Douglas's (1991) analysis of pollution and taboo. On this view the abominations of Leviticus – those biblical beatitudes on hygienic propriety – make sense only when we understand that 'holiness' or purity 'requires that different classes of things shall not be confused' which 'means keeping distinct the categories of creation' (1991: 53) particularly the animal and the human. This is testimony to the unsettling and disturbing nature of the anomalous. It helps to explain the sociological processes that consign disabled people to the marginal role of the stranger (Hughes, 2002). The animal represents the unrestrained and impulsive in man, and it is these very characteristics that civilisation seeks to abrogate. Elias (2000: 384) notes that 'offences against the prevailing pattern of drive and affect control, any letting go' by members of a civilised society is unacceptable and meets with strong disapproval.

The ontological insecurities of modernity become projected onto disabled people and, therefore, the positivity, wisdom and strength that Nietzsche recognises in the – so called – 'unfit' become obscured. Socially, disabled people come to represent those who cannot practice self-restraint and, as the 'threshold of repugnance' (Elias, 2000: 97–9) narrows, they are 'rounded-up' and 'herded' into institutions. The confinement of disability – in the nineteenth century – marks the supreme moment of its passage into interdiction, when the desire for social homogeneity – so characteristic of modernity – finally admits to itself that its civilising tendencies must be marked by clear corporeal prohibitions and that certain categories of bodies/minds must be removed from polite society so that it can realise the hygienic utopia inscribed in the civilising process. The punitive norm embodied in the hegemonic drive towards an homogeneous and hygienic culture demands many sacrifices. By the middle of the nineteenth century any 'thing' and every 'thing' anomalous was a potential lamb to the slaughter. Cora Kaplan (2000: 302) describes how the 'history of defect' in the early part of the twentieth century became 'a pretext for genocide', and she notes that disability has proved a significant challenge to the ethic of tolerance that underlies modern liberalism. In this context, Georges Bataille's (1985) argument for a 'heterology' – a science that rescues the victims of homogenising modernity – might have been written as a manifesto for disabled people. They, after all, have had to put up with the 'civilising process' in which the embedding of ever more prescriptive norms of bodily comportment confirms disability as a social contaminant, calling, more or less explicitly, for a 'disgust response' to its presence. Consequently, disabled people are 'sacrificed' (to use a term much loved by Bataille) on the grounds that they are devoid of the kind of comportment that is a pre-requisite for appropriate social participation. The residue of disgust – the *angar* and *anguista* – that is a product of the civilising process is, thereby, mobilised as social policy. It forms a kind of Dickensian clean-up operation that sweeps disabled people off the streets and into the carceral spaces that soon come to be dominated by medical custodians and their strategies for bodily or mental correction.

Sociogenesis as correction

There is another way to deal with disability, a technical (usually) medical solution designed to assuage the excess of corporeality, the 'surplus of life' (Kolnai, 2004) that upsets the 'civilised' observer. This is the anthropophagic strategy, the possibility of rescuing disability from the abyss of unacceptable difference, through correction, rehabilitation, through finding ways to conceal or heal the 'ontological deficit' (Hughes, 2007). The quest to correct the disabled body is about making disability and non-disability identical, about transforming the pathological into the normal.

In ableist culture, the bodily forms of disabled people are marked, not just by constitutional pathology but also by aesthetic unruliness. Disability represents deficit in competence and beauty. 'Eugenics', for example, 'promised to make humanity not just strong and smart but beautiful as well' (Pernick, 1997: 91). The ontological disparagement of disability in the modern period is a double-edged sword. It thrusts and slashes in the quotidian spaces of the civilising world. Medical and aesthetic prejudice work in combination to produce the view that disabled people's 'inabilities' and 'deficiencies' are products of the natural distribution of competence and beauty rather than the social organisation of opportunity. Insofar as one cannot exchange what one has not got or (easily) transform a deficit into a credit, the disabled body is blocked in its possibilities to acquire cultural, economic or symbolic capital (see Blackmore and Hodgkins in this volume). Correction/rehabilitation involves the attempted erasure of deficits of credibility that are simultaneously mechanical and undesirable. To be 'what not to be' is to be a stakeholder at the margins of the human community with few opportunities to escape misrecognition and exile. 'Correction' offers a tangible promise of redemption, through – to steal a phrase from Bourdieu (1984: 251) – 'ontological promotion'.

Making able (rehabilitation) offers an alternative to long-term or permanent incarceration in quasi-medical institutions. Henri-Jacques Stiker (2000: 128) argues that rehabilitation 'marks the appearance of a culture that attempts to complete the act of identification, of making identical' and that, 'this act will cause the disabled to disappear and with them all that is lacking, in order to drown them, dissolve them in the greater and single social whole'. The dynamic of the disgust response – down to the removal of the aversive object – is, in a concrete way, reproduced in the practice of rehabilitation. Modern professional therapeutic practice is designed to normalise in the name of sameness. Aside from the positive value that it can and does have for many, it represents an assault on bodily difference and embodies an assumption that the norm (of wholeness) is redemptive. Winance (2007: 627) notes that in France from the 1950s onwards, 'the term handicap' relates to 'divergence from a norm ... of social performance' and refers to a disabled person who, through medical means, is 'to be re-adapted'. Rehabilitation also signifies betterment indicating a moral element to correction. Rehabilitation is an offer of ontological promotion, an invitation to join the community of civilised persons. Assumptions about civilised bodily performances are clearly evident in the field of therapy and rehabilitation. Aides that facilitate the 'up-right' stance and comportment of people with mobility impairments are regarded as tools for enhancing physical capital. The difference between *homo erectus* and 'his' slouched, primate predecessors might have a quite a lot to do with our disdain for those who do not 'walk tall' as well as with the pervasive (non-disabled) view that a wheelchair is a place of confinement rather than a vehicle of liberation. The medical term prosthesis is derived from the Greek word meaning 'addition', suggesting nature in deficit. 'In a literal sense', note Mitchell and Snyder (2000: 6), 'a prosthesis seeks to accomplish an illusion', perhaps a deceit. It covers-up. It attempts to represent what an individual is – at the level of biology and ontology – so that she can be embraced by a community that will not tolerate her as she is. Therapies improve and correct, some cure. The goal of speech and language therapy, for example, is to transform 'deficit communicators' by providing them with the tools to develop 'civilised' speech patterns. Recipients of the therapy are taught – like the heroine of George Bernard Shaw's *Pygmalion* –to embody the protocols of 'competent communication' and be able, therefore, to participate effectively in civil social encounters. The person with the speech impairment is presented as a portent of social mess. To offend against protocol attracts aversion. Yet, these protocols are themselves carnally informed and arise from the ways in which non-disabled bodies leave their imprint – the imprint of normalcy – on the forms of communication that come to be defined as acceptable. Impairment, in these normalised social spaces, is always an ontological lack. Rehabilitation – from the Latin '*habilitare*', 'to make able' – is a corrective, a pedagogical solution to our aversion for the disruption caused by an ontological splinter in the otherwise perfect fleshy fabric of a slick social encounter. Speech impairment is treated as a creeping unruliness that threatens civility. From a 'non-disabled' perspective, the corrupting presence of ontological deficit is a source of moral apprehension.

Disabled people can attempt to erase their difference by 'passing as normal' (Goffman, 1969) – a form of ontological bluff that is profoundly precarious. In equating social competence with the concealment of corporeal difference, disabled people trade pride in who they are for the rewards of assimilation. Elias understands this all too well. Passing, from his perspective, can be explained by 'fear of degradation and is underpinned by the alignment of one's super-ego with' the social demands for 'self-constraint' (Elias, 2000: 414). Given the pervasiveness of ableism and the 'tyranny of normalcy', one can understand why this can be regarded as an attractive bargain. The 'right side' of civility is an attractive place to be. One of the ways to sustain credibility as a disabled person seems to be by convincing others that one is not what one is. Yet the cost of this civilising, ontological strategy can be high. Its attraction hinges on the extent to which its protagonist internalises – as shame – the disgust response that, she assumes, she will invoke if her impairment is not 'corrected' by concealment. However, if the concealed impairment is exposed and the protective mantle of 'passing' collapses, the individual is caught in a deceit that may have profoundly negative consequences for her social relationships.

Conclusion

Elias (2000: 118) refers to the 'weeding out of the natural functions from public life' and in this regard, those who do not have their affects moulded to a degree acceptable to their peers will be regarded as objects of disgust and reduced to objectifying categories such as the 'sick', the 'pathological' or the 'perverse' (Elias, 2000: 120). This categorical ensemble forms the modernist, negative medical and moral evaluations that have, like stray dogs, followed disabled people around barking out testimonials to their ontological failures and indiscretions.

Modern life has become troubled, increasingly –according to Elias – by whatever reminds us of our animal origins and our visceral dispositions and by those objects and events that trigger disgust. Disgust thrives on difference because it is provoked by what is 'opposed to (the) norm, direction or plan of life' (Kolnai, 2004: 72). Difference can be corrected, tidied away and if it proves to be more troublesome, then a more radical strategy (of elimination) can be deployed (Bauman, 1989). The holocaust is the obvious and most extreme example of the 'disposal of contaminants' but the desire to eliminate difference in general or disability in particular can register in all sorts of unexpected places. As this passage from the *Diary of Virginia Wolf* indicates, the eugenic sensibility can manifest itself in the most 'progressive' minds:

> On the tow path we met and had to pass a long line of imbeciles. Everyone in that long line was a miserable shuffling idiotic creature, with no forehead or no chin and imbecile grin, or a wild suspicious stare. It was perfectly horrible. They should certainly be killed.
> (Bell and McMellie, 1982: 13)

Of course, one need have no qualms about killing these wild, repulsive creatures. It is clear that they exhibit no tangible sign of humanity to trouble the conscience of a would-be executioner. Wolf, appalled by her sister's 'imbecility', by the shadow of a sibling presence that she could not embrace, sees only an anthropoemic solution. Minor correction will suffice for Eliza Doolittle just as speech therapy will help to tidy up the social mess associated with speech impairment, but for the more disturbing proximity of 'imbecility', a more radical solution is required. We use social policy to decontaminate and cleanse the social body in a host of different ways, and we can correct individual bodies to make them more tolerable, sanitised and even virtuous. And all in the name of civility!

In modernity the response to disability has been based on either the anthropoemic strategy of elimination/banishment and/or the anthropophagic strategy of rectifying and correcting anomalies (Hughes, 1999: 2002). The *emic* in anthropoemic is instructive. It means to expel or vomit and therefore has its 'roots' in a bodily function that is associated most closely and most dramatically with the disgust response. However, both strategies – the anthropophagic as well as the anthropoemic – are testimony to the aesthetic and existential anxiety (Hahn, 1986) that underpins the non-disabled response to disability and to the tyranny and violence of ableism which invests so much discursive and emotional energy in seeking to convince that the 'clean and proper body' is 'the barometer against which all biology's are assessed and compared' (Mitchell and Snyder, 2000: 29). Ableism is a child of the civilising process. Non-disabled individuals embody and enact ableism by clinging onto 'normalcy' and disavowing their fragile, transient, visceral, identities. In so doing, they add bricks and mortar to the 'invisible wall' (Elias, 2000: 258) of affects that invalidates disability.

Note

1. Elias is intrigued by the link between *sociogenesis* and *psychogenesis* or the way in which culture and personality develop such that they collude and become enmeshed. The former refers to social structure and the latter to personality structure. Indeed, some commentators note that the central and most important message of the 'civilising process' is its thesis that 'personality structure' and 'socio-political structure' are 'not only intertwined but mutually instrumental in each other's occurrence' (Bauman, 1979: 121).

References

Agamben, G. (2004). *The Open: Man and Animal* (translated by Kevin Attell). Stanford, CA: Stanford University Press.
Bataille, G. (1985). *Visions of Excess: Selected Writings 1927–39*, trans. A. Stoekl, Manchester: Manchester University Press.
Bauman, Z. (1979). 'The Phenomenon of Norbert Elias'. *Sociology*, 13, 117–25.
Bauman, Z. (1989). *Modernity and the Holocaust*. Oxford: Polity.
Bell, A. and McMellie, A. (eds) (1982). *The Diary of Virginia Woolf*. New York: Harcourt.
Bourdieu, P. (1984). *Distinction: A Social Critique of the Judgement of Taste*. London: Routledge and Kegan Paul.
Canguilhem, G. (1991). *The Normal and the Pathological*. New York: Zone Books.
Campbell, F. A. K. (2001). 'Inciting Legal Fictions: Disability's Date with Ontology and the Ableist Body of Law'. *Griffith Law Review* 10 (1), 42–61.
Campbell, F. A. K. (2008). 'Exploring Internalised Ableism Using Critical Race Theory'. *Disability & Society*, 23 (2), 151–62.

Davis, L. (1995). *Enforcing Normalcy: Disability, Deafness and the Body*. London: Verso.

Davis, L. (2000). 'Dr Johnston, Amelia and the Discourse of Disability'. In H. Deutsch and F. Nussbaum (eds), *Defects: Engendering the Modern Body*. Ann Arbor: University of Michigan Press.

Deutsch, H. and Nussbaum, F. (eds) (2000). *Defects: Engendering the Modern Body*. Ann Arbor: University of Michigan Press.

Douglas, M. (1991). *Purity and Danger: An Analysis of the Concepts of Pollution and Taboo*. London: Routledge.

Elias, N. (2000). *The Civilising Process*. Oxford: Blackwell.

Fiedler, L. (1978). *Freaks: Myths and Images of the Secret Self*. New York: Simon and Schuster.

Garland-Thomson, D. (1995). *The Eye of the Beholder: Deformity and Disability in the Graeco-Roman World*. Ithica, New York: Cornell University Press.

Garland-Thomson, R. (1997). *Extraordinary Bodies: Figuring Physical Disability in American culture and Literature*. New York: Columbia University Press.

Goffman, E. (1969). *Stigma: Notes on the Management of Spoiled Identity*. Harmondsworth: Penguin.

Heidegger, M. (1993). Letter on humanism. In D. Farell Krell (ed.), *Basic Writings*. London: Harper Collins.

Heidegger, M. (1995). *The Fundamental Concepts of Metaphysics* (translated by W. McNeil and N. Walker). Bloomington: Indiana University Press.

Hahn, H. (1986). 'Public Support for Rehabilitation Programmes: The Analysis of US Disability Policy'. *Disability, Handicap and Society*, 1 (2), 25–38.

Hughes, B. (1999). 'The Constitution of Impairment: Modernity and the Aesthetic of Oppression'. *Disability & Society*, 14 (2), 155–72.

Hughes, B. (2000). 'Medicine and the Aesthetic Invalidation of Disabled People'. *Disability & Society*, 15 (4), 555–68.

Hughes, B. (2002). 'Bauman's Strangers: Disability, Impairment and the Cultures of Modernity and Postmodernity'. *Disability & Society*, 17 (5), 571–84.

Hughes, B. (2007). 'Being Disabled: Towards a Critical Social Ontology for Disability Studies'. *Disability & Society*, 22 (7), 673–84.

Kaplan, C. (2000). 'Liberalism, Feminism and Defect'. In H. Deutsch and F. Nussbaum (eds), *Defects: Engendering the Modern Body*. Ann Arbor: University of Michigan Press.

Kolnai, A. (2004). *On Disgust*.Chicago and La Salle, IL: Open Court.

Kristeva, J. (1982). *Powers of Horror: An Essay on Abjection* (translated by L. Roudiez). New York: Columbia University Press.

Miller, W. (1997). *Anatomy of Disgust*. Cambridge MA: Harvard University Press.

Mitchell, D. and Snyder, S. (2000). *Narrative Prosthesis: Disability and the Dependencies of Discourse*. Ann Arbor: University of Michigan Press.

Nussbaum, M. (2004). *Hiding from Humanity: Disgust, Shame and the Law*. Princeton: Princeton University Press.

Park, K. and Daston, L. (1981). 'Unnatural Conceptions: The Study of Monsters in Sixteenth and Seventeenth Century France and England'. *Past and Present*, 92, 51–73.

Paterson, K. and Hughes, B. (1999). 'Disability Studies and Phenomenology: The Carnal Politics of Everyday Life'. *Disability & Society*, 14 (5), 597–610.

Pernick, M. (1997). 'Defining the Defective – Eugenics, Aesthetics and Mass Culture in Early Twentieth Century America'. In D. Mitchell and S. Snyder (eds), *The Body and Physical Difference*. Ann Arbor: University of Michigan Press.

Preistley, M. (2003). *Disability: A Life Course Approach*. Cambridge: Polity Press.

Reave, D. (2008). 'Biopolitics and Bare Life: Does the Impaired Body Provide Contemporary Examples of Homo Sacer'. In K. Kristiansen, T. Shakespeare and S. Vehmas (eds), *Arguing about Disability: Philosophical Perspectives*. London: Routledge.

Rozin, P. and Fallon, A. (1987). 'A Perspective on Disgust'. *Psychological Review*, 94, 23–41.

Shildrick, M. (1997). *Leaky Bodies and Boundaries: Feminism, Postmodernism and (Bio)Ethics*. London: Routledge.

Shildrick, M. (2002). *Embodying the Monster: Encounters with the Vulnerable Self*. London: Sage.

Stainton, T. (2008). 'Reason, Grace and Charity: Augustine and the Impact of Church Doctrine on the Construction of Intellectual Disability'. *Disability & Society*, 23 (5), 485–96.

Stiker, J. H. (2000). *A History of Disability*. Ann Arbor: University of Michigan Press.

Winance, M. (2007). 'Being Normally Different? Changes to Normalisation Processes: From Alignment to Work on the Norm'. *Disability & Society*, 22 (6), 625–38.

Winzer, M. (1997). 'Disability and Society before the 18th Century: Dread and Despair'. In L. Davis (ed.), *The Disability Studies Reader*. New York: Routledge, 75–109.

3
Commodifying Autism: The Cultural Contexts of 'Disability' in the Academy

Rebecca Mallett and Katherine Runswick-Cole

> A commodity appears at first sight, a very trivial thing, and easily understood. Its analysis shows that it is, in reality, a very queer thing.
>
> —(Marx, 1954: 76)

Introduction

The cultural presence of autism has grown vastly over the past few decades, with the impairment becoming the subject of films (e.g. *Rain Man*, 1998; *Snow Cake*, 2006), novels (e.g. *Curious Incident of the Dog in the Night-Time*, 2003), autobiographies (e.g. Grandin, 1996; Lawson, 2000), museum exhibitions (e.g. *Welcome to Our World ... Living with Autism*, 2011) and newspaper articles (e.g. McNeil, 2009; Alleyne, 2010). In turn, these have attracted the attention of academics in the humanities and social sciences (for instance, Greenwell, 2004; Murray, 2008; Davidson and Smith, 2009). Such considerations acknowledge, as Murray (2008: xvii) does, that autism can be considered 'compellingly attractive in the way it presents human otherness'. However, although autism as a mysterious and fascinating style of human difference has been explored for what it reveals of popular understandings, the fascination signaled by its emergence and proliferation as an academic presence has not been scrutinised. In this chapter we are interested in approaching autism *critically*. We seek to understand the cultural contexts of this academic presence and think through its implications. By positioning academia as part of contemporary consumer culture, we borrow from Marxist-inspired theories to conceptualise the processes by which 'seemingly the most enigmatic of conditions' (Murray, 2008: xvi) has become produced, traded and consumed within the social sciences.

To do this, we utilise theories of *commodification*. We argue that such theories offer a way of understanding how autism has become a *thing-like form* within academia. We then move to outline autism as a capitalist commodity and think through the different parties involved in the process of its production. We discuss the role of desire and use the concept of *commodity fetishism* to explore what we buy (into) when autism is purchased. Through this theorising, we end by arguing that the persistent presence of autism as a largely unproblematised entity within academia, and within the study of disability in particular, works to jeopardise the continued emancipation of disabled people.

Autism's academic presence: Theorising the cultural contexts of knowledge

The ideas for this chapter stem from repeated conversations between the authors over cups of coffee in draughty corridors at research conferences. Over the past few years, we have noticed, with some concern, that one impairment was being spoken about much more than any other. If we consider the titles of sessions at some recent disability conferences, we can sense a pattern emerging. At the 'Present Difference: The Cultural Production of Disability Conference 2010' in Manchester, there were three sessions which mentioned an impairment label in their title: 'Representing Autism I'; 'The Social Identities of Learning Disabled People'; and 'Representing Autism II'. At the 'Society of Disability Studies (SDS) 2009 Conference' in Arizona, there were two sessions which centred on a specific impairment category: 'Neuro-Diversity: Autism and Disability' and 'Autism as Teacher'. Similarly, the 2010 SDS conference had three sessions which included an impairment label in their title: 'Autism I'; 'Autism II'; and 'Intellectual Disability'. While other papers at these conferences no doubt talked about other impairments, when a specific impairment was named it was more often than not *autism*.

At these conferences at least, it seemed that autism aroused widespread interest and we could not shake the feeling that certain sessions were being branded, marketed and sold as being about autism. This was particularly curious to us because autism seemed to be receiving a lot of attention in an area of academia which aimed to interrogate disability in the social world and work towards the emancipation of *all* disabled people. Such an agenda is summed up by Pfeiffer and Yoshida (1995: 480) when they describe the key distinguishable feature of this realm of study as a commitment to a shift in focus 'away from a prevention/treatment/remediation paradigm to a social/cultural/political paradigm'. It seemed odd then that certain sessions were concerned with specific impairments as defined by the very paradigm (prevention/treatment/remediation) the area purported to be shifting away from.

Puzzled by this seemingly unquestioned proliferation of autism in the academy, this chapter is an exploration of what we did next and provides a demonstration of how turning to social theory can, following Tanya Titchkosky (2008), help understand the meanings made of disability within contemporary culture. However, while Titchkosky (2008: 12) wishes to resist 'the temptation to simplify by rendering disability into a definable objectified *thing*', we seek to pay attention to those moments when disability (as represented here by the category autism) stubbornly appears, remains and proliferates as a *thing*.

We suggest that one way of explaining the processes by which autism has gained and maintained an undisturbed academic presence is by taking seriously the cultural contexts of knowledge and arguing that, far from being neutral, knowledge is constructed and procured through varied social, cultural and economic contingencies. To do this, we employ a critical theory approach which can be said to be 'committed to unveiling the political stakes that anchor cultural practices' (Conquergood, 1991: 179) and which we later define as the practice of *defetishisation*. It is important to note here that within *cultural* practices, Conquergood includes 'research and scholarly' practices.

Despite being described as one of the most difficult words to define (Jackson, 1989), some have argued that 'it is precisely because "culture" has no clear referent that it becomes such a useful tool' (Mitchell, 1995: 106). In this chapter, we approach culture through critical theory, in particular Marxist theory, in order to better understand the complex ways in which meanings are generated, disseminated and maintained at a given time and place. Our time and place is contemporary academia, in particular, recent social science research activity around disability and although we have tried to restrict our discussion to the academy in the UK, given the cross-fertilisation of ideas and researchers, this has not been completely possible.

Paying attention to social, cultural and economic contexts is not altogether new within the study of disability, but among those who have deployed similar approaches, categories of impairment have not been subjected to analysis. Finkelstein (1980), for instance, discussed how responses to impairment changed as the economic and technological capabilities of society changed; Oliver (1990) linked the emergence of disability to the rise of capitalist society; and Gleeson (1999) looked at how the socio-spatial marginalisation of disabled people occurred as industrialisation increasingly demanded the ability to be geographically mobile; but all leave categories of impairment relatively undisturbed. This concern with the conditions of economic production and the sociocultural organisation which stems from them is sometimes referred to as a *political economy* approach. It has been utilised across the disciplines and is often associated with some level of historical analysis of how particular forms of society emerge and are sustained. Although we would consider our approach to be derived from a political economy perspective, due to the relatively short confines of a book chapter we cannot offer an extensive historical analysis and have chosen instead to consider our present moment. We also seek to depart from the previous disability-related studies in this area which proceed along lines similar to Albrecht and Bury (2001: 598) when they comment:

> Molecular biologists and geneticists are leading the way in identifying the organic basis for impairment while political economists explore the social production and responses to disability.

We argue that rather than bracket off impairment as an 'organic' entity best dealt with by scientists, we should use political economy's analytical tools to interrogate 'impairment' from a sociocultural perspective. For us, this entails asking what part contemporary capitalist consumer culture plays in the making of 'disability'.

By focusing on the academic presence of one impairment category, we will explore whether theories of *commodification* can help us understand how certain sets of disability knowledge, for us those around autism, are produced and seem to be thriving at this particular point in time. Ever since Marx's critique of commodification appeared at the beginning of the first volume of *Capital* (Jackson, 1999), use of the idea has been widespread. We contend, like Castree (2001: 1519), that although 'the signifier "Marxism" is now so polysemic as to be virtually incoherent ... it can still usefully denote a set of explanatory and political resources that are relinquished only at a considerable cost'. This chapter does not have the space to enter into debates about the finer points of Marx's contentions or engage in debates over the (mis)use of his work by those who have followed. Instead, we are interested in the ideas of *commodification*, and later *commodity fetishism*, as 'explanatory and political resources' for contributing to the defetishisation of the place of autism in the academy.

To that end, there has been a small amount of critical engagement with the production of autism knowledges such as work on the construction of autism by Nadesan (2005) and of Asperger Syndrome by Molloy and Vasil (2002). Others have called into question the coherence of tests for autism (McGuire and Michalko, 2009) and have examined the political activism surrounding neurodiversity (Ortega, 2009). However, despite injecting valuable and much overdue critique into the study of autism, and laying the groundwork for what could be called Critical Autism Studies, little has been said about the amount of discussion autism is generating.

As we can only explore a small fraction of this potentially fruitful area, our specific aim is to contribute to the theorisation of the ways in which present cultural contexts produce autism in the academy in certain ways – as *thing-like form*, as a commodity and as a unsatisfied desire. As we will discuss, these all overlap and mutually constitute an academic presence which, when defetishised, reveals a threat to the broader project of emancipation. Before we move on to outline capitalist commodification within academia in more detail, we start, in the next section, by considering the significant part played by the processes of *abstraction* in carving out autism as a *thing*.

Autism as thing: Becoming commodity through abstraction

As part of addressing autism's presence in the academy, we acknowledge that academia is part of the contemporary world and that one of the ways of understanding how that world is maintained is as one increasingly characterised by consumer culture. By that we mean that culture is driven by the social arrangement in which the buying and selling of goods and services is not only the predominant activity of everyday life but is also an important arbiter of social organisation, significance and control. Slater (1997: 101) has commented that today 'more of social life is produced in a thing-like form' and this notion of 'thing-like forms' fits well with the idea that disability is often 'demarcated and encoded as some "thing" found wrong in individuals' (Titchkosky, 2008: 133). As we have argued elsewhere (Mallett and Runswick-Cole, 2010), impairment labels often act as a shorthand for the identification and explication of a specific impairment 'thing', and thereby play a part in packaging corporeal difference. In this section we consider definitions, possible causes and the diagnosis of autism. Despite revealing a complex and highly contested 'thing', the processes of *abstraction* (the assigning of real and discernable characteristics to an entity across a range other entities) can be seen to not only to create autism as a 'thing', but, specifically, as a commoditised 'thing'.

Autism is often described as a 'devastating developmental disorder' (Happe, 1999: 216), or a 'neurological abnormality' (Frith, 2003: 1) 'due to a physical dysfunction of the brain' (National Autistic Society, 1998: 26). People labeled as having autism are considered to share three main areas of difficulty, otherwise known as the 'triad of impairments' (Wing, 1991). These are difficulty with social communication, social interaction and social imagination. Other related characteristics of autism have been described as a love of routines; sensory sensitivity; special (sometimes described as obsessive) interests; and learning disabilities. The main clinical features, as noted by Burgoine and Wing (1983), include: lack of empathy, one-sided interaction, little or no ability to form friendships, pedantic speech, poor non-verbal communication, intense absorption in certain subjects and odd postures. In this view, autism was 'discovered' in the 1940s by two psychiatrists working independently. Kanner (1943), in the US, made observations of children he considered to be autistic in his paper 'Autistic Disturbances of Affective Contact', and Hans Asperger (1944), in Austria, made observations in which he also chose to use the label *autism*.

Yet, the UK National Autistic Society's (NAS) current definition reflects a shift in thinking. The NAS define autism as a lifelong developmental disorder; however, autism is also referred to as an autism spectrum disorder (ASD). The NAS uses the word 'spectrum' because 'while all people with autism share three main areas of difficulty, their condition will affect them in very different ways. Some are able to live relatively 'everyday' lives; others will require a lifetime of specialist support' (NAS, 2008: n.p.).

In addition to the conceptualisation of autism existing on a spectrum, the category autism has also been divided into subcategories including Asperger Syndrome (AS), able and High Functioning Autism (HFA). People labelled with AS are characterised by at least average intelligence (an IQ of above 70) with no significant language delay up to the age of five (Attwood, 2000, 2007). Yet, uncertainty surrounds the hazy edges between AS, able and HFA with the labels often used interchangeably (Attwood, 2000). Indeed the shift to describe autism as a 'spectrum disorder', the variance in interpretations of diagnostic criteria of AS, and the absence of consensus among practitioners in clinical practice on 'patterns of symptoms being referred to as AS, High-Functioning Autism and Autism Spectrum [condition]' (Molloy and Vasil, 2002: 661) point to the slipperiness of autism as a category, even within the medical paradigm.

Similarly, explanations of the causes of autism are many and varied, ranging from blaming 'refrigerator mothers' to mercury in childhood vaccines (Bettleheim, 1967; Wakefield et al., 1998). There have also been claims of diagnostic 'trendiness' where the identification of autism is thought to be on the rise because it is seen as a fashionable label which carries with it access to resources (Baker, 2006). However, despite the popular urge to find a biological basis, as illustrated by campaigns such as *Autism Speaks*[1] in the US, currently there is no generally accepted biomedical cause.

Despite the uncertainty in cause, explanation and definition, here we begin to glimpse the commodifying processes by which natural materials are transformed into culturally useful objects (Miller, 2003). Castree (2003: 281) describes *abstraction* as the process by which 'the qualitative specificity of any individualised thing (a person, a seed, a gene or what-have-you) is assimilated to the qualitative homogeneity of a broader type or process'. It can be argued that, the diagnostic category of autism is a product of individual people with individual behaviours being absorbed into a uniform and standardised 'type', albeit a slippery 'type'. This is consistent with Robertson's (2000) concept of *functional abstraction* where individual cases (by which we mean, people) are considered as instantiations of the generic category of autism which 'stands over and above them' (Castree, 2003: 281). In order to demonstrate *functional abstraction* in process, Robertson (2000: 472) explored the 'formal assessment methodologies and taxonomic systems' which work to commodify 'wetlands', in doing so he comments:

> Taxonomic classification systems provide both an imposed order and a common language for scientists … assessment methodologies involve paper forms, filled out on a brief visit to a site, which allow the assessor to total up a 'score' for a given site.
>
> (Robertson, 2000: 473)

If Robertson's description is re-read as a diagnostic assessment, the role of *abstraction* in the process by which individuals are identified as autistic also becomes significant. A number of instruments for diagnosing autism have been developed and are becoming more widely used. Each diagnostic tool sets out to translate observable behaviours into behavioural indicators, for example, 'lack of empathy', 'pedantic repetitive speech' and 'poor non verbal communication' (Attwood, 2000: 15) are all presented as 'observable behaviours' which are 'behavioural indicators' for a diagnosis of autism. The American Psychiatric Association's (1994) Diagnostic and Statistical Manual fourth revision (DSM IV),[2] often used by professionals, outlines the diagnostic criteria necessary for a diagnosis of autism. The Autism Diagnostic Interview (ADI) is a semi-structured interview designed to be completed by parents and caregivers of autistic persons (Le-Couteur et al., 1986).

The uptake of diagnostic instruments point again to the influence and success of *abstraction*. Definitions, debating possible causes and diagnostic assessment only make sense if the process is at work and autism has been, at some level, coherently separated out as a 'discrete ontological' entity with its 'own qualitative specificities' (Castree, 2003: 280). Counter-intuitively, the uncertainty discussed earlier can also be deemed to be part of these processes. If they are recast as battles over lines of abstraction, they can be understood as attempts to further the value of autism by improving the product. This is in keeping with Slater (1997: 105) who, following George Simmel, associates modern productivity with 'increasing differentiation of goods and increasing refinement and discrimination in tastes, needs and experiences'.

The significance of this can be understood if we consider it alongside the second form of *abstraction* suggested by Robertson (2000), that of *spatial abstraction*. Castree (2003: 281, emphasis in original) describes this as 'any individualized thing in one place being treated as *really the same* as an apparently similar thing located elsewhere'. Considered through these ideas, autism is not only revealed as a homogeneous 'thing' which is separated from and 'stands over and above' individuals and their specific sociocultural contexts, but also an entity which has incredible potential to travel across spaces. In other words, it has the capacity to be relevant to mass national and international markets.

In this section we have briefly outlined the processes by which autism can be considered to have become abstracted as a 'thing'. In the next section, we delve deeper into the process of commodification and narrow our focus to concentrate on *what* is being commodified.

Autism as academic commodity: Trading knowledges

Recent research on commodification has included considerations of: education (Dreyer and Kouzmin, 2009); science (Toleubayev et al., 2010); tourism (Cousins et al., 2009); health care (Timmermans and Almeling, 2009); the trade in body parts (Sharp, 2009) and intimacy (Constable, 2009). What they share with earlier work is a focus on the processes of commodification as the ways in which 'things' and social relations are affected by the market. In the following sections, we will explore the roles of labour and desire in the processes by which 'things' become established as commodities, but for now we want to concentrate on *what* is being commodified when autism becomes a 'thing' in the academy. We are aware that within the commercial autism industry, interventions and treatment programmes, such as Applied Behaviour Analysis, Relationship Development Interaction and the Son-Rise programme, are traded for profit. We also acknowledge that autism can be said to play a continuing role in selling cultural products such as the film *Rain Man* (1988) and the made-for-TV-movie *Temple Grandin* (2010). However, our interest is in academia's role in the processes by which autism is increasingly exchanged, and here the literature on commodification has again been helpful.

An area where the application of commodification theory has been particularly fruitful is in understanding changing socio-economic relationships with nature. In Robertson's (2000: 466) discussion of the commodification of wetlands, he comments that the process of commodification 'involves an abstraction from materiality of the unique object to an exchangeable medium which signifies the object'; this suggests that the *how* (the medium) rather than the *what* (the object) is significant. When Noel Castree (2003) identifies six ways in which nature is being commodified, he includes one which is very useful for our purposes. The sixth way in which nature is being commodifed according to Castree (2003) is *informationally*, as knowledge which is produced, traded and consumed; this comes closest to how we wish to theorise the exchange of knowledge around autism. Similarly, Thornes and Randalls (2007), when talking about the commodification of the atmosphere, discuss the production and exchange of data, information or predictions about the atmosphere used by providers of weather forecasts and insurers.

If we consider academia to be a marketplace of knowledge (Ball, 2004; Caplow and McGee, 2001) and focus on how knowledge about autism is being exchanged, in terms of courses, conferences, research centres and published research, it is clear that over the past few years, *informationally*, autism has become big business. In 2008 the UK hosted a number of conferences which took autism as their sole focus; they included: 'Autism Neuroscience Conference' (University of Cambridge); 'The National Autistic Society (NAS) Conference'; '7th Annual International Meeting for Autism Research (IMFAR) Conference'; 'Asperger Syndrome: Moving Forward Together' (Sheffield Hallam University); and 'International Conference on Autism in Cardiff' (Autism Cymru).

By 2010 a number of universities in the UK had established centres focusing on autism; these include: *Autism Centre for Education and*

Research (University of Birmingham); *Autism Research Centre* (University of Cambridge); Wales *Autism Research Centre* (University of Cardiff); *Autism Centre* (Sheffield Hallam University); and *Autism Research Unit* (University of Sunderland). There is a UK-based charity called *Research Autism*, which funds research into three priority areas: interventions, including biomedical interventions, autism and mental health, autism and challenging behaviour (www.researchautism.net).

With the increase in knowledge generation surrounding autism, a number of higher education institutions now offer autism-specific courses and therefore offer qualifications in autism. Taking a snapshot in August 2010, those institutions in the UK included Birmingham; Bristol; Cambridge; Sheffield Hallam; Strathclyde; and Sunderland.

In terms of the publication of research, there are a number of scholarly and practitioner journals based in the UK which are autism focused. These include *Autism: The International Journal of Research and Practice* (published in association with NAS) and *Good Autism Practice*. At the time of writing, the *Tizard Learning Disability Review* is advertising a themed issue on autism in 2011, the *Journal of Inclusive Practice* published its themed issue in 2009 and, in 2010, six out of the seven editions of the leading disability studies journal *Disability and Society* included an article on either autism or Asperger Syndrome.

The number and range of individual research publications on autism or Asperger Syndrome is vast. Using the search term autism, the search engine *Google Scholar* offers 249,000 articles with autism in them,[3] including Madriaga et al.'s (2008) study on the experiences of people labelled with Asperger Syndrome in higher education; Jones and Harwood's (2009) analysis of print media representations of autism; and Ryan's (2010) discussion of experiences, support and information needs of parents of children diagnosed with autism, particularly in relation to the use of public spaces.

While many of these are valuable contributions to knowledge and many have very tangible impacts on lived experiences, we want to problematise this expanse of study into autism, especially within social science. We seek to conceptualise courses, conferences, centres and publications as examples of autism being *informationally* exchanged and consumed. Although the monetary procurement which distinguishes capitalist exchange is readily apparent in moments such as when autism-as-information is purchased as a qualification, less explicit elements of what Castree (2003) calls *alienability* and *privatisation* – both key processes in the capitalist commodification process – are also present.

Alienability refers to a commodity being 'physically and ethically "detached" from its seller' (Castree, 2003: 280), as we will discuss in more detail. The process by which knowledge about autism can be detached from those labelled with autism is relatively simple and individual people quickly become disassociated from the knowledges they have provided. The recognised right to academic authorship of conference papers and publications as well as the institutional employment of academics, ownership of courses and conferment of qualifications also echoes Castree's (2003: 279) summary of the process of *privatisation* as the 'assignation of legal title to a named individual, group or institution. The title gives more-or-less exclusive rights to the owner to dispose of that which is named by the title as they wish'. Following this, knowledge about autism, or rather autism as an *information-thing*, can be considered not only a commodity but a distinctly capitalist commodity. Castree (2003: 279) goes on to say that 'the exchange of things either via or for money cannot occur unless those things belong to different parties who are free to alienate those things'. This leads us to consider the different parties involved in these processes as well as the role of *alienation*. The latter will ultimately help us to explore the possible implications of the commodification of autism for the emancipatory agendas of many studies into disability.

Producing autism: Labour and the processes of alienation

In differentiating the different parties, the first problem to be faced is who is who in the academic marketplace of autism information. As these theories on commodification owe a debt to Marx, the role call should be easy. They are the capitalists; we are the proletariat. We provide our labour and become subjugated into their capitalist system, in which they take the surplus from our labour and produce a profit. In this simplified version it is easy to follow the power within the production of autism as an *information-thing*. Professionals (often medical), practitioners, experts and academics hold the power as they own the means of knowledge production. Patients, families and autistic individuals do not. Time, bodies, selves, symptoms, behaviours and experiences are provided, often free of charge within clinical or research settings, to be medicalised and pathologised in order to produce knowledges which can be repackaged by the professionals, practitioners, experts and academics and reproduced for consumption to another set of patients, families and individuals. This view could be said to be supported by Oliver's (1990: 42) comment that 'what needs to be considered next is the way the individualisation of life under capitalism has contributed to the individualisation of disability and the role of powerful groups, notably, the medical profession, in this process'.

But the contemporary world is not this simple, and neither is Marxist theory nor the relationship between different parties in the cycles of production and consumption. Within the process of production, considering the relationships between capital and labour as dialectic (in dialogue) means that the production of capital only appears to be the responsibility of one party, the capitalists. In reality, it is the actualisation of labour power that produces the capital, that then faces the labourer as a distanced object. This is often referred to as the process of *alienation*, or as Castree (2003: 282) terms it *displacement*, in which 'something [appears], phenomenally, as something other than itself'. The concept of alienation is considered as characteristic of contemporary consumer culture, and Slater (1997: 104–5) describes a state where 'individuals are unable to recognise these objects as the products of their own labour' as fundamental to the process of capitalist commodity consumption.

So for us, although information about autism appears to be the sole responsibility of medical and allied professions, *in reality* the situation is much more complex. If we think about the labour of medical professionals and practitioners as well as the labour of individuals and families, both sets of labourers are labouring to abstract and produce autism as a 'thing'. The 'instruments of labour' (Marx, 1954) may well include the mind and bodies, symptoms and behaviours of those with the label autism but also include the labours of the medical professionals and practitioners. This is even more complicated if we add in the academic labours involved in producing autism *informationally*. Following medical-labour, autism is 'ready for immediate consumption' but goes on to 'serve as raw material for a further product' (Marx, 1954: 177) such as a research paper on how to include children with the label of autism in mainstream education. In all these scenarios, the process of *alienation* is at work as labourers are distanced from the product of their labours. They all face autism as a distant object, a *thing*, rather than as the product their mutual labours or, even more significantly, as 'externalizations of their own subjectivity' (Slater, 1997: 105).

With the binary between expert on and person labelled with autism collapsed, we begin to see how the world in which we live and work is mutually constituted. We are all labourers, and by virtue of being labourers, we are also all consumers (Slater, 1997); there are no clear cut parties in this process. Albrecht's (1992) analysis of the US disability-business also concluded that while stakeholder groups could be identified, they were mutually dependent. This becomes particularly important for us later because it requires that we all acknowledge our implication in these processes and removes the possibility of simply decrying and/or disregarding the dominance of a medical paradigm. However, first we consider further how desire and the concept of *commodity fetishism* helps understand how the market works to sustain this alienation between subjects (labourers) and objects (autism) through the promise of usefulness.

Desiring autism: The role of promise in commodity fetishism

From the number of courses, conferences and research centres devoted to it, autism appears to have value. The raw materials that have been used to create that value can be said to be the time, bodies, selves, symptoms, behaviours and experiences provided by families and individuals, utilised by and added to by the time, bodies, selves of professionals, practitioners, experts and academics. As we discussed above, the source and conversion of that value via 'concrete acts of making and doing' (Slater, 1997: 115) is made invisible through *alienation*; as Marx states, 'the process disappears in the product' (Marx, 1954: 176). The significance of this is that labourers, and thereby consumers, perceive products like autism to be beyond human making or changing and as such the commodity is perceived as a fixed, static and ahistorical 'thing' (Slater, 1997). This is the process of *fetishism*, a concept Marx took from the study of religion to mean the 'capacity of humanity to ignore the fact that we create our own material culture and instead treat commodities as though they come to us as the products of some other force' (Miller, 2003: 360). In other words, the labourer and the consumer *only* perceive the product and its value in its ready-made form. This has been called 'the fantastic form' (Marx, 1976: 165) or to use Rose's (1978: 47) term, 'the phantasmagorical form'. This highlights the importance of the point of consumption. As Marx (1954: 173) states, in order for labour to reappear in a commodity, the labourer must 'expend it on something useful, on something capable of satisfying a want of some sort', it raises the question – what *want* is autism satisfying?

The insights of W. F. Haug (1986) are really helpful here. He discusses how market exchange depends on the consumer's self-acknowledged need for the object. However, at the moment of exchange, the precise object has not yet been experienced therefore it is instead the *promise* of its use-value that is bought into. For Haug the promise is established through its appearance which helps us to refine our question to – what is the *promise* of autism? What leads us to buy (into) it? We argue that for all the uncertainty surrounding autism, it is the promise of coherent explanations that makes us buy (into) it. We argue that it is the promise of useful information. Predominately biomedical but also social, political and economic practices have created a situation where expert medical professionals produce autism as a 'thing' because they perceive a need for certain behaviours and symptoms to be explained. Practitioners and academics consume such knowledge in their efforts to create knowledge which fulfils the perceived need for informed interventions in certain situations (e.g. the classroom). Parents and families help produce autism in their interactions with the medical profession and consume autism in order to understand and better care for their loved ones, indeed to be a good parent depends on consumption of such knowledge. Individuals, often in the role of patient, also consume such knowledge in efforts to better understand themselves. Thus the circular logic of a self-sustaining commodity chain is established through the power of promise.

What is revealed here is that although autism is consumed differently at different times in the commodification cycle, it remains identifiably autism throughout; the phantasmagorical form remains intact. Even when the neurodiversity movement reject negative, tragic and deficit aspects of medicine in order to better define themselves, autism is still consumed through medical knowledges. The ability of neurology to explain autism as 'thing' is not questioned; medicine is merely requested to change its focus (see Ortega, 2009) and autism as an abstracted biomedical entity remains relatively undisturbed.

The unremitting nature of this promise, or rather the persistence of the phantasmagorical form, also helps explain the growth in autism. As the promise of the commodity is never fully fulfilled, temporary satisfaction gives way to the need to consume again and the self-sustaining commodity chain is maintained. Slater (1997: 125), following Marcuse, speaks to this when he comments: 'identified so utterly with the commodities on offer, modern subjects cannot see alternatives or perceive the limited nature of satisfaction within the commodity system'. For the final sections, we explore the implications of, and possible responses to, this inability to recognise the limited nature of satisfaction.

Defetishising autism: Thinking, reading and watching academic presences

> Think we must. Let us think in offices; in omnibuses; while we are standing in the crowd watching Coronations and Lord Mayor's Shows; let us think as we pass the Cenotaph; and in Whitehall; in the gallery of the House of Commons; in the Law Courts; let us think at baptisms and marriages and funerals. Let us never cease from thinking – what is this 'civilization' in which we find ourselves? What are these professions and why should we make money out of them? Where in short is it leading us, the procession of the sons of educated men?
>
> (Woolf, 1938: 62–3, cited in England, 1994: 80)

Using the words of the novelist and essayist Virginia Woolf, Kim England begins her exploration of the importance of paying attention to how the academic discipline of geography is *made* by those involved in it. Here, we argue that we need to pay attention to how *we* make the study of disability by participating in it as, for example, students, lecturers or researchers. In doing so, we respond to Woolf and England (1994: 80) when they ask us to 'consider the structure of our social relations and how we are accountable for them and how our actions perpetuate those relations'. A similar call has been made by Tanya Titchkosky (2008: 3) when she demands that we 'watch our watchings' and 'read our readings'. For us, it has meant asking hard questions and being prepared to not like the answers.

In this section, we explore the implications of impairment labels, such as autism, remaining unquestioned within academia and advocate increased thinking, reading and watching via the use of *defetishisation* as a critical practice (Castree, 2001). If the term *fetish* 'implies our capacity to deny what we should know about manufacture and to treat goods as autonomous from their origins' (Miller, 2003: 360), then *defetishisation* is the process by which we acknowledge our denial and work through the consequences of that acknowledgement.

Firstly, the commodification of a certain category cannot help but valorise one brand of impairment over another. It could be argued that autism now occupies a top spot in the hierarchy of impairments, attracting research funding, university courses, services and resources that less famous, less certain and less commodified impairments cannot hope to attract. Castree's (2003: 288) description of *commodification effects*, where the commodification of one entity impacts upon nearby and related non-commodities, is pertinent here. An example occurs in Murray's (2008: 5) recent book where he recognises that autism is 'only one condition among many that needs to have its place within cultural narratives explained' but still autism *is* the one which is having its cultural narratives explained, thereby leaving the narratives of other states of corporeal difference unexplained.

Secondly, as we have demonstrated, as the commodified category of autism remains fetishised, the dominance of medical perspectives on disability is maintained. This leads to a rather uncomfortable deduction for anyone who considers the academic study of disability to be committed to the emancipation of disabled people *from* the tyranny of medical discourses. When we discuss autism as a *thing*, when we hold sessions about it, establish research centres around it or write articles on it, we are implicated in sustaining the fetish. We suggest that instead, researchers and students of disability nurture a state of critical consciousness by utilising tools from social theory because, for the reasons stated above, it is only when we recognise the role of *our* labour in the production and commodification of autism and practice *defetishisation* that we can contribute to the transformation of society and participate in efforts towards the continued emancipation of *all* disabled people. This leads us to conclude by outlining what a *defetishisation* of autism can offer to people with the label autism.

Conclusions

In this chapter we have argued that the increasing academic presence of autism can be explored by conceptualising it as 'thing-like form'. From there we sketched out how autism becomes a capitalist commodity; we thought through the different parties involved in the process by which labour becomes distanced from the moment of production; and we discussed the importance of promise to understanding the purchasing of autism. We ended by arguing that such defetishising theorising suggests that the persistent presence of autism reveals a significant threat to the part academia can play in the continued emancipation of disabled people.

As disability theorists are often accused of failing to consider the impact of their work on disabled people (Barnes, 2010), and as Lennard Davis (2008) does at the end of his cultural history of Obsessive Compulsive Disorder (OCD), we finish by asking the most important question – what does all this mean for a person labelled with a commodified impairment? We do not intend to present commodification as wholly a bad thing (Jackson, 1999) but as Robertson (2000: 466) is at pains to remind us, we 'should never lose sight of the social work involved in abstraction and commodification'. While some of this 'social work' can be considered valuable, and commodification can be deemed as potentially enabling for people labelled with autism, we contend that this is not without clear and present dangers.

The NAS's campaign in the UK for autism awareness[4] has promoted understanding and tolerance in the wider community of what is often called autistic difference. However, the promise such campaigns offer, like the commodifed promise of autism itself, can only ever satisfy the consumer temporarily. Inevitably many of the symptoms and behaviours of individuals with the label of autism remain unexplained and this dissatisfaction leads to the further production, trading and consumption of autism as consumers search for a better product.

Furthermore, as the dominance of medical perspectives are maintained, the dangers of individuals labelled with autism becoming dissolved into, and in some cases buying into, an inescapable, fixed and totalising autism identity are all too obvious. As Robertson (2000: 466) states, 'commodification involves an act of reference in which, through exchange, the abstraction is treated by actors as equivalent to the concrete'. The resulting experience of a 'concrete' label being considered before, and at times, instead of, the person echoes the distancing we have been discussing.

We are aware that Marxism is far from theoretically fashionable, but maintain, as Miller (2003) does, that this is not because the issues it deals with have gone away. For us, its explanatory power helps makes sense of those repeated conversations over cups of coffee in draughty corridors at research conferences. We have only explored a fraction of what the theory of *commodification* could offer to the elucidation of the academic presence of autism but hope that we have demonstrated the benefits of *defetishisation* as a critical practice and the need to labour towards, rather than against, 'the reinscription of the larger humanity we share as both workers and consumers' (Miller, 2003: 371).

Acknowledgements

We would like to thank the editors and John Rees for their insightful and extremely valuable comments on various drafts of this chapter. And we are especially grateful to William Runswick-Cole for inspiring us to think through the commodification of autism.

48   *Commodifying Autism*

Notes

1. Autism Speaks: http://www.autismspeaks.org/.
2. At the time of writing, DSM IV is being revised and there has been a proposal to delete Asperger Syndrome from DSM V.
3. Search carried out 21 November 2010.
4. There have been a number of campaigns from the NAS promoting autism awareness in the UK over recent years including *Think Differently About Autism* and *You Need to Know* (www.nas.org.uk).

References

Albrecht, G. (1992). *The Disability Business: Rehabilitation in America*. Newbury Park, CA: Sage.
Albrecht, G. and Bury, M. (2001). 'The Political Economy of the Disability Marketplace'. In G. L. Albrecht, K. D. Seelman and M. Bury (eds), *Handbook of Disability Studies*. Thousand Oaks/London/Delhi: Sage.
Alleyne, R. (2010). 'Brain Scan Could Diagnose Autism Early'. *Daily Telegraph*, January, http://www.telegraph.co.uk/health/healthnews/6951699/Brain-scan-could-diagnose-autism-early.html, date accessed 21 November 2010.
American Psychiatric Association (1994). *Diagnostic and Statistical Manual of Mental Disorder* (fourth edition). Washington, DC: American Psychiatric Association.
Asperger, H. (1944). *Die Autistischen Psychopathen, In Kindesalter, Archiv. Fur Psychiatrie und Nervenkrankheiten*, 117, 76–136.
Attwood, T. (2000). *Asperger's Syndrome: A Guide for Parents and Professional*. London: Jessica Kingsley.
Attwood, T. (2007). *The Complete Guide to Asperger's Syndrome*. London: Jessica Kingsley.
Ball, S. (2004). 'Education for Sale! The Commodification of Everything?' The Annual Lecture, Department of Education and Professional Studies, King's College, London, June, http://www.kcl.ac.uk/content/1/c6/05/16/42/lecture-ball.pdf, date accessed 13 September 2010.
Baker, D. L. (2006). 'Neurodiversity, Neurological Disability and the Public Sector: Notes on the Autism Spectrum'. *Disability and Society*, 21 (1), 15–29.
Barnes, C. (2010). 'Book Review Arguing about Disability: Philosophical Perspectives, edited by Kristjana Kristiansen, Simo Vehmas and Tom Shakespeare, London, Routledge, 2010'. *Disability and Society*, 25 (1), 123–5.
Bettleheim, B. (1967). *The Empty Fortress: Infantile Autism and the Birth of the Self*. New York: The Free Press.
Burgoine, E. and Wing, L. (1983). 'Identical Triplets with Asperger's Syndrome'. *British Journal of Psychiatry*, 33 (7), 1169–82.
Caplow, T. and McGee, R. (2001). *The Academia Marketplace*. New Jersey: Transaction.
Castree, N. (2001). 'Commodity Fetishism: Geographical Imaginations and Imaginative Geographies'. *Environment and Planning A*, 33, 1519–25.
Castree, N. (2003). 'Commodifying What Nature?' *Progress in Human Geography*, 27 (3), 273–97.
Conquergood, D. (1991). 'Rethinking Ethnography: Towards a Critical Cultural Politics'. *Communication Monographs*, 58, http://www.csun.edu/~vcspc00g/603/RethinkingEthnography-DC.pdf, date accessed 3 December 2010.

Constable, N. (2009). 'The Commodification of Intimacy: Marriage, Sex, and Reproductive Labor'. *Annual Review of Anthropology*, 38, 49–64.

Cousins, J., Evans, J. and Sadler, J. (2009). 'Selling Conservation? Scientific Legitimacy and the Commodification of Conservation Tourism'. *Ecology and Society*, 14, http://www.ecologyandsociety.org/vol14/iss1/art32/, date accessed 4 December 2010.

Davidson, J. and Smith, M. (2009). 'Autistic Autobiographies and More-than-Human Emotional Geographies'. *Environment and Planning D: Society and Space*, 27, 898–916.

Davis, L. J. (2008). *Obsession: A Cultural History*. Chicago/London: University of Chicago Press.

Dreyer, W. and Kouzmin, A. (2009). 'The Commodification of Tertiary Education within a Knowledge Economy'. *Journal of Economic and Social Policy*, 13 (1), http://epubs.scu.edu.au/jesp/vol13/iss1/1, date accessed 3 December 2010.

England, K. V. L. (1994). 'Getting Personal: Reflexivity, Positionality, and Feminist Research'. *Professional Geographer*, 46 (1), 80–9.

Finkelstein, V. (1980). *Attitudes and Disabled People: Issues for Discussion*. New York: World Rehabilitation Fund.

Frith, U. (2003). *Autism: Understanding the Enigma*. Oxford: Blackwell.

Gleeson, B. (1999). *Geographies of Disability*. London: Routledge.

Grandin, T. (1996). *Thinking in Pictures: And Other Reports from My Life with Autism*. New York: Vintage Books.

Greenwell, B. (2004). 'The Curious Incidence of Novels about Asperger's Syndrome'. *Children's Literature in Education*, 35 (3), 271–284.

Haddon, M. (2003). *Curious Incident of the Dog in the Night-Time*. London: Jonathan Cape.

Happe, F. (1999). 'Cognitive Deficit or Cognitive Style?' *Trends in Cognitive Sciences*, 3 (6), 216–21.

Haug, W. F. (1986). *Critique of Commodity Aesthetics: Appearance, Sexuality and Advertising in Capitalist Society*. Minneapolis: Minnesota University Press.

Jackson, P. (1989). *Maps of Meaning: An Introduction to Cultural Geography*. London: Routledge.

Jackson, P. (1999). 'Commodity Cultures: The Traffic in Things'. *Transactions of the Institute of British Geographers*, 24 (1), 95–108.

Jones, S. C. and Harwood, V. (2009). 'Representations of Autism in Australian Print Media'. *Disability and Society*, 24 (1), 5–18.

Kanner, L. (1943). 'Autistic Disturbances of Affective Contact'. *Nervous Child 2*, 217–50.

Lawson, W. (2000). *Life Behind Glass: A Personal Account of Autism Spectrum Disorder*. London: Jessica Kingsley.

Le- Couteur, A., Bailey, A., Goode, S., Pickles, A., Robertson, S., Gottesman, I. and Rutter, M. (1986). 'A Broader Phenotpye of Autism – The Clinical Spectrum in Twins'. *Journal of Child Psychology and Psychiatry*, 37, 177–86.

Madriaga, M., Goodley, D., Hodge, N. and Martin, N. (2008). *Enabling Transition into University for Students with Asperger Syndrome*, http://www.heacademy.ac.uk/projects/detail/projectfinder/projects/pf2971lr, date accessed on 21 November 2010.

Mallett, R. and Runswick-Cole, K. (2010). 'Knowing Me, Knowing You, Aha!: Does the Urge to Know Impairment Reveal an Urge to Know Normal?' Critical Disability Studies Conference 'Theorizing Normalcy and the Mundane', 12–13 May, Manchester, UK.

Marx, K. (1954). *Capital – Book One: The Process of Production of Capital*. London: Lawrence and Wishart.

Marx, K. (1976). *Capital*, Vol 1. London: Penguin/New Left Review.

McGuire, A. and Michalko, R. (2009). 'Minds Between Us: Autism, Mindblindness and the Uncertainty of Communication'. *Educational Philosophy and Theory*, http://onlinelibrary.wiley.com/doi/10.1111/j.1469-5812.2009.00537.x/full, date accessed 12 September 2010.

McNeil, D. (2009). 'Outbreak of Autism or Statistical fluke?' *New York Times*, March, http://www.nytimes.com/2009/03/17/health/17auti.html, date accessed 21 November 2010.

Miller, D. (2003). 'Could the Internet Defetishise the Commodity?' *Environment and Planning D: Society and Space* 21, 359–72.

Mitchell, D. (1995). 'There's No Such Thing as Culture: Towards a Reconceptualisation of the Idea of Culture in Geography'. *Transactions of the Institute of British Geographers*, 20 (1), 102–116.

Molloy, H. and Vasil, L. (2002). 'The Social Construction of Asperger Syndrome: The Pathologising of Difference?' *Disability and Society*, 17, 659–69.

Murray, S. (2008). *Representing Autism: Culture, Narrative, Fascination*. Liverpool: Liverpool University Press.

Nadesan, M. H. (2005). *Constructing Autism: Unraveling the 'Truth' and Constructing the Social*. Abingdon: Routledge.

National Autistic Society (1998). *The Autistic Spectrum – A Handbook 1999*. London: National Autistic Society.

National Autistic Society (2008). *What is Autism?* http://www.autism.org.uk/about-autism/autism-and-asperger-syndrome-an-introduction/what-is-autism.aspx, date accessed 12 November 2010.

Oliver, M. (1990). *The Politics of Disablement*. London: Macmillan.

Ortega, F. (2009). 'The Cerebral Subject and the Challenge of Neurodiversity'. *BioSocieties*, 4, 425–45.

Pfeiffer, D. and Yoshida, K. (1995). 'Teaching Disability Studies in Canada and the USA'. *Disability and Society*, 10 (4), 475–500.

Rain Man (1988). Dir. Barry Levinson.

Robertson, M. M. (2000). 'No Net Loss: Wetland Restoration and the Incomplete Capitalization of Nature'. *Antipode*, 32 (4), 463–93.

Rose, G. (1978). *The Melancholy Science: An Introduction to the Thoughts of Theodor W. Adorno*. London: Macmillian.

Ryan, S. (2010). 'Meltdowns, Surveillance and Managing Emotions: Going Out with Children with Autism'. *Health and Place*, 16 (5), 868–75.

Sharp, L. A. (2009). *Bodies, Commodities and Biotechnologies: Death, Mourning and Scientific Desire in the Realm of Human Organ Transfer*. New York: Colombia University Press.

Slater, D. (1997). *Consumer Culture and Modernity*. Cambridge: Polity.

Snow Cake (2006) Dir. Marc Evans.

Temple Grandin (2010) Dir. Mick Jackson.

Timmermans, S. and Almeling, R. (2009). 'Objectification, Standardization, and Commodification in Health Care: A Conceptual Readjustment'. *Social Science and Medicine*, 69 (1), 21–7.

Thornes, J. E. and Randalls, S. (2007). 'Commodifying the Atmosphere: "Pennies from heaven?"' *Geografiska Annaler*, 89A (4), 1–13.

Titchkosky, T. (2008). *Reading and Writing Disability Differently: The Textured Life of Embodiment*. Toronto: University of Toronto Press.

Toleubayev, K., Jansen, K. and van Huis, A. (2010). 'Commodification of Science and the Production of Public Goods: Plant Protection Research in Kazakhstan'. *Research Policy*, 39 (3), 411–21.

Wakefield, A. J., Murch, S. H. and Anthony, A. (1998). 'Ileal-Lymphoid-Nodular Hyperplasia, Non-Specific Colitis, and Pervasive Developmental Disorder in Children'. *Lancet*, 351 (9103), 637–41.

Welcome to Our World ... Living with Autism (2011) V&A Museum of Childhood, London, March.

Wing, L. (1991). 'Asperger Syndrome: A Clinical Account'. *Psychological Medicine*, 11, 143–55.

4
Disability and the Majority World: A Neocolonial Approach

Shaun Grech

Introduction

Global guesstimates suggest that around 80 per cent of the planet's 650 million disabled people are located in the so-called Global South, the bulk in rural areas and most suffer the brunt of disproportionate poverty. In spite of this, disability studies remains profoundly WENA (West European and North American) and focused exclusively on urban post-industrialist settings. In spite of this, its theories and tenets such as the social model of disability are consistently exported to a Global South it never intended to address. As the imperialistic trail of Western knowledge and practices legitimises this process, debates are perpetually re/neocolonised, discourses are simplified and generalised, contexts (places and spaces), cultures and histories (temporalities) homogenised, and many critical issues ignored or intentionally resisted. They become ontological invisibility. Disability studies becomes complicit in the neocolonising of the Southern space. This chapter is inspired by elements of post-structuralism and Latin American writings on coloniality/neocolonialism (Coronil, 2000, 2008; Quijano, 2008) and seeks to explore and critically discuss some of the gaps that emerge when attempting to articulate a critical debate around disability in the majority world. The chapter takes on the call by some to decolonise methodologies (Tuhiwai Smith, 2002), as well as thought and debate (Fanon, 1967; Meekosha, 2008; Goodley, 2010). It concludes that a critical disability studies that is open, situated around prioritising, engaging with and learning about the Global South in its full complexity is necessary, a project I term *Critical Global Disability Studies*.

Neocolonised spaces – neocolonised bodies

In recent years, postcolonial theories and concepts have injected much needed theoretical and analytical breadth into the study of disability (see Ghai, 2002; Sherry, 2007). In this chapter, I move beyond the postcolonial, towards the neocolonial, in a bid to emphasise that decolonisation in much of the Global South has not meant the end of empires, but simply the shift from 'global colonialism' to 'global coloniality' (Grosfoguel, 2008: 8). This necessitates a strong focus on the colonial encounter, not only as a historical event that has come and gone, but one that provides the foundations for the continuing contemporary material, discursive, epistemological and ontological domination of Southern spaces and bodies.

History remains one of the critical instruments creating the ideological–cultural conditions that facilitate and maintain relations of domination in contemporary times. Tuhiwai Smith (2002: 34) is direct: 'history is mostly about power. It is the story of the powerful and how they became powerful, and then how they use their power to keep them in positions in which they can continue to dominate others'. The colonial encounter/invasion is perhaps the only common experience in the complex, fragmented and heterogeneous histories of the Global South, but it is all too often bypassed in the linear and Eurocentric materialist accounts of universal history – pre-capitalism/capitalism with nothing before or in between (see for example Oliver, 1990, 1996; Barnes, 2009).[1] Santos (2007: 39) in fact questions the 'monoculture of linear time' in materialist accounts, proposing instead 'an ecology of temporalities' permitting differential spaces, their own distinct time lines.

Indeed, the colonial encounter stretching back to the late fifteenth century, with the domination of the Atlantic commercial circuit (of silver, gold and other products destined for the world market) by the Portuguese and the Spanish, is not simply an abstraction. Quijano's (2008) much cited work on the coloniality of power, in fact, highlights how coloniality is constitutive of modernity, implying that modernity not only came earlier than the eighteenth-century European enlightenment, but was instituted through a project of racial exploitation, division of labour and extraction favouring the European empires. Any serious materialist critique, therefore, cannot possibly bypass the colonial encounter, because it is constitutive of 'the historical development of modern society and of capitalism' (Lander, 2000: 35). As Coronil (2000: 93, my translation) emphasises, coloniality is 'the dark side of European capitalism; it cannot be reduced to a footnote in its biography'. We need a materialist analysis capable of stretching back its timelines, therefore, to redress its Eurocentric view of capitalism (and the overall analysis) as a European project, fabricated within the European space, and only then, spread to the world's 'backward' peripheries. This view of history and capitalism is dangerous because it casts into ontological oblivion the invasion, domination, subordination and oppression of the Global South and its people, and the introduction of 'racial "Otherness" as the ideological key to domination' (Green, 2003: 23). Race and racism, therefore, are not only instrumental, but indeed constitutive of the colonial encounter and hence also of capitalist accumulation, and cannot be eliminated from the analysis.

Disabled people, like others, do not exist outside this history and were impacted as part of the subaltern. The colonial constructions of, and approaches to, disability seep into and make up the contemporary disability landscape (including the transmission/imposition of knowledge and practices) (see Grech, 2011). In the colonial enterprise, notions of 'defectiveness and sub-normality', for example, were employed to legitimise the broad subjugation of the colonised subjects – 'intellectual normality and disability as self-evident – one the ideal and the other in need of a cure' (Kliewer and Fitzgerald, 2001, cited in Wehbi et al., 2009: 414). These measures often isolated disabled people, were a cause of extraordinary suffering, and destroyed traditional forms of care within communities. The focus on production and exportation for the world market (founded on the extraction of labour through slavery or serfdom) also implied that those who were seen as unfit (among them disabled people) or schismatic to the European presence and order had to be normalised (to function and produce), or else subjugated and isolated.

Colonialism is buried deep in the psyche of the colonised because people speak from their particular locations within power structures, past and present. There are some that have never changed, their knowledge always situated, their narratives often shared-past, present and future. These are the geopolitics of their knowledge. Overall, these marginalised imaginaries and subjugated spaces need differential epistemologies and methodologies.

More broadly, colonialism provides the ontological, material, spatial, global and political backdrop for the contemporary contexts we talk about – the Global South. Colonialism and its dynamics, effects and manifestations are in fact recreated and perpetuated in the *neocolonial*. While Ashcroft et al. (2002: 216) concludes that 'perhaps the ultimate and unavoidable future of postcolonial studies lies in its relation to globalization', this statement reads more as an apology, than a statement of intent. Dirlik (1994: 339) observes how the concept of the 'postcolonial is applicable not to all of the postcolonial period, but only to that period after colonialism when, among other things, a forgetting of its effects has begun to set in'. It is in fact interesting to note that other than the work of Edward Said (1993), mainstream postcolonial theory continues to elide the term imperialism, one that usefully brings together colonialism, neocolonialism and present strategies of Western intervention. In response to this and others, a corpus of Latin American writings[2] emerged much earlier than postcolonial studies (partly based on the earlier colonial period and independence), emphasising instead that 'we are still living under the same regime' (Mignolo, 2008: 249) – a global coloniality. The broader implication of the coloniality of power is that decolonisation not only has not fully occurred, but will remain perpetually incomplete unless the racial, ethnic, sexual, cultural, economic and the many other power disparities are shifted.

Disabled people exist, live, operate and are constrained by coloniality in its multiple forms, where the contemporary modes of domination are not simply the aftermath of a domination that was, but instead one that remains the necessary lifeline for those dominating (discursively and materially), and that perpetuate the inscription of the history of difference and subjugation. Disabled bodies are therefore repositioned as neocolonised subjects, or better still *neocolonised bodies* – the bodies positioned at the anxious intersection of the economic, the cultural and political, the global and the local. These are the docile bodies ruled over indefinitely by virtue of and through their specific geopolitical, historical and ontological location. Neo-liberal globalisation and the economic policies, ideologies and unequal trade relationships favouring metropolitan countries embody the neocolonial. As Coronil (2008: 416) notes, neo-liberal globalisation represents the shift from Eurocentrism to 'globalcentrism', a process that 'dissolves the West into the market and crystallises it in less visible transnational modules of concentrated financial and political power'. Neo-liberalism for majority world countries, overridden by debt, is hardly a choice, imposed through standardised policy reforms or rather structural adjustments programmes (SAPs) as a condition to obtain a loan from the World Bank or IMF. Deceptively renamed Poverty Reduction Strategy Papers (PRSPs) in 1999, the fundamentalist one-size-fits-all neo-liberal package remains the same, and has become synonymous with 'development' and often comprises: the infamous 'roll back the state' and cutbacks in public sector expenditure; liberalisation of markets; and mass privatisation. These continue to increase poverty, suffering and inequality (between and within countries); lead to unemployment and conflict; constrain the fragile economies of the Global South, and overall regenerate the domination of Western empires, and sustain the logic and path of racial differentiation.

Disabled people are not spared the effects of these neo-liberal impositions. Elsewhere (see Grech, 2009) I argue that these are in fact antithetical to inclusive development because they (among others) destroy livelihoods (e.g. push out small-scale farmers unable to compete with subsidised imports); reduce access to health care and other basic services (e.g. schools); shatter critical family support (e.g. when family members are forced to migrate, often the healthier and stronger ones); are a source of environmental degradation and destruction (and hence degenerating living and working spaces) and so on. Importantly, neo-liberal globalisation strengthens economic growth as the ultimate end of the development enterprise, the pre-requisite of which is the disciplining and normalising of bodies to produce, the *homo oeconomicus* predicated on the production of docile bodies.

Neo-liberal globalisation emerges as much more than an economic theory and associated practices, but is instead 'a hegemonic discourse of a civilising model ... supported in specific historical-cultural conditions' (Lander, 2000: 11, my translation). While materialist accounts in disability studies brush over the subject through some or other narrative about what they refer to as 'free market economics', it is hard to miss the ultra simplistic and extreme Eurocentrism of this analysis, especially in that transposed to the majority world from the Western comfort zones (see for example Barnes, 2009). What emerges in these accounts is an utter failure to consider the workings of global markets in practice, and how free markets in the UK are not the same as those imposed on the Global South, the latter the playground for global politics, where Western empires are constantly recreated and perpetuated. The debate should instead be about colonialism, global capitalism, material and ontological domination of the Global South, international (rather than exclusively national) markets and international division of labour and nations and geopolitics, without ever losing sight of imperialism. A decent knowledge of how these work, the politics, parties involved (e.g. the IMF, WTO and their respective histories, functions etc.), the architecture of neo-liberal impositions (e.g. PRSPs), and more broadly global economics remain sadly lacking in these few West/Eurocentric materialist accounts attempting to extend/impose their standard rhetoric to the Global South. This knowledge is required at the very least to be able to speak the language of a development sector packed with economists, and to present a critique that is global, informed, relevant and timely so that demands to include disabled people are not simply shot down by even more excuses using more global economics jargon.

Neo-liberal globalisation is only one mechanism embodying and perpetuating the neocolonial. Wars and violence remain clear examples. Often steered by the Western hand, violent conflict remains a major cause of impairment and death throughout the world and shatters the lives of those who live through it: loss of livelihoods and shelter; interrupted education; ill-health and disease; displacement; psychological trauma; and a plethora of other impacts experienced more harshly by certain populations, among them disabled people. The neocolonial also emerges and breathes through the environmental degradation – a major source of poverty, destitution and ill-health – caused by rich countries, and again among the hardest hit are disabled people. Research, media and other representations such as movies, documentaries, books and development discourse also embody and perpetuate the neocolonial. These blatant or subliminal messages, are insidious in constructing a Southern subject that is degenerate, sexual, ignorant, violent, uncivilized- calling for, and even desiring an illuminated and civilized intervention that can only be offered by the Western hand. Developing and humanizing the Other, therefore becomes a moral obligation. Overall, these and other aspects of what is positioned as the neocolonial, the intersections between global politics, global power and economic asymmetries and inequalities and disability remain largely overlooked in the Western disability studies, focused on these Western spaces, some strands more insular than others.

From the global–historical to the local

As one moves from the global and historical to the local, contextual and other aspects of the Global South are cast even further into ontological oblivion. Paradoxically, the majority world is talked about but with little or no engagement with the complex and heterogeneous socio-economic, political and cultural landscapes that make up these spaces. For many disability theorists, the majority world is simply an object of curiosity and study, written about from the detached comfort of their Western offices. From this position, all the world is made to look the same, simplified, reduced and homogenised, which in turn permits the sale of one's own epistemologies to everyone, everywhere. What does not fit is removed, rejected or resisted, while the politics of location of these Western writings that ultimately make their imposition complicit in the neocolonial are conveniently shelved. In this scenario, few are the attempts to learn about aspects of the contexts we talk about, despite the fact that disabled people and their families live in them and they shape their experiences, possibilities and barriers. This is the reality they are bound to speak about, because like others they do not live in a vacuum.

Poverty is a critical defining aspect of this space, but this is little more than an abused term. While it is the assumed (and disproportionate) presence of this poverty that draws researchers to the majority world in the first place (a space that exists at least ontologically as something separate from the West), this complex term is simply brushed over, taken as a given, rarely conceptualised or assumed to be the same everywhere. All that defies, veers from or resists the Western individualist, welfarist, secular, urban, industrial space known by many Western disability theorists is ignored. One may include here a number of examples: around 55 per cent of the population in the Global South live in rural areas; some 80 per cent depend on agriculture and 75 per cent of the extreme poor are located in these rural areas (IFAD, 2001; World Bank, 2008). Complex and diverse livelihood strategies and activities (rather than one job), which are not always remunerated (e.g. labour in kind), and are almost always in the informal sector, are also pursued by the poor in the bid to seek security. This means that most of the poor are not registered, do not pay income tax or insurance, and are not entitled to benefits, meeting the frequent absence of a welfare system and other universal social protection measures (e.g. health, disability benefits etc.). Many poor people, particularly in rural areas, are often both producers and consumers. Between 50 per cent and 70 per cent of the budget of a poor household is used simply to purchase food, compared to 10 per cent to 15 per cent in rich countries (FAO, 2008).

By positioning disability within these impoverished spaces, a myriad of issues that are hardly ever talked about emerge. I discuss *some* of these in the rest of this chapter. This is not a comprehensive listing but simply marks one attempt at generating much needed questioning and critical debate.

Defining disability across cultures: No simple affair

The definition of disability remains hugely controversial. The category 'disability' is itself a Western construct that emerged in particular historical circumstances in Europe, and has only recently penetrated the majority world through 'surveys, research projects, rehabilitation programs and government policy' (Whyte and Ingstad, 1995: 7). Disability issues in the Global South also importantly remain embedded in the colonial, and in the construction of neocolonial terrains and identities described above. Overall, a homogeneous category called 'disabled' does not exist, and the meanings of disability (and also 'non-disability') vary among disabled people. Meaning is dependent on the hybrid contexts in which disability is placed, and any attempt to understand what disability means in specific spaces involves first engaging with what is valued in these same social, political, economic, cultural and ontological locations. Wasserman's (2001: 229) questions are pertinent: 'what valued roles and functions are limited by impairments?' and 'what is valuable about the activities that these same impairments limit to a certain extent?' These activities form part of what comes to be understood as full personhood[3] in specific contexts and temporalities. It is against this background that the meaning of disability is shaped, lived and experienced. Disability takes shape in the context of the hegemony of 'normality': 'to understand the disabled body, one must return to the concept of the norm, the normal body' (Davis, 2010: 3).

But contexts vary even within one country at the most micro levels, and are themselves dynamic. This means that so too does the landscape of personhood, including what is regarded as of value in personhood. When these change, so too do bodily interactions, experiences and hence the meaning of impairment. Furthermore, so too do individual, family, social and other circumstances. These transformations make the definition of disability as well as the disability experience complex and intensely heterogeneous. This runs parallel to the position adopted by many feminists who have engaged with 'the multiple subject positions of each individual' (Mann, 1994: 159). One may include here a broad range of aspects (themselves dynamic and interacting). These should include: the type of impairment; quantities and quality of health care (and associated costs); the presence of other health conditions (e.g. HIV/AIDS) and/or impairments; prices and price hikes (e.g. of food and medication); family (if any) composition and number of dependents (compared to those engaged in remunerated activities); rurality and geographic isolation; types of livelihood; age; class (or caste); role in the household economy (e.g. household head/main income earner); presence of extended family and communities; ill-health and disability among other family members (that could absorb resources or affect financial inflows); status and citizenship (e.g. refugees); conflict (past or present); organisational or other formal support; religious and other beliefs; and so on. If contexts and circumstances vary and are not static, so is the meaning of disability *fluid, dynamic and shifting, constantly (re)negotiated*. Disability across cultures can hardly be encapsulated in all embracing models, whether the social or medical model or by any other universalising discourse.

Beyond oppression: The homogenising of the Southern subject and space and the complexity of the disability experience

Despite the difficulties, if not impossibility, of encapsulating disability comprehensively across space and time, the attempts at simplifying and unifying the disability experience dissipate into the majority world debate. Disability studies and its tenets, especially the social model, have reached hegemonic status in the disability and development/majority world cacophony. This process has been facilitated by the virtual abandonment of disability issues in development studies and practice; the monopolisation of most things disability by the Western disability studies; and an inherent assumption that disability theories and writings from the West (specifically the UK) are transferrable across cultures, peoples, contexts and histories by academics or development and other international organisations keen to emulate the dominant discourse and sing along to the popular/knowing Western tune. The notorious efforts of the Western historical materialist strand, sometimes vigilant, insular, bent on defining the disability experience as one of oppression, neatly tucked into the social model package, lead to the wholesale transnational exportation of ideas wholesale transnational exportation/ domination (see for example Barnes, 2009). Backing this exportation of epistemologies is the inherent assumption that theories and writings from the West (in this case the UK) are transferrable to the rest, sustained by the continued Western imperialism in knowledge production and its dissemination (see Grech, 2011).

This exportation of epistemologies from North to South, what Alatas (2003: 601) calls 'academic neo-imperialism' or 'academic neo-colonialism', has severe analytical consequences, and comes yet again with gross generalisations, simplifications, omissions and neocolonising tones when confronted with a range of (different?) realities. For example, the standard discourse that all disabled people are oppressed everywhere forsakes critical engagement with the varying attitudes and behaviours towards disabled people, and how these are mediated by a host of socio-economic, cultural, political, personal, situational, and many other variables, themselves dynamic and changing. Substantial evidence highlights a wide range of responses and attitudes to disabled people, ranging from positive to negative along a wide and varied continuum and varying between as well as within countries (see for example Ingstad and Whyte, 1995, 2007).

Understanding differential attitudes and behaviours on the ground necessitates firstly an understanding of the meaning of full personhood, how the disabled person relates to this, and how this experience is impacted and/or mediated by aspects such as the type of impairment. It is highly unlikely for example that a person with dyslexia would be oppressed in a community where livelihoods involve agricultural labour and/or construction. Furthermore, not all societies consider the same attitudes and behaviours to be discriminatory and/or oppressive, and depicting a person as oppressed if he/she does not consider himself/herself to be, may be little more than singling him/her out as a 'special' case, and subjecting him/her to the controlling and disabling gaze and intervention, but this time reframed as a question of individual rights.

To suggest that ill-treatment is all that faces disabled people in majority world countries neglects and overshadows the agency, resilience, love and care of families who continue to ensure the survival of their own disabled members, their efforts constrained only by extreme poverty, not lack of concern, and/or negative attitudes. The disablism of poverty is all too often rendered invisible. I argue elsewhere (see Grech, 2008, 2011) that whole households are often cast into spiralling and intergenerational chronic poverty as a result of disability, with the implication that we should be examining the impacts and barriers confronting *disabled families* rather than (exclusively) disabled individuals. Overall, my argument is not about ignoring ill-treatment when it does exist. It is simply about giving back these families the same agency, heterogeneity, resilience and humanity awarded to (or taken for granted among) Western families. It is about making sure that these strengths are understood, learnt from and built upon, and never ignored or trampled on, whether discursively or materially.

More broadly, the exclusive focus on ill-treatment does little to reverse the demonising of majority world cultures and their people. Discourse, Foucault (1980) demonstrates, is bound to and reflects power. It suggests a space where power and knowledge become intertwined. Discourse about and directed at the Global South is invariably external, produced by the 'superior West', and, like the colonial enterprise, predicated on the homogenising of its people as inferior, in need of correction, uncivilised. This discourse produces the Southern subject and location, legitimises the exercise of power and domination over it, and results in practices of thinking and acting. Escobar, for example, emphasises how 'development proceeded by creating abnormalities ('the poor' 'the malnourished'), which it would then treat or reform' (1995: 343).[4] He goes on to note that 'development relies on the perpetual recognition and disavowal of difference' (1995: 54). In a similar fashion, Spivak (1988: 289) refers to the 'worlding' of what is today called the 'third world', imperialistic epistemic violence naturalising the subjugation of the Southern space.

Generalisations and even myths about disabled people and their treatment in these 'backward' and 'uncivilised' cultures are not lacking in Western literature: hidden, killed, abandoned, and neglected; there is no evidence of local events or literature and no testimonies in European languages to indicate that anything ever happened before the colonisers arrived[5] (see also Ingstad, 1995; Miles, 2007). Overall, this discourse is not dissimilar to Western feminist discourse in the 1970s consistently depicting 'third world' women as passive, powerless, backward and uneducated, discourse that enraged their Southern counterparts (see for example Mohanty, 1991). A discourse that demeans Southern subjects is also detrimental at another level, because it deflects attention from ill-treatment, oppression and subjugation of disabled people in the West, as these spaces are constructed as infinitely more 'civilised', 'developed', 'caring', even 'human'. In practice paternalism, dependency, neglect, violations of rights and violence against disabled people are ubiquitous. Recent years have in fact seen substantial literature emerging around disability hate crimes (see Sherry, 2010). In spite of this, today, it is far from common for anyone to claim that in Europe (or indeed the UK), disabled people are hidden, killed and neglected. On the other hand, when transposed to the majority world, this statement becomes not only palatable, but also justified, if not *expected*.

Hybrid spaces, hybrid lives

The hybrid that emerges in the Global South, and which forces us to problematise boundaries and totalising forms of cultural understandings and notions of national identity, place and space (both historically and in contemporary times) among others, is also often ignored in the disability and majority world debate. Where do agrarian societies fit in the materialist pre-capitalist/capitalist dichotomy? How does this model explain a situation in which a substantial proportion of livelihoods remain dependent on home-based subsistence production? The majority world and the spaces within are not immune to the penetration of Western ideologies, influences, work and consumption patterns and so on. García-Canclini's (2005) work on hybrid cultures emphasises the cultural mixtures or hybridisations between what he calls the old (the traditional) and the new (the modern), providing powerful analytical power to the condition of societies and people at various intersections and crossroads. As he explains, 'neither the "paradigm" of imitation, nor that of originality ... nor the one that lazily wants to explain us by the "marvellously real" or a Latin American surrealism, are able to account for our hybrid cultures' (García-Canclini, 2005: 6). People operate at various and interacting margins, of capitalism, globalisation, markets, interventions and so on. For example the poor often have one foot in the market and the other in subsistence, which means that they enter and exit the market and still survive, but are not wholly immune to its pressures (e.g. price hikes of staple foods). The hybrid is also manifest in the presence of non-unitary households, not necessarily blood-related and not always sharing access and control over resources. This suggests a renegotiation of what we understand by family, a re-examination of households of different formations and compositions, relationships, control of assets, and even conflicting interests.

Hybridity does not imply the domestication, elimination or 'sell-out' of the traditional in favour of the modern, since these beliefs and practices are often employed as counter-hegemonic forces or simply as enablers of survival. Despite its physically arduous nature, agricultural work performed by the rural poor redeems itself by providing a wider breadth of tasks, less specialised, and less formal than those in urban areas and cities. Some of these tasks can also be performed by disabled people (e.g. sowing, fertilising etc.). This is especially the case when families (and communities) work together as the basic unit of production and live in close proximity; working conditions are flexible (e.g. family members compensate each other's labour); and activities are largely subsistence (rather than market) oriented.

Hybridity usefully steers our thinking away from an over-glorification of the local and the traditional, and the view of these spaces and people as impenetrable to global influences and unwilling/unable to participate (although acknowledging this is often on unequal terms) or as simply assimilated or antagonistic to global factors and processes. Furthermore, it implies that local people may not necessarily want to revert to whatever is perceived as pre-modern, pre-industrial, pre-capitalist, or anything perceived as pure or pre-hybrid (if this ever existed at all). Instead, they may be constantly borrowing and negotiating in the process of transculturation. A number of questions arise and they have a variety of implications for disabled people. Where do these local people and spaces fit within the materialist construction of universal history, and how realistic is the project of removing capitalism when this is already incorporated within the hybrid? Can ignoring hybridity be dangerous when it is within the hybrid that communities often renew themselves, when it is within the local that the global is processed and experienced, and within and through which meaning (e.g. of disability and poverty) develops, and strategies for survival are negotiated? How do these hybrid post/neocolonial spaces connect with the disabled body, itself hybrid and cyborg, constituted by 'transgressed boundaries, potent fusions, and dangerous possibilities' (Haraway, 1985: 69) that refute dominant ontologies, epistemologies and discourse. Can we do without a type of disability studies prepared to be hybrid, inter/transdisciplinary, adopting the philosophical nomadism highlighted by Braidotti, the vision of the subject that is non-unitary, and a philosophy 'played out on this juxtaposition of Sameness and specular Otherness'? (2006: 21).

Impairment and bodies of pain

In true social model form, the body is also recast into the folds of the forbidden. But while the this dichotomisation of impairment and disability generated much critique in the West (see for example Hughes and Paterson, 1997; Shakespeare, 2006), it still remains – other than for a few notable exceptions (see for example Ghai 2002, 2006; Grech 2009, 2011) – to be addressed in the disability and majority world debate.

The body, the repository of the personal and the social and of pain, becomes harder to ignore in contexts of extreme poverty, where livelihoods (and indeed most activities) are predicated on physical strength and when health care is often absent or at best fragmented. The body and its materiality – '*the intentional experiencing body*' (Marks, 1999: 129, italics in original) – can hardly ever shift out of focus. Siebers (2008: 64), taking the lead from Butler's (1993) rebuttal of constructionism, insists that

> [p]hysical pain is highly unpredictable and raw as reality. It pits the mind against the body in ways that make the opposition between thought and ideology in most current body theory seem trivial ... Pain is not a friend to humanity. It is not a secret resource for political change. It is

not a well of delight for the individual. Theories that encourage these interpretations are not only unrealistic about pain; they contribute to the ideology of ability, marginalizing people with disabilities.

In contexts such as the ones in the Global South, it is not surprising that disabled people may look for the abhorred medical 'fixing' because they are hardly subjected to the medical gaze; their disabled bodies are often rendered docile by extraordinary, unmedicated pain, and the desperate need to work to ensure survival means the priority is refocused on achieving previous body functioning. The need to pay attention to what Davis and Watson (2002: 165) call 'the material consequences, the here and now of having an impairment' cannot be sufficiently emphasised. In more practical terms, health care and associated services need to be desperately drawn in, especially in the poorer rural areas, and any factors and processes (including discourse) pushing them away or devaluing them diminished or removed where possible. Medicalisation, if anything, needs to be politicised.

Societal responses, reactions and relationships are also articulated around bodies, strengthening the notion that impairment cannot be simply abandoned. Bodies are already profoundly social – 'bodily facts do not exist outside this setting, but only make sense within the social and cultural practices that constitute everyday life' (Rothfield, 2005: 38). Price and Shildrick (2002: 63) neatly sum this up as the relationship between bodies, 'the interactions of our bodies and their mutually constitutive effects of one on another ... the recognition that our sense of self, and how we orientate ourselves to the world, is irrevocably tied up with the bodies of those around us'. Different impairments are also associated with different forms as well as manifestations of disablism (Thomas and Corker, 2002: 20). This leads to the examination of hierarchies of impairments and how these interact with contextual, attitudinal and circumstantial landscapes.

Ignoring bodies means making the stories emanating from them invisible. While some criticise personal accounts of the disability or impairment experience, claiming it deflects attention from the political struggle to change the world, poor people in the majority world struggle to have a voice. Ultimately we know people and contexts through narratives. One is hard pressed to question: How can one change a world he/she knows little or nothing about? Can this be at all possible by refuting voices, concerns and lives? Can eliminating the body, diminish and/or remove the daily resistances (discursive and material) achieved and achievable by and through these bodies? Said (1993: xiii) notes that while 'stories are at the heart of what explorers and novelists say about strange regions of the world; they also become the method colonized people use to assert their own identity and the existence of their own history'. Closing this space therefore epitomises little more than the neocolonisation of disabled people by Western theorists, themselves well medicated, a silencing no different from the biopolitical regimentation of bodies by the processes of medicalisation and institutionalisation much criticised by these same materialists.

Faith, beliefs, religion: Readings beyond secular spaces

A lacuna is more than evident when it comes to faith, beliefs and religion. It is symptomatic of the broader secularism that also permeates disability studies and forms the basis of the supposed universal, disembodied and decontextualised knowledge that has so much currency. Tomalin (2006: 95) highlights the secularism in development suggesting that it is built on the 'modernist assumption that religion will disappear once people become economically advanced, and a new-found rationality supersedes "primitive superstition" and "backward" religious worldviews'.

While rights, policies and legislation have replaced God in the toolkit of the secular, in many cultures and societies, faith and religion remain important constituents of people's economic, political, social and embodied reality (see for example Miles, 1995). Religions remain critical sources of meaning influencing people's views about the world and their role within it. Disability is thoroughly immersed in this meaning system. As Hutchinson (2006: 7) concedes, religious beliefs are unlikely to vanish, since 'bodies remain imbued in struggles fostered by the irrefutable ontological certainties of fragility and finitude'. For poor people, this fragility rarely slips out of focus. They are positioned in perilous living and working spaces, where the prospect of death of self, of family, of loved ones or acquaintances is constantly lived. Disability therefore reinforces fragility and death as lived themes. While the emphasis on the body and embodied reality is multiple and strong, the constant reminder of how easily the body is impaired and dies, in the narratives of some religions, may also deflect focus from this temporary vehicle of life, this material and discursive repository, and death be therefore perceived as liberating. As Siebers (2010: 328) puts it, 'the association of the body with human mortality and fragility, however, forces a general distrust of the knowledge embodied in it'. References that demean the finite earthly body are many, for example, in both the Bible and the Quran:

> This is how it will be when the dead are raised to life. When the body is buried, it is mortal; when raised it will be immortal. When buried, it is ugly and weak; when raised it will be beautiful and strong. When buried it is a physical body; when raised it will be a spiritual body. There is, of course, a physical body, so there has to be a spiritual body.
>
> (Corinthians 15: 35–6, 42–4)

> The souls of the deceased people do not disappear after death, these souls are living in the so called (Barzakh), waiting for the judgement day, but the bodies spoil on earth (ground).
>
> (Quran)

Beliefs can also become a critical source of resilience and resistance (even psychological) for disabled people and their families or may compensate for the paucity of other resources such as medical support (to which the poor, particularly in the majority world often have scarce access). Belief and faith also impact the attitudes and behaviours of others (e.g. families and community members). Evidence such as that provided by Ingstad and Grut (2007), for example, illustrates how religious congregations in Kenya offer critical resource for families of disabled people by providing both meaning and material help. Religious congregations may therefore strengthen the communities of support upon which poor people depend.

But religion and belief can also have a negative impact on disabled people and their families. Ghai's (2002) account of the construction of disability in India as an individual condition, for example, focuses on the idea that impairment has to be endured as payback for sins committed in the past. Poverty and suffering are sometimes constructed as the will of God by those in powerful positions (e.g. politicians as well as clerics). This helps to maintain the status quo and to quell spiritual sources of resistance. This extends from the Christianising mission in colonial times, a compliance bought and sold cheaply as the way to the coloniser's heaven, on the coloniser's terms and conditions; the coloniser became God: unchallenged and omnipotent.

Unfortunately, there is little engagement with the themes of religion and faith in disability studies, in particular materialist accounts. This is gross negligence because religion remains a fundamental constituent of people's social and embodied reality, forms a critical part of people's narratives, and cannot ever be ignored. While the Europeans conquered with the Bible in one hand and a gun in the other, the stronghold of Christianity, for example, today lies in a South (notoriously Latin America) that seems bent on throwing it back to a West that appears to have lost the beliefs it used to oppress and subjugate with, a faith it now replaced by one in economics, open markets and secular individualised spaces.

Conclusions

In this chapter, I have discussed some of the critical issues and gaps that arise in the debate around disability in the Global South. The debate continues to be dominated by strands of Western disability studies and legitimised by Western academic/epistemic imperialism. We urgently need to decolonise this debate through a *Critical Global Disability Studies* willing to emphasise uncertainty, contingency and (self)reflexivity that encourages a great deal of questioning and learning. We need to learn about the histories and contexts we are talking about at the most micro levels, and to do so without undermining the complexity, heterogeneity and dynamic nature of these spaces, and how they remain bound to global asymmetries of power – the neocolonial.

What is required above all is the ability to step back and acknowledge that recycling Western disability studies and its tenets will simply not do. We need to move towards the space that Einstein and Shildrick (2009: 293) call 'postconventional', meaning 'openness to the unknown', informed by a willingness to embrace an 'epistemology of ignorance'. A critical global disability studies to me is therefore (and critically) about decolonising debates, about making 'present and credible, suppressed, marginalised and disaccredited knowledges' (Santos, 2007: 16), especially those by critical Southern thinkers, activists, and the disabled poor themselves, in particular those that dissent from the dominant debate. But, first of all, we need to decolonise thought, our own dominant epistemologies, our minds, and to open a space where dialogue transcends disciplinary, geo-political, epistemological and other boundaries. Critical global disability studies is not simply an interdisciplinary but a transdisciplinary project.

Notes

1. This omission is perhaps compounded by a postcolonial critique that remains limited to ethnicity, race and gender, but which continues to flagrantly bypass disability in its analysis.
2. These writings are often placed under the heading 'Latin American Cultural Studies', the bulk of which are written and available exclusively in Spanish.
3. While personhood is a complicated term, it is used here in its broadest sense to imply what it means to be a full person as considered by the individual and those around him/her in specific contexts, through which meanings are developed, shared, sometimes imposed, negotiated and renegotiated, using material, ideological, spiritual and other means.
4. Development is a hugely contested term, and there is no universally agreed definition. The term in this chapter is used to refer to discourse and intervention (whether at research, policy, programme), power-loaded, historically contingent and not benign. I am sympathetic with the views of writers in the post-development tradition (e.g. Sachs, 1992; Escobar, 1995), who see development as a Western creation maintaining and initiating another cycle of imperialism, benefiting their own purposes, to the detriment of poor people.
5. The issue of language is itself a reflection of the Eurocentric bias towards the written text and the hegemony of the alphabet, at the expense of other non-lettered means of communication, for example, maps, calendars, oral narratives and pictures in sixteenth- and seventeenth-century Mesoamerica.

References

Alatas, S. H. (2003). 'Academic Dependency and the Global Division of Labour in the Social Sciences'. *Current Sociology*, 51, 599–633.
Ashcroft, B., Griffiths, G. and Tiffin, H. (2002). 'Introduction to the Second Edition'. In B. Ashcroft, G. Griffiths and H. Tiffin (eds) *The Post-Colonial Studies Reader* (pp. 5–8). Oxford: Routledge.

Barnes, C. (2009). 'Disability in a Majority World Context: A Materialist Account', paper to be presented at the Disability and Economy Conference, Manchester Metropolitan University, Manchester, 29–30 April 2009.

Braidotti, R. (2006). *Transpositions: On Nomadic Ethics*. Cambridge: Polity.

Butler, J. (1993). *Bodies That Matter: On the Discursive Limits of Sex*. London: Routledge.

Coronil, F. (2000). 'Naturaleza del poscolonialismo: del eurocentrismo al globocentrismo'. In E Lander (ed.), *La colonialidad del saber: eurocentrismo y ciencias sociales- Perspectivas latinoamericanas* (pp. 87–112, 93, my translation). Buenos Aires: CLACSO.

Coronil, F. (2008). 'Elephants in the Americas? Latin American Postcolonial Studies and Global Decolonization'. In M. Moraña, E. Dussel and C. A. Jáuregui (eds) *Coloniality at Large: Latin America and the Postcolonial Debate* (pp. 396–416). US: Duke University Press.

Davis, L. J. (ed.) (2010). 'Constructing Normalcy'. In L. J. Davis (ed.) *The Disability Studies Reader* (pp. 3–19). New York and London: Routledge.

Davis, J. and Watson, N. (2002). 'Counteracting Stereotypes of Disability: Disabled Children and Resistance'. In M. Coker and T. Shakespeare (eds) *Disability/ Postmodernity: Embodying Disability Theory* (pp. 159–74). London: Continuum.

Dirlik, A. (1994). 'The Postcolonial Aura: Third World Criticism in the Age of Global Capitalism'. *Critical Inquiry*, 20 (2), 328–56.

Escobar, A. (1995). *Encountering Development: The Making and Unmaking of the Third World*. Princeton: Princeton University Press.

Fanon, F. (1967). *The Wretched of the Earth*. New York: Grove Press.

Food and Agricultural Organization (FAO) (2008). 'Soaring Food Prices: Facts, Perspectives, Impacts and Actions Required', paper for the High-Level Conference on World Food Security: The Challenges of Climate Change and Bioenergy, Rome, 3–5 June 2008.

Foucault, M. (1980). *Power/Knowledge*. New York: Pantheon Books.

García-Canclini, N. (2005). *Hybrid Cultures: Strategies for Entering and Leaving Modernity*. Minneapolis: University of Minnesota Press.

Ghai, A. (2002). 'Disability in the Indian Context: Post-Colonial Perspectives'. In M. Corker and T. Shakespeare (eds) *Disability/Postmodernity: Embordying Disability Theory* (pp. 88–100). London: Continuum.

Ghai, A. (2006). *(Dis)embodied Form: Issues of Disabled Women*. Delhi: Shakti Books.

Goodley, D. (2010). *Disability Studies: An Interdisciplinary Introduction*. London: Sage.

Green, L. (2003). 'Notes on Mayan Youth and Rural Industrialization in Guatemala'. *Critique of Anthropology*, 23(1), 51–73.

Grech, S. (2008). 'Living with Disability in Rural Guatemala: Exploring Connections and Impacts on Poverty'. *International Journal of Disability, Community and Rehabilitation*, 7(2), http://www.ijdcr.ca/VOL07_02_CAN/articles/grech.shtml, accessed 24 August 2010.

Grech, S. (2009). 'Disability, Poverty and Development: Critical Reflections on the Majority World Debate'. *Disability & Society*, 24 (6), 771–85.

Grech, S. (2011). 'Recolonising Debates or Perpetuated Coloniality? Decentering the Spaces of Disability, Development and Community in the Majority World'. *International Journal of Inclusive Education*, 15 (1), 87–100.

Grosfoguel, R. (2008). 'Transmodernity, Border Thinking, and Global Coloniality'. *Eurozine*, 1–23.

Haraway, D. (1985). 'A Manifesto for Cyborgs: Science, Technology and Socialist Feminism in the 1980s'. *Socialist Review*, 80, 65–107.

Hughes, B. and Paterson, K. (1997). 'The Social Model of Disability and the Disappearing Body: Towards a Sociology of Impairment'. *Disability & Society*, 12 (3), 325–40.

Hutchinson, N. (2006). 'Disabling Beliefs? Impaired Embodiment in the Religious Tradition of the West'. *Body & Society*, 12 (4), 1–23.

IFAD (2001). *Rural Poverty Report 2001*. Rome: IFAD.

Ingstad, B. (1995). 'Public Discourses in Rehabilitation: From Norway to Botswana'. In B. Ingstad and S. R. Whyte (eds) *Disability and Culture* (pp. 174–95). Berkeley: University of California Press.

Ingstad, B. and Grut, L. (2007). *See Me, and Do Not Forget Me: People with Disabilities in Kenya*. Oslo: SINTEF.

Ingstad, B. and S. R. Whyte (eds) (1995). *Disability and Culture*. Berkeley: University of California Press.

Ingstad, B. and S. R. Whyte (eds) (2007). *Disability in Local and Global Worlds*. Berkeley: University of California Press.

Lander, E. (2000). 'Ciencias socials: saberes coloniales y *eurocéntricos*'. In E Lander (ed.), *La colonialidad del saber: eurocentrismo y ciencias sociales- Perspectivas latino-americanas* (pp. 11–40). Buenos Aires: CLACSO.

Mann, P. S. (1994). *Micro-Politics – Agency in a Postfeminist Era*. Minneapolis: University of Minneapolis Press.

Marks, D. (1999). *Disability: Controversial Debates and Psychosocial Perspectives*. London: Routledge.

Meekosha, H. (2008). 'Contextualizing Disability: Developing Southern/ Global Theory'. Keynote paper delivered at the 4th Biennial Disability Studies Conference, Lancaster University, 2–4 September 2008, Lancaster UK.

Mignolo, W. (2008). 'The Geopolitics of Knowledge and the Colonial Difference'. In M. Moraña, E. Dussel and C. Jauregui (eds) *Coloniality at Large: Latin America and the Postcolonial Debate* (pp. 225–58). Durham: Duke University Press.

Miles, M. (1995). 'Disability in an Eastern Religious Context: Historical Perspectives'. *Disability and Society*, 10 (1), 49–69.

Miles, M. (2007). *International Strategies for Disability-Related Work in Developing Countries: Historical, Modern and Critical Reflections*, http://www.independentliving.org/docs7/miles200701.html, accessed 24 November 2010.

Mohanty, C. T. (1991). 'Cartographies of Struggle: Third World Women and the Politics of Feminism'. In C. T. Mohanty, A. Russo and L. Torres (eds) *Cartographies of Struggle: Third World Women and the Politics of Feminism* (pp. 1–47). Indianapolis: Indiana University Press.

Oliver, M. (1990). *The Politics of Disablement*. Basingstoke: Macmillan.

Oliver, M. (1996). *Understanding Disability: From Theory to Practice*. Basingstoke: Macmillan.

Price, J. and Shildrick, M. (2002). 'Bodies Together, Ethics and Disability'. In M. Coker and T. Shakespeare (eds) *Disability/Postmodernity: Embodying Disability Theory* (pp. 62–76). London: Continuum.

Quijano, A. (2008). 'Coloniality of Power, Eurocentrism, and Social Classification'. In M. Moraña, E. Dussel and C. A. Jáuregui (eds) *Coloniality at Large: Latin America and the Postcolonial Debate* (pp. 181–224). Durham: Duke University Press.

Riddell, R. (2004). 'Approaches to Poverty: A Note from the "Development" Perspective. International Council on Human Rights Policy Researchers'. Meeting on Poverty, Development, Rights, Geneva, 24–25 November.

Rothfield, P. (2005). 'Attending to Difference: Phenomenology and Bioethics'. In M. Schildrick (ed.) *Ethics of the Body: Postconventional Challenges*. Cambridge, MA: MIT Press.

Sachs, W. (ed.) (1992). *The Development Dictionary: A Guide to Knowledge as Power*. London: Zed.

Said, E. (1993). *Cultural and Imperialism*. London: Vintage.

Santos, B. D. (2007). 'Beyond Abyssal Thinking: From Global Lines to Ecologies of Knowledges'. *Eurozine*, 1–33.

Shakespeare, T. (2006). *Disability Rights and Wrongs*. London and New York: Routledge.

Sherry, M. (2007). '(Post)colonising Disability'. *Wagadu*, Volume 4, Intersecting Gender and Disability Perspectives in Rethinking Postcolonial Identities, 10–22.

Sherry, M. (2010). *Disability Hate Crimes: Does Anyone Really Hate Disabled People?* London: Ashgate.

Siebers, T. (2008). *Disability Theory (Corporealities: Discourses of Disability)*. Ann Arbor: University of Michigan Press.

Siebers, T. (2010). 'Disability and the Theory of Complex Embodiment – For Identity Politics in a New Register'. In L. J. Davis (ed.) *The Disability Studies Reader* (pp. 316–35). New York and London: Routledge.

Spivak, G. C. (1988). 'Can the Subaltern Speak?' In C. Nelson and L. Grossberg (eds) *Marxism and the Interpretation of Culture*. Urbana: University of Illinois Press.

Thomas, C. and Corker, M. (2002). 'A Journey around the Social Model'. In M. Corker and T. Shakespeare (eds) *Disability/Postmodernity: Embodying Disability Theory* (pp. 18–31). London: Continuum.

Tomalin, E. (2006). 'Religion and a Rights-Based Approach to Development'. *Progress in Development Studies*, 6 (2), 93–108.

Tuhiwai Smith, L. (2002). *Decolonizing Methodologies: Research and Indigenous Peoples*. London: Zed Books

Wasserman (2001). 'Philosophical Issues in the Definition and Social Response to Disability'. In G. L. Albrecht, K. D. Seelman and M. Bury (eds) *Handbook of Disability Studies* (pp. 219–51). Thousand Oaks, CA: Sage.

Wehbi, S., Elin, L. and El-Lahib, Y. (2009). 'Neo-colonial Discourse and Disability: The Case of Canadian International Development NGOs'. *Community Development Journal*, 45 (4), 404–22.

Whyte, S. R. and Ingstad, B. (1995). 'Disability and Culture: An Overview'. In B. Ingstad and S. R. Whyte (eds) *Disability and Culture* (pp. 3–32). Berkeley: University of California Press.

World Bank (2008). *Global Monitoring Report 2008 – MDGs and the Environment: Agenda for Inclusive and Sustainable Development*. Washington, DC: The World Bank.

5

Discourses of Disabled Peoples' Organisations: Foucault, Bourdieu and Future Perspectives

Theo Blackmore and Stephen Lee Hodgkins

Introduction

This chapter considers the discourses of disabled peoples' organisations (DPOs). Drawing on the work of Michel Foucault and Pierre Bourdieu, we explore the rise of the disabled people's movement in recent history, the development of DPOs and their gradual colonisation, moving from a radical political and social movement to pseudo-government agents. Using notions of power and resistance from Foucault, and capital, field and habitus from Bourdieu, opportunities and challenges for DPOs are explored. These are critically considered in terms of the implications for the project of impairment-management, inclusion and the preservation of the cultures of disabled bodies, minds and identities.

Disabled Peoples' Organisations in the UK

The history of disabled people and their organisations in the UK is a very brief one. There are clear instances where collectives of disabled people have mobilised for political aims – for example, war veteran protests, or the blind workers' strike in Derry, Northern Ireland in 1939 (O' Cathain, 2006). The first manifestations of political activism by disabled people can be traced to the nineteenth century (Braddock and Parish, 2001: 13). One of the first self-advocacy organisations was the 1890 British Deaf and Dumb Association (BDDA). The BDDA initially organised in direct response to the International Congress's sign language ban, and the view that deaf persons did not need to be involved in matters concerned with them. This political movement sharply contrasted with the contemporaneous exploitation of disabled people as freak show attractions, and the ascendancy of the eugenics era (Braddock and Parish, 2001).

In the nineteenth century, disability became a subject of study and research (Alt, 2005). This moved the experience of disability away from the subjective, individual experience towards an objective stance which dehumanised the experience of disability. Braddock and Parish describe the nineteenth century as the century of institutions and interventions (Braddock and Parish, 2001: 39). Schools and institutions for persons with physical disabilities, deafness, blindness, mental illness and intellectual disability took root throughout Europe and North America. Professionals developed differential diagnosis to particularise disability and devised treatment interventions and educational schemes focused on specific impairments. The medical notion of defining and classifying disability became thoroughly accepted in this century. However, the segregation of individuals with similar impairments also afforded disabled people opportunities to begin to develop group identities. By the close of the nineteenth century, deaf people advocating for manual education and control of their own schools had begun to coalesce into the first disability political action groups. The emergence of this militant positioning can be seen elsewhere, such as the blind workers' protest on 28 February 1939 in Derry, Northern Ireland (O' Cathain, 2006). Led by McDermott and McGoven protesters marched from their workplace to the town hall with banners reading 'Blind, but not to the hard facts of life' as an action against the low pay and poor employment conditions.

However, with disability conceptualised as an extraordinary medical problem came the view that biophysical 'abnormality' or 'maladaptation' leads to, or is the cause of, social 'abnormality' or 'maladaptation' (Hughes, 2002: 60). In other words, to be defined as a 'flawed' body is simultaneously to be defined as incapable of adequate social participation. The increasing segregation of disabled people into separate provision, away from the mainstream of life, would have reinforced and strengthened this link between physical and social maladaptation. This dominant discourse about disability led to the eugenics movement in Europe and America, and the sterilisation and segregation of large numbers of disabled people (Braddock and Parish, 2001: 38–9). Nazi Germany offers the most extreme example of the eugenics movement, where about 200,000 people, in particular those with a mental illness or congenital malformation, were exterminated in the hospitals and death camps because of their disability (Ravaud and Stiker, 2001: 502).

It was not until the 1960s–1970s in the UK, with the rise of liberatory identity politics, that disabled people began to self-organise in a significant way and offer an alternative discourse of the body and mind. In the 1960s and 1970s there was a very strong tradition of charitable fundraising in the disability sector, which was controlled by non-disabled people, and relied solely on projecting the disabled body and mind as deserving and needy. Anti-discrimination legislation had yet to be created. DPOs – created, controlled and populated by disabled people – began to challenge the established medicalised, individualistic and tragic disability discourses. DPOs were, and are, created and controlled by disabled people in response to needs and wants, defined by themselves, for themselves. This created a unique organisational culture that embraced and valued the voices and experiences of disabled people from the perspective of equality and dignity.

The story of the lobby by disabled people in the UK begins with Paul Hunt's (1972) letter to *The Guardian* newspaper, which led to the creation of the Union of the Physically Impaired Against Segregation (UPIAS) and the beginnings of the social model of disability (Pfeiffer, 2000) as expressed in the UPIAS Fundamental Principles of Disability (1975). This document is regarded as the 'year zero' (Shakespeare, 2006: 14) of the social model of disability in the UK. Other organisations led and controlled by disabled people formed around the latter part of the twentieth century included the Disablement Income Group in 1965, Disablement Information and Advice Line in 1978, the United Kingdom Disabled People's Council (UKDPC, formerly British Council of Disabled People, BCODP) in 1981, the Direct Action Network in 1993 and others. Each contributed to an increased recognition of disability as a collective identity marker and minority grouping that was subject to prejudice, discrimination and exclusion. These organisations provided community development and leadership for disabled people, often developing solutions and running projects to advocate inclusion and equality.

To root this new political and social movement firmly within the control of disabled people, strict guidelines were created to define DPOs, their constituents and their authenticity. The BCODP, later known as the UKDPC, defines a DPO as

> an organisation whose constitution requires it to have a membership and managing board with a majority of disabled people, and whose objectives are the rights and equality of disabled people. DPOs subscribe to the social model of disability and are committed to the human rights of disabled people. DPOs work for the empowerment of disabled people either implicitly or explicitly.
>
> (UKDPC, 2010: 1)

In the 1970s the disability rights movement took a very firm stance about whether an organisation could truly call it an organisation 'of' or 'for' disabled people. The BCODP created stipulations for organisations 'of' disabled people to include a management committee made up of a majority of disabled people.

In England, DPOs have experienced significant growth and diversification since the 1970s. The UK has an ever-increasing number of voluntary sector organisations, ranging from small community groups to international charities with bases in many countries. DPOs represent a minority within this sector, with the estimated number of DPOs in England ranging between 650 and 1000.[1] Their impact has been huge, furthering a radical social policy agenda and redefining meanings of social care, independent living and inclusion. Within current government legislation and initiatives there is a drive to populate public services with DPOs, to root statutory services within the populations served, and to drive forward the project of inclusion for disabled people. DPOs are currently positioned as essential drivers for social policy reform. This can be seen as the professionalisation of DPOs and represents their colonisation as pseudo-governmental bodies. It can also be seen as an attempt to mainstream aspects of the disabled body, mind and lifestyle through state-guided intervention.

In 1972 at the University of California, Berkeley, US, the first Centre for Independent Living (CIL) was established initially as a self-help group run by disabled people to increase participation and access to the academic experience. From this the development of local CILs were seen as relevant for improving the lives of disabled people. Significant also was the American Congressional amendment of the Rehabilitation Act 1978 to establish 'comprehensive services for independent living' (Barnes, Mercer and Shakespeare, 1999: 148). By the 1980s British DPOs, the Derbyshire Coalition of Disabled People and the Hampshire Coalition of Disabled People had each developed CILs, the latter forming largely out of 'Project 81'.

Project 81 was a 'consumer-directed housing and care' initiative, managed by disabled people. Here a group of disabled people convinced the local authorities that the financing of residential care could be re-appropriated and used to resource community support options (Barnes, Mercer and Shakespeare, 1999: 149). Disabled people convinced the local authority to hand over money and resources directly to disabled people, instead of merely paying for them to live in care settings. This set a new, radical social policy standard and brought together social care professionals and disabled people to create a new policy initiative. This specific initiative marked the birth of the independent living movement in the UK and can be seen as responsible for the introduction of the current 'personalisation' agenda and approach to social care reform.

The European Network on Independent Living was formed in 1989, following which the UKDPC set up the United Kingdom Independent Living Committee to forward the campaign for disabled peoples' right to independent living. In 1996 the National Centre for Independent Living was set up by UKDPC to focus specifically on policy development and to lobby government on direct payments, which was put on the statute books through the Community Care (Direct Payments) Act in 1996.[2] As a result many local DPOs were awarded contracts to deliver direct payment support services to disabled people. These contracts have contributed to significant growth and sustainability for DPOs. This echoed the call by Vic Finkelstein for disability professions to become truly allied to the community and set a radical social policy standard, whereby passive users move to the role of active self-direct support managers (Finkelstein, 1999). A key text 'Independent Futures' (Barnes and Mercer, 2006) critically evaluated disabled people-led services, identified challenges facing their development, and listed the added value such organisations bring to the delivery of support services for disabled people. Independent living has proved to be a powerfully resistive discourse charging the issue of impairment with much political capital (Barnes, 2002).

We will now explore some key concepts from the work of Michel Foucault and Pierre Bourdieu, and then apply these understandings to current issues concerning DPOs in the UK. Foucault's work is relevant to DPOs through his commentary on power and resistance, and how oppressive norms of knowledge can be critically reworked and their meaning undone so as to understand alternatives such as disabled peoples' collective identity and the way their organisations have established activities around social model principles in recent years. The work of Bourdieu is useful in this respect in the way it provides explanatory power for the capital resources at play within human actions and interactions. These capital transactions can be fruitfully examined internally within DPOs and their everyday acts, as well as externally within capital transactions between DPOs and other organisations and the world at large that contribute to social change and policy reform.

Michel Foucault (1926–1984)

While Michel Foucault lived with HIV and produced two significant volumes, *The Birth of the Clinic* (1963) and *Madness and Civilisation* (1961), that give a history of the development of structural conditions that made visible and oppressed the 'abnormal' body and mind, he was not known in his lifetime as a disabled person, neither personally nor politically. Since his death however, a number of studies have considered the relevance of Foucault's work to the phenomena of disability and impairment (see Tremain, 2005). Foucault's work has also generated a critical qualitative research method know as foucauldian discourse analysis (Carabine, 2001). This offers a lens through which to identify and read discourses as both subject to, and productive of, aspects of power and knowledge. For Foucault, discourses are considered as systems of representations and signifiers.

Key to Foucault's work is the drive to question everything, particularly spelling that which is considered natural and inevitable. He asserts his stance as 'hyper or pessimistic activism' (Tremain, 2005: vii) and although his work can be positioned as structuralist and/or post-structuralist, as he rejected these labels he is perhaps better considered a critical theorist. This resistance to traditional philosophical categories and positions, along with his overall rejection of objectivity, in any form, has invoked critique and disapproval. Part of the criticism is that Foucault's work is nihilistic and suggests a passivity in relation to human action, conduct and politics. However, there is value in his work in the way in which his ideas illuminate the darker aspects of social control and regulation, through which we can become aware of everyday dangers that permeate human oppression, and so make 'ethico-political' choices to resist them (Tremain, 2005).

Central to the work of Foucault is the relationship between power, knowledge and discourse. For Foucault, power is a productive and shared resource, operating across the realm of social life, ever persistent in the transmission of knowledge forms and regimes of truth. In this way the expression of power through human action is never centrally located, nor is it specific. Neither is it only negative, seeking to control, but can be reformative, generating pleasurable alternatives. Power circulates through a web of human social relations, connecting and engaging people as both the oppressed and the oppressor, the liberated and the liberator, the ethical and the unethical, the powerful and the powerless.

Foucault further asserted certain types of power, such as biopower and disciplinary power (see Foucault, 1972, 1975, 1976). Biopower is a technology emerging in the late eighteenth century for managing populations by surveillance and record keeping of births, deaths, reproduction and dysfunction. Disciplinary power is the mechanism or training of the actions of bodies to produce and regulate desired behaviours, through the construction of particular space, time and structure, such as the construction of psychiatry and the establishment of the asylum (Foucault, 1961). Only through power is truth, and the knowledge of truth, achieved and maintained as a realistic and factual aspect of the human experience. Power organises and wields itself to be known as true, through a regime of truth, or truth game. Thus humans can never know objective truth, because its very expression is also an assertion of social control. We never tell the truth, rather we reveal ourselves according to our variable positioning in space, time and structure. Such as the reluctance of humans to accept mental health issues as an inevitable aspect of human life, rather than something that must be treated, managed and corrected (Foucault, 1961). Crucially, Foucault also asserted that linked to power is also resistance to it. Power can be subverted and reclaimed into positions of resistance that rework oppression and create everyday opportunities for equality and liberation to emerge. Contrary to the nihilist criticism Foucault receives, this suggests that no matter how powerful or oppressive a system maybe, it can be resisted. The social model, the disability discrimination act and direct payments can be seen as moments of disabled peoples' resistance to their degradation and institutionalisation. This is because, in line with Foucault's thinking, resistance can be seen as ultimately an expression of power. Power is taken as agentic and relative, not centralist nor oppositional but part of, and connected to unique struggles and fluctuations in truth values.

For Foucault power/knowledge are expressed through discourse. Discourse, is a system of representation and signifiers, where rules and practices apply to set the tone and detail of what, and how topics and concepts can be constructed. This includes the text and spoken words, but also other signs, forms and mediums of expression, such as the body, or a map. However, language is not to be taken as value neutral, nor merely a linguistic concept, but rather considered as a form of social action and knowledge practice (Foucault, 1972). Discourse provides a way of speaking and knowing things through language. Statements or concepts of certain knowledge objects, such as disability, that drift towards or support common institutional strategies or ideological patterns are drawn from shared repertoires and discursive formations. Therefore, 'the statement (*of disability*) is not in itself a unit (*of reality or meaning*), but a function that cuts across a domain of structures and possible unities, and which reveals them, with concrete contents in time and space' (Foucault, 1972: 87, *our italics*). It is only discourse that produces units and objects of knowledge, does so it certain ways, without which meaning about them cannot exist. This does not deny our realities, say disability, but rather reminds us that they are versions of it, variable, influenced and related to actions in previous times, spaces and structures. So, disability discourses are cultural discourses.

Through a Foucauldian lens therefore, disabled people and their impairments become artefacts of knowledge interaction immersed in historical, social and political structures that have been instrumental in regulating and organising the human body and mind within a context of economy, civil society and community. Foucault's work reveals disabled people as subject to the power of the norm regulating systems that favour ability and rationality and posit the discursive boundaries and pathologies of dysfunctional bodies and minds. The contribution of Foucauldian theory to disabled peoples' lives has been argued elsewhere as limited in that it has a tendency to presume disabled people are merely subjected to power, and not agents of it (Hughes, 2005). This overlooks, as Hughes suggests, the reconstruction of disabled peoples' status and equality that liberatory social movements have achieved in recent years. Disabled people have organised themselves as a voice of change through the formation of a political collective movement and establishment of their formal organisations. Using Foucault, the actions and achievements of DPOs can be read as resisting and countering disability oppression, as well as being part of the production of both emancipatory and disciplinary power. These are not just in the grand ideas, such as the social model or legislative change, but also in the personal moments of acceptance and pride about impairment that DPOs work constantly to communicate in their daily work. However, part of the difficulty with Foucault's work is found in its dark and nihilistic implication of humankind. Indeed as he stated 'not everything is bad, but everything is dangerous' (Tremain, 2005: vii) suggesting the need to be ever watchful of ourselves as simultaneously both the oppressed and the oppressor. But this is not a bad thing to bear in mind. For DPOs it is an important message to reflect upon as they increase their activities to deliver services for disabled people and are written into state governing policy.

We will now examine the work of Pierre Bourdieu.

Pierre Bourdieu (1930–2000)

Pierre Bourdieu focused on an individual's use of resources, or capital, within communities of interest, to resist and adapt. Bourdieu's work has been used in many disparate fields since his death to illuminate the dynamics of social conduct and interaction, and has had an enormous impact on a variety of different fields of academic enquiry (Fowler, 2003: 487). Bourdieu's theory of practice uses the notions of field, capital and habitus to explain and understand human action and interaction. In his 1979 work *Distinction: A Social Critique of the Judgment of Taste*, Bourdieu produced an equation that expresses 'practice' as the combined effect of habitus, capital and field.

To explore Bourdieu's theory of practice in relation to DPOs, we will start with 'field'.

Bourdieu represents the objective world as field. Field is defined as 'a network, or a configuration, of objective relations between positions objectively defined' (Bourdieu and Wacquant, 1992: 72–3). For our analysis we can construct many different fields within which DPOs operate, from the macrocosmic, national field of governmental legislation and policy initiatives, to the local level of individual DPOs interacting with their local authority, with other DPOs, User Led Organisations (ULOs, see UKDPC, 2010) and other third-sector service providers (depending on the field-specific, local project).

The second element of Bourdieu's theory of practice is the notion of capital. For Bourdieu, the social world is accumulated history – he states that if the social world is not to be reduced to a discontinuous series of instantaneous mechanical equilibria between agents who are treated as interchangeable particles, one must reintroduce into it the notion of capital (Bourdieu, 1983: 242). And this means capital in all its forms, and not solely in the one form recognised by economic theory. All forms of capital can be accumulated, or lost, from one moment to the next.

Bourdieu uses many different forms of capital, both explicitly and implicitly, in his work. The notion of capital relates to resources that can be 'traded' or exchanged for other useful resources. The traditional notion of capital relates to economic capital, whereby money can be exchanged for particular, useful goods or services. For this study we will define three different forms of capital in relation to the work of DPOs.

Economic capital relates to the financial resources held by, or accessible to, DPOs. Some DPOs have relatively large amounts of financial capital at their disposal. Those operating on a regional level that deliver independent living services, like advocacy, direct payments or employment support have been most financially successful and can boast annual incomes of £2 million+. Others however can be unfunded, or have a relatively small annual income of up to £15k (Disability LIB, 2007).

Social capital relates to social networks and connections between individuals and organisations. These social connections, or ties, can facilitate, or hinder, the transmission of useful resources to a DPO. This is where the adage 'it's not what you know but who you know' comes from. DPO social capital can derive from the contacts between a DPO and its stakeholders. These stakeholders include disabled people, disability services, state policy-makers and budget holders, other equality and voluntary sector organisations/bodies, and the wider society and community.

Cultural capital relates to the skills and knowledge held within the DPOs. This includes the understanding of the social model, disability equality training, access auditing, disability arts, pride and also the resources to connect and share positive identities with other disabled people.

Bourdieu used capital to illustrate relationships of power within field-specific settings. By examining the capital resources of DPOs, we can reveal the ever-changing locations of power and influence in the various fields.

The third element of Bourdieu's (1977: 77) theory of practice is the notion of habitus. This is a description of the individual's internal make up, what Bourdieu calls their savoir faire. This can include several aspects of a DPO, including its internal workings, and how and what it does (e.g. does the DPO employ disabled people? What is the underlying ethos of the DPO – is it a campaigning body, a service delivery body, an arts organisation, or a combination of these things? etc); its public face (e.g. how does the DPO present itself to the world? Does it look professional? etc.). The organisational habitus will vary from DPO to DPO. Each will have its own, specific habitus.

The three elements of field, capital and habitus all influence, and are influenced by, individually and in combination, the way the DPO acts and interacts with the world. This reciprocality exists throughout a DPO's fields of interaction, and is ultimately illustrated by the DPO sector's creation of the social model of disability as a result of the interactions of the fields on individual disabled people. This social model of disability eventually influenced and changed the fields within which DPOs operate. Bourdieu illustrates this influence and reciprocality through the metaphor of the 'Game'.

The game

Bourdieu conceptualises the accumulation, or loss, of power and influence in the language of the game (Bourdieu, 1979). This reflects his belief that the location of power and influence within human activity is relational, and in a constant state of flux and change.

This is a very useful analogy to make in relation to understanding DPO activity, and it deserves some explanation. In a card game (the field of interaction), the players (DPOs) are all dealt cards (capital) (Lareau and McNamara, 1999: 39). However, each card and each hand has different values. Moreover, the value of each hand shifts according to the explicit rules of the game (the field of interaction) that is being played (as well as the way the game is being enacted). In other words, a good hand for blackjack may be a less valuable hand for gin rummy. In addition to having a different set of cards (capital), each player relies on a different set of skills (habitus) to play the cards (activate the capital). By folding the hand, a player may not activate his or her capital or may play the cards (activate the capital) expertly according to the rules of the given game. In another game, the same player may be dealt the same hand, yet because of a lack of knowledge of the rules of the game, play the hand poorly.

Bourdieu's analogy of the game is useful when examining DPO activity, as it can illustrate which games the DPO plays well, and which ones it plays less well. This can help to describe how power shifts from the government agencies to the DPO, and vice versa, or from one DPO to another or other voluntary sector organisation, or from DPOs to disabled people.

Disabled Peoples' Organisations: Power and capital

Having briefly outlined Foucault's notions of power and resistance, and the capital, field and habitus of Bourdieu, we will now consider this in further detail in relation to the DPO context. This explores the rise of disabled people's resistance in recent history, the discourse of independent living, the development of DPOs as radical social movement organisations to their professionalisation as pseudo-government agencies and the challenges this poses.

In 1972 the UPIAS was formed as a direct result of Paul Hunt's letter to *The Guardian* newspaper. This organisation had clear, political goals, namely to change the way that disability was perceived and responded to within civil society. Again, like the BDDA the members of the group came from similar backgrounds in that at least two of the organisation's membership were living in segregated settings. In the case of both of these organisations the shared social experiences brought these people together to share social and cultural capitals and influence political change. The habitus of these early DPOs was political. It is clear that the practice of these early DPOs is an effect of actions and interactions which are shaped simultaneously and in equal measure by the habitus and capital of agents, as well as the context and dynamism constituted by their shared participation in a common field.

The political organisation of disabled people over about four decades in the UK has contributed to an increase in campaigns and the active promotion of disability equality. The uniting factor behind these organisations was the increasing desire for official recognition, and acceptance, of the social model of disability as a counter position to the excessive surveillance and gaze of medicine over the bodies, minds and lifestyles of disabled people.

Notable in this history is the UK anti telethon demonstrations of the 1990s recorded in the disability current affairs TV programme '1 in four'. Outside the LWT studios in London over the weekend of nationally broadcast TV fundraising, disabled people came together and chanted 'choices and rights' and 'rights not charity'. The footage captures the now Baroness Jane Campbell of Surbiton, Mike Oliver, the first Professor of Disability Studies, Activist Johnny Crescendo and TV presenter Chris Tarrant. This represents a key moment of resistance mobilised by a collective of disabled people. What was refuted was the representation of disabled people as helpless, needy and dependent. The protest is interesting as it is not about the closure of factories, loss of jobs or withdrawal of benefits. It is about challenging mainstream representations of disabled people as unfortunate and pitiful. This is one of many examples of disabled people exerting power and resistance, forcing virtual fractures in traditional benevolent discourses of disability, and a collective organisation that challenges discrimination and enshrines the human rights of diverse bodies, minds and lifestyles.

An 'independent living' approach to disabled peoples' support and inclusion asserts the distinction between 'physical' dependency and 'social' dependency. The former is linked to impairment and the latter to not having control over one's life due to reliance on others for support (Morris, 1992, 2004). The discourse of independent living challenges the ideology of disabled people as dependent and repositions the boundaries of autonomy and human agency. Disabled peoples' independent living needs include achieving accessibility in all areas of the everyday: environment, transport systems, information, housing, education, employment, provision of equipment, technical aids, personal assistance, self-advocacy (through advocacy, counselling and peer support) and economy (Morris, 1992, 2004).

Bourdieu's theory of practice suggests the position in which a DPO finds itself can be dependent on a set of factors over which the DPO has control, and also on other factors that DPOs cannot control. The very early days of the disabled peoples' movement in the UK, with the creation of the BDDA and actions such as the blind workers' protest of 1939 (O Cathain, 2006), show how organisations can be contextual, responding to field-specific and clearly identified needs. Groups of disabled people formed as a result of the common fields in which they found themselves and their common interest in changing these fields. They created a strong sense of shared social capital, created new forms of cultural capital based around their disability activism, and reacted to change the field. The people who came together to form these organisations had similar backgrounds and situations, in that they were living and working in segregated settings. This segregation helped create the strong bonds of social capital links between the individuals, leading to a sense of shared purpose.

The independent living discourse is radically different from previous discourses which position disabled people as passive recipients of services – including residential accommodation – which is created, and directed, by non-disabled people. The discourse has shifted to place the disabled person at the heart of his or her own life, in control and making key decisions. It is through the political mobilisation of disabled people as a movement that this discourse was appropriated, changed and re-posited. In their appropriation of the discourse DPOs changed the discourse cultural capital, and redefined the policy debates. Over time these new discourses, new debates and new understandings have been re-appropriated by the political elites, in an attempt to maintain political and structural dominance. It is a measure of the success of the DPO political and social movement that these mainstream political parties are now using phrases such as 'Nothing about us without us' within their own political discourse.

A significant achievement of DPOs is that their emergence has marked out the self-defined, authentic voice of impairment, and offers new terms of reference for disability knowledge. Through the positing of an alternative disability discourse, enshrining the language of barriers within the social model of disability and the rallying slogans of 'rights not charity', 'choices and rights' and 'nothing about us without us', DPOs forced new understandings into traditional disability discourses. DPOs represent the creation of new political, social and artistic bodies, with discourses that give impairment the opportunity to be reimagined, viewed as resourceful, and endowed with economic, cultural and social capitals. Through a Foucauldain lens this can be seen as representing a specific resistance to power forms concerned with the disability subject and context (see Dreyfus and Rabinow, 1982).

By examining the movement of capital, we can see how DPO power and control shift over time. When holding the reigns of power and control, DPOs can influence the policies and attitudes of the broader population. For example before the 1970s, power was located away from DPOs. Disabled people were often institutionalised, living, working and being educated in institutional settings. During the 1970s, DPOs began to seize capital and power, by forming organisations and making sure their voices were heard. DPOs shaped the way disability is conceptualised, giving voice to medical and social model discourses. This was the first time that disabled people articulated their versions and interpretations of disability. Over time DPOs became recognised as the places where expertise in relation to disability and disabled people were located. DPOs became centres of disability cultural capital. As social capital relationships between DPOs and local and central government, and other organisations, were strengthened, the social, health and education agendas began their transformation. Disability cultural capital shaped these agendas from one of exclusion as the norm, to one of inclusion as the norm.

As future policy initiatives are developed, implemented and communicated as more efficient and effective ways of enabling independence, disabled people and their organisations will be involved in the creation of new professions and institutions. The extent to which these will be successful is dependent upon on how representative and allied the new professions and institutions remain to the community. Mike Oliver (2009) alerts us to the recent rise of a compromised disability industry, the breakdown of disabled peoples' culture, and thus the loss of voice and ownership of their diverse bodies, lives and minds.

From a cursory glance at the political situation in the UK, it appears that the local, regional and national fields within which DPOs operate are constantly changing. For example at the time of writing (November 2010) we are in the middle of several major policy shifts in the social care field. These have come about from a combination of the previous Labour government's Personalisation agenda (e.g. Improving the life chances of disabled people 2005, Putting People First 2007, Right to Control Trailblazers 2010), together with the new coalition government's attempts to dramatically reduce departmental spending. The Personalisation agenda explicitly encourages ULOs and DPOs to become service delivery structures. As a result many DPOs have entered into contractual relationships with their local authority, and have consequently moved from being agents provocateurs, campaigning for change, to become trusted local authority allies.

As the broader policy discourse shifts, those DPOs which are most able to make similar discourse shifts to align themselves with the broader dialogue stand to benefit the most. In order to be effective within this political discourse each DPO needs to establish strong social capital links with their local authority. These contacts are often made between individuals, rather than between specified job descriptions. As staff move – and local authority staff tend to move far more frequently than the staff within DPOs – these contacts can be broken. This can make it very hard to sustain relationships, and to create firm foundations on which to build contractual relationships. And as the policy discourse shifts from government to government, the cultural capital required in an organisation also shifts.

The more nimble DPOs which are able to make these shifts will be better able to take advantage of new opportunities, including new funding streams, that become available. These DPOs are often relatively large, professional, and can be constituted as companies limited by guarantee. They often access several funding streams simultaneously, and manage their affairs very professionally through paid staff. At the same time many DPOs are battling with the continuing need for campaigning activity, often against government agencies, while also receiving funding from them. This can create a discourse friction within an organisation, which on the one hand needs to be close to a local authority to establish good working relationships, and on the other hand also maintain a distance to be able to campaign, perhaps against the same authority.

The political field can have massive consequences for how a DPO operates. Add to this the economic field, where all organisations, from government departments to smaller, voluntary sector organisations, are struggling for funding. This difficult financial situation is forcing organisations to create new ways of working, to restructure internally, and to provide services in new ways. There is little consistency in regional field activity across the

UK. Some local government areas and regions deliver a plethora of services through DPO partners, while others do very little or no such activity. While central government policy currently encourages DPO participation, local government may not. Through national bodies and organisations DPOs may attempt to influence change, though there are very few formal channels through which this influence can be enacted on a national scale. It therefore falls upon individual DPOs to adapt to shifting political, economic and regional field variations, or to fail. Indeed while the current personalisation agenda provides new opportunities for DPOs, it has also increased competition and there are recent examples of established DPOs closing as they lose contracts to other DPOs.

So the field, capital and habitus relationships between, and within, DPOs, local authorities and other players in the broader game are in a constant state of flux and change. The dynamism within Bourdieu's theory of practice is useful here, in that field, capital and habitus are constantly engaging and re-engaging to create dynamic fluid situations, where adaptability and discourse realignment are continuously required. The DPOs who are able to engage in this fluid discourse will be the DPOs that are able to thrive in these situations. The DPOs that are able to present a stable façade to the outside world, while managing change effectively and coherently, will be the DPOs that succeed. The DPOs that can invest in their internal habitus development to accommodate this constant change will be the DPOs that survive.

For the past 20 years in the UK the government and other institutions have begun to re-seize the political disability discourse, capital and power and to shape the agenda to suit their needs (see Burton and Kagan, 2006). In an attempt to mainstream disability equality, the government colonised the social model, adopting it throughout various departments, and using it to justify their shaping, and cutting, of social and health care provision. For example the current Personalisation agenda has the social model at its core. For the UK government Personalisation represents the destruction of the power and control of the state, through the dismantling of the structures of the state, particularly in relation to disability and disabled people. Residential institutions are closed in favour of individual living in community settings, special schools are closed in favour of mainstream education, and much disability medical provision – for example physiotherapy services – is restructured to offer an individual service rather than group activity. The individual is the expert, while structural changes allow for downsizing and even elimination of entire departments. As the field is changed, and as capital resources shift and change, so the DPO habitus has had to change. There is a continuing professionalisation of the DPO sector with many organisations changing from small-scale social gatherings into major budget holders with million pound plus annual turnovers.

The assimilation of the social model and independent living discourses by traditional disability charities and government represents the colonisation of the disabled peoples' social movement and the emergence of a disabling corporatism. For Foucault this reflects the operation of power, and in this case, disabled peoples' resistance to it. This is partly a result of the success and clarity of disabled peoples' articulation of their voices and experiences in recent years, but also because disability is as much about impairment as it is about a significant industry. In this way the discourses and principalities of disabled people are not only mapped upon their bodies, lives and minds but also in the economic resources and regulations that govern their actual and potential actions.

Conclusion

This chapter has considered discourses of DPOs. Using notions of power and resistance from Foucault, and capital, field and habitus from Bourdieu, the emergence of DPOs and their challenge to the negative positioning of impairment and articulation of inclusive and independent living alternatives were explored. While DPOs have much to be proud of and celebrate, inclusion and equality is far from achieved and realised by the diverse range and broad community of disabled people. As mainstream political and financial opportunities for disabled people and DPOs increase, new struggles will no doubt emerge. Inequality is clouded within colonised spaces that attend to corporate interests and attempt to rebrand the disabled body, mind and lifestyle as part of the political and economic project of impairment management and inclusion. As disabled peoples' visibility and palatability have increased, the discourses of their organisations have been embraced in policy and industry. However, the emergence of disabling corporatism, as Oliver (2009) terms it, suggests the assimilation of disabled peoples' discourses, that is, social model and independent living, have lost their once radical ethos.

This 'corporatisation' is double edged, for while it enables the development of inclusion technologies, it subsumes the independent bodies, minds and lives into a broader economic agenda of service consumption. Further work that maps crucial texts and moments that politicise the oppression of impairment and expose the abuses may be useful to illuminate everyday practices and processes that invalidate the human diversity. Considering the dilemmas of disabled peoples' identity and the mainstreaming of disability, a new language of resistance is required to further the inclusion agenda. This is so that the broadest collective of people who are associated with impairment and disability can come together and push for positive social change. This will include how disability rights work for older people, disabled prisoners, those with addictions and others with unfamiliar disability identities.

Perhaps this new language of resistance should emphasise crimes and breaches of human rights articles now that the UK has signed the Convention of Rights of Disabled People and is thus obliged to ensure compliance. However, there are challenges and it should be noted that the articulation of any new language of resistance is a discursive construction, so will be only work to represent a specific position for particular audience and thus be subject to rebuttal and dispute by mainstream views. Therefore it not only risks being cosseted as authentic cultural capital by those on the inside wanting out, but also assimilated and colonised by those on the outside wanting in. This becomes then not something of resistance, but rather a new style of power, and its potential to radicalise inclusion policies is lost as disabled people find they have now come full circle, the danger being that the once radical, resistive ideas of disabled people, are now turned against themselves as some find acceptance in the mainstream through the success of their organisations, but others with social disputed characteristics remain marginalised, ignored and excluded.

Notes

1. Actual numbers of DPOs in UK are unknown. Estimates of those being between 650 and 1000+ are based on Maynard-Campbell, Maynard and Winchecombe (2007) and Disability LIB (2007).
2. Rather than having the state provide social care services, direct payments are a financial resource given to some disabled people which they use to organise and fund their own support provision.

References

Alt, C. (2005). 'The Birth of the Clinic'. *Nursing Standard*, 19 (47): 36–48.

Barnes, C. (2002). 'Introduction: Disability, Policy and Politics'. *Policy & Politics*, 30 (3): 311–18.

Barnes, C. and Mercer, G. (2006). *Independent. Futures: Creating User Led Disability Services in a Disabling Society*. Bristol: The Policy Press.

Barnes, C. Mercer, G. and Shakespeare, T. (1999). *Exploring Disability: A Sociological Introduction*. Cambridge: Polity Press.

Bourdieu, Pierre (1977). *Reproduction in Education, Society and Culture*. London: Sage Publications.

Bourdieu, Pierre (1979). *Distinction: A Social Critique of the Judgment of Taste* (translated by Richard Nice). London: Routledge.

Bourdieu, Pierre (1983). *The Forms of Capital* (translated by Richard Nice), http://www.viet-studies.org/Bourdieu_capital.htm.

Bourdieu, P. and Wacquant, L. J. D. (1992, Reprinted 2005). *An Invitation to Reflexive Sociology*. Cambridge: Polity Press.

Braddock, David, L. and Parish, Susan L. (2001). 'An Institutional History of Disability'. In G. L. Albrecht, K. D. Seelman, M. Bury, *Handbook of Disability Studies*. London: Sage Publications.

Burton, M. and Kagan, C. (2006). 'Decoding Valuing People'. *Disability & Society*, 21 (4): 299–313.

Carabine, J. (2001). 'Unmarried Motherhood 1830–1990: A Genealogical Analysis'. In M. Wetherell, S. Taylor and S. J. Yates, *Discourse as Data*. London. Sage Publications Limited.

Department of Health (DOH) (2001). 'Valuing People a New Strategy for Learning Disability', www.archive.official-documents.co.uk/document/cm50/5086/5086. pdf, accessed 19 March 2012.

Department of Health (DOH) (2007). '"Putting People First": A Shared Vision and Commitment to the Transformation of Adult Social Care', http://www.dh.gov. uk/en/Publicationsandstatistics/Publications/PublicationsPolicyAndGuidance/DH_ 081118, accessed August 2010.

Disability LIB (2007). 'Thriving and Surviving: Challenges and Opportunities for Disabled People's Organisations in the 21st Century', http://www.disabilitylib.org. uk/images/stories/DisabilityLIB_report.pdf, accessed August 2010.

Dreyfus, H. and Rabinow, P. (1982). *Michel Foucault: Beyond Structuralism and Hermeneutics*. Chicago: Chicago University Press.

Finkelstein, V. (1999). 'A Profession Allied to the Community: The Disabled People's Trade Union'. In E. Stone (ed.) *Disability and Development: Learning from Action and Research on Disability in the Majority World*. Leeds: The Disability Press.

Foucault, M. (1961). *Madness and Civilization*. Routledge, London.

Foucault, M. (1963). *The Birth of the Clinic*. Routledge, London.

Foucault, M. (1972). *The Archaeology of Knowledge*. New York: Pantheon.

Foucault, M. (1975). *Discipline and Punish: The Birth of the Prison*. New York: Random House.

Foucault, M. (1976). *The History of Sexuality Vol. 1: The Will to Knowledge*. London: Penguin.

Fowler, B. (2003). 'Reading Pierre Bourdieu's Masculine Domination: Notes Towards An Intersectional Analysis of Gender, Culture and Class'. *Cultural Studies*, 17 (3/4), 468–94.

Hughes, B. (2002). 'Disability and the Body'. In C. Barnes, M. Oliver and L. Barton (eds), *Disability Studies Today*. Cambridge: Polity Press.

Hughes, B. (2005). 'What Can a Foucauldian Analysis Contribute to Disability Theory?' In S. Tremain (ed.) *Foucault and the Government of Disability*. US: The University of Michigan Press.

Hunt, P. (1972). Letter to *The Guardian*, http://www.leeds.ac.uk/disability-studies/ archiveuk/Hunt/Hunt%201.pdf, accessed 19 March 2012.

Lareau, A. and McNamara Horvat, E. (1999). 'Moments of Social Inclusion and Exclusion Race, Class, and Cultural Capital in Family-School Relationships'. *Sociology of Education*, 72 (1), 37–53.

Maynard-Campbell, S., Maynard, A. and Winchcombe, M. (2007). 'Mapping the Capacity and Potential for User-Led Organisations (ULO) in England'. Department of Health, http://www.dh.gov.uk/en/Publicationsandstatistics/Publications/Publica tionsPolicyAndGuidance/DH_078538, accessed August 2010.

Morris, J. (1992). *Independent Lives: Community Care and Disabled People*. London, Macmillan.

Morris, J. (2004). 'Independent Living and Community Care: A Disempowering Framework'. *Disability & Society*, 19 (5): 427–42.

O' Cathain, M. (2006). 'Blind, But Not to the Hard Facts of Life: The Blind Workers' Struggle in Derry, 1928–1940'. In T. Meade and D. Serlin (eds) *Radical History Review: Disability History*. Durham, NC: Duke University Press.

Oliver, M. (2009). *Understanding Disability: From Theory to Practice* (second edition). Hampshire: Palgrave Macmillan.

Pfeiffer, D. (2000). 'A Comment on the Social Model(s)'. *Disability Studies Quarterly*, 22 (4): 234–35.

Prime Minister's Strategy Unit (2005). 'Improving the Life Chances of Disabled People'. London: The Stationery Office.

Ravaud, J-F. and Stiker, H-J. (2001). 'Inclusion/Exclusion: An Analysis of Historical and Cultural Meanings'. In G. L. Albrecht, K. D. Seelman, M. Bury, *Handbook of Disability Studies*. London: Sage Publications.

Shakespeare, T. (2006). *Disability Rights and Wrongs*. London: Routledge.

Tremain, S. (ed.) (2005). *Foucault and the Government of Disability*. US: The University of Michigan Press.

United Kingdom Disabled Peoples Council (UKDPC) (2010). DPOs vs ULOs helpsheet, http://www.ukdpc.net/library/DPOs%20v%20ULO%20Helpsheet1.pdf, accessed August 2010.

Part II
Bodies

6
Cyborgs, Cripples and iCrip: Reflections on the Contribution of Haraway to Disability Studies

Donna Reeve

Introduction

Although Haraway's cyborg has been widely used in feminist science studies and other fields, 'disabled cyborgs' are largely absent (see Moser, 2000, 2005 for conspicuous exceptions). Ironically, while the cyborg is supposedly about 'transgressed boundaries' and 'potent fusions', the starting point in any cyborg discussion is inevitably a 'fully functioning human and a fully functioning machine' (Quinlan and Bates, 2009: 51), an assumption which remains invisible and unquestioned. One of the reasons why there has been little utilisation of the transgressive cyborg figure within disability studies to date is because of a well-documented history of how technology was problematically associated with normalisation, rehabilitation and cure (Goodley, 2011).

This chapter will revisit Haraway's *A Cyborg Manifesto* (1991) in order to explore what the cyborg can offer disability studies. Opinions in disability studies are currently divided (Kafer, 2009): some argue that cyborg theory cannot offer solutions for the material disadvantage faced by disabled people in society; others see the cyborg as providing a way of understanding the lack of a fixed boundary between disabled and non-disabled people. As well as presenting these debates, this chapter will also consider other ways of using cyborg theory to make sense of the lived experience of impaired people who have intimate relationships with technology, such as people with prosthetics and implants or who use assistive devices such as wheelchairs.

After presenting a summary of Haraway's key work, I look at the *lived experience* of impaired cyborgs and then briefly touch on *cultural* representations of disability and cyborgs within science fiction. Finally I discuss what the 'impaired cyborg' can offer disability studies through engagement with theoretical understandings of embodiment, identity and disabled/non-disabled binaries.

'A Cyborg Manifesto'

It was back in 1960 that the term 'cyborg' – cyb(ernetic) + org(anism) – first entered the lexicon. As a result of the US space research programme, the first cyborg was a rat that had been fitted with an osmotic pump under the skin which automatically dispensed chemicals without any intervention by the organism (Clynes and Kline, 1995 [1960]). These scientific advances ran parallel with the popular culture of the time as science fiction, films and novels were quick to exploit the image of the cyborg, an entity which was neither human, animal or machine (Kafer, 2009). Now, 50 years later, cyborgs have proliferated into every facet of everyday life and culture (for more information see Gray, 1995, 2002) and 'cyborgization' is evident today in the everyday ways that people use technology – the commuter using a mobile phone, the teenager plugged into their iPod and someone interacting with others in *Second Life*, a virtual software-driven world accessed using the Internet.

However, for the purposes of this chapter I want to draw on the work of Donna Haraway. In *A Cyborg Manifesto* (1991) Haraway used the concept of the cyborg as a way for feminism to engage with rapid advances in science and technology and to move beyond the impasse of standpoint feminism. Suggesting that Foucault's notion of biopower provided a 'flaccid premonition' (Haraway, 1991: 149) of how contemporary technoscience would impact on people and their lives, Haraway instead analyses the position of women *now*, asking what it means to be a subject in a post-industrial power framework. Haraway argues that advanced capitalism has spawned an 'informatics of domination' which is based on social relations of science and technology that underpin a new global technoculture. *A Cyborg Manifesto* introduces the cyborg as a

> cybernetic organism, a hybrid of machine and organism, a creature of social reality as well as a creature of fiction.
>
> (Haraway, 1991: 149)

Haraway points out that by the late twentieth century,

> we are all chimeras, theorized and fabricated hybrids of machine and organism; in short, we are all cyborgs. The cyborg is our ontology; it gives us our politics.
>
> (Haraway, 1991: 150)

The cyborg can be found in the transgression of the human–animal boundary, such as the implantation of human cancer cells into mice (OncoMouse™). The blurring of physical and non-physical boundaries provides another site for cyborgisation, as reflected in sexual practices on the Internet (Netsex) which may or may not involve a real blood-and-flesh partner (Gray, 2002). Internet encounters may be virtual, but the resulting friendships can be real, supporting Haraway's assertion that 'the virtual isn't immaterial. Anyone who thinks it is, is nuts' (Gane, 2006: 147). Finally, and most importantly for this chapter, the cyborg can also be found in the transgression of the human–machine boundary as in people with prosthetic limbs, implants or artificial organs.

In *A Cyborg Manifesto* Haraway uses her feminist theory of cyborg politics to offer a way forward in the face of fragmentation in traditional identity politics.

> There is nothing about being 'female' that naturally binds women. ... Gender, race, or class consciousness is an achievement forced on us by the terrible historical experience of the contradictory social realities of patriarchy, colonialism, and capitalism.
>
> (Haraway, 1991: 155)

Haraway suggests that rather than searching for a new essential unity, cyborg feminism identifies a new political struggle which is about coalitions rather than divisions, working towards affinity rather than identity (see also the chapter in this volume by Roets and Braidotti which considers the contribution of Deleuze to disability studies).

In addition, the cyborg is an individual and the whole, representing 'transgressed boundaries, potent fusions, and dangerous possibilities' (Haraway, 1991: 154). The hybrid figure of the cyborg blurs categorical distinctions such as human/machine, human/animal and nature/culture and moves beyond the dualisms which contribute to the domination of those marked as Other. Cyborgs can unsettle the existing order by creating new modes of 'resistance and recoupling' (Haraway, 1991: 154) which undermine the implicit hierarchies within these dualisms. This theoretical approach raises new ethical and epistemological questions; for example, how does the cyborg (often seen as posthuman) question what it means to be human?

I have briefly identified some of the key points about the cyborg figure described by Haraway in *A Cyborg Manifesto*. While she engages with issues of difference such as gender, ethnicity and class, her discussion about disability is restricted to a passing comment that many disabled people are already cyborg.

> Perhaps paraplegics and other severely handicapped people can (and sometimes do) have the most intense experiences of complex hybridization with other communication devices.
>
> (Haraway, 1991: 178)

This omission is particularly striking when one takes into account the fact that Haraway's father was disabled from childhood which meant he used underarm crutches to walk (Haraway, 2008). While Haraway talks about the cyborg relationship her father had with his crutches and various wheelchairs, there is no discussion of *disability* per se; this seems odd given that it is likely she grew up with a father who would probably have experienced environmental barriers of some kind during his life as a crutch user before the disability rights movement started in the US in the 1970s.

While there is potential value in exploring disability within the larger 'bodies' of cyberculture, the Internet and telecommunications technologies, such as disability activists working together across the world via Internet technology (Goodley, 2011), that has been set aside for another day. This chapter sets out to revisit the figure of the *individual* cyborg and to consider its relevance for disability studies in the twenty-first century.

The impaired body as contemporary cyborg

For people with impairments, the hybridisation of machine/human or animal/human is often synonymous with lived experience, particularly for those with physical or sensory impairments (which will form the focus for this chapter). Potential cyborg figures can be seen in the wheelchair user, the person with a cochlear implant, artificial leg or pacemaker or someone who uses an assistance dog. In this section I want to look at the issues which are raised if the impaired body is viewed as a potential contemporary cyborg.

Access to cyborg technology

There have been various criticisms within disability studies about the cavalier use of impaired bodies within mainstream theorising about cyborgs. For example Mitchell and Snyder describe how *A Cyborg Manifesto* provides an example of how

> disabled people exemplify, *in a footnote*, the self-evident cyborgs of modernity – transhuman subjects who rework the nature/culture divide.
> (Mitchell and Snyder, 1997: 28–9, my emphasis)

This footnoting is common; discussion of prosthetics and impaired bodies is often limited to consideration of how technology either restores functionality or normalises the person with little discussion of the cultural/social implications of prosthetics, or of the lived experience of body and prosthetic. Discussions of the connections between 'cyborg' and 'disabled' are rarely made (Campbell, 2009).

Mitchell and Snyder (1997) also point out the insensitivity that many social theorists and philosophers display when using impaired bodies and technology to illustrate cyborg thinking. It is all very well to fantasise about the couplings of human and technology which have developed over time to include prosthetics, implants, artificial organs and technological aids – human trials will start by 2012 on a prosthetic arm which is directly controlled by micro arrays which have been implanted into the brain (Drummond, 2010). This is close to the stuff of science fiction. But at the same time, disabled people are among the poorest group in society and so access to adequate prosthetics or technology so that they can participate in society as an 'active citizen' is seriously curtailed (Mitchell and Snyder, 1997). Therefore improvements in technology do not always relate to improvements in the quality of life of disabled people because

> [t]echnology is always already social – which in our culture means it is shaped and informed by market forces and the requirements of powerful vested interests.
>
> (Cromby and Standen, 1999)

This leads to hierarchies in 'who gets what prosthetic'; while an injured US soldier receives a high-tech prosthetic arm costing $18000 (Page, 2007), a civilian who has lost a leg because of illness is assessed by US insurance companies based on what is necessary to get between the bed and toilet.

> No other aspect of daily living other than using the bathroom is considered 'necessary', which means your basic prosthetic given to most amputees – a stick with a rubber foot as a leg, or a stick with a hook on the end as an arm, has fundamentally not changed since WWII.
>
> (Mullins, 2009b)

This could be seen as reinforcing the existing hierarchies in culture about the relative worth of different impairments (Deal, 2003); thus acquiring an impairment through fighting for one's country is more worthy than that caused through illness. For a politics of cyborg bodies to be envisioned, then, certain questions need to be asked, including:

> Does everyone have the 'right' to become any kind of cyborg body? Or are these 'rights' economically determined?
>
> (González, 2000: 65)

People with impairments do not have automatic 'rights' to become the cyborg body they want because these 'rights' *are* economically determined and tied up with other factors such as hierarchies of impairment as well as gender, class and ethnicity. This is analogous to the stratification of women and people from ethnic minority groups into lower socio-economic groups in the world as a result of the development of new social relations of technology (Haraway, 1991).

As part of her critique of the post-structural disabled subject, Erevelles (2001) argues strongly that there is danger in viewing disabled subjects as being able to

> seek a pleasurable survival as a border-crosser in the ironic political myth of a cyborgean materiality.

(Erevelles, 2001: 97)

While many disabled people do have intimate relationships with technology, guide dogs and ventilators which are necessary to everyday survival, this playful transgressing of boundaries so favoured by Haraway and subsequent theorists neglects the materiality of *disablism*, in other words, the social practices and cultural beliefs that underpin the disadvantage and exclusion experienced by people with impairments (Thomas, 2007: 13). The ease with which cyborg politics offers a new language and possibilities for marginalised groups risks erasing the *actual* struggles that many disabled people face for economic survival, especially in the majority world. Here the extreme poverty in some countries is exacerbated by the high numbers of people who become amputees as a result of war and landmines (Yeo and Moore, 2003) – cyborg politics would appear to have little relevance to these disabled people struggling simply to survive.

Reality of living as a cyborg

Another criticism which has been made by scholars in disability studies is that the cyborg imagined by Haraway fails to take account of the *reality* of living with a body which is hybridised with technology. As Siebers (2008) puts it so well:

> Haraway's cyborgs are spunky, irreverent, and sexy; they accept with glee the ability to transgress old boundaries between machine and animal, male and female, and mind and body. ... [However] Haraway is so preoccupied with power and ability that she forgets what disability is. Prostheses always increase the cyborg's abilities; they are a source only of new powers, never of problems. The cyborg is always more than human – and never risks to be seen as subhuman. To put it simply, the cyborg is not disabled.

(Siebers, 2008: 63)

Siebers describes how his plastic leg brace helps ease the pain in his lower back, but in summer it chafes his calf causing pain and soreness. Long-term wheelchair users can develop painful shoulder problems in later life and implanted devices such as nerve cord stimulators can have wires break and batteries that need replacing; these are examples of 'impairment effects' (Thomas, 2007: 136), restrictions of activity due to bodily variation and ways of managing that difference, rather than from externally imposed disablism. In addition to these physical problems that prosthetics can cause, there are also potential psycho-emotional barriers. For example, while using a wheelchair can be enabling, allowing the user to move more freely in space, that person then becomes subject to the prejudices that exist in society about the perceived inabilities of wheelchair users (Cromby and Standen, 1999). This example of psycho-emotional disablism (Reeve, 2006, 2008; Thomas, 2007) is a form of social oppression that undermines emotional well-being, self-esteem and ontological security, impacting on 'being' rather than 'doing' as seen in examples of structural disablism such as inaccessible buildings. This experience of psycho-emotional disablism may make someone decide to abandon their prosthetic because they do not want to be marked out as different and subject to stigma; this has implications for professionals such as physiotherapists who need to rework their notion of 'non-compliance' through the lens of psycho-emotional disablism.

Another form of psycho-emotional disablism can emerge when people feel 'forced' to use a prosthetic or assistive device because of the reactions of others. For example, there is social pressure on women to wear a prosthetic or have breast reconstruction surgery following breast cancer (Herndl, 2002); not only does this retain the cultural image of women as feminine but it also hides the unspeakable spectre of cancer from public view. People using prosthetic devices can be stared at by strangers which is another example of psycho-emotional disablism. Alongside questions about how someone lost their hand, for example, there are also questions about how the mechanical hand works (Garland-Thomson, 2009). Some people choose to wear an 'aesthetic prosthetic' which has no function, but helps reduce this experience of psycho-emotional disablism.

It is not just impaired bodies that have been seen as potential cyborgs – increasingly the ageing body can also be seen as a cyborg if one considers the use of stents, pacemakers, artificial hips and so on, that are offered to shore up worn out joints and other body parts near their sell-by date. Ihde (2008) who self-identifies as a 'partial cyborg' has written an excellent paper describing how these prosthetics do not work as well as the original body part and so they are 'quasi-transparent'. Although implants such as replacement hip and knee joints are common operations in the UK at least, they have a limited lifespan in practice and so people delay surgery as long as possible, aiming for 'late life, rather than mid-life cyborg parts!' (Ihde, 2008: 400). Although prosthetics 'fall far short of the bionic technofantasies so often projected in popular culture' (Ihde, 2008: 403), adopting cyborg options is one common way of attempting to counteract the processes of ageing.

Surveillance, control and dependence

Cyborg technology keeps pace with the times and I now want to turn my attention to other more subtle consequences that highly computerised technological aids might have for their impaired users. Surveillance of disabled people is not new; the work of Foucault has been used to explain the workings of disciplinary power to exclude disabled people through systems of surveillance underpinned by medical definitions of (ab)normal bodies and minds (Tremain, 2005); see also the chapter in this book by Hodgkins and Blackmore. Cromby and Standen (1999) describe a 'caring house' which contains sensors, pressure pads and other devices which are linked to a central computer system, allowing for movement and activity in the building to be monitored and to call for assistance if the occupant appears to have fallen or become ill. Although this form of 'telecare' allows someone to live independently, the personal price paid is the loss of privacy because of the 24-hour surveillance by technology – 'care' has been morphed into surveillance. As countries seek to reduce the cost of their social care of disabled and older people, it is likely that telecare solutions will increasingly be offered instead of personal care solutions (Mort, Roberts and Milligan, 2009).

Wheelchairs are also becoming more technologically advanced with some incorporating 'remote presence' technology. If the user feels that they are about to have an epileptic seizure then they press a button and in

> the best 'Thunderbirds' tradition, the operator [at the remote base] then uses the joystick to drive the wheelchair and its occupant home again.
>
> (Cromby and Standen, 1999: 107)

Therefore this wheelchair reflects elements of both surveillance and total control because once the button has been pressed, the remote operator has complete control of the wheelchair's movements. Like the example of telecare, surveillance and safety are co-present, overriding the right of the disabled user to have access to privacy and the acts of spontaneous intimacy which are available to other people. The disabled person is also dependent on the remote base (the 'carer') not to misuse this technology – surveillance and control at this level are only one step removed from the panopticon, an institution designed to allow the omnipresent gaze of authority on inmates who did not know when they were being watched (Foucault, 1977).

The final issue of dependency is multifaceted. While we are all dependent on technology in the minority world for everyday life to function, for disabled people, moving towards *dependence on technology* can be one way of achieving *independence* to become an active citizen (Gray, 2002), for example, relying on increasingly technological wheelchairs and other assistive devices. Consequently a power failure is not simply inconvenient – it can be life threatening if one is dependent on artificial organs which work outside the body. In addition, software failures in implanted medical devices pose additional risks to life (Sandler et al., 2010). Like other forms of technology, obsolescence and monopolies are other potential problems and the more complex the assistive device is, the more likely one is to be tied into networks and institutions to support that device. Consequently, 'people with disabilities [would] become hostages to the machines that help them.' (Cromby and Standen, 1999: 108). These issues of surveillance, control and dependency were well illustrated in a study of disabled teenagers who used AAC (Augmentative and Alternative Communication):

> Thus, although the teenagers are enabled by their technology in some very positive ways, as was reflected by their verdicts that VOCAs [voice output communication aids] were 'magic', 'fantastic', 'great', and 'help me say what I want', they are also simultaneously very dependent on the technology and sometimes at the mercy either of it, or the people who manage it for them.
>
> (Wickendon, 2010: 240)

Thus technological assistance was a double-edged sword which left the teenagers 'being technology enabled and technology dependent' (Wickendon, 2010: 240).

Cyborgs in film and literature: The example of Lila Black

I now want to briefly look at how cyborgs and disability have been represented in contemporary culture because this has an impact on how others – disabled and non-disabled people – view cyborg bodies.

> [C]yborgs are everywhere and multiplying ... It's not just Robocop, it is our grandmother with a pacemaker. Not just Geordi [in *Star Trek: The Next Generation*] but also our colleague with the myloelectric prosthetic arm.
>
> (Gray, Mentor and Figueroa-Sarriera, 1995: 2)

Therefore although disability is rarely discussed in cyborg literature, nonetheless the connections between disabled people and cultural icons are made when the word 'cyborg' is mentioned.

In *A Cyborg Manifesto* Haraway argues that writers are 'theorists for cyborgs' (Haraway, 1991: 173) because they offer accounts of what it means to be embodied in a highly technological society and hence of the politics associated with cyborg bodies. Haraway draws on the short story 'The Ship Who Sang' by Anne McCaffrey which relates the story of Helva, a disabled child who is transformed into a space ship. Cheyne (2010) has analysed this story from a disability studies perspective and shows that although the most common interpretation of the story is that it represents a positive message about disability, this hides various disabling discourses. Unfortunately Haraway uses the literary connection with 'The Ship Who Sang' to support her suggestion that 'severely handicapped' people have the most intense experiences of hybridisation with technology and then adds that

> Gender, sexuality, embodiment, skill: all were reconstituted in the story. Why should our bodies end at the skin, or include at best other beings encapsulated by skin?
>
> (Haraway, 1991: 178)

As Cheyne wryly comments, 'How could such a text be anything other than positive about disability?' (Cheyne, 2010: 8). While other cyborg theory and cyberculture writers have analysed 'The Ship Who Sang', attention has been on the gender rather than disability issues in the story. So the one example of literature which Haraway refers to, which features disability, is used to support the contention that being transformed into a cyborg (if one is impaired) can only be 'A Good Thing' (Cheyne, 2010: 8).

While there is an established body of work on the analysis of how disability representations in film such as the 'evil cripple' influence how disabled people are seen in society, it is in the genre of science fiction films that the search for perfect bodies and medical cure comes to fruition (Cheu, 2002). As medical technology and genetic engineering have developed, so have the futuristic ideas of a society where 'disability' is eradicated by the intervention of technology to cure and treat impairment. In films such as *Blade Runner* and *Gattaca* Cheu shows how disability is associated with the stigmatised identity of a 'second-class citizen', but in *The Matrix*, disability becomes a socially constructed concept. Meekosha (1999) has analysed the film *Alien Resurrection* and points out that identity and corporeality have a complex and troubled relationship. Classification systems have always existed in some form or another to mark out and separate the 'insiders' from the 'outsiders'; this is exemplified in the scene where Ripley discovers her 'failed' clones in the laboratory. All of these human/alien hybrids embody common images of disability – '"the deformed", "the spastic", "the disfigured", "the limbless"' (Meekosha, 1999: 26) – and cry out for Ripley to end their pain by killing them. Meekosha argues that by becoming Dr Death, Ripley is reproducing the 'voluntary euthanasia' scenarios which allow the ending of life on the basis of negative assumptions about the worth and value of disabled people's lives. Consequently Meekosha doubts that cyborgs offer a vision of the future in which impaired bodies will have transcended 'normalcy' to become part of the variation of beings who are part of society.

In the same way that the disabled body is assumed to be asexual, cyborgs such as the Terminator or RoboCop, who feature in the 1980s films *The Terminator* and *RoboCop* respectively, are portrayed as asexual, lacking human emotions and are represented as more machine than human (Cherney, 2001). Cherney contrasts this with David Cronenburg's controversial film *Crash* which features a cyborg who is both disabled and sexy – Gabrielle who wears a short skirt and fishnet stockings along with her leg calipers. In contrast to the ableist perception of disabled women as asexual and passive, Gabrielle is shown in the film as a beautiful woman who is erotic and highly desirable. Scars and prostheses in this film are seen as sexually desirable rather than stigmatising marks, thereby forcing 'ableist viewers to rethink their erotic gaze' (Cherney, 2001: 177). Although the film does risk fetishising the impaired body, Cherney argues that the need to challenge ableist assumptions about disability/sexuality through films such as *Crash* make the risk worthwhile.

The final example I want to introduce is that of the character Lila Black in the *Quantum Gravity* series written by Justina Robson (2006, 2007, 2008, 2009), who has a reputation for writing feminist science fiction that explores the blurred boundaries between human and technology, hybridity and subject formation (Mitchell, 2006). Throughout the stories, Lila battles with emotional insecurity and struggles to make sense of her rebuilt body – part human, part robot, part AI. Lila describes being careful sitting down so that the weight of her prosthetic legs does not break furniture. Initially at least, she dresses to hide her metal prosthetic parts so that she does not have to deal with the stares of other people. She also has to return to the Agency to restore her ammunition stocks and for ongoing medical treatment and maintenance; she has pain and discomfort.

But over time, she becomes aware that the interface where her flesh meets metal is changing into something new, slowly converting human flesh into machine; she worries about what will happen at the instant she moves past her 'final moment of existence as a human being' (Robson, 2008: 192). Lila tracks down her medical records for the cyborg procedure she underwent, as she tries to make sense of what was done to her body and the violence of this act is brought home sharply:

> Where ordinary women would have their babies, she held a copy of a star [reactor power source] that could burn on long after any of her weak flesh body had gone.
>
> (Robson, 2008: 128)

In some ways Lila is like one of Haraway's cyborgs, 'spunky, irreverent, and sexy' (Siebers, 2008: 63), but she is also vulnerable and human. She does not reproduce the dominant discourses of femininity and queers heterosexuality somewhat by having two lovers – an elf and a demon. Thus compared to characters such as the *Bionic Woman* (Quinlan and Bates, 2009), Lila presents a more sophisticated representation of overlapping images of disability, gender and cyborg. Disability is occasionally present; impairment and impairment effects are part of her story. Therefore Lila presents a more realistic account of living as a cyborg, with all its inherent problems, which is closer to the lived experience of disability and impairment than is usual with science fiction cyborgs.

*i*Crip: The impaired cyborg as disabled, non-disabled or something other?

Earlier I suggested that impaired people with their intimate associations with technology both inside and outside the body in many ways are 'already cyborg'. Add in the relationships between disabled people and a variety of (usually) canine 'companion species' who act as hearing, seeing and sensing support animals for their impaired owner and it is possible to see examples of blurred human/machine and human/animal boundaries. While these relationships are not always as simple in practice – constrained by access to material resources and vulnerable to interruption caused by breakdown or chafing body parts – nonetheless they are still examples of cyborgs in everyday life. Now that I have discussed some of the cultural representations of cyborgs and the messages they give about disability, I want to consider what all this means for the categories of disabled/non-disabled, abnormal/normal and what, if anything, this can offer disability studies.

Cure, 'fix' and the 'twilight zone': The experience of cochlear implants

One of the obvious criticisms of cyborg theory and disability which I have not mentioned is that it risks reinforcing the individual model of disability because of the way in which

> cyborg theory's celebration of technological intervention and human/ machine couplings perpetuates the ableist assumption that disabled bodies are broken and require 'fixing'.
>
> (Kafer, 2009: 224)

This reinforces a rehabilitation discourse of medicine and although it might be possible to fix the impaired body, it is argued that this particular cyborg body will continue to be stigmatised and seen as 'half a human being' (Barnes and Mercer, 2003: 83). This has not been helped by Haraway's silence about the relationship between disabled people and cyborgs (Campbell, 2009). The case of cochlear implants which were hailed as a 'cure' for deafness is one such example of 'fixing impairment' (for a more detailed discussion see chapter 5 in Campbell, 2009). The promotional literature for cochlear implants stressed how the device would enable the user to straddle both the hearing and deaf communities. Instead, this has led to the creation of 'hybrids, who are destined to exist in the "twilight zone" of the hearing and Deaf worlds' (Campbell, 2009: 95). Although people who have had the cochlear implant surgery can supposedly 'return' to the deaf world by removing the external component of the device, in reality these people feel that they are only temporary visitors to the deaf community. Additionally, the hearing outcomes vary for each person and will never return hearing to 'normal'; cochlear implants do not provide 'bionic ears' with enhanced hearing abilities as implied by cultural science fiction narratives.

It seems to me that the arguments about whether or not (and how) impaired bodies should be modified by relationships with technology are analogous to those associated with the contentious issue of 'cure' (Shakespeare, 2006). Technology can never totally remove impairment, but it can help reduce the effects of impairment. There is still an imperative for society to be challenged and changed to include disabled people as equal citizens at all levels – this is outside the remit of cyborg technology. Technology should never be forced on someone as a 'fix', and they need to be fully informed about the decisions they are making, especially when surgery is involved. While the 'benefits' of cochlear implants are debateable, there is no doubt that other implants such as pacemakers and artificial hips go a long way towards *reducing impairments*; prosthetics, wheelchairs and other aids such as VOCA do not change the impairment but *reduce impairment effects* – in both cases they allow the individual to participate more fully in social life, especially given the reality that we still do not live in a fully accessible society (Cherney, 2001). However as I have noted previously, the use of these technologies comes with their own problems and are not equally available to all.

Unsettling of the 'normal'

In disability studies there is a strong argument that viewing the impaired body as a contemporary cyborg reinforces the discourses of normal/abnormal because of the way technology (informed by medicine) tends to recreate the 'normal' body. But this assumption ignores the aspects of cyborg theory that should enable the 'rethinking [of] normal society, normal bodies, and normal relationships with technology' (Cherney, 2001: 169). How instead might the relationships of impaired people and technology unsettle the everyday understandings of 'normal'?

One good example of this unsettling of the 'normal' is seen in the two sprinters, Oscar Pistorius and Aimee Mullins, both of whom run with lower limb prosthetics made from carbon fibre. These 'Cheetah Legs' had been used for 15 years by amputee sprinters, but it was only when Pistorius entered a track event in 2007 and came second in a field of non-disabled runners that he was 'deemed *too* abled' (Mullins, 2009d, emphasis in original). Athletics in particular has always been the domain of the physically perfect body. These cultural messages about the desirability and value of 'normal' bodies contrast with the denigration and devaluation of those bodies which are 'abnormal'. Therefore Pistorius with his request (and proven ability) to compete (and win) against non-disabled athletes is 'encroaching on hallowed ideological territory' (Swartz and Watermeyer, 2008: 189) because he is directly challenging the notion that success in mainstream athletics is only for those with perfect 'normal' bodies.

Moreover, programmable prosthetic legs are on the horizon and these will be able to be configured to emulate the thresholds that reflect flesh-and-bone legs. So while this might mean that the legs could be configured to a 'normal' setting defined by an Olympic standard to allow the user to race alongside other non-disabled athletes, there will be no such rules in the Paralympics.

> In an ironic, amazing cultural flip, you will see runners in the Paralympics going faster than those in the Olympics. Now won't *that* be an interesting comment on 'dis'ability?
>
> (Mullins, 2009d, emphasis in original)

So Pistorius and his Cheetah Legs are directly challenging the boundary between disabled and non-disabled bodies, and his request to participate in the Olympics reveals a *cyborg anxiety* at not only the level of top athletics, but more fundamentally, at the implications this could have for body culture and notions of 'othering' (Swartz and Watermeyer, 2008).

Embodiment and technology

Within disability studies, there has been a growing interest in the role of the body and impairment in understanding the experience of disablism; some of the other chapters in this book reflect this trend. What happens to the 'body' when prosthetic devices, assistance aids and the like enter the equation? For someone with a visual impairment, a long white cane can enable them to negotiate the built environment – the cane is not simply an object but becomes an additional tactile organ, providing feedback on objects and surfaces at ground level (Iwakuma, 2002). Similarly wheelchair users describe how the chair becomes a 'part of them' (Winance, 2006).

> She also objects strongly if anyone leans on her chair, as if they are leaning on her body without permission.
>
> (Marie described in Wickendon, 2010: 236)

A phenomenologically trained academic who also uses a hi-tech prosthesis commented:

> Indeed, in learning to use the prosthesis, I found that *looking objectively* at my leg in the mirror as an exteriorized thing – a piece of technology – to be thought about and manipulated did not help me to improve my balance and gait so much as did *subjectively feeling* through all of my body the weight and rhythm of the leg in a gestalt of intentional motor activity.
>
> (Sobchack, 2004 cited in Ihde, 2008: 399, emphasis in original)

In these cyborg examples, the Cartesian dualisms of body and mind start to become unstable; Campbell (2009) suggests that technology is

> characterological ... in its unification and transmogrification of the corporeal and psychic life of the person with disability.
>
> (Campbell, 2009: 54)

Therefore living with technology impacts on the lived experience of disabled people at the level of both body and mind, irrespective of whether the technology is outside or inside the body (Ihde, 2008). Becoming cyborg in this manner can also alter the body – 'I am now part chair, with some capabilities that exceed my original specifications' (Hockenberry, 2001: 105). While it is possible for the prosthesis, cane or wheelchair to become part of the embodied experience of the world, this fusion is nonetheless contingent because technology can fail, thereby revealing the illusion of this melding. In the same way that corporeal bodies are only brought into the foreground of our attention when injury or illness occurs, the electric wheelchair, VOCA technology or hi-tech prosthetic leg can be taken for granted until it breaks or becomes unreliable. This is very close to other phenomenological accounts of the body (such as Iwakuma, 2002) and the 'dys-appearing' body (Paterson and Hughes, 1999).

iCrip: New ways of being?

I now want to end by seeing the potential that technology has for destabilising the categories of 'disabled' and 'non-disabled'. As I have shown in the sections above, the impaired cyborg is not always seen as disabled – it depends on the kind of prosthetic or implant – which in turn is informed by cultural images, visibility, economics and how common and readily available the technology is for people with impairments. For example, someone who has an artificial knee joint fitted is much less likely to see themselves as disabled (or be seen by others as disabled) than someone who uses VOCA to communicate with others. Having a pacemaker fitted is almost a 'normal' aspect of ageing like needing reading glasses – it is not a marker of disability. Compare this to the example of this competent wheelchair user, who, despite being able to 'coast flat out and slalom effortlessly around pedestrians' (Hockenberry, 2001: 103), continues to have a fixed ontological status as disabled. Thus the prosthetic is endowed with cultural and social meanings which in turn impact on identity and subjectivity.

The cultural images of cyborgs discussed earlier can be used to advantage by those who use prosthetics. Aimee Mullins, mentioned earlier, is an actress and fashion model, as well as an athlete; as someone who travels widely, she has learnt to travel wearing her carbon fibre 'RoboCop' legs rather than her cosmetic looking legs (Mullins, 2009b). When the metal detectors at the airport go off, lifting trouser legs to reveal these obvious prosthetics leads to less explaining (and potential misunderstanding) than if she appeared to have 'normal' legs – the word 'prosthetic' is unlikely to appear in your average tourist dictionary. She also described how when wearing her RoboCop legs, she finds that children, rather than being fearful or staring, are 'drawn like a magnet to them, accompanied by a list of very astute questions' (Mullins, 2009c). In her opinion, it is the exposure to cultural images such as RoboCop which 'familiarises' the unfamiliar and results in engagement rather than avoidance by others.

So I do not agree that it is *inevitable* that the impaired cyborg will be stigmatised and seen as 'half a human being' (Barnes and Mercer, 2003: 83). As technology improves and becomes available to more people, new possibilities can emerge.

> A prosthetic limb doesn't represent the need to replace loss anymore. It can stand as a symbol that the wearer has the power to create whatever it is that they want to create in that space. So people that society once considered to be disabled can now become the architects of their own identities and indeed continue to change those identities by designing their bodies from a place of empowerment.
>
> (Mullins, 2009a)

While acknowledging the very privileged situation Mullins is in with respect to access to prosthetics, nonetheless her point about people being able to redesign their bodies and challenge who is seen as 'disabled' is empowering and a good example of what I will term *i*Crip. The use of the prefix '*i*' is to allow the reclaimed Crip word (McRuer, 2006) to be conjoined with technology, to represent the twenty-first century impaired cyborg (inspired by the name of the 'iLimb' prosthetic [Page, 2007]).

According to Haraway, cyborg identity is established on transgressing boundaries, in particular the discourses of otherness which result in binaries that maintain the illusion of the invulnerable autonomous subject. If the cyborg is 'never an either-or but always both' (Gane, 2006: 153), *i*Crip represents new ways of being which are (non)disabled and (ab)normal. So for example, the ways in which impaired people incorporate their wheelchairs, prosthetics and canes into their corporeal and psychic sense of self produces new ways of being which are both (non)disabled and (ab)normal, which are *i*Crip. But *i*Crip is not always a productive outcome if one considers the 'twilight world' between the deaf and hearing worlds inhabited by some people with cochlear implants discussed earlier. In addition, *i*Crip is subject to the problems associated with living as a human–machine hybrid discussed previously in this chapter, such as surveillance, stratification and hierarchies, control and dependence.

I have tried to show how *i*Crip changes as technology becomes more freely available, better fitting (in other words, fits the purpose better both physically and psychologically) and grows to be more culturally acceptable.

Rather than seeing technology as 'fixing' impaired people in normative ways (and therefore to be rejected), it is more productive to see the new ways of being in the world that emerge from living as cyborg. Haraway's cyborg has the potential to

> open up productive ways of thinking about subjectivity, gender [or disability] and the materiality of a physical body.
>
> (Balsamo, 2000: 157)

When considering the ways in which the impaired body meshes with technology to become a cyborg, it is possible to see the ambiguity which results from what is then (ab)normal or (dis)abled as reflected in the case of Oscar Pistorius as well as new embodied ways of being in the world.

Finally, what does this mean for identity politics? In the UK, from where I am writing, the disabled people's movement has achieved a great deal for disabled people, such as anti-discrimination legislation with more disabled people in mainstream society than 40 years ago. However, like other social movements, it is not representative of all disabled people in society; often people with chronic illnesses see themselves as 'ill' not disabled, and older people see their difficulties associated with their age rather than because of disabling barriers (Grewal et al., 2002). In many ways disabled people represent another diverse group, like women, who might have more cohesion if they came together as a group based on political kinship and affinity, rather than any imagined 'disability identity' (Kafer, 2009). Therefore it might be possible to rethink the category of 'disabled people' as a 'cyborg identity, a potent subjectivity synthesized from fusions of outside identities' (Haraway, 1991: 174), which could better include those 'disabled people' who are currently absent such as older people and those with chronic illness. Similarly, it would be useful to consider what organisations of *i*Crip could achieve politically, culturally and socially through their ability to produce new ways of being which are not necessarily 'disabled'.

Conclusions

Although Haraway's cyborg theory has rarely engaged with disability, other than as a metaphor or footnote (McRuer, 2006), in this chapter I have tried to use it literally, to look at the reality which many people with impairments experience when living with a variety of prosthetics, implants, artificial organs and technological aids. I have described some of the issues which are raised by the experience of living in an intimate relationship with technology and how this is never straightforward for most disabled people. The experience of living as a contemporary cyborg, a fusion of human and machine raises many issues which tend not to feature in accounts of cyborg theory outside disability studies: the unequal distribution of technology to those who could use it, the compromises people make to live with it such as pain as well as vulnerability to surveillance, control and dependency. At this point I would be inclined to agree with Kirkup (2000) who commented that the value of the 'gendered cyborg' was limited:

> Its usefulness for cultural deconstruction of gender has become apparent, but its usefulness as a tool for material change is yet to be proved.
>
> (Kirkup, 2000: 5)

I agree with other disability studies writers who believe that in the case of disability cyborg theory is unlikely to prove a way forward for reducing the material poverty and exclusion experienced by disabled people.

I do not agree that this therefore renders cyborg theory irrelevant to disability studies, to be dismissed as 'extravagant flights of academic fancy' (Barnes and Mercer, 2003: 83). Some academics suggest that the cyborgisation of impaired bodies is simply the individual model in disguise – after all it is the individual that is being 'fixed' to adapt to the environment through the application of artificial limbs. But not all cyborg adaptions are seen in this way – for example, artificial organs which keep someone alive on the transplant list, or stents and artificial hips. Rather than 'throw the baby out with the bathwater', I have used cyborg theory to look at embodiment and to illustrate the way in which impaired cyborgs are potentially able to unsettle the binary divisions between normal/abnormal, non-disabled/disabled as exemplified by *i*Crip. Living with technology as many disabled people do potentially offers new ways of being and can directly challenge what is 'normal', particularly when the prosthetic or assistance device supplied 'does the job well' both physically and psychologically. So while the cyborg world has its risks of ignoring the material realities of disablism, it could also offer hope for the future:

> In place of the security of a rigid categorisation that has bred intolerance, persecution and the putative mastery of strange and unfamiliar others, there is the opportunity of positive transformation in our ontological and epistemological models.
>
> (Shildrick, 2002: 128)

Cyborg theorists may have neglected disability; but disability studies can use cyborg theory to look at embodiment and subjectivity in new and productive ways, as suggested through the figure of *i*Crip.

References

Balsamo, A. (2000). 'Reading Cyborgs Writing Feminism'. In G. Kirkup, L. Janes, K. Woodward and F. Hovenden (eds), *The Gendered Cyborg: A Reader* (pp. 148–58). London: Routledge in association with The Open University.

Barnes, C. and Mercer, G. (2003). *Disability*. Cambridge: Polity Press.

Campbell, F. A. K. (2009). *Contours of Ableism: The Production of Disability and Ableness*. Basingstoke: Palgrave Macmillan.

Cherney, J. L. (2001). 'Sexy Cyborgs: Disability and Erotic Politics in Cronenberg's *Crash*'. In C. R. Smit and A. Enns (eds), *Screening Disability: Essays on Cinema and Disability* (pp. 165–80). Lanham, MA: University Press of America.

Cheu, J. (2002). 'De-Gene-Erates, Replicants and Other Aliens: (Re)Defining Disability in Futuristic Film'. In M. Corker and T. Shakespeare (eds), *Disability/Postmodernity: Embodying Disability Theory* (pp. 198–212). London: Continuum.

Cheyne, R. (2010). '"She was born a thing": Disability, the Cyborg and the Posthuman in Anne McCaffrey's "The Ship Who Sang"', paper presented at Present Difference, Manchester Metropolitan University, 6–7 January.

Clynes, M. E. and Kline, N. S. (1995 [1960]). 'Cyborgs and Space'. In C. H. Gray (ed.), *The Cyborg Handbook* (pp. 29–33). New York & London: Routledge.

Cromby, J. and Standen, P. (1999). 'Cyborgs and Stigma: Technology, Disability, Subjectivity'. In A. Gordo-Lopez and I. Parker (eds), *Cyberpsychology* (pp. 95–112). London: Routledge.

Deal, M. (2003). 'Disabled People's Attitudes Toward Other Impairment Groups: A Hierarchy of Impairments'. *Disability & Society*, 18 (7), 897–910.

Drummond, K. (2010). *Human Trials Next for Darpa's Mind-Controlled Artificial Arm*, Wired, http://www.wired.com/dangerroom/2010/07/human-trials-ahead-for-darpas-mind-controlled-artificial-arm/, accessed 16 July 2010.

Erevelles, N. (2001). 'In Search of the Disabled Subject'. In J. Wilson and C. Lewiecki-Wilson (eds), *Embodied Rhetorics: Disability in Language and Culture* (pp. 92–111). Carbondale and Edwardsville, IL: Southern Illinois University Press.

Foucault, M. (1977). *Discipline and Punish: The Birth of the Prison* (translated A. Sheridan). London: Allen Lane. Originally published in France as *Surveiller et punir: Naissance de la prison* by Paris: Editions Gallimard in 1975. Reprint referenced Harmondsworth: Penguin Books, 1991.

Gane, N. (2006). 'When We Have Never Been Human, What Is To Be Done?: Interview with Donna Haraway'. *Theory, Culture & Society*, 23 (7–8), 135–58.

Garland-Thomson, R. (2009). *Staring: How We Look*. Oxford: Oxford University Press.

González, J. (2000). 'Envisioning Cyborg Bodies: Notes from Current Research'. In G. Kirkup, L. Janes, K. Woodward and F. Hovenden (eds), *The Gendered Cyborg: A Reader* (pp. 58–73). London: Routledge in association with The Open University.

Goodley, D. (2011). *Disability Studies: An Interdisciplinary Approach*. London: Sage.

Gray, C. H. (ed.) (1995). *The Cyborg Handbook*. New York & London: Routledge.

Gray, C. H. (ed.) (2002). *Cyborg Citizen: Politics in the Posthuman Age*. London: Routledge.

Gray, C. H., Mentor, S. and Figueroa-Sarriera, H. J. (1995). 'Cyborgology: Constructing the Knowledge of Cybernetic Organisms'. In C. H. Gray (ed.), *The Cyborg Handbook* (pp. 1–14). New York & London: Routledge.

Grewal, I., Joy, S., Lewis, J., Swales, K. and Woodfield, K. (2002). 'Disabled for Life? Attitudes Towards, and Experiences of Disability in Britain (DWP Research Report 173)'. Leeds: Corporate Document Services.

Haraway, D. J. (1991). *Simians, Cyborgs and Women: The Reinvention of Nature*. London: Free Association Books.

Haraway, D. J. (2008). *When Species Meet*. Minneapolis, MN: University of Minnesota Press.

110   *Cyborgs, Cripples and iCrip*

Herndl, D. P. (2002). 'Reconstructing the Posthuman Feminist Body Twenty Years after Audre Lorde's *Cancer Journals*'. In S. L. Snyder, B. J. Brueggemann and R. Garland-Thomson (eds), *Disability Studies: Enabling the Humanities* (pp. 144–55). New York: The Modern Language Association of America.

Hockenberry, J. (2001). 'The Next Brainiacs'. *Wired*, 9 (8), 94–105.

Ihde, D. (2008). 'Aging: I Don't Want to Be a Cyborg!' *Phenomenology and the Cognitive Sciences*, 7 (3), 397–404.

Iwakuma, M. (2002). 'The Body as Embodiment: An Investigation of the Body by Merleau-Ponty'. In M. Corker and T. Shakespeare (eds), *Disability/Postmodernity: Embodying Disability Theory* (pp. 76–87). London: Continuum.

Kafer, A. (2009). 'Cyborg'. In S. Burch (ed.), *Encyclopedia of U.S. Disability History* (pp. 223–4). New York: Facts on File.

Kirkup, G. (2000). 'Introduction to Part One'. In G. Kirkup, L. Janes, K. Woodward and F. Hovenden (eds), *The Gendered Cyborg: A Reader* (pp. 3–10). London: Routledge in association with The Open University.

McRuer, R. (2006). *Crip Theory: Cultural Signs of Queerness and Disability*. New York: New York University Press.

Meekosha, H. (1999). 'Superchicks, Clones, Cyborgs, and Cripples: Cinema and Messages of Bodily Transformations'. *Social Alternatives*, 18 (1), 24–8.

Mitchell, D. T. and Snyder, S. L. (1997). 'Introduction: Disability Studies and the Double Bind of Representation'. In D. T. Mitchell and S. L. Snyder (eds), *The Body and Physical Difference: Discourses of Disability* (pp. 1–31). Ann Arbor, MI: University of Michigan Press.

Mitchell, K. (2006). 'Bodies that Matter: Science Fiction, Technoculture, and the Gendered Body'. *Science Fiction Studies*, 33 (1), 109–28.

Mort, M., Roberts, C. and Milligan, C. (2009). 'Ageing, Technology and the Home: A Critical Project'. *ALTER – European Journal of Disability Research / Revue Européenne de Recherche sur le Handicap*, 3 (2), 85–9.

Moser, I. (2000). 'Against Normalisation: Subverting Norms of Ability and Disability'. *Science as Culture*, 9 (2), 201–40.

Moser, I. (2005). 'On Becoming Disabled and Articulating Alternatives: The Multiple Modes of Ordering Disability and Their Interferences'. *Cultural Studies*, 19 (6), 667–700.

Mullins, A. (2009a). 'Aimee Mullins and Her 12 Pairs of Legs'. TED Conferences, http://www.ted.com/index.php/talks/aimee_mullins_prosthetic_aesthetics.html#, accessed 14 December 2009.

Mullins, A. (2009b). 'Is Choosing a Prosthesis So Different than Picking a Pair of Glasses?' [Internet], Gizmodo, http://gizmodo.com/5401408/is-choosing-a-prosthesis-so-different-than-picking-a-pair-of-glasses, accessed 8 July 2010.

Mullins, A. (2009c). 'Normal was Never Cool: Inception of Perception', [Internet], Gizmodo, http://gizmodo.com/5404227/normal-was-never-cool-inception-of-perception, accessed 28 July 2010.

Mullins, A. (2009d). 'Racing on Carbon Fiber Legs: How Abled Should We Be?', [Internet], Gizmodo, http://gizmodo.com/5403322/racing-on-carbon-fiber-legs-how-abled-should-we-be, accessed 11 January 2010.

Page, L. (2007). '"Cyborg-Style "ilimb" Hand a Big Hit with Iraq Veterans: "Soldiers Love The Robotic Look"'. *The Register*, http://www.theregister.co.uk/2007/07/18/robo_hand_gets_big_hand/, accessed 15 July 2010.

Paterson, K. and Hughes, B. (1999). 'Disability Studies and Phenomenology: The Carnal Politics of Everyday Life'. *Disability & Society*, 14 (5), 597–610.

Quinlan, M. M. and Bates, B. R. (2009). *'Bionic Woman* (2007): Gender, Disability and Cyborgs'. *Journal of Research in Special Educational Needs*, 9 (1), 48–58.

Reeve, D. (2006). 'Towards a Psychology of Disability: The Emotional Effects of Living in a Disabling Society'. In D. Goodley and R. Lawthom (eds), *Disability and Psychology: Critical Introductions and Reflections* (pp. 94–107). London: Palgrave Macmillan.

Reeve, D. (2008). 'Negotiating Disability in Everyday Life: The Experience of Psycho-Emotional Disablism'. Ph.D. Thesis, Lancaster University.

Robson, J. (2006). *Keeping It Real*. London: Gollancz.

Robson, J. (2007). *Selling Out*. London: Gollancz.

Robson, J. (2008). *Going Under*. London: Gollancz.

Robson, J. (2009). *Chasing the Dragon*. London: Gollancz.

Sandler, K., Ohrstrom, L., Moy, L. and McVay, R. (2010). *Killed by Code: Software Transparency in Implantable Medical Devices*. New York: Software Freedom Law Center.

Shakespeare, T. (2006). *Disability Rights and Wrongs*. Abingdon: Routledge.

Shildrick, M. (2002). *Embodying the Monster: Encounters with the Vulnerable Self*. London: Sage.

Siebers, T. (2008). *Disability Theory*. Ann Arbor, MI: University of Michigan Press.

Swartz, L. and Watermeyer, B. (2008). 'Cyborg Anxiety: Oscar Pistorius and the Boundaries of What It Means to Be Human'. *Disability & Society*, 23 (2), 187–90.

Thomas, C. (2007). *Sociologies of Disability and Illness: Contested Ideas in Disability Studies and Medical Sociology*. Basingstoke: Palgrave Macmillan.

Tremain, S. (ed.) (2005). *Foucault and the Government of Disability*. Ann Arbor, MI: University of Michigan Press.

Wickendon, M. (2010). 'Teenage Worlds, Different Voices: An Ethnographic Study of Identity and the Lifeworlds of Disabled Teenagers who use AAC'. Ph.D. Thesis, The University of Sheffield.

Winance, M. (2006). 'Trying Out the Wheelchair: The Mutual Shaping of People and Devices through Adjustment'. *Science, Technology, & Human Values*, 31 (1), 52–72.

Yeo, R. and Moore, K. (2003). 'Including Disabled People in Poverty Reduction Work: "Nothing about us, without us"'. *World Development*, 31 (3), 571–90.

7
Theory, Impairment and Impersonal Singularities: Deleuze, Guattari and Agamben

James Overboe

Introduction

Since the Enlightenment with the displacing of God with 'man' [*sic*] as the primary architect of society, differing marginalised people have struggled to be included in this realm of citizenship with rights and responsibilities. Since the 1960s with the advent of identity politics, marginalised groups stake out their claim of legitimacy under the rubric of citizenship. Disability activism and by extension disability studies has followed feminism, queer movements, and antiracism in adopting this method of social change. Yet, this model of self-actualised individuals within a group membership with its reliance upon liberalism to some degree disavows impairments that coexist with the disabled identity. I draw on the theoretical works of Gilles Deleuze, Felix Guattari and Giorgio Agamben to illuminate how impersonal singularities can affirm impairments, and offer another way to express life.

Impersonal or pre-individual singularities are the materiality of life that provides the basis for life. The impersonal or pre-individual vitalism originates at birth as life without a conscious self expressed, it sustains itself at least until, and possibly beyond, death. By simply I do expressed, not mean to diminish the vitalism of this impersonal or pre-individual life. In *The Deleuze Connections*, John Rajchman (2000) asserts that impersonal singularities are the essence of life. The multiplicity of singularities provides the materiality from which the self is constituted. But within this constitution the vagueness of life is sacrificed in the name of certitude and identity. Yet, as Rajchman (2000: 84) suggests, it is precisely the vagueness of indeterminate and impersonal lives that opens up space for new possibilities of life.

Although they take us from our 'selves' or 'persons', in another sense they are what are most peculiar to us or about us. For 'a life' is always singular. It is made up of 'singularities' that are 'pre-individual' or 'sub-individual' which are then linked to others in a plan or 'plane' that is impersonal, like the 'it' in 'it's raining', which is the condition of the singularity of a life ... The vagueness of a [singular] life is thus not a deficiency to be corrected, but rather a resource or reserve of other possibilities, our connections.

Yet, I do not want to leave the impression that impersonal or pre-individual singularities are present only at the beginning or near end of life. They coexist with the personal with cognition and intent that is part of the residual humanistic registry (identified by Colebrook below). This generative vitalism a pre-individual or impersonal (genius) life force has a co-presence with the personal (ego) from birth to death. In *Profanations*, commenting on the concept of Genius, Agamben (2007: 11) asserts:

> Comprehending the conception of man [sic] implicit in Genius means understanding that man [sic] is not only an ego and individual consciousness, but rather that from birth to death he is accompanied by an impersonal pre-individual element. Man [sic] is thus a single being with two phases; he is a being that results from the complex dialectic between a part that has yet to be individuated and lived and another part that is marked by fate and individual experience. But the impersonal, non-individual part is not a past we have left behind once and for all and that we may eventually recall in memory; it is still present in us, still with us, near to us and inseparable from us, for good or bad.

Life simply is a force field of tensions whose antithetical poles are Genius and Ego. Giorgio Agamben (2007: 13) maintains, 'This field is traversed by two conjoined but opposed forces; one that moves from the individual to the impersonal and another that moves from the impersonal to the individual. The two forces coexist, intersect, separate, but can neither emancipate themselves completely from each other nor identify with each other perfectly.' For the purposes of this chapter, I privilege the impersonal registry over the personal registry. In this sense I am employing a Nietzschean transvaluation (Deleuze, 2006: 63) by reversing the belief that the personal register is the ultimate way to live a life' and instead offer the merits of a pre-individual life for consideration by the field of disability studies on its right. Moreover, the point of this chapter is to illumine how impersonal singularities affirm impairments and can lead to a fuller life expressed through the vitality of disability.

Identity politics, personhood and the human registry

Michel Foucault (1984: 124–5) asserts that the liberal rhetoric of individualism is based upon a belief in a 'founding subject' who gives meaning to a so-called empty world, judging, categorising and shaping this world. Agreeing with Foucault, Richard Jones (1990: 81) asserts that since the seventeenth century liberal individualism has been dominant in Western discourse. Bill Hughes (1999: 163) argues that the vision of the white-able-bodied-heterosexual male defines 'truth' through a description of the world based on one specific experience of it. This view has authority that allows its proponents to invalidate other embodiments, as they affirm their own.

As Zola (1991a) and Oliver (1990) and others point out, the disability movement is indebted to the civil rights, feminism and the various queer movements for establishing the various differences of identity central to social change. Moreover, these prior social movements critiqued the Eurocentric, masculine, heterosexist view of the Cartesian body/mind split that arbitrarily privileges the latter over the former. The Cartesian dualism was fabricated to justify the European man of reason as superior to other lesser bodies including women, racialised others, queer people and 'the disabled'.

The concept of identity politics remains the dominant discourse within disability studies. As in most social movements, in disability studies it has been important for disabled people to tell their own stories (to claim their voice). But this is not simply a disabled person's so-called overcoming narrative. In *Disability, Self and Society*, Tanya Titchkosky (2006: 7) asserts that within disability studies, autobiography is employed to provide a counter-narrative to the hegemonic view that privileges ableness. To that end, she analyses how the meaning of disability is constituted by various social actors and institutions, and later demonstrates how disabled people reinterpret and explicate the oppression they experience. In her later work, *Reading and Writing Disability Differently*, Titchkosky (2007: 25) writes, 'What matters for my project is *how* the given meanings surrounding disability are noticed in the here and now of everyday life. What matters is *how* disability is spoken about, narrated, and thereby made present in our lives'.

To develop a counter-narrative presupposes an identity reclaimed through narrative. Simi Linton (2006) speaks to the fluidity of identity in this narrative. Commenting upon the increased use of the terminology 'disabled people' as opposed to the term 'person with a disability' since 1990, Linton (2006: 163) notes,

> Beginning in the early 90s *disabled people* [italics in original] has been increasingly used in disability studies and disability rights circles when referring to the constituency group. Rather than maintaining disability as a secondary characteristic, *disabled* [italics in original] has become a marker of the identity that the individual or group wish to highlight or call attention to.

Ironically, disability studies echoes the Cartesian split by arbitrarily creating a division between impairment and disability, an illusion to solve the problem of what to do with the messiness of our bodies, minds and sensibilities that detract from our being considered worthy of being a person, a citizen, or for that matter being fully human. Just as the Cartesian fabrication has been proven to be detrimental to the understanding of how life manifests itself by privileging the mind over the body, I argue the arbitrary split between disability and impairment privileges the rationally controlled disabled person, thus creating a personae that fundamentally is a facsimile of the 'able' personae and supplants the vivacity of a disabled life expressed through impairment.

While I respect proponents of a disabled identity for social change, I am concerned that we will disavow the vivacity of our impairments in order to be recognised as having the prerequisites of a group identity in the (neo)liberal mould, that is – self-directed, independent citizens with the same rights and responsibilities associated with able people. In some sense are disabled people not selling themselves short if they accept this Faustian bargain? Because of our respective impairments will we always remain 'unreasonable facsimiles' of the able, white, masculine, heterosexual prototype that admittedly is flawed but its illusion of being the standard for humanity still resonates. Instead, could we not affirm disabled lives expressed without the (neo)liberal baggage?

Similarly, in her article, Fiona Kumari Campbell (2008: 160) implores disabled people to employ two strategies. First, in keeping with Titchkosky's counter-storytelling, Campbell (2008: 160) encourages disabled people to tell stories about embracing impairment and framing success in terms of 'because of disability' rather than the 'in spite of disability' ableist rhetoric. The second strategy asks disabled people to reject the seduction of liberalism and affirm impairment.

In my own academic writing career I continue to affirm impairments, as well as warning about the dangers of the seductive lure of liberalism (see Overboe, 1999, 2007a, 2007b). In my last writing (Overboe, 2009) and presently in this chapter, I am suggesting that perhaps disability studies needs to shift from the personal registry associated with humanism to the impersonal registry associated with the inhuman as another avenue to affirm impairment and critique liberalism. Let me be clear, I am not criticising either Titchkosky or Campbell for their positions; in fact we need more nuanced critiques of liberalism and more affirmation of impairments in counter-narratives. Instead my focus is on the impersonal singularities associated with impairment.

Impairment and embodiment

Jim Ferris argues against transcending the materiality of disability even if we have to embrace pain. Ferris (2008: 249) writes:

> My dialogue with Laura [Ferguson] about pain is the foundation for this piece. Sometimes we talk in similar ways, about loving our bodies,

about the importance of delving into them as we experience pain. But fundamentally our perspectives on pain and the body are quite different. She wants ultimately to transcend pain, transcend the body, to feel the body turn to light. Me, I want the meat of the body, the blood and guts, the pleasure of eating and shitting and fucking and fucking again, and if some pain is the price to pay for these, then so be it. So be it. I would much rather feel the world, taste it and smell it and wear it even as it wears me out – I'd much rather have my painful smelly dirty ultimately uncontrollable body than transcend my corporeal being. I'd rather leave transcending for after I am done with this body. To me, transcending is the line we've all been fed all our lives – your reward will come in the next life, so shut up and suffer, and by the way here's some discrimination thrown in. No thank you. Laura and I agree that the only way is through – I think perhaps the goal of thoroughness is what is at issue. I don't want to live in a Platonic heaven of ideas – let's eat. And fuck. Transcendence through fucking.

The arthritis in my left hip is getting worse. The pain is up, my range of motion is down, and I'm afraid that at some point I'm not going to be able to use it anymore. That I'll be too fucked to fuck. That scares me, but not into the arms of transcendence.

Ferris enthusiastically grounds life in the materiality and messiness of impairment and rejects transcending the body. Similarly, Irving Zola (1991b) argues for his assorted impairments – polio, carpel tunnel syndrome, arthritis, diabetes – to be acknowledged as important aspects that helped shape his life and attributed success. Zola (1991b: 2) writes,

I want at the very least to bring these personal bodily experiences closer to my center – not to claim that they constitute all of who I am, but that they are a central part of my identity; not that they explain all that I have accomplished, but that they are essential to understanding what I have done.

How do we bring the body Zola and Ferris write about back to disability studies? Or more correctly how do we move beyond the body that is restricted and weighted down by the notion of representation and identity – these empty phrases like empty calories that may do more harm than good? A body bloated by its reliance upon the dialectic to explain, to understand, to organise and give meaning to life, as manifested in the subsequent necessity for its 'politics of recognition' (Grosz, 2010). A 'politics of recognition' that through the dialectical process creates vacuous identities and representations that transcend the messiness that is a crippled life that Zola and Ferris, albeit to differing degrees, both wish to embrace. Perhaps we have to search deeper and question the taken-for-granted humanism with its reliance upon achieving personhood.

As disabled people (and by extension the discipline of disability studies) can we risk easing off on the reliance upon, and its attachment to, the 'I' with its (hopeful) progression to be anointed to the status of personhood? Continually garroting life, squeezing out and discarding any expression of vitality that fails to enhance the 'nobility' of personhood? For many marginalised people achieving personhood along with its rights and status has been a 'crown jewel' worthy of attainment by any (new) social movements. I can just hear the murmur of protest beginning – after all, copious amounts of sweat and blood has been spilled in achieving the status of personhood for former gimps, cripples, crazies, spastics, blind and assorted others who previously were labeled 'unfortunates' or 'damaged goods' (Bauman, 1988).

Can we not recognise the sterility in being 'unreasonable facsimiles of ableness' striving for that 'brass ring of normality' while disavowing the messiness of our impairments (Overboe, 1999)? Hoping that the effects of our impairment don't become noticed as if 'discharge' or 'ooze' from a sore. Thus, exposing the fallacy of being the able-cripple (Wade, 1997) and in doing so allowing the able-centric others (including some disabled people) to recognise our taken-for granted so-called limitations and pass judgement upon us. For the power resides in those that adhere to and naturalise able-centric thinking cloaked in the 'pure' concept of being a 'person just like everyone else'. Perhaps we need a radical shift and recognise the affirmation of impairment originating from the vitality of impersonal singularities within an inhuman registry.

The emphasis upon identity politics squarely situates disability studies within the human registry associated with personhood. Let me shift the conversation to the inhuman registry associated with an impersonal singularities that constitute both the 'normative' biological system as well as constituting impairments. The impersonal singularities of impairment especially break in, thieve, steal away, causing havoc and ultimately expressing life.

In order to affirm these impersonal singularities, we must first critique the taken-for-granted twin concepts of identity and representation. Melissa McMahon (2005: 43) writes, 'The function of the concept of identity, as Deleuze presents it in Difference and Repetition, is that of "managing" difference', consequently the notion of identity developed from the need to differentiate the disabled from the able people. The subcategories of disability, cerebral palsy, autism, psychiatric disabilities are representations and categorisations that fail to see the vitality of assorted impairments. The vitality of impairment is discarded and rejected unless overcome, as it is deemed detrimental to achieving the full status of personhood.

Within the impersonal registry there is no need for the exactness or representation required of identity. In fact the vitality of the impersonal singularities of impairment cannot be pinned down. The 'thisness' or 'haecceity' of a life expressed is ever elusive and in that respect is and remains impersonal. For example within the human or personal registry the interpellation of name cerebral palsy pathologises my spasms, and my life. In the inhuman, impersonal or pre-individual registry so-called spasms are singularities, a generative source and vitality for a life.

In respect of 'identity in concept', Deleuze (1994: 266) writes, 'To restore difference in thought is to untie this first knot which consists of representing difference through the identity of the concept and the thinking subject.' By untying this knot that garrottes the materiality of impairment and impersonal singularities that constitute this matter, we can begin to see our impairments as impersonal singularities, as generative sources – as a *thisness* of life rather than as detractors from identity. Second, for Deleuze difference is subordinated to resemblance. In effect many disabled people disavow and attempt to overcome their impairments in order to resemble productive members of society with the same privileges and obligations as the 'able' others. If we affirm the difference of impairment not in terms of comparison or resemblance to 'able' others, but simply as a life (as it is) expressed we open up the possibility to live our lives beyond the normative shadows (see Overboe, 2007a, 2007b) of ableism and disableism that restrict disabled people.

According to Deleuze (1994: 266) difference has been represented as opposition and limitation, which has led to hierarchical levels that have been counterproductive for people. For example, in his discussion about opposition and revolution, Deleuze (1994: 268) writes, 'Contradiction is not the weapon of the proletariat but, rather, the manner in which the bourgeoisie defends and preserves itself, the shadow behind which it maintains its claim to decide what the problems are.' Thus, framed within a dichotomy the oppressed are always responding to the oppressor in the name of resistance. Addressing the question of resistance, Linda Martin Alcoff (1999: 67) writes,

> There is a kind of quest purity in the attempt to maintain only a resistance which is itself defined as a reaction to power rather than a fight for power. Resistance so circumscribed suggests a desire to inhabit a space free from criticism, responsibility, and accountability, to be always a critic never the advocate.

Always 'reacting against' ableism and disableism, rather than 'fighting for' the affirmation of my assorted impairments left me feeling empty. When articulating positions from the dichotomy of ability and disability, I felt restricted by the incessant need to respond to the normative shadow of ableness that was omnipresent in discussions, and influenced the parameters for the 'rules of engagement', as well as the means of articulation. In order to advocate, I emphasise impersonal singularities of impairment that exist on a plane of life other than the dialectic of ability and disability.

Impersonal vitalism and the inhuman registry

The spectre of being a person, subject or self haunts the discipline of disability studies. Similarly, from a theoretical perspective queer theory must break itself free from selfhood and subjectivity, Claire Colebrook (2010a: 11) writes,

> For Deleuze, true thought and true theory; a real break with the normative image of "man" – must include *both* the intuition of the ground from which sense, truth and problems emerge, *and* must fulfill the promise of transcendental inquiry, which has all too often fallen back upon a self or subject who subtends theory.

Disability studies' true thought and true theory must break free from the normative image of the able-cripple that has too often fallen back on the notion of self or subject who subtends theory. And in doing so allow for the generative source of impairment to flourish as a life.

Colebrook (2010a: 11) continues,

> Contrary to a popular idea of a simple anti-humanism Deleuze does not simply reject the intuition of essences, the eternal, genesis, and grounds; on the contrary, his work is best understood as an argument in favour of a true or superior transcendentalism which would think beyond the residual humanism maintained both by forms of Kantian critique and by popular notions of community and interrogation.
>
> (Deleuze, 1994: 197)

With its genesis in the social movement of the disabled community, disability studies as an academic discipline continues to be haunted by a residual humanism in its reification of a 'politics of recognition' as a prerequisite for notions of community and social change. Can disability studies move beyond both the residue of humanism and its reliance solely upon the self? In what way might the materiality or matter of those impairments be a generative source of a superior transcendentalism or in a somewhat ironic twist a Nietzchean 'greater health'? (Overboe, 1999).

In order to move beyond this residue of humanism, we have to consider life as existing without being confined to the concepts of the person or individual, and instead embrace the inhuman aspects of ourselves. Gilles Deleuze (2004b: 143) asserts, 'Whenever we write, we speak as someone else. And it is a particular form that speaks through us.' Through most of human existence we have been stuck between two oscillating forms the individual coextensive with being that expresses God and the person who is coextensive with representation. Offering a third option with its basis in pre-individual, impersonal singularities, Deleuze (2004b: 143) elaborates,

> For a long time we were stuck with the alternative, either you are persons or individuals, or you sink back into an undifferentiated sea of anonymity. Today, however, we are uncovering a world of pre-individual, impersonal singularities. They are not reducible to individuals or persons, nor to a sea without difference. These singularities are mobile, they break in, thieving, and stealing away, alternating back and forth, like anarchy crowned, inhabiting a nomad space. There is a big difference between partitioning a fixed space among sedentary individuals according to boundaries or enclosures, and distributing singularities in an open space without enclosures or properties.

In another text, *Pure Immanence, Essays on a Life*, Deleuze illustrates how impersonal singularities are manifested in the social world. Deleuze (2005: 30) writes,

> They connect with one another in a manner entirely different from how individuals connect. It even seems that a singular life might do without any individuality, with-out any other concomitant that individualises it. For example, very small children all resemble one another and have hardly any individuality, but they have singularities, a smile, a gesture, a funny face – not subjective qualities. Small children, through all their sufferings and weakness, are infused with an immanent life that is pure and even bliss.

Later Deleuze considers how an impersonal singularity has significance as we are near death. In his analysis of the near-death scene of a despicable man, in the Charles Dickens novel *Our Mutual Friend*, Deleuze (2005: 28–9) writes,

> The life of the individual gives way to an impersonal and yet singular life that releases a pure event freed from the accidents of internal and external life, that is, from the subjectivity and objectivity of what happens. ... It is a haecceity no longer of individuation but of singularization, a life of pure immanence, neutral, beyond good and evil, for it was only the subject that incarnated it in the midst of things that made it good or bad. The life of such individuality fades away in favour of a singular life immanent to a man who no longer has a name, though he can be mistaken for no other. A singular essence, a life.

Referring to the above quote, in *Potentialities, Collected Essays in Philosophy*, Giorgio Agamben (1999: 229) states, 'The place of this separable life is neither in this world nor in the next, but between the two, in a kind of happy netherland that it seems to leave only reluctantly'.

From their social location as able-centric people both Deleuze and Agamben in their discussion about the pre-individual or impersonal singularities invoke a normative and able interpretation of the grotesque. From the perspective of disability studies, Lennard Davis (1997: 10) argues that the ideal body was an artistic representation of a compilation of preferred body parts of living models. During pre-modern times this idealised body could never be achieved but was to be admired. Conversely, the common people were the opposite of this ideal body because of their imperfect bodies were labelled as 'grotesque'. However, even this grotesque population excluded disabled people. Davis (1997: 11) asserts, 'The grotesque permeated culture and signified common humanity, whereas the disabled body, a later concept, was formulated as by definition excluded from culture, society, the norm.'

Within a disabled life expressed some of the impersonal singularities of the grotesque exist but supplement the impersonal singularities that combine, constituting various impairments within disabled bodies. To paraphrase Rajchman (2000), the vagueness of an impaired life is thus not a deficiency to be corrected, but rather a resource or reserve of other possibilities, our connections. Deleuze and Guattari see the secrecy of impersonal singularities as producers of life. Colebrook (2010b: 298) writes,

[F]or Deleuze and Guattari the secrecy that defines life is that which produces relations and which repeats itself. Life is not reducible to the extended and recognisable terms that it produces, but this does not mean that there is an absolute secret so much as a proliferating secrecy, the emission or unfolding of relations the virtual force of which can never be given once and for all. One is not separated from or responsible for this unnameable secret, for precisely through the recognition of virtual life one can overcome subjectivism.

In addition Colebrook cites Deleuze and Guattari (1987: 280)

To be present at the dawn of the world. Such is the link between imperceptibility, indiscernibility, and impersonality – the three virtues. To reduce oneself to an abstract line, a trait, in order to find one's zone of indiscernibility with other traits, and in this way to enter the haecceity and impersonality of the creator.

Agamben (1996: 30) argues that 'the concept of people does not refer to a unitary subject. It is an oscillation between two opposite poles, People as a whole refers to an integral body politic whereby life becomes politicized. And people as a subset a fragmentary multiplicity of needy and excluded bodies.' Agamben (1996: 30) adds, 'The concept of people pretends to be inclusive with no remainder. While simultaneously an exclusive known to afford no hope.' At one extreme, people were anointed to the total state of sovereignty, at the other end, total banishment. These banished people are considered to be under the 'state of exception' (Agamben, 1998: 26–7).

For example, I personify the extreme binaries of the concept of people by being anointed to both the total state of sovereignty, and at the other end, total banishment. My status as an associate professor gives me the status of being worthy of sovereignty. While my spasms and lack of body control perceived by many to indicate a lack of intellectual ability has often relegated me to a bare life existing because of the benevolence of others or institutions. Ironically, my impairments (the collective impersonal singularities) I believe are a generative source of my academic success. Moreover, I argue that within these impersonal singularities of impairment, there may be a multitude of vitality unable to be expressed because of the restrictive nature of the human register with its reliance upon identity, representation and personhood. Moreover, 'normative shadows' inhibit these impersonal singularities of impairment. Affirming these impersonal singularities allows for possibilities of a life beyond the restrictive able grid with its normative shadows. Yet most others read me as a person who has overcome his disability.

Yet desires that emanate from these impersonal singularities of impairment often are exposed. Addressing the erotics of exposure, Michael Hardt (2002: 80) writes,

> Erotic exposure, paradoxically, does not really involve seeing and being seen. In fact, exposure subverts a certain regime of vision. The exposed flesh does not reveal a secret self that had been hidden, but rather dissolves any self that could be apprehended. We not only have nothing left to hide, we no longer present any separate thing for the eyes to grasp. We become imperceptible. In the erotic we lose ourselves, or rather we abandon our discontinuity in a naked and divine communion.

Hardt (2002: 80–1) continues,

> Exposed flesh is not transgression but scandal. In other words, exposure does indeed oppose and negate the norms of propriety, but its effect does not depend on that opposition as a support. Violation or the norm is not primary to exposure; the negation is secondary, an afterthought, an accident. It turns its back on the norm – that is its great offence. Exposure operates in ignorance of the norm, and thus conducts, in the only way possible, its real destruction.

Usually within the context of the human registry, exposure of impairment is the unveiling of a 'pathological' secret. But within the desires of impersonal singularities that manifest impairment, exposure is another way to dissolve the self and affirm an alternate life expressed. Similarly, an exposed impairment is not a transgression (a response to ableism) but scandal. Impairment exposed does oppose and negate the norms of what constitutes an 'able' life, but its effect is not dependent upon the opposition to the able norm to define it. Violation of the able norms is not primary to the exposure of impersonal singularities culminating in impairments; the negation (of the propriety of ableness) is secondary, an afterthought, an accident. The exposed impairments manifested by impersonal singularities operate in ignorance of the able norms and dare I say the human register grounded in personhood. It turns its back on the norm – that is its greatest offence. These impersonal singularities exposed operate in ignorance of the (able) norm, and thus conducts, in the only way possible, the real destruction of the hegemonic position that the human register is the only worthwhile expression of life.

Conclusion

This volume is about the theory, but perhaps there is too much ink spilt on the discourse of theory that takes for granted an 'I' that 'makes sense' of the world. While I am spilling ink or writing about theory, I would like to shift the discussion from personhood, identity and representation and the associated politics of recognition with its basis in the dialectic to the impersonal vitalism or singularities as a generative force for life itself, moving away from the incessant need for disabled people to claim or carve out a place for their personhood to be legitimised and recognised by themselves or 'able' others. The sole reliance upon the self as the representation of (human) life will dissipate. What the impersonal singularities offer is another perspective on life – an imperceptible life.

As Jami Weinstein (2008: 26) asserts, 'This feminist move toward the imperceptible, suggested by Grosz, would take the following form':

> Instead of a politics of recognition, in which subjected groups and minorities strive for a validated and affirmed place in public life, feminist politics should, I believe, now consider the affirmation of a politics of imperceptibility, leaving its traces and effects everywhere but never being able to be identified with a person, group, or organization. It is not a politics of visibility, of recognition and of self-validation, but a process of self-marking that constitutes oneself in the very model of that which oppresses and opposes the subject. The imperceptible is that which the inhuman musters.
>
> (Grosz, 2005: 194 as cited in Weinstein, 2008: 26)

Can theory as practised in disability studies learn from the unfulfilled promise of feminist theory (as Grosz suggests), and affirm the 'politics of imperceptibility' through impairment. Creating a milieu for the freeing of the impersonal singularities that form impairment leaving its traces and affects as a generative force for life expressed. Resulting in the dissipation of both representation and identity that perhaps unintentionally restrict life. Understanding impairment not as an entity that inhibits life but like other impersonal singularities provides the vitality and is the basis for *a life* expressed. This requires the able-cripple (Wade, 1997) to step aside and allow space for the proliferation of impersonal singularities including those associated with impairments to form assemblages that continually constitute life expressed.

Gilles Deleuze and Felix Guattari wanted their work to be used, not simply understood. This chapter is not a complete rumination of how Deleuze and Guattari's or Agamben's work can illuminate theory within disability studies. Nevertheless, it does question the privileging of the predominant view that we must achieve social change through identity politics. And it offers an alternative vitality, that of the inhuman registry with its impersonal singularities including impairments that offer new possibilities for *a life*.

Pragmatically speaking I ask the readers these following questions. Does the pressure of striving for 'recognition' as a person has you metaphorically 'walking on egg shells'? Now that you have been included into the 'brethen' of 'able' personhood, do you worry about falling back to and losing the privileges of personhood through greater or different impairment(s)? How does the affirmation of impairments affect social change within disability studies, and your life specifically? Are you willing to risk losing your identity that has always been a response to ableness and instead let the proliferation of singularities flourish?

A word of caution, in Deleuzian terms affirmation does not mean a positive outcome. For Deleuze outcomes are too prescriptive thus affirmation is simply life expressed. Yet this is not a zero sum game of this or that: the human and inhuman registers coexist. The personal and impersonal singularities intermingle and again the latter is the basis for the former. The point is to facilitate within disability studies a theoretical appreciation of impersonal singularities generally, and more specifically those that provide the mortar for the development of impairments. By affirming singularities associated with impairment, hopefully we can move towards generating new life, and new possibilities for ourselves and other disabled people.

Perhaps even more radically can disabled lives affirm the joy in our supposed impairment, perhaps by embracing the impersonal life rather than reaching for the brass ring of normality? In sum, rather than striving for heroic endurance, perhaps many disabled people would be wiser to follow a Nietzschean path and affirm fate and avoid a life of *ressentiment* (Deleuze, 2004a, 2006) to find joy in the fate of the impersonal singularities of impairment. For example, from a Deleuzian perspective on amor fati, I now see my birth as an event where my spasms are singularities that affirm the impersonal life, rather than as the birth of an individual afflicted with impairments. Whenever the onset of impairment whether at birth or acquired later, is it possible for disabled people and disability studies as a discipline to embrace the event and avoid *ressentiment* in the proliferation of impersonal singularities that signals a burgeoning life to come as it is expressed?

References

Agamben, G. (1996). *Means Without Ends: Notes on Politics* (translated by V. Binetti and C. Cesario). Minneaapolis: University of Minnesota Press.
Agamben, G. (1998). *Homer Sacer: Sovereign Power and Bare Life* (translated by D. Heller-Roazan). Stanford: Stanford University Press.
Agamben, G. (1999). *Potentialities: Collected Essays on Philosophy* (translated by D. Heller-Roazan). Stanford: Stanford University Press.
Agamben, G. (2007). *Profanations* (translated by J. Fort). Brooklyn: Zone Books.
Alcoff, L. Martin (1999). 'Becoming an Epistemologist'. In Elisabeth Grosz (ed.), *Becomings: Explorations in Time, Memory, and Futures* (pp. 55–75). Ithaca: Cornell University Press.
Bauman, Z. (1988). *Freedom*. Markham: Fitzhenry & Whiteside.
Campbell, F. K. (2008). 'Exploring Internalized Ableism Using Critical Race Theory'. *Disability & Society*, 23 (2), 151–62.
Colebrook, C. (2010a). 'On the Very Impossibility of Queer Theory'. In C. Nigianni and M. Storr (eds), *Deleuze and Queer Theory* (pp. 11–23). Endinburgh: Edinburgh University Press.
Colebrook, C. (2010b). 'The Secret of Theory'. *Deleuze Studies*, 4, November, 287–300.
Davis, L. J. (1997). 'Constructing Normalcy: The Bell Curve, the Novel, and the Invention of the Disabled Body in the Nineteeth Century'. In Lennard J. Davis (ed.), *The Disability Studies Reader* (pp. 9–28). New York: Routledge.
Deleuze, G. (1994). *Difference and Repetition* (translated by Paul Patton). New York: Columbia University Press.
Deleuze, G. (1997). *Essays Critical and Clinical* (translated by D. W. Smith and M. A. Greco). Minneapolis: University of Minnesota Press.
Deleuze, G. (2004a). *The Logic of Sense* (translated by M. Lester and C. Stivale) (edited by Constas V. Boundas). New York: Continuum.
Deleuze, G. (2004b). *Desert Islands: And Other Texts 1953–74* (translated by M. Taormina) (edited by D. Lapoujade). New York: Semiotext(e).
Deleuze, G. (2005). *Pure Immanence: Essays on a Life* (translated by A. Boyman). New York: Zone Books.
Deleuze, G. (2006). *Nietzsche and Philosophy* (translated by H. Tomlinson). New York: Columbia University Press.
Deleuze, G. and Guattari, F. (1987). *A Thousand Plateaus: Capitalism and Schizophrenia* (translated by B. Massumi). Minneapolis: University of Minnesota Press.
Deleuze, G. and Guattari, F. (1994). *What is Philosophy?* (translated by H. Tomlinson and G. Burchill). New York: Columbia University Press.
Ferris, J. (2008). 'Just Try Having None: Transforming, Transmuting, Transcending, Transfixing, Transfiguring, Transcribing Pain'. *Text and Performance Quarterly*, 28 (1/2), pp. 242–55.
Foucault, M. (1984). 'The Order of Discourse'. In M. J. Shapiro (ed.), *Language and Politics* (pp. 108–38). New York: University Press.

Grosz, E. A. (2010). 'The Practice of Feminist Theory'. *Differences*, 21 (1), 94–108.
Hardt, M. (2002). 'Exposure: Pasolini in the Flesh'. In B. Massumi (ed.), *A Shock to Thought: Expression after Deleuze and Guattari* (pp. 77–84). New York: Routledge.
Hughes, B. (1999). 'The Constitution of Impairment: Modernity and the Aesthetic of Impairment'. *Disability & Society*, 4 (2), 155–72.
Jones, R. (1990). 'Educational Practices and Scientific Knowledges: A Genealogical Reinterpretation of the Emergence of Physiology in Post-Revolutionary France'. In Stephen Ball (ed.), *Foucault and Education: Disciplines and Knowledge* (pp. 29–53). New York: Routledge.
Linton, S. (2006). 'Reassigning Meaning'. In L. J. Davis (ed.), *The Disability Studies Reader* (second edition) (pp. 161–72). New York: Routledge.
McMahon, M. (2005). 'Difference, repetition'. In C. Stivale (ed.), *Gilles Deleuze: Key Concepts* (pp. 42–52). Montreal & Kingston: McGill-Queens University Press.
Oliver, M. (1990). *The Politics of Disablement: A Sociological Approach*. New York: St. Martin's Press.
Overboe, J. (1999). '"Difference in Itself": Validating the Lived Experience of Disabled People'. *Body & Society*, 5 (4) December, 17–29.
Overboe, J. (2007a). 'Disability and Genetics: Affirming the Bare Life (the State of Exception)'. In 'Genes and Society: Looking Back on the Future'. Special issue of *Canadian Review of Sociology*, 44 (2), 219–35.
Overboe, J. (2007b). 'Vitalism: Subjectivity Exceeding Racism, Sexism, and (Psychiatric) Ableism'. In 'Intersecting Gender and Disability Perspectives in Rethinking Postcolonial Identities'. Special issue of *Wagadu, Journal of Transnational Women's and Gender Studies*, 4, Summer, 22–34.
Overboe, J. (2009) 'Affirming an Impersonal Life: A Different Register for Disability Studies'. In 'Deleuze, Disability, and Difference'. Special issue of *Journal of Literary & Cultural Disability Studies*, 3 (3).
Rajchman, J. (2000). *The Deleuze Connections*. Cambridge, MA: MIT Press.
Titchkosky, T. (2006). *Disability, Self, and Society*. Toronto: University of Toronto Press.
Titchkosky, T. (2007). *Reading & Writing Disability Differently: The Textured Life of Embodiment*. Toronto: University of Toronto Press.
Wade, C. M. (1997). 'I AM NOT THE'. In L. J. Davis (ed.), *The Disability Studies Reader*, New York: Routledge (p. 408).
Weinstein, J. (2008). 'Introduction II', Deleuze and Gender. *Deleuze Studies*, 2 (Issue Supplement: December), 20–33.
Zola, I. K. (1991a). 'Self, Identity and the Naming Question: Reflections on the Language of Disability'. *Social Science and Medicine*, 36 (2), 167–73.
Zola, I. K. (1991b). 'Bringing Our Bodies and Ourselves Back In: Reflections on a Past, Present, and Future: "Medical Sociology"'. *Journal of Health and Social Behavior*, 32 (1, March), 1–16.

8
The Body as the Problem of Individuality: A Phenomenological Disability Studies Approach

Tanya Titchkosky and Rod Michalko

Introduction

Disability, as Paul Abberley (1998: 93) reminds us, is interesting often only as a problem. Or as Bill Hughes (2007: 673) puts it, 'almost by definition, [we] assume disability to be ontologically problematic, and many disabled people feel that many of the people with whom they interact in everyday situations treat them as if they are invisible, repulsive or "not all there"'. What interests us from a phenomenological perspective is that the contemporary scene of disability framed as 'problem' typically generates the requirement for explanation and amelioration, but little else. Thus, this chapter examines the hegemonic taken-for-granted character of the disability-as-a-problem frame.

We aim to show how this frame is produced against a background of a notion of the 'natural' or 'normal' body, that is, a body conceived of by science as in need, and worthy, of description – how does it work, what are its essential features? The disabled body, in contrast, is conceived of as requiring explanation – what went wrong, how can it be fixed and brought back to normalcy? Yet, the questions 'what went wrong and what should be done?' are based on the reproduction of the frame 'disability as a problem' and leave this frame completely unexamined. Questioning the 'facticity' (Heidegger, 1962) of the problem-of-disability means reflecting on the oft-used, overdeterministic and under-theorised frame 'disability is a problem in need of a solution' as itself a solution to some implicit problem. That disability is conceptualised as a problem is what we take to be our problem in need of theorising. In other words, conceiving of disability as a problem in need of a solution may be treated as a response to an implicit version of disability, a response that acts as a solution to the question 'What is disability?' This approach permits us to ask, what sort of problem do contemporary times need disability to be? And, what is the meaning of human embodiment that grounds the unquestioned status of disability as a problem?

The field of disability studies says, and says often, that such frames constitute disability as an individual problem of tragic proportions requiring only individualised redress. But, from a phenomenological perspective, knowing this and showing this are not the same. We aim, then, to show how disability is made into an individual problem of tragic proportions and this returns us to the question of the normalised embodied contours of individuality itself. As disability is made into a problem, what is made of the human condition harnessed to the workings of a culture that seeks to service 'normal' individuals? A disability studies approach informed by phenomenology can contribute to understanding the consequences of the contemporary 'demand' on us to understand identity as our individual 'task' and 'duty' (Bauman, 2004: 18–19). We will further draw out these issues by conducting an exploration of how the phenomenon of disability-as-problem composes university life while teasing out how the language of the problem reflects the educational world views that arise through the lived bodies that we are. In so doing, we offer a reflection regarding what a phenomenological approach does in order to do what it does and to say what it says and then show this at work in the university milieu.

Disability as problem

Framing disability as a problem in need of a solution takes many different forms. The biomedical world view, for example, conceives of disability as the 'body-gone-wrong' (Michalko, 2002: 120) and, if living a life of disability is to be achieved at all, this body should be treated in a way that permits it to 'look' and act as 'normal' as possible. This treatment, or better, this interpretive work, is achieved through such contemporary ideologies as medicine, rehabilitation and education, especially that of the 'special' kind.

Still another form of the disability-as-problem frame is the erasure of disability through the privileging of personhood – a framing of disabled people as 'like everyone else' but only *like* and not *as* everyone else since, within this frame, personhood is not located in disability but against it (Titchkosky, 2001). This frame suggests that disabled people can 'resemble' non-disabled others even though they are other to non-disability regardless of the fidelity of the resemblance. Disability may participate in normalcy, but it can never be normal, let alone be valuable, enjoyable or necessary.

Framed in these ways disability is represented and experienced as a kind of partially protected liability precariously perched on the edge of liveable life (Butler, 2009: 9, 43). The disciplinary infrastructures and technologies engaged in these ways of framing disability are powerful and global in their character and reach (Titchkosky and Aubrecht, 2009). The disciplinary research-based regimes, such as medicine and education, do not typically address what it means to constitute the phenomenon of disability in this singular and unified way. The sociopolitical act of framing disability as a problem in need of a solution does not engage itself, it does not question what it makes when it makes disability a problem – this way of framing disability is not reflexive and this now becomes *our* problem.

Phenomenology is a way to frame disability as a scene (Butler, 1993: 23) where the meaning of the human condition of embodiment can be brought into consciousness for reflective consideration – a task we regard as essential to any political possibility of forging something new since the new is tied to rethinking our most basic ways of framing embodiment. The desire for something 'new' is grounded in the sense of the unexpected potentiality that resides in all forms of human action as well as in the politicalised sense that disabled people face extreme forms of devaluation within cultures animated by limited and limiting conceptions of embodiment that themselves leave much to be desired. The possibility of forging something new is intimately interwoven with questioning what is typically assumed to be beyond question; questioning what is otherwise taken as a given serves as a reflexive reframing of our lives together as bodied beings. We turn our analysis towards a fuller discussion of the phenomenological conception of the 'frame' and of framing with regard to disability.

Disability-frameworks and phenomenology

The world comes to us and we receive it always-already 'framed'. Like all other phenomena, disability comes to us in a frame and this frame 'works' as a guide and even as a rule for recognising the phenomenon of disability. We recognise disability in others and in ourselves insofar as disability-frameworks guide us to these recognitions and work to rule them. Even though we recognise disability, we do not easily recognise its frames nor the framework that provides for such recognition. Nonetheless, we are conscious of disability insofar as there are disability frames for and of such consciousness. Disability consciousness typically entails experiencing disability as always-already a problem, located in individuals.

Edmund Husserl tells us that a function of understanding is 'ruling in concealment, i.e., ruling as constitutive of the always already developed and always further developing meaning-configuration "intuitively given surrounding world"' (Husserl, 1970: 104). The world surrounds us, according to Husserl, and it is intuitively given to us. The world comes to us always configured (framed) as meaning – the world always means. Or as Maurice Merleau-Ponty (1945: xxii) says, 'Because we are in the world, we are *condemned to meaning.*' Meaning is the rule and it constitutes a world, including all that belongs in and to it, that comes to us as 'given' and intuitively so. As such, we take the reality of the world for granted. It is this 'rule' of the taken-for-granted world that is concealed from us when we experience the world. We perceive the world that surrounds us but we do not 'see' the frameworks that constitute this world as configured in and by meaning.

This world includes a multitude of frameworks and perspectives, some of which are in agreement with one another, others in conflict. Whether our perspectives on the world agree or not, we do agree in a taken-for-granted way that there is a world about which to have perspectives. Husserl calls the taken-for-granted world, the perspectives we have on it, and our experience in it, the 'life-world', the *Lebenswelt*. He writes that the life-world:

> is always already there, existing in advance for us, the 'ground' of all praxis whether theoretical or extra theoretical. The world is pre-given to us, the waking, the always somehow practically interested subjects, not occasionally but always and necessarily as the universal field of all actual and possible praxis, as horizon. To live is always to live-in-certainty-of-the-world. Waking life is being awake to the world ... The world is pre-given thereby, in every case, in such a way that individual things are given.
>
> (Husserl, 1970: 142–3)

We take for granted, irrespective of individual differences and perspectives, that we live our lives in a shared life-world. As different as perspectives and world views may be, they do share in common the sense that the world is 'just there', a world on which we have a view and have a perspective(s).

We orient to this taken-for-granted life-world through what Edmund Husserl (1970) and Alfred Schutz (1973) call the 'natural attitude'. The world is just 'naturally' there and we are as 'naturally' there as is the world. Living in the 'natural attitude', means living with a sense that 'of course' that is just the way things are. We know, too, that we did not invent this world, that it came before us or, in Husserl's words, that it exists in advance, for us, and that it will, barring any environmental catastrophe, exist after us. Nor did we invent disability; it was there before we came into the world and before any of us became disabled. We may disagree on the meaning or genesis of disability – for some disability is a biological anomaly, for others an accident or happenstance and for still others, disability is an occasion that tests and demonstrates the human spirit's capacity to adapt and overcome, and for yet others disability is the result of inappropriate responses by society to impairment – but what we do not disagree on is that disability exists and, of course, we know it when we 'see' it.

All human practice, everything we say and do is said and done on the ground and under the auspices of the life-world. Governments change, revolutions happen and our individual lives change and do so radically at times and all of this attests to the certainty that we do affect the world – human agency exists as certainly as does the world. 'Things change', the adage goes; 'the only thing that stays the same, is change', it continues.

Sustaining the 'given-ness' of the world, the sense that it is naturally just there for all to perceive, is an activity in which we are constantly involved (Sacks, 1984). The world, change and human agency are given to us and received by us as naturally occurring phenomena. These phenomena are seemingly so natural to us that we readily give an explanatory account for those times they do not occur. We make sense of the world even when it is disrupted and every disruption is remedied through the sense-making character of the natural attitude (Garfinkel, 1967; Weiss, 2008). 'I think you're in denial, you have to get past this and move forward.' 'Some people just don't see that things have to change, they're brainwashed by society and the media.' 'What you need is a reality check.' Despite the mundane character of these accounts, they do dramatically demonstrate how we act to sustain the taken-for-granted and natural character of the life-world.

We are continuously providing an account, albeit in a taken-for-granted way, for the existence and possibility of world views, different and conflicting as they may be. We all have a world view. We perceive the world from a perspective or 'standpoint'. We are socially positioned in the world, and from the perspective of contemporary versions of identity, for example, we are so positioned through categories such as race, gender, sexuality, social class, and sometimes even disability. These social categories position us and give us a standpoint, a perspective from which to view the world. We also view the world from the 'point of view' of our interests, concerns, anxieties, aspirations and the like (Ahmed, 2004a, 2004b). The way people are positioned in the world, then, generates not only multiple perspectives but multiple realities.

While we do experience the world differently from one another depending upon our sense of our social identity and upon our differences and interests, we also experience the world in common with one another insofar as we assume that everyone would 'see' the world as we do if they were in our position (standpoint), and that we would 'see' the world the way others do if we were in theirs. This means that frames reconcile difference by making the perception of a disruption or a difference into a signifier of the same, as originating in the intuitively given life-world. How we understand and know the world and its phenomena is potentially understood and known by 'everyone' – everyone, that is, who shares our social position, everyone who shares in our taken-for-granted sense of being anyone. People knowing the world 'in common' is provided for by the assumed potentiality of shareable perspectives, or what Schutz (1973: 11) calls 'reciprocity of perspectives', the 'interchangeability of standpoints', or as what we have been calling frames or frameworks. Schutz expands this phenomenological notion of shareable frames.

What is supposed to be known in common by everyone who shares our system of relevances is the way of life considered to be the natural, the good, the right one by the members of the 'in group'; as such, it is at the origin of the many recipes for handling things (and each other) in order to come to terms with typified situations, of the folk ways and mores, of 'traditional behaviour', ... of the 'of course statements' believed to be valid by the in-group in spite of their inconsistencies, briefly, of the 'relative natural aspect of the world'.

(Schutz, 1973: 13)

Living in the midst of others, at times we experience a sort of 'belongingness', a sense of belonging in and to a group, a social space, not as someone marginal to this group and space, but as someone integral to them and thus as someone who is valuable. What we conceive to be relevant is now understood as a shared perspective and as relevant to everyone 'in the know' and thus what is relevant and valuable is understood under the rubric of a 'system' rather than that of 'individual idiosyncrasy'. In this way, our perspective on the world becomes understood, as Schutz tells us, as something natural, good and right. From this 'system of relevances', socially put together or constructed through our assumption of the 'reciprocity of perspectives', flows all other aspects of our individual and collective lives. And, perhaps most important, we come to understand ourselves as naturally belonging in and to this world.

It is, then, this taken-for-granted life-world and the natural attitude that represents, for us, the genesis of disability frameworks. It is within and from this conception of human life that disability experience, whether our own or that of others, springs and frames disability as a meaning-full phenomenon. Disability is a frame that can, upon analysis, teach us much about the life-world that generates it. But herein lies an irony – disability is framed as a phenomenon located and locatable only outside of the taken-for-granted life-world as well as outside the natural attitude. Disability is thus understood as marginal to the common-sense world and, as such, as outside intuitively given reality. Disability is one source of what Schutz (1973: 228 [see also Michalko, 1998: 29–34]) calls the 'fundamental anxiety' insofar as disability can, and often does, disrupt the taken-for-granted character of the world and our life in it.

Disability, framed as a problem, becomes one of the fundamental 'unnatural aspects' of the otherwise natural, good and right way of being-in-the-world. Disability disrupts and, even threatens, what Schutz calls 'the relative natural aspect of the world'. What disability often represents is the taken-for-granted sense of the unnatural, of the value-less and of that which does not belong – or, to take liberties with Schutz's words, disability is framed as the unnatural, the bad and the wrong way of being-in-the-world. With this framework as background, this chapter now turns to an examination of some of the ways disability is conceived of and treated as just this sort of radical and disruptive problem, a problem naturalised as such.

Disability as a problem in need of a solution

The perception of a problem brings with it the requirement for a solution even though and, somewhat paradoxically, problem is an expected and taken-for-granted aspect of the life-world. Problems are inevitable (Butler, 1999: vii) and a life free of problems is inconceivable. Everyone has problems – some serious, some not so serious, some trivial and some catastrophic – but everyone has problems. We are not required to search for problems, for they 'naturally' occur in the round of everyday life. In the face of our inevitable problems, we are, however, expected to search for solutions.

The search for a solution to the problem of disability is inevitable and not optional since disability is understood within this framework as generating the requirement for a solution and thus the search. Disability is understood as a problem insofar as it represents a disruption to the 'natural-order-of-things' with its concomitant requirement to restore this order, an activity understood as the 'need' to solve the problem of disability. Cure, of course, is the quintessential solution to disability conceived of as a problem. But many disabilities resist curative measures and become, in the vernacular of the day, 'permanent'. Now, we have a more serious problem – what to do about and how to live with disability as a 'permanent problem', or how to solve the permanent problem of disability.

The solution to the permanent problem of disability, the one favoured today, is normalisation which takes shape through remedial treatments such as rehabilitation, special education and the like. Since the problem of disability is located in the world and is so often permanently, the solution becomes one of 'normalising' disability, thus 'making' it a 'normal' part of the natural-order-of-things. Normalising disability is one way of making it identical with the taken-for-granted life-world where this act of 'making identical' serves to socially produce the life-world as identifying with disability as one of the many problems that are inevitable, again, naturally so. Through the social act of normalisation, disability becomes *merely* a problem that some people have. Ironically, being 'merely' a problem requires that disability never comes to consciousness as anything but a problem. Thus, the rule of finding a solution to the always-already problem of disability is a singular unified response to disability with which individuals are routinely and ordinarily engaged. We already know, and obviously so, that disability simply *is* a problem in need of a solution and to admit an alternative approach can be as disruptive as is the onset of impairment or as is the attempt to manoeuvre in a world prepared only for a 'non-impaired carnality' (Paterson and Hughes, 1997: 607, 604).

The ubiquity of the frame of disability-as-problem for individuals means making disability identical not only as problem but also in its solution. Henri-Jacques Stiker speaks of the act of making disability identical in this way.

This act [of identification and of making identical] will cause the disabled to disappear and with them all that is lacking, in order to assimilate them, drown them, dissolve them in the greater and single social whole.

(Stiker, 1999: 128)

Making disability identical is not the same as making disabled people identical to those who are not disabled, nor does it allow non-disabled people to identify with disabled people. Instead, the act of making identical generates the common-sense understanding of disability as part of the life-world and, as such, identifies disability as a phenomenon among the plethora of phenomena making up the taken-for-granted world. Making disability identical, however, does not make disability 'equal' to other phenomena; on the contrary, it makes disability one of the less favoured problems to have.

As one of the least favoured problems to have, the contemporary act of making identical – an act marked by the advent of rehabilitation and special education – seeks, in its identification with the world, to make disability disappear, particularly the lack that disability is thought to be. In this way, as Stiker says, disabled people can be assimilated or, more poignantly, be drowned, dissolved 'in the greater and single social whole'. Given that disability is merely a problem, any alternative interpretation is, like disability itself, also drowned, but with this annihilation of alterity comes the achievement of a 'normal' approach to the problem of disability. This is one reason why Hughes (2007: 680, 681) argues that 'The real problem in this existential mire is not disability but non-disability ... The normative, invulnerable body of disabilist modernity [the greater and single social whole] that is the problem.' This interpretation, however, admits an alternative view, a view which is typically drowned in the single social whole by asking 'But what is your problem? What do you need? How can we help?'

There is still another aspect of framing disability as a problem in need of a solution, an aspect found in the idea of problem itself. The phenomenon of problem, while generating the sense that problems are inevitable and all people have them, also releases the possibility for people themselves to be understood as a problem. Thus, while everyone has problems, not everyone *is* a problem. Disability is not only a problem that some of us have, we are also *the* problem that others have. Not just disability, but disabled people become one of the myriad of problems that others can have. Disability and disabled people are in the world since they can be nowhere else. But insofar as disability represents a disruption and even a threat to the taken-for-granted way that bodies, minds, senses and emotions should be, a threat to unquestioned versions of normalcy, disability represents a problem to the taken-for-granted character of the life-world. In this way, we (disabled people) become a problem to and for the world as it is conceived and lived by others understood as 'normal'.

At the turn of the twentieth century and theorising the lives (souls) of 'Black folks', W. E. B. DuBois (1903: 1) writes, 'being a problem is a strange experience'. As with race, disability's 'being', its ontology, is 'problem' (Erevelles and Minear, 2010: 128). Disability becomes a problem that the world and others have and, as such, the need for a solution to the problem of disability is born. Solutions share in the singular commitment to, as Stiker puts it, making disability disappear. Questioning the taken-for-granted good of making disability disappear relies upon a two-ness or, in DuBois's (ibid.) terms, a double-consciousness regarding disability experience and the experience of disability. Within the contemporary biomedical ideological paradigm, disabled people do experience their disabilities as a problem, as the body, mind, senses or emotions gone wrong. This is one way and, a dominant one at that, for us (disabled people) to experience our disabilities. Then, there is another way; disabled people experience the ways non-disabled others experience us. We experience their experience, or better, we experience ourselves through their experience of us. Through the contemporary frame of disability-as-problem, we experience ourselves as having a problem and we also have the 'strange experience' of being a problem to and for others.

The strangeness of the experience of problem is, then, manifold. There is the strangeness of gaining a double-consciousness of embodiment and its essentially social character. That is, I understand my disability to be a problem for me, and I understand it as such for you; and between having a problem and being a problem there is the problem of needing to seek a solution to one, the other and to both, in a life-world that understands disability only and forever as problem. So too there is the strangeness of bringing to consciousness the frames that are otherwise taken-for-granted – I perceive that you (and even I) see me only in the shape of a problem and am 'stunned' into self-recognition as such (Paterson and Hughes, 1997: 603). Stranger still is the sense in which disability is assumed to be objectively a problem, loosed from any subjective interpretation, and thus disruptive of the normal order of daily life. This is also part of the strange experience of being a problem that is typically assimilated and dissolved into the social whole through the pursuit of normalcy – the only normal solution is to drown any interest in the ways in which normalcy is produced and, instead, return, as quickly and as closely as possible, to the replication of normalcy.

Experiencing disability as a problem that some people have and simultaneously a problem that everyone has represents the dominant ideological frame through which disability experience is mediated. Some of us are a problem to the society, its institutions and settings. That disabled people experience their lives in this way is crucial, if not essential, for the ways in which society and its institutions develop solutions to the problem of disability. Any solution developed within this framework, of course, serves to politically and socially sustain the cultural conception of disability as a problem and thus to make it disappear, to drown it, in the single social whole that contains the inevitability of problems as an integral feature of its social organisation. It is important that we phenomenologically uncover the problem to which the conception 'disability is a problem in need of a solution' is itself a solution. To this end, and as a way to further exemplify our phenomenological approach, we turn to an examination of one way that the university formulates the problem that is disability.

Including 'Them'

Like all other appearances, the appearance of disability must be noticed for its appearance to count as apparent. Noticing requires more than 'looking' insofar as it is taken-for-granted cultural frameworks that permit us to 'see' what we are 'looking at'. What do we 'see' when we experience someone using a wheelchair or someone who is blind or when someone tells us they have a learning disability? Typically, what we 'see', is a problem. But what sort of a problem and thus what sort of a solution do we perceive? The contemporary space of the university, in our case the University of Toronto, does have a way of 'seeing' and thus of noticing disability. As a way to expli-cate this 'way' we turn to an examination of how the university conceives of disabled students.

<u>Accessibility Services, St. George Campus</u>

The role of accessibility services is to facilitate the inclusion of students with disabilities into all aspects of university life. Our focus is on skills development, especially in the areas of self-advocacy and academic skills. Services are provided to students with a documented disability. It can be physical, sensory, a learning disability, or a mental health disorder.

Accessibility Services is responsible for facilitating the inclusion of stu-dents with disabilities into university life. Specifically, accessibility serv-ices is responsible for:
• Receiving and retaining documentation from a medical professional or specialist which identifies your disability. (This documentation is kept in confidence with the service.)
• Providing information and advice to students, student applicants, uni-versity departments, and individual staff members on accommodation strategies.
• Providing or facilitating services such as alternative test and examina-tion arrangements, note-taking services.
• Assessment for adaptive equipment and assistive devices.
• Assessment for learning disabilities, coordination of interpreters and intervener services, and liaison and referral on and off campus.
• The office is also a resource for instructors who require information in order to meet the needs of students in their classes. The office also plays an educational role; raising the awareness of students with dis-abilities among staff, faculty, and students at the university and wider community. (Accessibility Services, University of Toronto, 2010).

The role of accessibility services, as it understands it, is to 'facilitate' the 'inclusion of students with disabilities into all aspects of university life'.

Students with disabilities are understood as *not* included into all aspects of university life despite the obvious 'fact' of their presence in university life. Present yet absent or included as an excludable type is the way that accessibility services frames and subsequently characterises the presence of disabled students in university life (Titchkosky, 2008). This frame constitutes disabled students as the problem of the lack of 'skills development' particularly those of self-advocacy and academic skills. Thus, the lack of skills marks the problem that disabled students are understood to be and skill development marks the solution. Disability thus becomes a technical problem in need of a technical solution and the problem of disability as a problem is itself a solution to the absent presence character of disability.

Accessibility services says that disability can be physical, sensory, a learning disability or a mental health disorder, and that students are eligible for services only if their disability is 'documented'. Student documentation of their own disabilities does not count as such. It is only medical professionals or specialists who are permitted (legitimately) to provide such documentary evidence. Evidence of a disability, therefore, can come only from the legitimated source of biomedicine. The notion of 'expertise' is invoked as a way to establish a disabled student's eligibility for yet another form of expertise, namely, accessibility services. 'Documentation', then, acts as an implicit social process to transform 'your disability' (point one above) into 'our disability' (see the remaining points above). This social process acts to delegitimise a disabled student as 'expert' and to legitimise professionals as such thus transforming disability into a problem that can be best remedied by 'expertise'. This represents yet another version of the problem-of-disability: disability is a 'thing' about which expertise can be gleaned and put into practice (Titchkosky and Michalko, 2009: 1–14). As an objective-problem-thing, a disabled student enters university life framed by the sensibility that there are those who 'know' his/her problem, expertly. Knowing oneself *as* disabled, then, is illusory insofar as a disabled 'one' is not constituted as an 'expert' on disability and given that 'knowing disability' is framed, in contemporary times, as some 'thing' to be 'expertly known' making all other ways of knowing disability superfluous.

It is a medical professional or specialist who provides documentation that, according to accessibility services, identifies your disability but this does more than merely 'identify' a disability in a student. The documentation of disability and the subsequent accessibility services practices may be read as the constitution and re-constitution of expertise as the paramount framework, and framer, of the conception of disability-as-problem. This framework gives rise not only to legitimate individual problems understood as a disability but also to individuals legitimated as in possession of such problems understood as 'people with disabilities'.

Disabled students have a problem, an individual one, and now that they are applying for entry into university, or are already here, or, as we suggest, have always been here, disabled students are now a problem for the university, disability is now a problem that the university has. The solution? Medical and subsequent accessibility services' expertise. While disabled students share some of the same needs that their non-disabled counterparts have, 'disability needs' are different. All students are understood as representing a 'deficit' with regard to not possessing or lacking the knowledge that universities have. Closing this gap, however, is not the same for all students. The university is the means for closing this gap, but disabled students experience this 'means' as a barrier and not as a solution to the 'knowledge deficit'.

The needs of disabled students are conceived of as different from their non-disabled counterparts or, in the vernacular of the day, they are 'special needs'. And these 'special needs' are met with special measures – the provision of information and advice to students, university staff and faculty regarding accommodation strategies, the provision of alternative examination arrangements and note-taking, the provision of adaptive technology, the provision of assessment for learning disabilities, sign language interpreters, the provision of awareness training to university staff and faculty regarding the 'special needs' of disabled students. And finally, the provision of, and staying true to medicine – indicated in the penultimate point above – the 'referral'.

The spatial and educational organisation of the university is not framed as a problem, instead, only disability is framed as such, and thus the problem of and with disability is conceived of as the problem of access. According to common-sense reasoning, disabled people 'because' of our disabilities do not typically have access to mainstream society and this problem is solved by society 'identifying and removing', as the saying goes, barriers to such access. But we have also demonstrated that this seemingly straightforward and simple conception of the disability problem/solution is much more complex than it initially seemed. We need only raise Titchkosky's (2011) question, 'Once we're in, what are we in for?' to provoke and reveal this complexity. On the heels of this question, we now conclude this chapter with an initial formulation of the problem to which the framework 'disability is a problem in need of a solution' is represented as a solution. We have also suggested that the university needs disability 'to be' a technical problem requiring a technical solution, and we will reflect on what we understand a phenomenological approach needs disability 'to be'.

Needing disability... to be

Finding a home in the university as a disabled person, within the problem/solution frame, means 'getting in' as an individual understood as having a personal problem. This problem finds its solution through the invocation of expert and technical intervention meted on to the life of the person with the problem who likewise is ordinarily expected to deal with their problem thereby gaining some distance from the status of 'being' a problem for self or for others. Disability thus becomes a stage or social space over and against which individuals achieve a sense of their individuality; it is that space where we can show each other we are oriented to the doing of ourselves as individuals but only so long as we conform to the normative sense that no life is to be found or forged 'in' disability. Hence, we need to stage our life as one 'with' disability rather than 'in' disability (Michalko, 1999: 172ff.).

Individuals deal (or not) with disability since disability is only a problem, thus the relatively recent identity category 'person with a disability'. In this way, a sense of obtaining the identity of person is achieved by containing disability within the frame of problem and letting nothing of disability slip into alternative relations between self and other which could potentially change the exclusionary prowess of everyday life. Disability is thus conceived of as the problem-background against which the figure of individuality is achieved; it is not, however, imagined as that scene where we might rethink and recast the normative order of individuality and thereby of everyday life.

The figure of individuality is framed as our normative task and duty creating disability as a problem and as a way to achieve our task of producing the startling reasonableness of a taken-for-granted sense of individuality. Disability now serves as the key scene for the re-achievement of the primacy of personhood understood as the development of an individual identity. In his work on the modern 'identity', Zgmunt Bauman (2004: 21, 32) says,

> Identity could only enter the Lebenswelt [life-world] as a task, as an *as-yet-unfulfilled, unfinished task,* a clarion call, a duty and an urge to act – and the nascent modern state did whatever it took to make such a duty obligatory for all people inside its territorial sovereignty (21) ... In the liquid modern setting of life, identities are perhaps the most common, most acute, most deeply felt and troublesome incarnations of *ambivalence* (32).

Within modernity, disability is framed as a space where the 'duty and urge to act' as an individual is expertly announced, technically organised, and bureaucratically arranged as a duty for all. Always constituted as a problem, and as one imagined as marginal to mainstream existence, disability becomes, ironically, central to the question of belonging and thus akin to a sacrificial space where all that disability could be is submerged, even annihilated, for the good of demonstrating the common ubiquity of an urge towards individuality. Insofar as disability is the problem over and against which we can demonstrate that we are worthy of belonging within modernity's structures of individuality, it is of paramount importance to conform to the sense that disability is merely and only a problem in need of a solution.

The structure of education, for example, has incorporated disability as a disembodied project of individual identity and the expertly identified 'person with a disability' becomes not only expected but also accepted within the modern organisation of belonging. In more general terms, Bauman (2004: 22) puts it this way, 'Whoever else you might have been or have aspired to become, it was the "appropriate institutions" of the state that had the final word. An uncertified identity was [is] a fraud'. As we showed, it is neither reasonable, nor natural, let alone good, to aspire to find life, that is 'real' embodied limits and possibilities, and thus identity in disability. Instead life is forged only and simply against it (adjusting) and as background (overcoming).

But herein lies a radical ambiguity, if not paradox. We come to the scene of embodied existence as people who, first and foremost, can act as though any bodily difference that could make a difference to being-in-the-world is merely the occasion to show each other the 'normal' achievement of a 'normative' sense of individualised identity as persons. Framed as people with a disability, individuals become those who do not live through their bodies, minds, senses or emotions, but with them and with the asserted claims to personhood. This is the sociopolitical consequences of understanding disability as problem in need of a solution that we now witness in almost all traces of disability conceptions today. In short, the problem to which 'disability is a problem in need of a solution' points is *individuality* – the problem of individuality generates the solution of 'disability is a problem in need of a solution'.

Now, what of phenomenology – what sort of problem has *it* made of disability and what does it need disability to be? Our chapter has demonstrated that whatever else disability might be it is lived as a problem in need of a solution and it is made present as a space to think about everyday life that makes disability present in this singular and unified fashion. It is both overdetermined by culture and, ironically, it is also thus an ideal place to reflect on how we make and organise devalued and excluded people in routine and ordinary ways. Disability is, in this sense, ambiguity incarnate, a rupture in the clarity and unquestioned flow of daily life, and thus almost a 'natural' starting place for thinking about the workings of culture.

From the perspective of a phenomenologically informed disability studies approach, the question is not one of asserting a better, more correct or more socially just definition of the situation called 'disability'. Instead, phenomenonology asks 'What is the phenomenon called disability?' It does not do so by asserting a definition, but by addressing how disability makes an appearance in the world and is lived. If disability is lived primarily as a problem in need of a solution, as we claim it is, then this is what phenomenology needs disability to be in order to pursue its commitment to question and theorise. Phenomenology needs disability to be a *life* lived in the natural attitude. This allows us to ask – what sorts of people are understood as living in the singularity of 'problem' and what sorts of cultures need to have so many of their people understood, managed and expertly controlled in regular and predictable ways? Disability, for phenomenology, becomes a place where such questions thrive.

By not taking disability for granted, it is possible to show how disability comes to appear as a problem and thus to reveal the frames, or what Husserl (1970: 104) refers to as the 'ruling concealment' that generates the 'need' to understand disability as a problem in the first place. The phenomenological urge is to find a way to hold in tension any of the ways that disability makes an appearance in everyday life as always-already part of what disability has been made to be so as to reveal how cultures make the problems they need. The need of a phenomenological approach in disability studies, then, is to understand disability as constituted as a space for critical cultural inquiry regarding the normative order that makes disability always-already a problem. And, herein lies the political potential of a phenomenological approach to disability and disability studies – the experience of disability, our own or that of others, becomes the scene where we can frame how we experience embodied existence and thus disability becomes a place where culture can be examined anew, again and again.

References

Accessibility Services (AS) (2010). University of Toronto, http://www.accessibility.utoronto.ca/about/rightsandresp.htm, accessed 29 July 2010.

Abberley, P. (1998). 'The Spectre at the Feast: Disabled People and Social Theory'. In T. Shakespeare (ed.), *The Disability Reader: Social Science Perspectives* (pp. 79–93). London: Cassell Academic.

Ahmed, S. (2004a). *The Cultural Politics of Emotio.* New York: Routledge.

Ahmed, S. (2004b). 'Collective Feelings: Or, the Impressions Left by Others'. *Theory, Culture & Society*, 21 (2): 25–42.

Bauman, Z. (2004). *Identity.* Malden, MA: Polity Press.

Butler, J. (1993). *Bodies that Matter: On the Discursive Limits of Sex.* New York: Routledge.

Butler, J. (1999). *Gender Trouble: Feminism and the Subversion of Identity.* New York: Routledge.

Butler, J. (2009). *Frames of War: When is Life Grievable?* New York: Verso Press.

DuBois, W. E. B. (1903). *The Souls of Black Folk.* Chicago: A. C. McClurg & Co.

Erevelles, N. and Minear, A. (2010). 'Unspeakable Offenses: Untangling Race and Disability in Discourses of Intersectionality'. *Journal of Literary & Cultural Disability Studies*, 4 (2), 127–45.

Garfinkel, H. (1967). *Studies in Ethnomethodology.* New Jersey: Prentice-Hall, Inc.

Heidegger, M. (1962). *Being and Time.* New York: Harper & Row.

Hughes, B. (2007). 'Being Disabled: Towards a Critical Social Ontology for Disability Studies'. *Disability & Society*, 22 (7), 673–84.

Husserl, E. (1970). *The Crisis of European Sciences and Transcendental Phenomenology: An Introduction to Phenomenological Philosophy.* Evanston: Northwestern University Press.

142   *The Body as the Problem of Individuality*

Merleau-Ponty, M. (1958 [1945]). *Phenomenology of Perception*. London: Routledge and Kegan Paul.
Michalko, R. (1998). *The Mystery of the Eye and the Shadow of Blindness*. Toronto: University of Toronto.
Michalko, R. (1999). *The Two in One: Walking with Smokie, Walking with Blindness*. Philadelphia: Temple University Press.
Michalko, R. (2002). *The Difference that Disability Makes*. Philadelphia: Temple University Press.
Paterson, K. and Hughes, B. (1997). 'The Social Model of Disability and the Disappearing Body: Towards a Sociology of Impairment'. *Disability & Society*, 12 (3), 325–40.
Sacks, H. (1984). 'On Doing "Being Ordinary"'. In J. Maxwell and J. Heritage (eds), *Structures of Social Action: Studies in Conversation Analysis* (pp. 413–30). Cambridge: Cambridge University Press.
Schutz, A. (1973). *Collected Papers I: The Problem of Social Reality*. The Hague: Martinus Nijoff.
Stiker, H. J. (1999). *The History of Disability*. Ann Arbor: University of Michigan Press.
Titchkosky, T. (2001). 'Disability – A Rose By Any Other Name? People First Language in Canadian Society'. *Canadian Review of Sociology and Anthropology*, 38 (2), 125–40.
Titchkosky, T. (2008). '"To Pee or Not to Pee?" Ordinary Talk about Extraordinary Exclusions in a University Environment'. *Canadian Journal of Sociology*, 33 (1), 37–60, *http://ejournals.library.ualberta.ca/index.php/CJS/article/view/1526/1058*, accessed 18 March 2012.
Titchkosky, T. (2011). *The Question of Access: Disability, Space, Meaning*. Toronto: University of Toronto Press.
Titchkosky, T. and Aubrecht, K. (2009). 'The Power of Anguish: Re-Mapping Mental Diversity with an Anti-colonial Compass'. In Arlo Kempf (ed.), *Breaching the Colonial Contract: Anti-Colonialism in the US and Canada* (pp. 179–99). New York: Springer.
Titchkosky, T. and Michalko, R. (2009). *Rethinking Normalcy: A Disability Studies Reader*. Toronto: Canadian Scholars/Women's Press.
Weiss, Gail. (2008). *Refiguring the Ordinary*. Bloomington: Indiana University Press.

9
Dancing with Disability: An Intersubjective Approach

Eimir McGrath

Introduction

Dancers with disabilities are rarely seen in professional dance performance, yet dance offers a potential means of changing exclusionary societal perceptions of disability. This chapter explores the placing of the disabled body within a dance context and investigates how this placement can be theorised in terms of inclusion, by using a framework based on contemporary attachment theory.

Dance provides a window into the very heart of a culture, highlighting the beliefs and perceptions that shape the everyday lives of people; dance also provides a means of critical evaluation and exploration of the possibilities for change within that culture. It follows that dance performance can be understood as both an expression of societal values and as a vehicle for initiating change (Dale et al., 2007: 107). These apparently contradictory roles make dance an intriguing site for exploring the placement of the physically disabled body in contemporary society, and for disrupting existing perceptions of physical disability as transgressive. The dance scholar Ann Cooper Albright states, 'When a disabled dancer takes the stage, he or she stakes a claim to a radical space, an unruly location where disparate assumptions about representation, subjectivity, and visual pleasure collide' (2001: 58). The microcosm of the performance space, this 'unruly location', can be used to bring about the disruption of exclusionary societal perceptions of disability, reframing the notion of difference by providing an experience, through the medium of dance, that is inclusive of different corporealities. This experience can be transformative rather than transgressive and in order to understand how this can come about, I will explore the relationship between dance performer and viewer through the lens of contemporary attachment theory as it has developed within the field of social neurobiology. This approach will examine how viewing dancers of differing corporealities can bring about a state of empathic attunement, where the humanity of the dancer is foremost and corporeal difference becomes merely an element of that dancer's embodied presence.

Firstly, the placing of the disabled body in relation to Western theatre dance will be contextualised by examining what has historically constituted a legitimate dancing body. Secondly, the disruption of this understanding of a legitimate dancing body will be examined, by tracing the changes that took place during the twentieth century which eventually facilitated the inclusion of differently abled bodies within professional dance. Finally, I will consider how contemporary attachment theory can provide a theoretical understanding of the process of viewing dance, and how this process can facilitate change.

The legitimate dancing body – shifting the boundaries

Since its inception as an art form, Western theatre dance has played a role in reflecting the political and social climate of its time, as well as providing a means of critical comment and resistance. Perceptions of what types of dancing bodies are acceptable in performance have been an integral part of this role and it is necessary to examine the placing of the body within Western theatre dance from a historical context, in order to fully understand the significance of having a disabled body being present on stage, both as reflective of existing social norms and as subversive, taking a critical stance in relation to those norms. The perceptions of what is an acceptable dancing body have changed drastically over the past century, influenced by the broadening of horizons within the Western dance aesthetic.

Historically, Western theatre dance performance has been dominated by the ballet canon, with its roots in the introduction of ballet in the sixteenth century as a codified form of French and Italian court dance. From the nineteenth century onwards, the emergence of Romantic ballet (Au, 2002)[1] led to the prevailing aesthetic considerations which required that all dancers should share a physique based on the construct of the sylph. The sylph represented the perfectly formed, highly trained corporeal presence that, in its transcendence of everyday movement, was the representation of all that was considered superior in both the embodied and in the ideological sense. Slim, long limbed, rigidly trained to achieve virtuosity, aiming to rise above the pedestrian movement of everyday life and offering an ideal based on ethereality, this body was the epitome of artistry. It was valued as such until the beginning of the twentieth century, when some dancers and choreographers moved away from this dominant form of theatre dance and began to explore different expressions of embodiment, looking to more naturalistic ways of moving which signified the beginning of what became known as modern dance.[2] Movement vocabularies were developed that went beyond the rigid technique of ballet and new genres emerged. Dancers and choreographers such as Isadora Duncan and Ruth St. Denis[3] questioned the rigidity of the ballet canon and began to create new ways of dancing where they emphasised the expression of inner feeling through movement, a very different experience for the audience as dance academic and choreographer Susan Leigh Foster points out:

> Psychological subject matter found authentic realization in the movement vocabularies of each choreographer. And the audiences, for the first time, were asked to identify with dancer and dance and to feel rather than see their own life experience on stage.
>
> (1986: 145)

However, over time these new approaches developed their own codified movement vocabularies and until the 1960s, Western theatre dance still tended to exclude all but the most able by setting very restrictive parameters in relation to the ideal physique. These restrictive parameters were so exclusionary that a large proportion of non-disabled people could not ever hope to reach the physical ideal required. The disabled body was so far removed from the notion of the perfect dancing body that there was no possible connection between dance and disability beyond the therapeutic.

The 1960s saw the emergence of postmodern dance with new works being created by the artists who formed the Judson Dance Theater in New York (1962).[4] These choreographers began to create works for untrained as well as trained bodies through the introduction of pedestrian (natural, unstylised) movement into performance; new approaches to dance composition and the use of contact improvisation[5] further extended the boundaries of Western theatre dance.

These radical changes brought about a shift within modern/postmodern dance towards a changed perception of the body type that can be accepted as a dancer, as well as a shift in perception of what constitutes dance. The introduction of pedestrian movement and contact improvisation into performance challenged the existing aesthetic of virtuosity and the accepted view that professional dance was confined to a few specific technique-based styles. As these technique-based styles had evolved at a time when practically all professional dancers were non-disabled, they generally did not offer a movement vocabulary that could be directly applied to the disabled body. Attempts to do so only led to negative comparisons, and the perception that the disabled dancer's performance was merely an approximation of the 'real thing', an attempt to define the transgressive body in terms of the normative. As Cooper Albright states: 'normalizing the disabled body doesn't serve to break down these dichotomies of social difference, it merely disguises them with an alternative discourse' (1997: 63).

The development of these new movement vocabularies (pedestrian movement and contact improvisation) supplied an entry point into professional dance for two fundamental reasons. Firstly, differing corporealities were unremarkable because there was no single, uniform notion of the type of body needed to use these vocabularies, and secondly, there was a fluidity to the vocabularies, they were not rigidly codified systems of movement as had previously dominated Western theatre dance. Since the beginning of the twentieth century, the emphasis had gradually shifted from being focussed on the external, objectifiable view of the dancing body to also allowing for a focus on the internal, subjective experience of the dancer that could be communicated to the viewer. But even with such a fundamental change in viewpoint that permitted the not so 'sylph-like' dancer to be considered acceptable in certain dance companies, the professional dance world was still dominated by the culturally prescribed body, the body that meets the requirements of what is readily identified as dancer embodying the 'sylph'.

However, this ever increasing broadening prepared the way for the development of integrated dance, a genre that is inclusive of all embodiments, at all levels, up to and including professional dance performance. Integration, from the Latin *integrare* (to make whole), implies an approach to dance that would be inclusive of all, regardless of differences in embodiment. In its widest context, integrated dance can encompass physical, sensory and intellectual ways of being in the world that are considered to be outside the normative. As this is too broad a spectrum for consideration within this chapter, the focus here is on physical embodiment.

Misconceptions and prejudices surrounding disability are deeply ingrained in the communal psyche and they create the narratives that define the transgressive body. Until the latter half of the twentieth century, the inclusion of the physically disabled body within the art of dance had nearly always been confined to the realm of therapy. This therapeutic approach mirrored the medical model's perception of disability which saw dance as a means of intervention, a vehicle for the achievement of other goals within the management and rehabilitation of the client, where disability was equated with illness. In more recent times, community dance provided an entry point for those with disabilities, again often with an underlying therapeutic interpretation of inclusion that provided a sense of 'charitable giving' for the non-disabled participants, who tended to see their role as supporting and enabling. Dance practitioner and educator Adam Benjamin talks of the difficulties in working with inclusive groups where some members perceive themselves as 'helpers':

> groups organised in this way will often attract or be initiated by those whose main area of interest is 'people with special needs', who are in all likelihood not disabled and who may well instil a caring/therapeutic ideology rather than a challenging/problem-solving one. ... The widening gap that opens between disabled and non-disabled participants is obscured beneath a cloak of good intentions.
>
> (Benjamin, 2002: 62)

Dance making and viewing in this context become vehicles for maintaining perceptions of the disabled body as being less than whole, with non-disabled participants providing a compensatory presence that will somehow redress this perceived lack with 'disabled people being helped to dance by non-disabled people, rather than as an exchange of equals' (ibid.).

Integrated dance, the way forward

Philosophical discourse has always been facilitated by the arts, and the emergence of integrated dance (dance that is inclusive of dancers both with and without disabilities) appeared to be a fundamental means of creating an inclusive ethos, by bridging the space between the abstract notion of inclusion and its actual realisation. However, dance is an art form that is defined by embodied presence and artists with physical disabilities, no matter which area of the arts they are active in, are often defined by their disabilities rather than their artistic talents. The creation of integrated dance came about in the 1970s, at a time when social justice and equality were being sought by marginalised groups and the disability rights movement was emerging in both the UK and the US.[6] As the genre developed over the next decade, integrated dance began to make the shift from community-based activities to professional dance performance. Companies such as *Axis* in San Francisco and *CandoCo* in London were formed, and began to produce works with a disability focus, highlighting the social and political issues inherent in living within a norm-based society. Unfortunately, as there was no existing structure to provide training for dancers with differently abled bodies, the physically disabled dancer was often untrained, the works produced often lacked artistic rigour and although generally well received by sympathetic audiences, there was little critical response, which was generally reflected in the reviews received for dance performance by integrated dance companies at the time. If the performance was reviewed at all (and a great deal were not), the focus of the review would tend to be on the dancer's disability and the 'heroic' aspect of overcoming disability in order to dance.[7] Benjamin made the point that often dance was presented that was 'formalised and regimented, seeming to infantilise the dancers rather than empower them; the complexity and the uniqueness of the dancers' movement remains untapped' (Benjamin, 2002: 68).

This has been an issue within integrated dance since its inception and has led to the interpretation of this form of dance as freak show performance[8] and victim art,[9] as well as the apparently more politically correct placement of the disabled dancer as 'heroic', overcoming adversity in an effort to more closely resemble the normate, and therefore outside the critical evaluation criteria reserved for non-disabled dancers. The development of integrated dance training, although still in its infancy, is bringing about a fundamental change in perceptions of dancers with disabilities. An increasing number of differently abled dancers have begun to emerge who have achieved a level of professional competence, and as this has coincided with the emergence of works created on differently abled bodies by talented choreographers, artistic integrity and aesthetic value are now becoming the driving force behind the development of new work by integrated dance companies. The emphasis is no longer on performance as political statement of the marginalisation experienced by disabled people. The dance produced cannot be neatly labelled, placed alongside other disability arts and given cultural recognition as being an approximation of dance performed by an incomplete, damaged body. The fracturing of the existing narrative of 'disabled dancer' by the emergence of dance works that no longer adhere to the classical canon[10] opens up the possibility for reframing an understanding of what constitutes a legitimate dancing body (Sandhal, Auslander, 2005).

With the advent of integrated dance that has artistic rigour and integrity, the previously dominant narratives of disability within dance can be let go, opening the way for a new understanding to be created that need not be constructed in terms of incomplete and damaged embodiment. The embodied presence of the disabled dancer is no longer so easily defined, it has become unknowable in terms of previously existing, culturally prescribed boundaries that divided the disabled dancer from the normate. In her exploration of the physical act of how we look at disabled bodies, Garland-Thomson speaks of our need to know, she states 'Human curiosity animates our modern world, revealing the tacit, taming the novel, and undertaking the unknown' (2009: 47). The dance academic and disability activist Petra Kuppers (2003) has considered the same desire to know, in terms of dance, when she writes about a filmdance performance (*The Fall*, Darshan Singh Buller, 1991) by Celeste Dandeker, co-founder and former artistic director of *CandoCo*. In her reading of *The Fall*, Kuppers holds that pre-existing narratives of disability and dance are shattered in this performance, leaving the viewer in a state of 'unknowing', needing to engage with Dandeker's performance in a different way in order to create a new understanding of that dancer's embodiment. As a performer with a disability, Dandeker's communication through movement requires the viewer to reassess presumptions about who can and cannot dance. Kuppers states, 'it is only in the shared acknowledgement of the disruption of *all* narratives by the unknowable personal that a communication is achieved' (2003: 103). If this is generalised to other dance performances, letting go of preconceived notions that create and uphold the narratives of disability leaves the way open for a revisioning of the relationship between disabled dancer and viewer, moving forward from the position of unknowing to a shared understanding.

The new communication that will ensue makes it possible for new parameters regarding dance performance and disability to be created. The nature of this communication between dancer and viewer now needs to be explored, in order to formulate an understanding of dance as a tool for facilitating changing societal perceptions of physical disability.

Relationship and attunement: Creating the dance of intersubjectivity

The relationship between those with and without disabilities is grounded in the symbolic frameworks that shape interactions within everyday life. These symbolic frameworks are culturally constructed (Carlson, 2007)[11] and reflect the hegemony of the normate body, where narratives of being are assimilated that place the disabled body in a transgressive position as outsider, supplying the necessary binary to the exclusionary notion of 'normal' (Kuppers, 2003). This position needs to be deconstructed if changed perceptions of disability are to come about. An understanding of difference needs to be created based on an acceptance of a continuum of ability that does not exclude, but rather encompasses all forms of embodiment. Letting go of existing cultural constructs cannot easily happen at a conscious level so alternative modes of connection need to be activated and this opens up the possibility of considering dance as one alternative mode, a communication that is somatically based rather than symbolically based. Through the intentional movement of dance, an interpersonal dialogue can be achieved that is not dependent on any other form of expression, neither words nor music are necessary (Hanna, 1979). The performance of dance in the company of another (whether as viewer or dancer) can be understood as a non-verbal communication, a connecting link between two individuals. It is this connection that provides the key to creating a new understanding of disability.

A review of a recent dance production, Heidi Latsky's *GIMP* (May, 2009),[12] gives an insight into the process by which this connection is made. *GIMP* was choreographed by Latsky as a result of her interest in expanding the boundaries of who can dance, and how. Throughout her career, Latsky has been involved in works that explore the edges of professional dance, beginning as a dancer with Bill T. Jones' company, then working in partnership with Larry Goldhuber, a dancer of very large physical proportions. In her own dance company, *Heidi Latsky Dance*, she has continued to explore the possibilities of stretching the boundaries. In her current work *The GIMP Project*, her organisational vision statement encapsulates her approach to dance and physical difference,[13] where she respects and values all corporealities and the consequent movement potential that can inform her choreography. In *GIMP*, Latsky choreographed for four professionally trained dancers and four dancers with physical disabilities. Reviewer Theodore Bale (2009) wrote:

> as a child, I was taught never to stare at disabled persons. I remained curious into adulthood, however, the dancers in *GIMP* not only break this common taboo, they make the situation reciprocal. They stare back at you. Subverting these well-established 'polite' conventions of gaze is the starting point for this event, which skillfully blends political inquiry,

psychology, and aesthetic explorations of form, structure, and dynamics. *GIMP* is without doubt a gleaming milestone in the progress of contemporary dance and theater, proving that the term 'disabled dancer' is an oxymoron.

Bale's experience of looking at disability within the context of dance performance changed his perception of how one is allowed to look at physical difference. He was able to go beyond the confines of social conditioning in order to look at dancers with disabilities and engage with their presence onstage as performers. This experience of prelinguistic connection with the other through the gaze can be the starting point at which viewer and performer can connect outside the constraints of a subjectivity coloured by culturally generated signification. The concept of the voyeuristic, dominant male gaze (Garland-Thomson, 2009: 41) has been widely applied in dance performance theory, based on the notion of a corporeal presence (the dancer) that can be objectified and stared at (by the viewer).

Albright states that the 'traditionally voyeuristic gaze can be both fractured and reconstructed by looking at bodies that radically question the ideal image of the dancer's physique' (1997: 58). Dancers with disabilities have the potential to bring about a transformation of this objectifying stare into an interactive gaze, redefining the relationship between the dancer and viewer. To explore how this can come about, we need to go back to the very beginnings of social engagement during infancy, where the basis of how each looks at the other is laid down. The infant engages the gaze of the caregiver and an interaction is initiated that brings the infant to a heightened level of arousal. When this level of arousal becomes unbearable, as it inevitably must because the infant is only learning to self regulate at an emotional level, the infant and caregiver disengage. The infant is given time to re-establish equilibrium. This ongoing interactional dance of the gaze provides a safe, holding environment in which the infant can grow towards psychic integration and separation from the primary caregiver as ego identity is formed (Schore, 2002). The sense of self is created through the recognition of the other, and so the act of looking becomes the basis for interpersonal synchrony. It is not until the gaze becomes socially regulated during early childhood that it turns into the stigmatising stare, and the child is taught to stifle what Garland-Thomson (2009) calls the baroque stare. The baroque stare is one of wonderment; it is not contained by rationality or desire for mastery; it is a recognition of the unknown, an intense engagement with the other. As such, it becomes a shared experience where both 'starer' and 'staree' are empowered to create new insights. This type of staring 'strives toward knowing by reducing unfamiliarity, if it is not short-circuited, it can be coaxed toward transformative interaction' (Garland-Thomson, 2009: 194). In viewing dance, permission is tacitly given to engage in the baroque stare, the stare of infancy and early childhood. Dance performance unravels the familiar ways of looking at disability – the blank stare that negates and makes invisible, or the knowledge-producing medical gaze when disability becomes hypervisible. The freedom to engage in the baroque stare when viewing dance opens up the possibility that the viewer can let go of existing perceptions in the creation of a new, shared understanding of the dancer's embodied presence, a 'transformative interaction' (ibid.) that gives rise to interpersonal synchrony. This is the experience that Bale spoke about in his review of *GIMP*.

How we look at each other is an integral part of developing an interpersonal relationship, and the use of the baroque stare opens the way for a revised interpersonal relationship to grow between disabled dancer and viewer within the performance space. The exploration of interpersonal relationships has been the focus of many diverse schools of thought. The philosopher Martin Buber speaks of the *I/Thou* relationship (1958) where mutuality is created between two people, a recognition of each other's humanity within a dialogic engagement. Buber states, 'the relation to the *Thou* is direct. No system of ideas, no foreknowledge, and no fancy intervene between *I* and *Thou*' (1958: 17). This immediacy of engagement is at the core of the relationship between dancer and viewer. Recent developments in neuroscience are uncovering the essentially social aspects of the human brain, demonstrating how we are 'hardwired' to seek interaction with others (Trevarthen, 2003; Cozolino, 2006), providing a scientific framework for Buber's philosophy. The one common thread that runs through all human interactions is the first experience of relationship that occurs between an infant and the primary caregiver (Hughes, 2007), and it is this primary experience that will form the basis of the relationship between dancer and viewer in the performance space.

The developmental psychologist Colwyn Trevarthen's research with newborn infants has shown that a baby as young as 20 minutes old will interact with an adult, 'demonstrating coherence of its intentionality and its awareness of a world outside the body, and especially a world that offers live company' (2003: 57). Patterns of interaction are gradually built, arising out of the infant's chaos of somatic experience. The infant's needs are overwhelming in their insistence to be met and the first experience of successful relationship is created around the meeting of these needs. This is the basis of attachment and mutuality upon which relationships with the other are constructed. It can be hypothesised that the microcosm of the dance performance space allows for a disintegration of socially constructed perceptions of disability and for the possibility of using dance as a means of reawakening this early, somatically based form of relationship building. In dance performance, there is the potential for viewer and dancer to experience this shared recognition of each other as human, without the cultural interpretations of the disabled body as outsider. For an infant, 'the meaning of the world can only be acquired in communication and collaboration with other people' (Trevarthen, 2003: 67). In dance performance, it is possible for new meanings to be constructed where dance is the medium of communication, putting aside the mediating influence of existing narratives of disability. These new meanings are created when empathic attunement occurs in the viewer, arising out of the intentional movement of the dance, and the embodied presence of the dancer, both of which will now be discussed.

The creation of empathic attunement

Neuroscientific research has begun to uncover the workings of the brain during infancy and the need for healthy attachment to precede optimal development of neural connections required for cognitive and emotional growth (Siegel, 1999; Cozolino, 2006). Predating this research, the psychiatrist Donald Winnicott (1964) formulated the idea that healthy attachment is based on the holding of the infant in both a literal and a figurative sense. Physical holding, proximity to the primary caregiver, provides a sense of well-being if that holding is attuned to the physicality of the infant. The sensitivity of the caregiver to the subtle physical cues of the child allows for an ongoing state of adjustment, where every shift in movement is accommodated within the safety of the holding. On a figurative level, empathic attunement between infant and caregiver fosters the development of relationship, as the caregiver reflects and responds to the infant's emotional state in each moment of interaction. These links between physical movement and empathic attunement, between action and the perception of action, and between cognitive processes and the development of emotional intelligence (Gallese et al., 2004; Cozolino, 2006; Siegel, 2007; Bläsing, 2010) are the core elements, from a neuroscientific perspective; of the value of dance performance as a site of change, 'it makes sense that more primitive somatic and motor activation serve as the infrastructure of emotion, cognition and abstract thought' (Cozolino, 2006: 204).

Following a path from the philosophy of Buber, passing through the psychoanalytic approach of Winnicott, we come to new neuroscientific insights that have been gained into the inner (intrapersonal) world of the individual as it pertains to the development of social interaction through seeing and experiencing others' physical movements and actions, especially the development of attunement and empathy in interpersonal relationships. This growth in understanding has come about following the pioneering work of Vittorio Gallese and his colleagues in studying the mirror neuron systems of the brain (Gallese, 2003; Gallese et al., 2004, 2007). This is an emerging branch of neuroscience and it is beyond the scope of this chapter to give anything but a very general, non-specialist overview of how it impacts on the creation of relationship within performance.[14] Mirror neurons were first discovered in 1996, when researchers noticed that a certain area of a monkey's brain fired not only when the monkey carried out an action, but also when it watched the same action being carried out by one of the researchers (Gallese et al., 1996). The monkey recognised the intention of the movement which elicited the neurological response, however this response did not happen when the monkey observed non-intentional, random movement. Daniel Siegel, in applying this principle to human behaviour, has developed this research in the field of interpersonal neurobiology through focussing on a study of mindfulness, where empathy and attunement to the other occurs through each attending to the other's intentions. The process that allows this to happen is the working of the mirror neuron system within the brain where humans create representations of other's minds; not only is the physical action seen, but the mental intention is also imagined.

We use our first five senses to take in the signals from another person. Then the mirror neuron system perceives these 'intentional states', and by way of the insula alters the limbic and body states to match those we are seeing in the other person. This is attunement and it creates emotional resonance.

(Seigel, 2007: 167)

Mirror neurons appear to be the link between empathy and body sensation. Through the dancer's postures, gestures, facial expressions and meaningful movements, emotional responses are elicited in the viewer (Gallese, 2003). This is the neurological foundation for the social nature of the human brain and is the basis of empathic attunement. Siegel states:

Mirror properties of the nervous system provide an important window into examining the nature of culture and how shared ritual behaviours within our families, schools, and communities enable us to resonate with each other's internal states, including intentions.

(2007: 167)

Dance is one such ritual behaviour and this is the essence of the power of dance performance from a neuroscientific stance. Rituals are an important part of everyday life, reinforcing social connections that bind individuals together into a community. Historically, rituals were created to mark significant events in the life of the community. The contemporary parallel can be seen in social events such as football matches or theatre performances. However, rituals also have another role within the community as they can be a site of transformation, 'ritual holds the generating source of culture and structure. Hence, by definition ritual is associated with social transitions' (Turner, 1988: 158). In the ritual of dance performance, the inclusion of the disabled dancer can be a transformative experience, bringing about cultural changes in perceptions of disability. The viewer is given the opportunity to recognise and become attuned to the dancer's humanity through the engagement of the mirror neuron system, regardless of whether or not that dancer has a disability. When linked with the baroque gaze and the reawakening of a somatically based relationship between dancer and viewer as already discussed, a new understanding of disability can be created that leads to acceptance arising out of empathic attunement. This partnership of the biological approach to understanding human behaviour, along with a psychological frame of reference grounded in attachment theory, has led to an expanded version of what it is to be human. These two approaches would previously have been considered almost mutually exclusive but with increased knowledge, there is an increased common ground where one field of study complements the other. Through a growing scientific as well as psychological and philosophical understanding of how we form interpersonal relationships, it is possible to consider how social structures can be utilised in bringing about societal change. By including dancers with physical disabilities in the dance performance space, viewers are confronted by the humanity of those dancers in a manner that is rarely accessible outside the ritual space of performance. The act of dancing brings the viewer to a state of mindfulness in relation to the dancer, which comes about as the viewer moves from a position of unknowing (which could be considered almost a default setting for many people when encountering disabled bodies, because of societal prejudice) to one of open wonder and engagement that leads to empathic attunement. This state of mindfulness opens the way for that performance to become transformative, changing perceptions of disability from a position of exclusion and abjection to a position of acceptance and inclusion.

Conclusion

Dance research has been described as:

> a barrierless inquiry that attempts to move beyond either-or to consider both-and; a wholistic activity in which insights emerge at the confluence of streams of feedback from body, mind, and spirit; and a synoptic discipline that weaves together a range of outlooks drawn from diverse fields.
>
> (Dale et al., 2007: 99)

In this chapter, the value of dance performance as a legitimate site for influencing societal perceptions of disability has been explored through a psychological approach, utilising attachment theory, a neuroscientific approach, utilising mirror neuron research, and through the use of disability theory, utilising the notion of the baroque stare, relatively diverse fields that all contribute to forming the argument that viewing a dance performance by a disabled dancer holds the potential to positively influence perceptions of disability.

The connection between the viewer's experience of watching dance and the internal emotional mechanisms that can be activated by this experience have been explored, through examining how we become empathically attuned to each other in a non linguistic way. These biological and psychological processes have their roots in early infant attachment behaviour. Trevarthen states, 'a baby begins life with a tremendous sensitivity to the rhythmic processes going on inside the mind of a mother or father' (2003: 64). This sensitivity is reflected also in a physical sense as well as a psychological sense, and the rhythmic movement of dance can be understood as the link between the viewer's current involvement in watching dance and that viewer's preverbal embodied experience. The psychoanalyst Suzanne Maiello (2001) has explored this link between attachment, the development of relationship and rhythmic movement. A connection exists between prenatal movement patterns, rhythmicity of maternal embodiment providing the music of the life dance, and the holding of the infant in early attachment/attunement patterns, where mirror neurons are creating the groundwork for the development of empathy through physical movement. At a prenatal level, a synchronicity is already being created between mother and foetus through the shared experience of biological and physical rhythms. The mother's heartbeat, breathing, the bodily actions of everyday life such as walking and the act of speech, all provide an interweaving of rhythm and movement that shape early experience. The intrauterine environment of auditory, vibratory, proprioceptive and kinaesthetic stimuli provide the earliest form of attunement. Postnatally, attunement is further developed as the mirror neuron system assists the creation of healthy attachment. When viewing dance performance, the activation of the mirror neuron system creates a somatic connection with the dancer that can awaken emotional responses in the viewer, as Dale states:

> The existence of such a class of neurons in humans has tremendous implications for dance, where dancers may tap into the mirror neurons systems of their observers to evoke a sensual and emotional experience.
> (Dale et al., 2007: 104)

This evocation of a sensual and emotional experience resonates with previous early experience of emotion, connecting with experience that has not been filtered through the signification process that comes into being with the acquisition of language. It is this creation of a state of empathic attunement in viewing dance performance, that is not bound by culturally acquired perceptions of disability, that can bring about change.

The proposition outlined in this chapter is that the reawakening of early attachment patterns, the use of the baroque gaze and the activation of the mirror neuron system creating a state of mindfulness are all aspects of viewing dance that have the potential to bring about changed perceptions of disability. This experience of psychological and physiological resonance is the basis of the relationship between the self and the other, before symbolic imprinting imposes a culturally driven interpretation of disability. Viewing the disabled body dancing creates the opportunity to experience empathic attunement, to deconstruct the notion of disability as transgressive by recognising the humanity of the dancer, and to experience the relationship as transformative, where physical diversity need no longer be disabling.

Notes

1. For an overview of the development of ballet from the court dances of the sixteenth century to the Romantic Ballet era of the nineteenth century, see Au (2002).
2. A general introduction to the rise of modern dance can be found in Au (2002: 87–102).
3. Susan Leigh Foster (1986: 145–56) examines the radical change from traditional, academic European ballet to modern/Expressionist dance with particular reference to these choreographers.
4. A broad overview of the postmodern dance movement can be found in 'The Metamorphosis of Form' in Au (2002: 155–73). Postmodern dance transformed the choreographic process. There was an intent by the Judson group to 'liberate the body and the dance from what they perceived as the psychological domination of the expressionists and the virtuoso orientation of the ballet' (Foster, 1986: 169). For a more detailed outline of this change in choreographic process, see Foster (1986: 169–81).
5. Contact improvisation is an 'improvised movement system based on the communication between two moving bodies and their combined relationship to the physical laws that govern their motion: gravity: momentum: friction and inertia' (Koegler, 1982: 103). The introduction of contact improvisation is generally attributed to Steve Paxton in 1972, a member of the Judson group. For a more detailed exploration of the the the impact of contact improvisation on the development of integrated dance, see Albright (2001: 62–5.)
6. See Benjamin (2002: 23–42) for a detailed discussion of the development of integrated dance within the historical framework discussed earlier in this chapter.
7. As Judith Smith (Artistic Director of *Axis*) reported, 'Originally, we got sympathy reviews and when we eventually got our first negative review, I was really relieved. I felt that people were finally taking us seriously. There was a lot of truth in what that particular review said and it started to fuel my wanting to work with other choreographers and raise the quality of our work.' (personal interview, San Francisco, 25 November 2003).
8. 'Freak' is synonymous with the non-normate body and in the freak show era from the mid-nineteenth to the mid-twentieth century, the freak became 'a generalized icon of corporeal and cultural otherness that verified the socio-political status quo and the figure of the unmarked normate, the ideal subject of democracy' (Garland-Thomson, 1997: 79). For an exploration of contemporary freak show performance, see Kuppers (2003: 31–48).
9. The label 'victim art' was first used by the dance critic Arlene Croce to describe a particular performance that did not meet with her notion of an acceptable aesthetic because it dealt with a social issue. When the choreographer Bill T Jones staged a performance of his work *Still/Here* (New York, 1994), Croce refused to either view or review the work. She did not attend the performance, but wrote a

critique in the *New Yorker* magazine (1994/5: 54–60), stating that as it dealt with social issues relating to the Aids epidemic, *Still/Here* was outside the realm of 'high art' and should not be considered in terms of aesthetic value. She stated that as a dance critic, she had learned to 'avoid dancers with obvious problems – overweight dancers old dancers, dancers with sickled feet or dancers with physical deformities' (1994/5: 55). Croce's article sparked a heated debate regarding the concept of 'high art' and had the effect of raising awareness of cultural perceptions of disease and disability.

10. Choreographers such as Lloyd Newson (DV8 Physical Theatre) and Mark Morris (Mark Morris Dance Group) use dancers with a wide range of physicalities that would be considered unsuitable by many other dance companies.
11. Semiotic theory provides a framework for understanding the role of signs in social life – the system whereby we create shared meanings. For an introduction to the use of semiotics within performance studies, see Carlson (2007: 13–25).
12. *GIMP* is a dance performance choreographed by Heidi Latsky, which includes dancers with and without disabilities. The performance reviewed by Theodore Bale took place at the Institute of Contemporary Art, Boston on 24 April 2009. An excerpt from the performance and more information about this work can be accessed at http://www.thegimpproject.com/gimp/.
13. Latsky's vision statement is as follows:

all bodies are recognized as viable, fascinating and expressive instruments; difference is upheld, not feared; increased understanding and communication take the place of isolation, alienation and lack of contact; people learn to 'live in' their own skin and do not detach from their bodies because of external and internally assimilated judgments and conventional standards; one is encouraged to 'own' one's body, value it and use it to be expressive and truthful in ways that are empowering, enriching and unique; a strong work ethic is valued and implemented; and a high standard of excellence is not only desired but is achieved through sustained work and focus.

Latsky, Heidi. *The GIMP Project* (2008–2010), http://www.thegimpproject.com/gimp/mission/, accessed 14 December 2010.

14. For a more detailed discussion, see 'Internal Attunement: Mirror Neurons, Resonance, and Attention to Intention' (Siegel, 2007: 164–88), and 'Imitation and Mirror Neurons: Monkey See Monkey Do' (Cozolino, 2006: 186–98).

References

Albright, Ann Cooper (1997). *Choreographing Difference: Body and Identity in Contemporary Dance.* Connecticut: Wesleyan University Press.
Albright, Ann Cooper (2001). 'Strategic Abilities: Negotiating the Disabled Body in Dance'. In Ann Dils and Ann Cooper Albright (eds), *Moving History/Dancing Cultures.* Connecticut: Wesleyan University Press.
Au, Susan (2002). *Ballet and Modern Dance.* London: Thames and Hudson.
Bale, Theodore (2009). *Heidi Latsky Dance Magazine.* New York: McFadden Performing Arts Media LLC, http://www.dancemagazine.com/reviews/May-2009/Heidi-Latsky, accessed 14 December 2010.
Benjamin, Adam (2002). *Making an Entrance.* London: Routledge.
Bläsing, Bettina (ed.) (2010). *The Neurocognition of Dance: Mind Movement and Motor Skills.* Sussex: Psychology Press.

Buber, Martin (1958). *I and Thou* (second edition) (translated by Ronald Gregor Smith). London: Continuum Books.

Carlson, Marvin (2007). 'Semiotics and Its Heritage'. In Janelle Reinelt and Joseph Roach, *Critical Theory and Performance* (pp. 13–25). Michigan: University of Michigan Press.

Cozolino, Louis (2006). *The Neuroscience of Human Relationships*. New York: Norton.

Croce, Arlene (1994). 'Discussing the Undiscussable'. *The New Yorker*, 26 December, 54–5.

Dale, Alexander, Hyatt, Janyce and Hollerman, Jeff (2007). 'The Neuroscience of Dance and the Dance of Neuroscience'. *Journal of Aesthetic Education*, 41 (3).

Foster, Susan Leigh (1986). 'Expressionist Dance in the Early Twentieth Century'. In *Reading Dancing: Bodies and Subjects in Contemporary American Dance* (pp. 145–56). Berkeley: University of California Press.

Gallese, Vittorio (2003). 'The Roots of Empathy: The Shared Manifold Hypothesis and the Neural Basis of Intersubjectivity'. *Psychopathology*, 36, 171–80.

Gallese, Vittorio, Fadiga, L., Fogassi, L. and Rittolatti, G. (1996). 'Action Recognition in the Pre Motor Cortex'. *Brain*, 119, 593–609.

Gallese, Vittorio, Keysers, C. and Rizzolatti, G. (2004). 'A Unifying View of the Basis of Social Cognition'. *Trends in Cognitive Sciences*, 8 (9), 396–403.

Gallese, Vittorio, Eagle, M. N. and Migone, P. (2007). 'Intentional Attunement: Mirror Neurons and the Neural Underpinnings of Interpersonal Relations'. *Journal of American Psychoanalytic Association*, 55 (March), 131–75.

Garland-Thomson, Rosemarie (2009). *Staring: How We Look*. New York: Oxford University Press.

Hanna, Judith Lynn (1979). *To Dance is Human: A Theory of Non Verbal Communication*. Austin: University of Texas Press.

Hughes, Daniel, A. (2007). *Attachment-Focussed Family Therapy*. New York: Norton.

Koegler, Horst (1982). *The Concise Oxford Dictionary of Ballet*. Oxford: Oxford University Press.

Kuppers, Petra (2003). *Disability and Contemporary Performance: Bodies on Edge*. New York: Routledge.

Maiello, Susan (2001). 'On Temporal Shapes: The Relation Between Primary Rhythmical Experience and the Quality Of Mental Links'. In Judith Edwards (ed.), *Being Alive: Building on the work of Anne Alvarez* (pp. 179–94). Sussex: Brunner Routledge.

Sandhal, Carrie and Auslander, Philip (2005). *Bodies in Commotion: Disability and Performance*. Ann Arbor: University of Michigan Press.

Siegel, Daniel (2007). *The Mindful Brain*. New York: W.W. Norton and Co. Inc.

Siegel, Daniel (1999). *The Developing Mind*. New York: Guilford Press.

Schore, Allan, N. (2002). 'The Neurobiology of Attachment and Early Personality Organization'. *Journal of Prenatal and Perinatal Psychology and Health*, 16 (3), 249–63.

Trevarthen, Colwyn (2003).'Neuroscience and Intrinsic Dynamics: Current Knowledge and Potential for Therapy'. In Jenny Corrigall and Heward Wilkinson (eds), *Revolutionary Connections: Psychotherapy and Neuroscience*. London: Karnac.

Turner, Victor (1988). *The Anthropology of Performance*. New York: P.A.J. Publications.

Winnicott, Donald, W. (1964). *The Child, the Family and the Outside World*. London: Penguin Books.

Part III
Subjectivities

10
Nomadology and Subjectivity: Deleuze, Guattari and Critical Disability Studies

Griet Roets and Rosi Braidotti

Introduction

Over the last two decades, impairment has become a tricky issue and remains under-theorised in disability studies (see Hughes and Paterson, 1997; Corker, 2001; Tremain, 2002). In the UK the social model of disability has dominated disability theory. In this frame of reference, a distinction is made between 'impairment' and 'disability'. In the social model of disability, impairment is conceptualised as *the lack or defect of a limb, organ or mechanism of the body*, and analyses focus on the ways in which 'disability' is created through the historical, social, economic, political, cultural and relational exclusion of people with 'impairments' (UPIAS, 1976; Oliver, 1990, 1996). For many disability theorists and activists, impairment refers to an individualised phenomenon and implies negativities, including pathology, pathos, social death, inertia, lack, limitation, loss, deficit and/or tragedy (Goodley and Roets, 2008). Even quite recently it is argued that, after all, impairment *is* a tragic, biological reality (Shakespeare, 2006). Our question consequently becomes: can we return impaired bodies to their material roots, which means adopting a unified vision of bodies and minds as pre-social, biological essences and unchanging phenomena without discrediting the social and political project of disability studies?

Therefore, in this chapter we theorise the impaired subject as social, embodied and non-dualistic. This shift of perspective implies the rejection of framing subjectivity in terms of reproducing the existing political order, and refutes the negative or lack-based definition of bodies that are constituted differently. In this vein, we criticise the politics of mourning and melancholia and the extent to which they dominate social theory, leaving limited scope for alternative theoretical approaches (Braidotti, 2010). In our view, also the disciplinary identity of disability studies has failed to dissociate from the collective mourning and melancholia, from the dominant understanding of impairment as loss, deficit, lack, tragedy and so on. Nevertheless, as soon as we attempt to theorise impairment as social, we encounter another tricky snake in the grass. Contemporary social theory still seems dominated by a socially constructivist vision of human embodiment which reduces the body to inert matter shaped by social, cultural and symbolic codes (Braidotti, 2010). It also assumes the primacy of a master code – be it a symbolic signifier, or a linguistically encoded grid of subjectification – which would somehow constitute the ultimate location of power. We oppose this binary and static view of mind–body interaction and propose instead a more dynamic process ontology of embodiment that assumes a vitalist vision. As an alternative to a politics of mourning and melancholia, we argue the case for a politics of affirmation inspired by Deleuze and Guattari's vitalist materialism, which could also redefine the terms of the debate about impairment and disability. In what follows, we look at the meaning of disability studies as a project of affirmative politics. This implies an exploration of (i) *alternative notions of ontology and epistemology*, (ii) *an expansion of our understanding of subjectivity as embodied, non-dualistic and nomadic*, and (iii) *a methodology* that makes our praxis nomadic and involves another way of forming subjectivity as transversal connections or assemblages with multiple others. Throughout the chapter, we illustrate how we engendered subjectivity as nomadic through engaging with the lives of people labeled as having 'intellectual disabilities'.

Alternative notions of ontology and epistemology

In the light of the disciplinary dilemma in disability studies over the nature of impairment, the *continental philosophy of bodily materialism* enables the establishment of alternative ontological and epistemological grounds. This approach inspires an affirmative politics of impairment. The politics of affirmation challenges disability theorists and activists to transcend biological determinism and essentialism, but also challenges social constructivism, in the narrow sense of the term, to rethink its dualistic opposition of self to society, of bodies to social norms and selves to others. To recapture impaired bodies and minds from the lost social space of pre-social ontology, a new balance needs to be struck. We argue that a political process ontology – or a version of the nature of being always in political process – is required. In search of such a balance we explore some particularly relevant concepts in Deleuze and Guattari's nomadic philosophy that were inspired by the work of Foucault and Canguilhelm.

Deleuze and Guattari call for a radical shift from an essentialist to anti-essentialist ontology by returning matter to a vitalist mode. The focus in this line of thought is on 'the politics of life itself as a relentlessly generative force' (Braidotti, 2010: 142). Matter is taken as intelligent, vital and self-organising. Important for disability studies is their analysis, in *A Thousand Plateaus: Capitalism and Schizophrenia* (1980), of Foucault's notion of power over life ('bio-power') and of Canguilhelm's notion of 'anomaly'. In that work, in chapter 10 'Becoming-Intense, Becoming-Animal, Becoming-Imperceptible', they clarify the very different origin and meaning of the Latin word *a-normal* and of the Greek word *anomalous*.

It has been noted that the origin of the word *anomal* ('anomalous'), an adjective that has fallen into disuse in French, is very different from that of *anormal* ('abnormal'): *a-normal*, a Latin adjective lacking a noun in French, refers to that which is outside rules or goes against the rules, whereas *an-omalie*, a Greek noun that has lost its adjective, designates the unequal, the coarse, the rough, the cutting edge of de-territorialization. The abnormal can be defined only in terms of characteristics, specific or generic; but the anomalous is a position or set of positions in relation to a multiplicity.

(Deleuze and Guattari, 1980: 269–70)

The Latin *a-normal* ('abnormal') draws us to a conceptualisation of ontology as biological essentialism and determinism that is radically challenged by Foucault when he introduces the notion of bio-power. Michel Foucault (1961, 1978) introduced the concept 'regimes of bio-power' to challenge the binary marking and disciplining of bodies and minds as ab/normal. According to Foucault, the body is a central player in the negotiation of power and the politics of bio-power is a rather brutal regime (Braidotti, 2006). Foucault argues in *The History of Sexuality*:

Nothing that was not ordered in terms of generation or transfigured by it ... did merit a hearing. It would be driven out, denied, and reduced to silence. Not only did it not exist, it had no right to exist and would be made to disappear upon its least manifestation – whether in acts or in words. [As such] ... modern puritanism imposed its triple edict of taboo, non-existence, and silence.

(Foucault, 1978: 4, italics added)

Foucault stresses that difference and 'otherness' – anything that is not ordered along the norm – is seen as inferiority; and bodies that are branded as 'other' are silently reduced to a disposable status (Braidotti, 2006). Also in the present, regimes of bio-power operate as ways of 'disciplining the body, normalizing behaviour, administering the life of populations' (Rajchman, 1985, quoted in Lather, 1991: 110). This means that particular bodies and subjects are categorised and excluded, and their respective ontology or nature of being acquires essentialist connotations which are assumed to be pre-given, universal and unchanging (Parker, 2003; Grosz, 2005).

Deleuze and Guattari (1980: 270) adopt Foucault's theorising when they affirm that 'the abnormal can be defined only in terms of characteristics, specific or generic'. Moreover, Foucault was particularly interested in the ways in which regimes of bio-power fed upon social and cultural discourses that, as key mechanisms in the process of social control, socially construct particular versions of self, personhood and subjectivity (Goodley et al., 2004). Ever since modernity, a vision of the subject as a unitary and rational self is pursued in knowledge production and the aim has been to control, govern and discipline the individual according to this norm. In this universalistic frame of reference, a binary logic of self–other reduces 'difference' to a pejorative and disqualified phenomenon (Braidotti, 2010). It can be argued that these politics of bio-power have invalidated in particular the impaired body and subject, making it ontologically deviant (Hughes, 1999). For example, McClimens (2003) traces a eugenicist discourse established in the late nineteenth and early twentieth century, which suggested that the agency of impaired human beings should be socially controlled for the purpose of improving the human race. The discourse was based on a vision of biologically 'pure' populations.

In our work, we observe that these sort of insights into the nature of impairment – illustrated sharply in the case of 'intellectual disabilities' – may be reflected in the growth of interventionist social sciences over the past century and, indeed, have influenced current practice (Roets, 2008). People with 'intellectual disabilities' were categorised as abnormal, deviant from the abstract standard of 'normal man', and their supposed intellectual inferiority was an important factor in the drive to remove them from the public sphere and 'treat' them in total institutions (Smith, 1999). Their culture was easily defined for them as a professional construct rooted in the eugenics movement, used to justify institutionalisation, sterilisation, and other repressive policies (Taylor, 1996). The policy of institutional segregation was reinforced by extreme measures, such as sterilisation, to control disabled people's fertility, and their supposed rampant and dangerous sexuality and to prevent marriage, sex and parenthood (May and Simpson, 2003). Those policies and practices depended in many senses upon eugenic and biological essentialism and determinism (Baroff, 2000; Kerr and Shakespeare, 2002) and were motivated by a desire to remove from society people with 'intellectual disabilities' who were thought to be a threat to the social order (Marks, 1999; Park and Redford, 1998). Moreover the ways in which contemporary ideas about women and men with 'intellectual disabilities' operate as taken-for-granted 'truths' suggest that it is important to trace back and reflect upon social and ideological influences that culminate in contemporary practices (Tremain, 2005; Roets, Adams and Van Hove, 2006).

Our position consists in using disability studies to challenge the politics of bio-power in the present. It situates the discursive field of disability studies as 'a discourse that has a great ability to circulate, a great aptitude for metamorphoses, a sort of strategic polyvalence'. Here Deleuze and Guattari's nomadic philosophy of life inspires 'a practice of pragmatics where ontology is overthrown, foundations are done away with and endings and beginnings are nullified' (Deleuze and Guattari, 1980: 28). They refer, in this context, to Canguilhelm's notion of *the anomalous*.

Georges Canguilhelm (a philosopher and historian of medical science and Michel Foucault's dissertation advisor, see Snyder and Mitchell, 2001: 373) situated the body and its hard, essentialist existence as a historically contingent phenomenon. In his work *The Normal and the Pathological* (translated in English in 1989), he emphasised adaptation over deviation. Canguilhelm asserted that bodies were not the product of averages and submissive to norms. They were interdependent vessels, not fixed essences that shaped and were shaped by their environments. The modernist myth of the norm of 'bodily perfection' thus becomes little more than a hostile imposition upon necessarily fluctuating organisms: 'a norm, or rule is what can be used to right, to square, to straighten. To set a norm (*normer*), to normalize, is to impose a requirement on an existence, a given whose variety, disparity – with regard to the requirement – present themselves as a hostile indeterminacy' (Canguilhelm, 1989: 239, quoted in Snyder and Mitchell, 2001: 373). As such, a norm functions to surrender every notion of deviance to the violence of devaluation. In contrast to the ab/*normal*, Canguilhelm argued for a notion of *anomaly*, which offered medicine (his own discipline as a medical historian) a more appropriate gauge than dysfunction and abnormality: 'rather than interpret *bodily and cognitive differences* in terms of their degree of deviation from a standardized norm, *anomaly recognized difference as the ... expression of a biologically diverse species adapting to the pressures of environmental and internal forces*' (Snyder and Mitchell, 2001: 373, italics added). As such, Canguilhelm argues for bio-diversity, for the self-generative, affirmative power of living matter at the core of a collective and anti-essentialist becoming (Braidotti, 2006: 53). The Greek concept *an-omalie* symbolises a version of political process ontology, which expresses a version of *being* that is *simultaneously becoming* in alliance with related being(s) (see Braidotti, 2006).

Also Deleuze and Guattari introduce the notion of *becoming-animal* when they argue that 'the anomalous is a position or set of positions in relation to a multiplicity' (Deleuze and Guattari, 1980: 270). Interestingly, Biesta (2011) reveals that the way in which societies are made operational is related to how we understand the status of the borders of the democratic order. It can be argued that a disabling society defines disabled people as outsiders; as 'those on the outside of this order are there either because they are unable to act rationally and/or morally ... or because they explicitly reject the standards of rationality and morality that characterize the political order' (Biesta, 2011: 145–46). This translates as an appeal for a re-conceptualisation of the nature of impaired bodies-and-minds as always in process, always in becoming and in relation to the collective: 'For the whole question is: what is exactly the nature of the anomalous? What function does it have in relation to the band, or the pack? [...] It is a phenomenon, but a phenomenon of bordering ... there is a borderline for each multiplicity' (Deleuze

and Guattari, 1980: 269–70). The way how this 'borderline' for each multiplicity – or say collective, society – is constructed can be seen as a very
powerful resource for valuing the notion of diversity *within* human kinds.
Approaching impairment as one of these borderlines can push disability
studies into surprising new horizons. Impaired bodies and minds can be
recast as driving forces that constitute a network of interconnection with
others (Braidotti, 2010). This implies not an us/them politics but one in
which human beings border/cluster in the collective. This point of view also
expands our understanding of subjectivity.

An expansion of our understanding of subjectivity: Nomadic subjects

> I am rooted, but I flow.
>
> (Virginia Woolf, quoted in Braidotti, 2002: 1)

In Deleuze and Guattari's theory of the subject, bodies and subjects are
socially created in the affirmative actualisation of the encounter between
subjects, entities and forces which mutually affect and exchange parts
of each other. Collective life is an engine for an affirmative becoming
(Braidotti, 2002). This is what is at stake in Deleuze and Guattari's nomadic
theory of the subject as becoming:

> A kind of order or apparent progressions can be established for *the seg-
> ments of becoming in which we find ourselves*; becoming-woman, becoming-
> child, becoming-animal, -vegetable, or mineral; becomings molecular of
> all kinds, *becoming-particles*. Fibres lead us from one to the other, transform
> one into the other as they pass through doors and across thresholds.
>
> (Deleuze and Guattari, 1980: 300)

Gilles Deleuze, in his influential oeuvre *Difference and Repetition* (1968) and
later with Félix Guattari in *A Thousand Plateaus* (1980), perceives the raw materials of existence as a nomadic distribution of being(s) constantly in flux:

> then there is a completely other distribution which must be called
> nomadic, a nomad *nomos*, without property, enclosure, or measure. Here,
> there is no longer a division of that which is distributed but rather a divi-
> sion among those who distribute *themselves* in an open space – a space
> which is unlimited, or at least without precise limits.
>
> (Deleuze, 1968: 45–6, italics in original)

We adopt this strand of Deleuze and Guattari's work because, as we have
argued, we need a social and political ontology at the centre of epistemologies
and social practices in which 'the "real", "the body", "being", "materiality",

"nature", those terms themselves are opened up to their becomings, to the temporal forces of endless change' (Grosz, 2005: 5).

Braidotti (1994, 2002, 2006) argues for the relevance of Deleuze and Guattari's nomadology and provides an alternative for the theoretical elimination of the materiality of the body by cross-reading it with the late psychoanalytic work of Luce Irigaray. As a feminist late psychoanalytic approach, Luce Irigaray challenges biological or psychic determinism and she introduces the body and mind as a social construction and creation in process (Grosz, 1994):

> It is indeterminate and indeterminable outside its social constitution as a body of a particular type. This implies that the body which it presumes and helps to explain is an open-ended, pliable set of significations, capable of being re-written, reconstituted, in quite other terms than those which mark it, and consequently capable of re-inscribing the forms of sexed identity and psychical subjectivity at work today.
>
> (Grosz, 1994: 61)

Bodies and minds are interrelated, in reconstructing and creating the self and relationships with others. Irigaray (1999) brings the body and mind back into play as a mobile set of differences, and her unstable 'I's' and 'you's' avoid fixed subject positions and can be used to complement Deleuze and Guattari's becomings:

> You are moving. You never stay still. You never stay. You never 'are'. How can I say 'you', when you are always other? How can I speak to you? You remain in flux, never congealing or solidifying. What will make that current flow into words? It is multiple, devoid of causes, meanings, simple qualities. Yet it cannot be decomposed. These movements cannot be described as the passage from a beginning to an end. These rivers flow into no single, definitive sea. These streams are without fixed banks, this body without fixed boundaries. This unceasing mobility. This life.

As such, Irigaray challenges 'the old dream of symmetry' (Irigaray, 1985, quoted in Corker, 1999: 635) which requires a stable and oppositional category of 'normalcy' and binary thought in disability studies and allows us to deconstruct the idea of a foundational character of impairment.

Here the affirmativite nature of Deleuzian-inspired theory intrigues as well as explains, because a logic of desire as a force of production and a fundamental flow of energy is introduced: 'You *must* produce the unconscious ... The unconscious is a substance which must be created, placed, made to flow, it is a social and political space which must be won' (Deleuze, 1975–95: 81, italics in original). In *Two Regimes of Madness*, Deleuze (1975–95) challenges traditional psychoanalytic practices which 'reduce and destroy the assemblage of the unconscious and its desire as lack' (ibid.: 79). Classic psychoanalysis, for example, is contaminated by an ontology of lack and guilt (Braidotti, 2002: 97–101). Desire, instead, is productive: desire creates desire, through multiplicities of desires. As such, the impaired subject is no longer impaired for it has lost its engagement with lack as an ontological premise in the logic of desire as a force of production, an intense, productive and fundamental flow of energy (Gibson, 2006: 189). It is a subject ever moving and becoming (Goodley, 2007).

We argue for the need to fold these philosophical frameworks together and develop a new nomadic scenario for disability studies. We suggest a new figuration of layered, embodied subjectivity of nomadic existence; this is central to the concepts of *becoming* that lie at the heart of Irigaray's and Deleuze and Guattari's philosophical concerns (Braidotti, 2002). Nomadic subjectivity is about the simultaneity of complex and multi-layered identities, as 'here is a need to re-name the subject as a multiple, open-ended and interconnected identity that occupies a variety of possible subject positions, at different places (spatially) and at different times (temporally), across a multiplicity of constructions of self (relationality)' (Braidotti, 1994: 158). Nomadology is a political project in which a new subjectivity is created which blurs boundaries and consists in erasing and recomposing the former boundaries between self and others (Braidotti, 2002: 119). This notion of subjectivity brings the impaired subject back into play as a moving set of differences, that capitalises on the energies of a heterogeneous, discontinuous and unconscious nature, of a multiple and nomadic subject with bodily, rupturing roots that transforms and reconfigures the self in a politicised and anti-essentialist way (see Goodley and Roets, 2008).

Interestingly, to understand subjectivity as nomadic requires methodological creativity and innovation. In what follows, we illustrate some particular methodological implications for disability studies research.

Methodology

The aim in nomadic methodology is that of affirmative differences or creative repetitions, which means *retelling, reconfiguring, and revisiting a concept, phenomenon, event, or location from different angles* (Braidotti, 2010). This is not merely a quantitative multiplication of options, but rather a qualitative leap of perspective that can generate a hybrid mixture of interpretations of the phenomenon in question. This is a situated method of tracking the qualitative, ontological shifts from generative chaos or indeterminate forms to actualised and determined forms, while avoiding the pitfall of essentialism. This method respects the visible and hidden complexities and uncertainties of the real-life world in which we are living. Further, these qualitative shifts call for an intensive form of interdisciplinarity and boundary-crossings among a range of discourses.

This nomadic methodology as proposed by Braidotti (2010) seems very relevant for disability studies. In the light of recent research activities (see Roets, 2008), inspired by this nomadic methodology, we have suggested a research methodology designed to produce and create detailed cartographies of the present in the lives of disabled people and in their becoming in relation with multiple others (Roets et al., 2009). We explored Deleuze and Guattari's concept of *drawing cartographies of the present* as a potentially innovative methodological and analytical approach to disrupt and destabilise the monolithic master narrative typically told about people with 'intellectual disabilities'. In the main, Deleuze and Guattari stimulate us in a creative experiment with a nomadic and vitalist version of reality and human nature (Braidotti, 2002: 73). 'Reality' can be approached and constructed through the interplay of different territories of knowing (Gergen, 1994). Deleuze and Guattari's perception of the map is a useful metaphor:

> The map fosters connections between fields ... The map is open and connectable to constant modification. It can be torn, reversed, adapted to any kind of mounting, *reworked by an individual, group, or social formation*. It can be drawn on a wall, conceived of as a work of art, *constructed as political action*.
>
> (Deleuze and Guattari, 1980: 13–14, our italics)

Moreover, a map has multiple entry points and embodies many dimensions and meanings: 'Perhaps one of the most important characteristics of ... [a] map [is that it] *has multiple entryways* as opposed to the tracing, which always goes back 'to the same'. The map has to do with *performance*' (Deleuze and Guattari, 1980: 13–14, our italics). Inspired by Deleuze and Guattari, Braidotti (2002) proposes the drawing of cartographies of the present as a powerful analytic resource to display the multiple ways in which a culture constructs subject positions (Parker, 2003; Grosz, 2005). Creating cartographies of the present seizes the opportunity to depict and include a multiplicity of meanings, perspectives and realities. Haraway (1991) points out that there is no single standpoint since every subject is embodied and embedded within sense-making processes and has access to multiple versions of socially created realities. This renewal of conceptual creativity is a project that needs real-life people in positions of discursive subjectivity (Braidotti, 1994), and its methodological requirement is to map and engender diverse accounts of the subjectivity of research subjects. As an illustration, we introduce an experiment with nomadology while doing research in the context of the self-advocacy network in Flanders (Belgium) (see Roets, 2008). We argue that making cartographies of disability activism in micro-political contexts might enable disability research to question and challenge the essentialist interpretation of impairment, and in particular of 'intellectual disabilities'.

In the particular context of doing disability research, the drawing of cartographies of the present prioritises both the discovery, in a disabling society, of contextual counter-narratives, and the documentation of lost glimpses of the humanity of disabled people (see Roets, Goodley and Van Hove, 2007). During our research, we used *life story research* and *ethnography* as relevant and complementary research techniques to map the storied and enacted self-advocacy of people with 'intellectual disabilities'. *Life story research* is recognised as a useful technique to foreground 'hidden' and activist lives and the voices of self-advocates (Booth and Booth, 1996). Doing life story research can explicate cultural, pluralist meanings and create new ones in a dialogue at a deep level of signification where the motive is to philosophise across difference. Such research is inspired by 'awe, awe at the mystery and complexity of human existence' (Corker, 2001: 42). As documented life stories deserve to be contextualised in actions and events and require reflection, we argue that this can be achieved by ethnographic accounts and field notes (Denzin, 1996). *Ethnography* is defined by Mutua and Swadener (2004: 16) as a form of narrative in which multiple identities and nomadic subjectivities can be explored. Reflexive and dynamic accounts of researchers might be very useful when they include the storied and enacted versions of the self-advocacy of people with 'intellectual disabilities' (Goodley and Van Hove, 2005).

We illustrate such an analysis in what follows. The storied and enacted self-advocacy of Robert, the president of the self-advocacy network in Flanders, is at the heart of the analysis that is composed by Griet, who worked as an advisor for self-advocates while doing research. We attempt to unveil Robert's subjectivity and his activism through our detailed ethnographic field notes.

At the big meeting Robert shows up, right under my nose, beaming, and his enormous square glasses (which almost cover his entire face) crooked on his nose, his cheeks red and his hair wild and spiky. I distinctly remember that Robert was the first core member I met when I started giving support to the self-advocacy group ten years ago and I was amazed by the immense wisdom that lay in his words and that suited his impressive wrinkled forehead. He wishes me good morning in his customary nose-to-nose way. I've learned to appreciate his special way of greeting; out of sheer happiness, when he first squeezes me with his strong bear-like hug, his penetrating green eyes full of interest fathoming the bottom of my soul: *'How are you?'* I reply in a good mood: *'Hello Mr. President, fine, and how are you?'*

This time Robert looks at me with surprise, attentively eyeing my new pair of small round glasses. *'Hey, where did you get those?'* he wonders, burning with curiosity. *'Ehm ... just bought them at the optician's!'* I reply, *'do you like them?'* Robert nods. He takes off his huge old-fashioned pair of glasses, puts them on my nose and then tries on my new pair. *'How is that?'* he asks seriously. I tell him, I think he's really cool now. All of a sudden he seems 36 again, his real age, instead of 45 or older ... Later that day there is a coffee break. Robert pulls my sleeve and wants to tell his story: *'I've got a story, about my old glasses. I got them from my uncle. I couldn't choose. My uncle had fabricated them himself. I got those glasses when I left school. I was 18 then. They destroyed my glasses at school. Those guys. My glasses had to be cheap. My uncle gave me those old glasses. Those guys at school were pestering me. They were making fun out of me. They called me punk, because my hair always looked so wild. They said I looked like a clown in a circus. This is why I had to have a very short haircut. I still have those glasses now.'*

I feel touched by Robert's story. When the coffee break is over, I tell Robert that if he wants to buy a new pair of glasses, I wouldn't mind joining him on a trip to the opticians. *'Would you like to buy a new pair of glasses, Robert? Just like the ones I have?'* I ask. He looks at me indignantly. *'That won't be possible! My caregivers won't be able to manage.'* An awkward silence falls.

At the time, I did not understand why he said this. These events, and more significant ones hidden in the complexity of his life and uncovered later, raised uncomfortable doubts on my part. Did I miss the point? Though I could not see through his glasses, the snippets and glimpses of his life world amazed me and his social spaces of resistance confused me. As the ethnographic extracts of his life story further unravelled, it was as if Robert's limited sense of agency did not frustrate him. In the analysis, three subject positions were identified, as 'grey mouse', 'big dreamer' and 'Mr. President'. This was Robert's own way to frame his life in his booklet *The Journey of Our Lives* that was spread in the self-advocacy network (see Schoeters with support of De Winne and Roets, 2007)

Grey mouse

At work in the sheltered workshop, Robert – clothed in the dustcoat of the worker ant – presents as a passive figure. He is *the grey mouse*, afraid to upset his supervisors.

While collecting core members' life stories and photos for one of the self-advocacy group's projects, a fellow advisor and I had travelled to the other side of the country to take some photos of Robert at work, in the sheltered workshop where he works fulltime. Strangely enough, at the very moment we arrived there, he was waiting for us in his dustcoat: He said: '*WE can't allow photos to be taken of the production process at the work floor.*'

Later he reveals his insider perspective. *At home I am another man than at work in the sheltered workshop. We have supervisors and team leaders. They supervise us. The only thing they notice is the work. They don't see us as human beings. We have to keep quiet and shut up, just as little kids. If we talk, they scold us. We do have breaks. We're allowed to talk then. Forty minutes of break for the entire day. I cannot change that, for I have to shut up. And even if I say something, they don't listen. They think I'm stupid. But I'm having my own thoughts about it. I keep working in my thoughts. I talk to myself. That makes me wiser. They boss us around. We are trifled with. That's a horse of another colour! It's a big mess there. Chaos. I have never been able to show my colleagues my talent. I can think very well.*

So I remained puzzled. Whose voice did we actually hear? Robert's or the one of his work leaders in the sheltered workshop? Robert seemed to feel pressure to behave 'properly' in response to the expectations of the non-disabled supervisors at work. On a more symbolic level, he consciously marks this outlaw culture by wearing enormous square glasses that hide his subject position of being a self-advocate at other moments in his life. Robert shows that he is very well aware of the 'rules of the game' in this disablist community, and that he knows how to resist. Almost ironically, he performs this 'role' in line with the stereotypical and essentialist view of being a person having 'intellectual disabilities'. But what did Robert really (want to) gain from his involvement with self-advocacy and support? After all, he paid the price for this? Did I need to encourage him to address *his* habits, *his* life world/s? Did *I* have to empower *him*? Perhaps I needed to respect him as a 'split subject'? Perhaps he really did embody the generally accepted stereotype that people with 'intellectual disabilities' were passive? Perhaps as an outsider/researcher the fault was mine?

Big dreamer

Robert marks his residence in a predominantly oppressive disability culture by wearing his enormous square glasses. In his room, however, he takes off his glasses, and dreams of a smooth disability culture and of travelling to Ghent as Mr President. Hidden between the story-lines of his everyday life, Robert articulates and enacts his resistance, his activist knowledge, his desire to make sense of his life. This is mirrored in Robert's invention of his subculture at home, where he isolates himself in his 'kingdom' and becomes the big dreamer.

Every day I make a trip around the world. My home is my place to think things over. There is my world of thoughts, my kingdom. It is my study room. Thinking is dreaming. I am a big dreamer. I think about what I want to do. I want to realize projects. I want to lead my movement in Ghent. Open other people's eyes. Look at me. I don't live in a home, I live at home. I feel at home in my house. My safe nest. But I'm alone there. Most people don't really care about me. The caregivers have no time. They only have time for groups. They have only a small amount of time for each guest. Each of us four disabled men living there gets the same amount of time. They don't make time for us either. We cannot build a relationship. I sometimes want to get out and explore the world outside. Get away from my house for a while. Alone. Off to Ghent, where I am Mr. President! It makes me feel like a world traveller. And that's where I want a new pair of glasses!

Mr President

The vitality of Robert's sense of agency appears to arise from his self-empowerment and resilience. If people do not support or listen to him, he invents creative strategies of resistance in order to regain a sense of control over his life.

About a year later Robert and I are taking a stroll through the city, getting some fresh air after a busy self-advocacy meeting with the core members. We often do that. He always loves to talk things over after meetings with someone and dot the i's and cross the t's. In fact, I've already completely forgotten the story about his glasses. All of a sudden, Robert grabs my arm and drags me along, I don't know what to make of it. Pearl Vision Optician's. With mischievous twinkles in his eyes, he says: *I'm going to buy a new pair of glasses here! I've been thinking about it really hard at home.*

That day I join him at the optician's where he is helped by a female shop assistant who tests his eyesight and checks his glasses. Meanwhile Robert and I spend an hour in the shop trying on all kinds of frames. We split our sides with laughter. At last he finds a round frame that suits him perfectly and makes him look mature and special. When he pays the deposit, the shop assistant frowns: *'Do you realize that your current glasses are very bad for your eyes, sir?'* she asks, eyeing me meaningfully and almost accusingly. He shakes his head and tells her the story of his uncle making those glasses when he was 18.

However, Robert only wanted to wear his old pair of glasses at work and home. He only used his new, trendy pair of glasses in Ghent, when he was Mr President.

One week later Robert and André (the Vice-President of the group) come to Ghent. *'Ah, there you are, Mr. President and Mr. Vice-President!'* I greet them at the railway station. I am already looking forward to see him show off his new pair of glasses. I get almost in shock when he greets me in his customary way and I notice that he is still wearing those old glasses that almost fall off his nose. *'Where are your new....?'* I ask him stupefied. I haven't finished my sentence yet when, as proud as a peacock, he takes his new pair of glasses out of the pocket of his jacket while telling the story to his friend André: *'I've chosen and bought my new pair of glasses all by myself. That is completely different. Those new glasses make me different. I look different, don't I? I am different. I look like a wise professor now.'*

When I ask him why he isn't actually wearing his new pair of glasses, he again explains – a little irritated by my continuous questions – that he's still using his old glasses at work and at home. Patiently, he points out that he doesn't want to upset his caregivers who might be shocked to find out that he bought a new pair of glasses with the money from his savings account: *In Ghent I do care what other people say or think. I don't care about people that trouble me. But in Ghent other people are concerned about me. They open my world. That makes a world of difference. They help me to get going. If I don't understand, they tell me the whole story.*

The analysis shows that *being* an impaired subject is not an all-encompassing identity. In that light, Biesta (2011: 145) differentiates between identity and subjectivity. Achieving an identity refers to the belief that 'only a stable and positive identity [can be] obtained through identification with an existing socio-political order'. Subjectivity, in contrast, refers to 'a process of subjecti-fication – a process in and through which political subjectivity is established and comes into existence or, to be more precise, a process through which new ways of doing and being come into existence' (Biesta, 2001: 150). The analysis pressures us to discover and respect Robert's subjectivity, as the moments at which he interrupts the existing social order in a nomadic way have political significance. The cartographic analysis of his subject posi-tions disrupts and destabilises the monolithic master narrative typically told about people with 'intellectual disabilities', and about Robert as one of 'them'. We can, all too easily, bury Robert's territories of activist knowledge under the blanket of a modernist grand narrative about 'intellectual disabili-ties'. Nevertheless, manifest in his socially created realities as *grey mouse, big dreamer* and *Mr President* are the ways in which Robert radically deconstructs and reconfigures the essentialist master narrative of 'intellectual disabilities'. He clearly resists settling into socially coded modes of thought and behav-iour (Braidotti, 1994) and is at his most powerful when he creates a nomadic subculture when for example he travels to Ghent to become Mr President of the self-advocacy network. As a complex subject, Robert creatively invents and reconfigures a multiplicity of nomadic selves to travel, to cross borders between the 'us' and 'them', and to move pragmatically, sometimes quietly, in the webs of power, knowledge and social relations that constitute disabling society.

Concluding reflections

In conclusion, we argue for disability studies as a project of affirmative politics that celebrates embodied diversity, and we propose an epistemology in which the possibility of relational interconnection between self and others are both central, dynamic and productive (Haraway, 1991). This produces a significant shift from a notion of an oppositional and split disabled/nondisabled dichotomy to an open-ended, relational vision of interdependent subjects. Following Deleuze and Guattari, we want to radically challenge essentialist perspectives on impairment and support their proposal for a multi-layered, dynamic and nomadic subject, that is embodied but dynamic, corporeal and in-process, one and multiple, that has to be built up over and over again. Therefore we situate our work in critical disability studies (see Garland-Thomson, 2005; Goodley, 2010). In this emerging interdisciplinary field, dynamic interplays between impaired bodies and minds and various aspects of contemporary politics, culture and society are theorised in order to de-naturalise pathological and essentialist understandings of impairment (see Corker and Shakespeare, 2002; Snyder, Brueggemann and Garland-Thomson, 2002; Snyder and Mitchell, 2006; Hughes, 2007; Price, 2007). We have recently argued that critical disability studies should not ignore 'impairment' as a pre-social, biological essence and unchanging phenomenon, but should theorise it in order to open up unexplored territories of our collective subjectivity (Goodley and Roets, 2008). From this perspective, we need more (ad)ventures in disability studies in which impaired bodies-and-minds are theorised as both complex and vitalist.

References

Baroff, G. (2000). 'Eugenics, "Baby Doe", and Peter Singer: Toward a More "Perfect" Society'. *Mental Retardation*, 38 (1), 73–7.
Biesta, G. (2011). 'The Ignorant Citizen: Mouffe, Ranciére, and the Subject of Democratic Education'. *Studies in Philosophy and Education*, 30 (2), 141–53.
Booth, T. and Booth, W. (1996). 'Sounds of Silence: Narrative Research with Inarticulate Subjects'. *Disability & Society*, 11 (1), 55–69.
Braidotti, R. (1994). *Nomadic Subjects*. New York: Columbia University Press.
Braidotti, R. (2002). *Metamorphoses. Towards a Materialist Theory of Becoming*. Cambridge: Polity Press.
Braidotti, R. (2006). *Transpositions: On Nomadic Ethics*. Cambridge: Polity Press.
Braidotti, R. (2010). 'Elemental Complexity and Relational Vitality: The Relevance of Nomadic Thought for Contemporary Science'. In P. Gaffney (ed.), *The Force of the Virtual*. Minneapolis and London: University of Minnesota Press.

Corker, M. (1999). 'Differences, Conflations and Foundations: The Limits of "Accurate" Theoretical Representation of Disabled People's Experiences'. *Disability & Society*, 14 (5): 627–42.

Corker, M. (2001). 'Sensing Disability'. *Hypatia*, 16 (4): 34–52.

Corker, M. and Shakespeare, T. (2002). *Disability/Postmodernity: Embodying Disability Theory*. London/New York: Continuum.

Deleuze, G. (1968). *Difference and Repetition*. London: Continuum.

Deleuze, G. (1975–95). *Two Regimes of Madness: Texts and Interviews*. New York: Smiotext(e).

Deleuze, G. and Guattari, F. (1980). *A Thousand Plateaus: Capitalism and Schizophrenia*. London: Continuum.

Denzin, N. K. (1996). *Interpretive Ethnography: Ethnographic Practices for the 21st Century*. London: Sage Publications.

Foucault, M. (1961). *Madness and Civilization: A History of Insanity in the Age of Reason*. London: Tavistock.

Foucault, M. (1978). *The History of Sexuality*. New York: Vintage Books.

Garland-Thomson, R. (2005). 'Feminist Disability Studies'. *Signs: Journal of Women in Culture and Society*, 30 (2), 1557–87.

Gergen, K. J. (1994). *Realities and Relationships: Soundings in Social Construction*. Boston: Harvard University Press.

Gibson, B. E. (2006). 'Disability, Connectivity and Transgressing the Autonomous Body'. *Journal of Medical Humanities*, 27, 187–96.

Goodley, D. (2007). 'Towards Socially Just Pedagogies: Deleuzoguattarian Critical Disability Studies'. *International Journal of Inclusive Education*, 11 (3), 317–34.

Goodley, D. (2010). *Disability Studies: An Interdisciplinary Introduction*. London: Sage Publications.

Goodley, D., Lawthom, R., Clough, P. and Moore, M. (2004). *Researching Life Stories: Method, Theory and Analyses in a Biographical Age*. London/New York: RoutledgeFalmer.

Goodley, D. and Roets, G. (2008). 'The (Be)comings and Goings of Developmental Disabilities: The Cultural Politics of "Impairment"'. *Discourse: Studies in the Cultural Politics of Education*, 29 (2), 241–57.

Goodley, D. and Van Hove, G. (2005). *Another Disability Studies Reader? People with Learning Difficulties and a Disabling World*. Leuven/Apeldoorn: Garant.

Grosz, E. (1994). *Volatile Bodies: Toward a Corporeal Feminism*. London: Routledge.

Grosz, E. (2005). *Time Travels: Feminism, Nature Power*. London: Duke University Press.

Haraway, D. (1991). *Simians, Cyborgs and Women: The Reinvention of Nature*. London: Free Association Books.

Hughes, B. (1999). 'The Constitution of Impairment: Modernity and the Aesthetic of Oppression'. *Disability & Society*, 14 (2), 155–72.

Hughes, B. (2007). 'Disability Activism: Social Model Stalwarts and Biological Citizens'. Presentation at the 8th European Sociological Association Conference 'Conflict, Citizenship and Civil Society', 3–6 September 2007.

Hughes, B. and Paterson, K. (1997). 'The Social Model of Disability and the Disappearing Body: Towards a Sociology of Impairment'. *Disability & Society*, 12 (3), 325–40.

Irigaray, L. (1999). 'When Our Lips Speak Together'. In J. Price and M. Shildrick (eds), *Feminist Theory and The Body: A Reader*. New York: Routledge.

Kerr, A. and Shakespeare, T. (2002). *Genetic Politics – from Eugenics to Genome*. Cheltenham: New Clarion Press.

Lather, P. (1991). *Getting Smart: Feminist Research and Pedagogy with/in the Postmodern*. New York: Routledge.

Marks, D. (1999). *Disability: Controversial Debates & Psychosocial Perspectives*. London: Routledge.

May, D. and Simpson, M. K. (2003). 'The Parent Trap: Marriage, Parenthood and Adulthood for People with Intellectual Disabilities'. *Critical Social Policy*, 23 (1), 25–43.

McClimens, A. (2003). 'The Organization of Difference: People with Intellectual Disabilities and the Social Model of Disability'. *Mental Retardation*, 41 (1), 35–46.

Mutua, K. and Swadener, B. B. (2004). *Decolonizing Research in Cross-Cultural Contexts: Critical Personal Narratives*. New York: State University of New York Press.

Oliver, M. (1990). *The Politics of Disablement*. Basingstoke: Palgrave Macmillan.

Oliver, M. (1996). 'A Sociology of Disability or a Disablist Sociology?' In L. Barton (ed.), *Disability & Society: Emerging Issues and Insights*. Essex: Longman.

Park, D. C. and Radford, J. P. (1998). 'From the Case Files: Reconstructing a History of Unvoluntary Sterilization'. *Disability & Society*, 13 (3), 317–42.

Parker, I. (2003). 'Discursive Resources in the Discourse Unit'. *Discourse Analysis Online*, 1 (1).

Price, J. E. (2007). 'Engaging Disability'. *Feminist Theory*, 8 (1), 77–89.

Roets, G. (2008). *Connecting Activism with Academia: A Postmodernist Feminist Perspective in Disability Studies*. Orthopedagogische reeks, Nr. 30.

Roets, G. (2009). 'Unravelling Mr. President's Nomadic Life: Travelling to Interdisciplinary Frontiers of Knowledge in Disability Studies'. *Disability & Society*, 24 (6), 689–701.

Roets, G., Adams, M. and Van Hove, G. (2006). 'Challenging the Monologue about Silent Sterilization: Implications for Self-Advocacy'. *British Journal of Learning Disabilities* (BJLD) Special edition on The History of Self-Advocacy for People with Learning Difficulties: International Comparisons, 34 (3), 167–74.

Roets, G., Goodley, D. and Van Hove, G. (2007). 'Narrative in a Nutshell: Sharing Hopes, Fears and Dreams with Self-Advocates'. *Intellectual and Developmental Disabilities (previously Mental Retardation)*, 45 (5), 323–34.

Roets, G., Roose, R., Claes, L., Verstraeten, M. and Vandekinderen, C. (2009). 'The Pointer Sisters: Creating Cartographies of the Present'. *Journal of Contemporary Ethnography*, 38 (6), 734–53.

Schoeters, L, with support of De Winne, C. and Roets, G. (2007). *The Journey of Our Lives*. Ghent: ONT/Vlaams Nationaal Agentschap Socrates, Grundtvig.

Shakespeare, T. (2006). *Disability Rights and Wrongs*. London/New York: Routledge.

Smith, P. (1999). 'Drawing New Maps: A Radical Cartography of Developmental Disabilities'. *Review of Educational Research*, 69 (2), 117–44.

Snyder, S. L., Brueggemann, B. J. and Garland-Thomson, R. (2002). *Disability Studies: Enabling the Humanities*. New York: The Modern Language Association of America.

Snyder, S. L. and Mitchell, D. T. (2001). 'Re-Engaging the Body: Disability Studies and the Resistance to Embodiment'. *Public Culture*, 13 (3), 367–89.

Snyder, S. L. and Mitchell, D. T. (2006). *Cultural Locations of Disability*. Chicago/London: University of Chicago Press.

Taylor, S. J. (1996). 'Disability Studies and Mental Retardation'. *Disability Studies Quarterly*, 16 (3), 4–13.

Tremain, S. (2002). 'On the Subject of Impairment'. In M. Corker and T. Shakespeare (eds), *Disability/Postmodernity: Embodying Disability Theory*. London/New York: Continuum.

Tremain, S. (2005). 'Foucault, Governmentality, and Critical Disability Theory: An Introduction'. In S. Tremain (ed.), *Foucault and the Government of Disability*. Michigan: University of Michigan Press.

UPIAS (1976). *Fundamental Principles of Disability*. London: Union of the Physically Impaired Against Segregation.

11
Jacques Lacan + Paul Hunt = Psychoanalytic Disability Studies

Dan Goodley

Introduction

This chapter explores the potential of drawing on psychoanalytic ideas to analyse disabling culture, to make sense of the influence of culture on subjectivities and to unleash possibilities for individual and collective resistance on the part of non/disabled people. The chapter introduces psychoanalysis as an enlightenment project that has informed cultural understandings of the psyche and subjectivity. To analyse psychoanalytic culture we will explore the approach of Lacanian psychoanalysis with a view to understanding the imaginary and symbolic elements of culture. Our intentions will become more specific as we analyse the precarious cultural foundations of ableist society and consider the ways in which disabled people come to occupy a prominent position of disavowal through which the processes of ableism can seep into everyday subjectivities. Simultaneously, possibilities for resistance will be identified, to challenge the cultural violence of ableism. We will then consider the chapter by the renowned British disability activist Paul Hunt, 'A Critical Condition', in the acclaimed book that he edited entitled *Stigma* (1966), and suggest that while this text has been held up as an exemplary critique of the sociopolitical conditions of disablism, it also bears the marks of a piece of critical psychoanalytic analysis, which identifies lack and possibility.

Psychoanalytic culture

Psychoanalysis is engaged with subjectivity: who we are, where we came from and where we might go. Psychoanalysis therefore has much to say about ontology. For Scott Lash (2001: 107), ontology is *the* focal point of contemporary society;

> We are obsessed with ... experiencing things, through being in the life-world with them, can open up knowledge of things-in-themselves. To

know things-in-themselves is to know them not epistemologically, but in their ontological structures.

We can trace this contemporaneous obsession back to historical projects of the self. Michel Foucault (1988) sketched out how the self became cherished by two historical traditions (1) Greco-Roman philosophy in the first and second centuries AD and (2) Christian spirituality and monastic principles (both of the Roman Empire). Both these historical epochs promoted particular practices of the self, each associated with renunciating one's sins: *askesis* (mastery of oneself), *melete* (imaging the articulation of possible events) and *gymnasia* (training oneself and rituals of purification and self-development). All of these are to found today, where enactment of them is no longer part of a renunciation of the self but the *constitution of the self* (Foucault, 1988: 49). The origin of the self has been documented in many histories of social science and philosophical expositions of the renaissance, imperialism, modernity, capitalism and patriarchy (Fox-Keller, 1962). Davis (1995, 2002) comments that a Cartesian dualism between mind and body flowed from the neoclassical seventeenth century philosophical works of Rene Descartes. Human subjectivity was deemed to be fundamentally different from the objective world of matter and bodies. The mind was an individual human freedom to be celebrated in contrast to the unruly body and the wild natural world. Such philosophical manifestos of the self accompanied changes in politics and religiosity. Where once God and monarchy were omnipotent, modern societies upheld civilisation and the underlying rationality of the sovereign citizen:

> [M]odernism is typically traced to the period in which culture moved from the so-called Dark Ages of medievalism (characterised by an unquestioning adherence to totalitarian Royal or religious decree) to the Enlightenment (promising the bounded and sacred sanctuary of the mind, autonomous capacities and the beginnings of systematic human science).
>
> (Gergen, 2001: 803–4)

Psychoanalysis can be viewed as an enlightenment project that played a very influential role in modern practices associated with constituting the self or psyche. The concepts of psychoanalysis – such as the unconscious, the ego, repression, Oedipus complex, projection, denial – are a common part of everyday parlance. And the practices of psychoanalysis – confession, dreamwork, sublimation, therapy and the couch – are to be found in cultural practices across the globe. This cultural and psychical 'trickle down' effect of psychoanalysis has led Parker (1997) to argue that we now live in a psychoanalytic culture: where these ideas and practices have seeped into elements of everyday life. Psychoanalysis constitutes discourses through which societal members are expected to see themselves and others. At its most barbaric psychoanalytic assumptions have promulgated a 'eugenics of mind' (Davis, 1995: 39) that seeks cleanliness of thought, conscious awareness (ego) over unconscious uncertainty (id) patrolled by an internalised sense of morality (superego). At its least damaging, psychoanalytic confession – for Foucault a continuation of catholic confession (Parker, 1997) – undergirds the most popular TV chat shows and reality programmes from Big Brother to Oprah. And it is in the making of these psychoanalytic discourses that we can understand how our selves – and those of others – are made. As Parker (1997: 8) has argued, psychoanalysis provides a reflection, compression and reduction of societal phenomena to the level of the individual that reveals something of the social, cultural and political nature of those phenomena. In this sense we remain mindful of Mitchell's (1974) feminist argument that psychoanalysis provides a description, not a prescription of society and all its inequities. As I have argued elsewhere (Goodley, 2011b), a turn to the psyche – and psychoanalysis's take upon it – is timely. Over the last few years there have been a number of interventions within disability studies that have started to take seriously the psyche and its place in a politicised view of disability. The psyche can be understood as a cultural artefact of contemporary society that individualises social problems. Individual, medical, bio-psychological, traditional, charity and moral models of disability locate social problems in the heads and bodies – the psyches – of (disabled) people. This leads to the commonly held view that disabling society is not the problem: the disabled individual is. In contrast, the psyche can be acknowledged as a complex tightened knot of the person and the social word, the self and other people, the individual and society. At the heart of this is the internalised experience of disablism: oppression is felt both psychically, subjectively and emotionally but is always socially, cultural, politically and economically produced. Questions are raised, then, not simply about 'the disabled psyche' but, more importantly, about 'the non-disabled psyche'. As I have argued in Goodley (2011a: 2) our interests should lie not with the psyches of disabled people but with the ways in which 'non-disabled people and disablist culture symbolise, characterise, construct, gaze at, project, split off, react, repress and direct images of impairment and disability in ways that subjugate and, at times, terrorise disabled people' while upholding the precarious autonomy of non-disabled people.

Lacanian psychoanalysis

We will now turn to one psychoanalytic school of thinking, that developed by Jacques Lacan. His theories have been used previously in disability studies, for example, in Frank's (1994) dealings with medical sociology, Davis's (1995) considerations of normalcy, Michalko's (2002) claims about 'disability-as-difference', Wilton's (2003) comparison of Lacan and Freud, Shildrick's (2004, 2007a, 2007b) critical account in relation to the body and Erevelles's (2005) reflections on education. A more developed account of Lacanian theory is provided by Goodley (2011a, see chapter 8). For the purposes of this chapter I will provide a brief synopsis of Lacanian ideas.

If, as Parker (n.d.) argues, one of the tasks of psychoanalysis is to map how bodies and bits of bodies are signified and positioned in relation to one another, then Lacanian psychoanalysis provides a persuasive narrative. The story starts with a familiar unit of analysis for psychoanalytic theory: the family, which Fanon (1993: 149) defines as the 'nation's workshop in which one is trained'. The family provides the context for the development of the child and their encounters with others.

For the first six months of life, the child is at one with her primary caregiver which is more often than not the mother. There is no sense of separation of the child's world from that of others. The child is a psychic scrambled egg: anarchically and chaotically organised (Grosz, 1999: 268). She is a mass of turbulent movements, of sprawling limbs or desiring entity, gazing and being gazed at, touching and being touched. What she sees is only hers and what she wants is what she desires. This is a time filled with fulfilling desires, a time of pure jouissance. This is the 'real' phase. Between six and 18 months the child starts the process of seeing herself as a separate entity, a self that is distinct from others around her. The experience that kicks off this distinction of self from other is found in the reflection of a mirror. The child sees her self in the mirror and becomes captivated by it. As well as seeing herself she notices significant distinct others (often the mother). The child recognises an image of herself as fixed, frozen, whole and unitary. This is an image of her body that contrasts markedly with the body she is living with in the real (which is an uncoordinated 'body in pieces'). The child therefore commits a misrecognition: she is transfixed by an image that is no more than a fantasy of wholeness. This is a necessary mistake: the reflection allows the child to say 'that is me' (Rose, 1986). This existential wholeness is constituted in relationships with others (Frank, 2000: 153); the key other being recognised as equally whole and separate is the mother, who admires the child's reflection in the mirror – valuing (nurturing) and desiring (loving) the child. The child gives up on the turbulence of the real phase by identifying with their own image (the whole 'me' in the mirror) and the image of the other (the mother): each supplying the child with an imaginary sense of mastery (Lacan, 1977). The 'imaginary' phase will have long-standing impacts on the child.

First, the child will never match up to the whole, independent, masterful image of themselves depicted in the imaginary. The real dependent, fragmented body of the real will remain within them forever (Davis, 1995: 142). They find their uncoordinated bodies lacking in relation to the frozen 'coordinated' image in the mirror. Second, the child will always lack that initial desire of the mother and therefore find the mother (and many others) lacking. Through this lack we are launched on a lifetime journey in which we attempt to seek out the fantasised original object (the mother) who desired us as we desired her. We desire an idealised other to see us as whole and total in their eyes. We become locked into a double quest: to find an image of ourselves as autonomous (like the original image in the mirror) and an other who desires us (in the ways our primary other – the mother – did). 'I look for admiration in the eyes of the other – the other corroborates in me my search for self-validation' (Fanon, 1993: 218).

The third phase of Lacanian psychoanalysis sees the child enter culture. The 'symbolic' appears between a year and a half and four years of life (Parker, 1997: 215). The child is thrown into the disorientating world of words where they are expected to speak of themselves and others as human subjects. The symbolic includes spoken, written and visual discourses. Where the imaginary permitted a distinction of one's self from an other, the symbolic phase allows the child to speak of this separation – of 'I', 'you' and 'them' – in an order outside the child. This phase is where the child begins the process of enculturation. But, just as the imaginary phase gave the child ontological insecurity (in terms of the failure to match up to the original image/fantasy of the autonomous self and the split away from the desire of and by the original m/other), these insecurities are multiplied exponentially in the symbolic: because of the sheer size and expanse of language.

Lacanian psychoanalysis has been captured by the following equation: 'Freud + Saussure = Lacan' (Parker, 1997). Hence, while there is a distinctly Freudian feel to the account of the child's encounters with the real (unconsciously responding to the pleasure principles of the oedipal mother–child dyad) and the imaginary (the development of a conscious ego, a sense of self as independent and an adherence to the reality principle), in the symbolic Lacan inserts a linguistic structuralist layer of thinking into his account of the development of subjectivity. At the heart of this analysis is the Saussurian semiotic concept of the sign. As the basic unit of language the sign is made up of a signifier (word or symbol) and signified (meaning). The signified (meaning) of a sign is understood 'only because of the relationship between two or more signifiers (words or symbols)' (Eagleton, 1983: 127). Hence, we could say that the sign 'disabled' gathers meaning through its contrasting meaning with the sign 'abled'. Signifiers, such as these, 🛉 ♿, are assigned opposing poles. One signifier 'cannot exist without implying the existence of the other' (Lindeman, 1997: 74). In complex cultures, however, signifiers are constantly shifting, in moving chains. Signifiers also have long histories to them. Many words associated with disability have damaged origins. The world vulnerable derives from the latin 'vulnus' or 'wound' (Turner, 2008: 13). The signifiers 'handicap', 'educational subnormal', 'foetal-alcohol syndrome', 'developmental delay' all come to occupy the place of 'disability' but are constantly being dislodged by one another and new signifiers. Discourse is never stable because signifiers are constantly shifting. Moreover, following Eagelton (1983: 127–9), meaning is never *present* in a signifier because the meaning (signified) of a signifier is a matter of what it is *not* ('disabled' is not 'abled') and each signifier is underscored by a host of other signifiers ('disabled' has to fend off 'handicap', 'educational subnormal', 'foetal-alcohol syndrome', 'developmental delay'). The onto-logical consequence for a child's entrance into language is insecurity. This is particularly so when a sign such as 'I' – seemingly a simple corresponding sign to who we are – is laden with uncertainty because there are potentially a million 'I's to be.

Hence, the 'I', initially alienated through the misrecognition of the fan-tasy of 'whole self' in the mirror phase, is now further alienated from itself, and from others, through its location in the symbolic ordering of subjects (Lacan, 1977). When we speak of 'I' (or use any signifier for that matter), we drown in a symbolic sea of signifiers that float around and through us, leav-ing us empty and incomplete. Like the mirror phase we remain phenomeno-logically severed from the 'I' of whom we now speak. In order to cope with this alienation, the child deals with it like any other threatening concept: it is repressed into the unconscious. Following Parker (1997: 167), while language provides us with the means to articulate who we are and what we desire, it simultaneously 'turns experience into something symbolically mediated and broken from that which it is supposed to be expressed, that which vanishes into the unconscious as a fantasy space' (Parker, 1997: 167). The unconscious is therefore made up of a network of signifiers – the under-side of language – which the child must repress in order to speak (ibid.). In this way the 'out there' of the symbolic (the speaking world, culture and communication) is alienating but so too is the 'in there' of the unconscious (infinite signifiers of the symbolic influencing what we say, how we desire and how we understand ourselves and others). The unconscious is therefore the discourse of the other: because language belongs to the population of others of the symbolic. As the child commences their journey into different positions in language, they speak of culture but in ways that lose themselves in the authorities of that culture. Indeed, we are alienated by the endless possibilities of speaking of ourselves and therefore find our place in the symbolic lacking.

Nevertheless, one's place within language and culture is not without sta-tus or position. Clearly, while language may alienate anyone, some cultural groups are permitted more access to the use of language. The symbolic gives rise to the emergence of moral authority as expressed in the 'third term' of the father. While the real and imaginary bore witness to the relationship between child and mother, the symbolic allows entrance of the law of the father or the 'phallus'. The child's integrity and control (la puissance) is encouraged through the authority of the phallus which demands severance of the mother–child dyad (the original jouissance), prohibits the unruly real (the desiring body 'outside' of culture) and promotes adherence to the symbolic order. The phallus denotes codes of behaviour and social laws, originally played out in the cultural microcosm of the family, that reflect wider demands of patriarchal societies. Moral status is conferred through entrance into the symbolic, in similar ways to the emergence of the super-ego in Freudian theory, in which psychical inventions of the phallus attempt to deny the threat posed to the subject by the jouissance of the other (Feher-Gurewich, 2001). Crucial to this denial of the original jouissance is an insistence on an acceptance of the authority – or la puissance – of the phallus. The phallus imbues the symbolic with certainty, dictating who can use language and who cannot (Rose, 1986).

A key marker of the phallus on the symbolic is the cultural separation of women and men in terms of what can be said and by whom. Following Tremain (2000: 293), the sexual division of labour and the psychological construction of desire are the foundations of a system of the production of human beings which vests men with rights in women that they do not have in themselves. In patriarchal – or phallocentric cultures and societies – women are either excluded by the symbolic or defined as exclusion (Rose, 1986). Women do not have power to use the symbolic but men do. The phallus separates men and women: 'there is no pre-discursive reality, no place prior to the law ... there is no feminine outside language' (Rose, 1989: 64). Following Goodley (2011a: 128–9), resolving the demands of the phallus

> involves an accent to the symbolic for boys pursuing masculinity (with a lifelong aim to gain the power of immersion within the symbolic, to find the phallus, to speak of 'I') and submission to the symbolic for girls embracing femininity (to be simply something to be desired by men). But for *all*, the phallus extends beyond sex/gender, acting as a master signifier – the One – that demands unconscious autonomy and slavery to the symbolic (Miller, 2008). Following Eagleton (1983), the phallocentric binary opposition of man/woman is reminiscent of patriarchal ideology, which requires the drawing of rigid boundaries, to maintain the dominant and exclude the alternative. The phallus lays the foundations for other ideologies including the heteronormative, occidental, capitalist and the able.

What should have come through in this brief exposition of Lacanian psychoanalysis are troubled notions of independence, autonomy and mastery that are envisioned in the real, imaginary and symbolic aspects of culture. I say troubled, because the cultural actor that is depicted in the writings of Lacanian analysts, is one that is struggling with and inevitably failing to match up to the ideals often associated with abliest culture. This identification of the myth of the masterful subject feeds into Campbell's (2008a,

2008b, 2009) recent work on ableism (see also Chapter 13 of this book). She argues that the task of disability theorists is to move attention away from disabled people onto the production, operation and maintenance of ableist-normativity (2008a: 1). Ableist processes create a corporeal standard which presumes able-bodiedness (not unlike the Lacanian subject imbued with la puissance of the imaginary) and purifies the ableist ideal (phallocentrically erected in the symbolic):

> Internalised ableism means that to emulate the norm, the disabled individual is required to embrace, indeed to assume, an 'identity' other than one's own. I am not implying that people have only one true or real essence. Indeed, identity formation is in a constant state of fluidity, multiplicity and (re) formation [but] ... the desire to emulate the Other (the norm) establishes and maintains a wide gap between those who are loathed and that which is desired.
>
> (Campbell, 2009: 21)

Ableist society upholds the *imaginary* autonomous, self-sufficient, whole-functioning citizen; promotes signifiers of ableist achievement, mastery and competence in *symbolic* culture; and crucially, denounces those who fail to match such ableist images and signs as *really* uncivilised, dis-abled, fragmented, dis-coordinated shells of humanity. Disabled people are their bodies and their minds. They are their impairments: broken bodies/minds, fragmented, incapable, dependent. Ableist cultures are staffed by individuals whose jobs are to correct the monstrous *real*ities of disabled people.

It is precisely because the phallocentric mastery of ableism is so empty and so lacking for everyone that attention is, instead, drawn from the 'able soul' (which we know we lack) to the 'disabled soul' (who reminds us all of the real fragmented within us, which we mourn). Disabled people become disavowed by ableist society. That is to say they are stared at and stared through, loved and hated, prompt fear and fascination: disavowed in ways that shift attention from the myth of one's own able corporeality (the lacking real body that fails to match the image in the mirror and the I of the symbolic) to the *real*ities of disabilities of others. For Michalko (2002) and Wilton (2003) here is the big lie of ableist society: *there* is where lack lies (in the disabled person) not here in ableist society (which is empty with promises of autonomy). The consequences for disabled people are huge, ranging from mundane, unhelpful encounters through to larger acts of cultural violence:

Vignettes of disavowal
When people comment on my impaired experience I am shocked, amused and angered all at once.

(Hewitt, 2004: 13)

You get that all the time people stare, people comment, or people ...
I would rather people said to me, 'What's wrong?' rather than just stare.
Then you can hear them as soon as you walk past, [whisper sounds].
                    (Jemma, mother of a disabled child reported
                                    in McLaughlin et al., 2008)

Don't worry about paying love, we don't charge for retards.
                    (comment from a fairground assistant to the mother
            of a disabled child, from Goodley and Runswick Cole, 2010)

Kennedy (1996: 123) reports of a paediatrician who on examining a child
with 'hypnotonic spastic quadriplegia' [*sic*] found vaginal injuries, anal
scars and a sexually transmitted disease. He reported, 'These symptoms
could be due to an obscure syndrome'.

How do you explain a missing hand to a child? Parents have complained
that a children's TV presenter with one hand is prompting awkward questions from young children ... a minority of parents expressed concern that
Ms Burnell's appearance was 'scaring' children. One father said he feared
it would give his daughter nightmares and a mother said her two-year-old
girl could not watch because she thought the presenter had been hurt.

Ms Burnell, 29, says she doesn't take this personally but these kind of
comments highlight the prejudice that disabled people face.
'Children come up to me in the street every day and say "What's that?"
I wouldn't say they're frightened but certainly they're inquisitive.'
'I would always take the time to explain to a child. All they want is an
explanation. They want to know "What's that?" and "What's happened?"
and "Why are you different?" And then they will move on.'
She hopes that her presence can show young children what they can
achieve on merit. But what parents say is up to them.
'I'd never comment on anyone's parenting or the time for them to have
a discussion with their child about disabilities.'
                            http://news.bbc.co.uk/1/hi/magazine/7906507.stm

Possibilities for resistance to cultural violence and mundane disablism lie in
the failings of us all in our relationships with the symbolic. For Wilton (2003)
we are *all* symbolically castrated in and through language: the phallus reminds
us that we are nothing (that we will never be part of language). We can only
hope to recognise that the phallus is unobtainable, to recognise that the phallus was smaller than we have been taught and that neither women nor men
can have it (Parker, n.d.). While the phallus is a master signifier, it is empty.
Following Rudberg (1997) and Parker (n.d.), the signified (for example, 'the
body', 'truth', 'autonomy') is always absent because the symbolic is constituted

by an infinite number of empty signifiers. They are empty because they never settle, never attach to a signified and therefore never become signs. The phallus is small because it is only a signifier. The task then is to use this emptiness as an opportunity to re-site or reassign oneself in the symbolic. While we may never escape the symbolic, we need to re/work it in ways that are authentic and more inclusive for us. For disabled people, this requires challenging the emptiness of the signifiers dis/abled in order to work up a disability culture. One of the first steps of this resistant process is articulated by Davis (1995: 157):

> [O]nly when disability is made visible as a compulsory term in a hegemonic process, only when the binary is exposed and the continuum acknowledged ... only then will normalcy cease being a term of enforcement in a somatic judicial system.

For Butler (1993) psychoanalysis allows one to rearticulate symbolic legitimacy: to seek dis-identification with the regulated, normed and secured schemas of normative society to revise the symbolic. This reworking of the symbolic is captured well in the piece by the famous British disability activist Paul Hunt to which I will now turn.

Psychoanalytic disability politics: The case of Paul Hunt's (1966) 'A Critical Condition'[1]

> Whether it is the 'species typical body' (in science), the 'normative citizen' (in political theory), the 'reasonable man' (in law), all these signifiers point to a fabrication that reaches into the very soul that sweeps us into life.
>
> (Campbell, 2009: 7)

Paul Hunt was an acclaimed British disability activist who was instrumental in the setting up of UPIAS (The Union of the Physically Impaired Against Segregation). According to the Manchester Coalition of Disabled People, UPIAS was founded in 1972.

> It was started by Paul Hunt when he wrote a letter to the Guardian[2] inviting disabled people to join with him to form a group to tackle disability. Paul formed his ideas whilst living in an institution. He and other residents had been involved in a long and bitter struggle with the authorities over the right of disabled people to have control over their lives. The group of people who responded to Paul's invitation, became UPIAS. Now what was unusual at this time, was that they decided to take some time, about 18 months, to discuss and consider disability before rushing into action, which was the more usual tendency. And so it was that UPIAS became the first disability liberation group in the UK, and one of the first in the world, and certainly the most advanced in the world.
>
> (GMCDP, n.d.)

Hunt's contribution to British disability politics has been immeasurable. One text in particular has been cited and reprinted in a number of texts, Hunt's (1966) 'A Critical Condition' (Shakespeare, 1998; Barnes et al., 1999; Finkelstein, 2004). This work has been celebrated as a foundational text of British social model materialist thinking (Barnes, 2007) and a key text behind Hunt's thinking (with Vic Finkelstein) about the social relational conditions of disability (Thomas, 2004). This particular piece was, for many of us in disability studies, a key original introductory text to what we now know as disability studies. Hunt's (1966) account is beautifully nuanced and scholarly in its deliberations, in which he tackles five interrelated aspects of the position of disabled people as *'unfortunate, useless, different, oppressed and sick'* (Hunt, 1966: 157, italics in the original). This is a political account but it is also a cultural and subjective one. What we can see in this piece, I would suggest, is the relevance and resonance of Lacanian ideas in exposing the problematics – and contradictions – of ableism and the promise of a cultural symbolic that is rearticulated by disabled people. Hunt describes a common view held by non-disabled people:

> The 'unfortunate person' is assumed to have wonderful and exceptional courage (although underneath this overt canonisation there is usually a degree of irritation and hostility which comes to light as moments of stress).
>
> (Hunt, 1966: 148)

This observation captures the components of *disavowal*: fascination with the exceptional 'otherness' of disabled people, in the face of adversity, alongside a simmering hostility. His account, too, offers an insight into the possibilities and pitfalls of being the Other – outside the *symbolic*:

> Our freedom from the competitive trappings that accompany work in our society may give us the opportunity to demonstrate its essential elements ... we can act as a symbol for the pre-eminent claims of non-utilitarian values ... And we of course afford people the chance to be generous in support of the needy, thus enabling them to give practical expression to their desire to go beyond the acquisitive instinct.
>
> (Hunt, 1966: 149–50)

To be 'outside' the dominant symbolic order – one associated with the good life of health, purity and certainty (Michalko, 2002) – provides opportunities for deconstructing these very values; 'we do not have to prove anything' (Hunt, 1966: 149). Hunt hints not only at the doubly empty nature of the symbolic for disabled people but also suggests that this puts disabled people in a radically subversive position. As Erevelles (2005: 426) has argued, disabled people may well be in the driving seat then when it comes to getting in touch with multiple repressed sites located in the unconscious that might regenerate multi-cultural, multi-classed and multi-gendered selves. Hunt reminds us of powerlessness that is deeply ingrained in the symbolic:

> An impaired and deformed body is a 'difference' that hits everyone hard at first. Inevitably it produces an instinctive revulsion, has a disturbing effect ... The disabled person's 'strangeness' can manifest and symbolize all differences between human beings ... for the able-bodied, normal world we are representatives of many of the things they most fear – tragedy, loss, dark and the unknown. Involuntarily, we walk – or more often sit – in the valley of the shadow of death ... a deformed and paralysed body attacks everyone's sense of well-being and invincibility.
>
> (Hunt, 1966:151–6)

This account by Hunt resonates hugely with the Lacanian analysis offered by Davis (1995: 139):

> The disabled body is a direct imago of the repressed fragmented body [of the real phase]. The disabled body causes a kind of hallucination of the mirror phase gone wrong. The subject [the non-disabled viewer or disabling culture more generally] looks at the disabled body and has a moment of cognitive dissonance, or should we say a moment of cognitive resonance with the earlier stage of fragmentation. Rather than seeing the whole body in the mirror, the subject sees the repressed fragmented body; rather than seeing the object of desire [the frozen, 'autonomous' image], as controlled by the Other [the mother], the subject sees the true self of the fragmented body ... the moi is threatened with a breaking-up, literally, of its structure, ... a reminder of its incompleteness.

The disabled body is signified as *real* and Hunt highlights the meconnaissance of the 'I' (of able society) and the production of the Other (the disabled individual and collective body) that is necessary for maintenance of the misrecognised autonomy. The devalued body is capable of generating deep ontological anxiety (Shildrick and Price, 1999: 6). The disabled body is a morthological imaginary – a psychic body map – which corresponds less with the 'realities' of the biological 'blood body' and more with the culture that has constituted it as lacking (ibid.). This places both disabled and non-disabled people in a place of inertia and neurosis, in similar ways to those experienced by Black people in White racist contexts:

> The negro [sic] will seek admittance to the white sanctuary ... the negro enslaved by his inferiority, the white man enslaved by his superiority alike behave in accordance with a neurotic orientation.
>
> (Fanon, 1993: 51–60)

As Gratton (2007: 8) puts it, 'the white other serves to define everything that is desirable; whiteness overtakes the imagination of the black, causing a schizophrenia of his being in the eyes of the white colonials'. The great lesson of Fanon is that we are estranged from ourselves (ibid.: 9). Equally, Hunt is very much aware of this enslavement of all by the impossibilities of autonomy. In one of the most clearly psychoanalytic passages of the piece, Hunt (1966: 157–8) asserts:

> [T]here are traces of a *desire* [my italics] to externalise evil, to find a scape-goat, in attitudes to the sick ... We are perhaps saying that society is sick if we can't face our *sickness* [Hunt's italics], if it does not overcome its natural fear and dislike of unpleasantness as manifested by disability.

In viewing disablism (sick society) as a manifestation of the symbolic (normal society), Hunt is scathing of the illusory original values of normality, able-bodiedness and progress. In this sense he critiques the sickness and deficiency of the (disabling) symbolic. Like another great activist Franz Fanon (1993), Hunt calls for an end to physical and mental colonialism (Gratton, 2007: 7). Abelist society holds on to its illusory plenitude through the disavowal of disabled people (Wilton, 2003: 383). He ends his analysis with a warning and a reaffirmation of the possibilities of speaking from the position of Other who is allowed access to an archaic form of expressiveness outside the symbolic (Rose, 1986: 63):

> For the disabled person with a fair intelligence or other gifts, perhaps the greatest temptation is to try to use them just to escape from his disabledness, to buy himself a place in the sun, a share in the illusory normal world where all is light and pleasure and happiness ... But if we deny our special relation to the dark in this way, we shall have ceased to recognise our most important asset as disabled people in society – the uncomfortable, subversive position from which we act as a living reproach to any scale of values that puts attributes or possessions beyond the person.
>
> (Hunt, 1966: 158–9)

Hunt urges us in true post-structuralist style to interrogate the ideal subject of society – the master signifier as erected by the phallus – aligning himself with some of the more politicised readings of psychoanalytic discourse and putting him ahead of many queer and feminist disability studies scholars writing today (Thomas, 2004). His reflections again resonate with those of Fanon, who argued:

> Black consciousness is immanent in its own eyes. I am not a potentiality of something. I am wholly what I am. I do not have to look for the

universal ... My negro [*sic*] consciousness does not hold itself out as lack.
It *is*.

(Fanon, 1993: 135)

This fits with the earlier conception from Parker that we can only hope
to recognise that the phallus is unobtainable – to recognise that the phallus was smaller than we thought and neither women nor men can have it
(Parker, n.d.). That is, we just are. Hunt reveals the limitations of ableist
discourse – the symbolic governed by the phallus – and asks disabled people
to think about their exclusion from the symbolic not as lack but as a place
of immanence and resistance.

Conclusions

If one of the tasks of contributors to this section of the book on subjectivities
is to open up unexplored territories and processes of subjectivity to re/concep-
tualise the self, psyche and the unconscious, then psychoanalysis and disability studies have much to say to one another. In this sense psychoanalysis can
offer ways of disengaging (disabled) individuals from a normalising and disciplining society (Gratton, 2007: 4). We should be wary of where these analyses
are directed. It is clear that a psychoanalytic culture will construct subjectivities on the part of its members in ways the conceal conflicts, tensions and
contradictions. Žižek (2008: 71) proclaims that 'only psychoanalysis that can
disclose the full contours of the shattering impact of modernity – that is,
capitalism combined with the hegemony of scientific discourse – on the way
our identity is grounded in symbolic identifications'. While we might not be
so taken with psychoanalysis, it is surely our task, as critical disability studies
scholars, to explore the symbolic foundations of disablism. With this task in
mind then, perhaps, psychoanalysis might be a useful ally.

Notes

1. While extracts from this chapter are taken from the original book, an on-line
   version of this chapter is available at: http://www.leeds.ac.uk/disability-studies/
   archiveuk/Hunt/a%20critical%20condition.pdf.
2. For a copy of the letter, visit http://www.leeds.ac.uk/disability-studies/archiveuk/
   Hunt/Hunt%201.pdf.

References

Barnes, C. (2007). 'Disability Activism and the Struggle for Change: Disability, Policy
and Politics in the UK'. *Education, Citizenship and Social Justice*, 2, 203–21.
Barnes, C., Mercer, G. and Shakespeare, T. (1999). *Exploring Disability*. London: Polity
Press.
Butler, J. (1993). *Bodies That Matter: On the Discursive Limits of Sex*. London: Routledge.

Campbell, F. K. (2008a). 'Refusing Able(ness): A Preliminary Conversation about Ableism'. *Media and Culture*, 11 (3). Online paper available at http://journal.media-culture.org. au/index.php/mcjournal/article/viewArticle/46, accessed 15 September 2011.

Campbell, F. K. (2008b). 'Exploring Internalized Ableism Using Critical Race Theory'. *Disability & Society*, 23 (2), 151–62.

Campbell, F. K. (2009). *Contours of Ableism: Territories, Objects, Disability and Desire*. London: Palgrave Macmillan.

Davis, L. J. (1995). *Enforcing Normalcy: Disability, Deafness, and the Body*. New York: Verso.

Davis, L. J. (2002). *Bending over Backwards: Disability, Dismodernism and Other Difficult Positions*. New York: New York University Press.

Eagleton, T. (1983). *Literary Theory: An Introduction*. Oxford: Blackwell.

Erevelles, N. (2005). 'Understanding Curriculum as Normalizing Text: Disability Studies Meets Curriculum Theory'. *Journal of Curriculum Studies*, 37 (4), 421–39.

Fanon, F. (1993). *Black Skins, White Masks* (third edition). London: Pluto Press.

Feher-Gurewich, J. (2001). 'Lacan in America'. *Journal of European Psychoanalysis*, 12–13, 1–5, http://www.psychomedia.it/jep/, accessed 20 November 2008.

Finkelstein, V. (2004). 'Representing Disability'. In J. Swain, V. Finkelstein, S. French and M. Oliver (eds), *Disabling Barriers – Enabling Environments* (pp. 13–20). London: Sage.

Foucault, M. (1988). 'Technologies of the Self'. In M. Foucault, P. Huck Gutman, P. Hutton and L. Martin (ed.), *Technologies of the Self: A Seminar with Michel Foucault* (pp. 16–49). London: Tavistock.

Fox-Keller, E. (1962). *Reflections on Gender and Science*. New Haven: Yale University Press.

Frank, A. (1994). 'Reclaiming an Orphan Genre: The First Person Narrative of Illness'. *Literature and Medicine*, 13 (1), 1–21.

Frank, A. (2000). 'Illness and Autobiographical Work: Dialogue as Narrative Destabilization'. *Qualitative Sociology*, 23 (1), 135–55.

Gergen, K. (2001). 'Psychological Science in a Postmodern World'. *American Psychologist*, 56 (10), 803–13.

Goodley, D. (2011a). *Disability Studies: An Interdisciplinary Introduction*. London: Sage.

Goodley, D. (2011b). 'Social Psychoanalytic Disability Studies'. *Disability & Society*, 26 (6), 715–28.

Goodley, D. and Runswick-Cole, K. (2010). 'Critical Psychology and Disabled Children'. Seminar presentation, 15 JanuaryUniversity Sheffield, School of Education.

Gratton, P. (2007). 'What are Psychoanalysts for in a Destitute Time? Kristeva and the Community in Revolt'. *Journal for Cultural Research*, 11 (1), 1–13.

Grosz, E. (1999). 'Psychoanalysis and the Body'. In J. Price and M. Shildrick (eds), *Feminist Theory and the Body* (pp. 267–72). Edinburgh: Edinburgh University Press.

GMCDP (n.d.). *UPIAS*, http://www.gmcdp.com/UPIAS.html, accessed 30 August 2009.

Hewitt, S. (2004). 'Sticks and Stones in a Boy'. In B. Guter and J. Killacky (eds), *Queer Crips: Disabled Gay Men and Their Stories* (pp. 117–20). New York: Haworth Press.

Hunt, P. (1966). 'A Critical Condition'. In P. Hunt (ed.), *Stigma: The Experience of Disability*. London: Geoffrey Chapman.

Kennedy, M. (1996). 'Thoughts about Self-Advocacy'. Article with Bonnie Shoultz, http://soeweb.syr.edu/, accessed 1 January 1995.

Lacan, J. (1977). *Ecrits: A Selection*. New York: Norton.

McLaughlin, J., Goodley, D., Clavering, E. and Fisher, P. (2008). *Families Raising Disabled Children: Enabling Care and Social Justice*. London: Palgrave Macmillan.

Michalko, R. (2002). *The Difference That Disability Makes*. Philadelphia: Temple University Press.

Miller, J. A. (2008). 'Objects a in the Analytic Experience', http://www.lacan.com/lacaniancompass9miller.htm/, retrieved 9 September 2008.

Mitchell, J. (1974). *Psychoanalysis and Feminism*. New York: Pantheon Books.

Lash, S. (2001). 'Technological Forms of Life'. *Theory, Culture and Society*, 18 (1), 105–20.

Parker, I. (1997). *Psychoanalytic Culture*. London: Sage.

Parker, I. (n.d). 'The Phallus is a Signifier', http://www.lacan.com/symptom8-articles/parker8.html/, 5 November 2008.

Rose, J. (1986). *Sexuality in the Field of Vision*. London: Verso.

Rudberg, M. (1997). 'The Researching Body: The Epistemophilic Body'. In K. Davis (ed.), *Embodied Practices: Feminist Perspectives on the Body* (pp. 182–202). London: Sage.

Shakespeare, T. (ed.) (1998). *The Disability Reader: Social Sciences Perspectives*. London: Cassell.

Shildrick, M. and Price, J. (1999). 'Openings on the Body: A Critical Introduction'. In J. Price and M. Shildrick (eds), *Feminist Theory and the Body* (pp. 1–14).

Shildrick, M. (2004). 'Queering Performativity: Disability after Deleuze'. *SCAN: Journal of Media Arts Culture*, 1 (3), 1–6, http://scan.net.au/scan/journal/display.php?journal_id=36, 2 January 2008.

Shildrick, M. (2007a). 'Dangerous Discourse: Anxiety, Desire and Disability'. *Studies in Gender & Sexuality*, 8 (3), 221–44.

Shildrick, M. (2007b). 'A Response to Bardach and Hannabach'. *Studies in Gender & Sexuality*, 8 (3), 263–8.

Thomas, C. (2004). 'How is Disability Understood? An Examination of Sociological Approaches'. *Disability & Society*, 19 (6), 569–83.

Turner, B. (2008). *The Body and Society* (third edition). London: Sage.

Tremain, S. (2000). 'Queering Disability Studies'. *Sexualities and Disability*, 18 (4), 291–9.

Wilton, R. D. (2003). 'Locating Physical Disability in Freudian and Lacanian Psychoanalysis: Problems and Prospects'. *Social & Cultural Geography*, 4 (3), 369–89.

12

Intellectual Disability Trouble: Foucault and Goffman on 'Challenging Behaviour'

Karl Nunkoosing and Mark Haydon-Laurelut

> Foucault proposed his various ideas of a structure that determines discourse and action from the top down. Goffman gave us the local incidents and idiosyncrasies that lead us from bottom up. Both are essential for understanding what I call making up people.
>
> (Hacking, 2004: 288)

Introduction

This chapter draws on the insights of Erving Goffman and Michel Foucault to analyse how the practices of the group home[1] for people with intellectual disabilities create trouble and professional work. The analysis finds its focus via an interrogation of referrals to health professionals. We find staff and people with intellectual disabilities negotiating webs of power as the latter engage in acts of resistance. These acts of resistance get constructed as challenging behaviour requiring the intervention of health professionals.

Constructing trouble

The total institution was not simply the place where people with intellectual disabilities used to live and work. It was also the place of work for several professions, such as physicians, psychologists, nurses, social workers, speech and language therapists and others engaged in regulating the lives of disabled people. The closure of institutions and their replacement with the group home as one of the places where men and women with intellectual disabilities live still involve these professionals in processes that construct disability. In the British context of intellectual disabilities, these professions operate in a collective called the Community Learning Disability Team (CLDT). Staff in group homes can call on the CLDT to assist them to manage men and women with intellectual disabilities deemed to be in need of expert help. They do so by means of writing referrals in which they describe the troublesome actions, often acts of resistance, of the man or woman with learning disabilities. These referrals link the group homes with external agents of control and are also important sources of data about what is going on in the lives of people with intellectual disabilities and the people who support them in group homes. We have previously examined referrals to a CLDT to explore discourses of challenging behaviour in these texts. Below are two of the referrals we studied about two men, Dennis and Harry. These are taken from actual referrals made to a CLDT. We use these referrals to illustrate the application of Goffman's and Foucault's insights to group homes for men and women with intellectual disabilities. Methodologically our work with these texts is guided by Critical Discourse Analysis (CDA) (Fairclough, 2001). CDA 'is critical in the sense that it aims to show non-obvious ways in which language is involved in social relations of power and domination, and in ideology. It is a resource which can be used in combination with others for researching change in contemporary social life' (Fairclough 2001: 229). CDA is a resistant and disruptive reading practice aimed at revealing how assumptions operate to serve vested interests. Our position is also informed by critical and social constructionist perspectives of intellectual disability and the lives of people who have been given this label (Goodley, 1996; Rapley, 2004; Roets, 2009; Swain et al., 2004).

Two referrals: Dennis and Harry

Dennis:

We have had another incident where Dennis has physically attacked a member of the care team. The last incident was in November (three years ago).

On this occasion it was clear that Dennis has targeted the member of staff, on all other occasions we have felt that Dennis 'just snapped'. We have worked with the CLDT (Community Learning Disability Team) to put PRN (PRN here refers to prescribed psychotropic drugs that can be used as necessary to control Dennis's behaviour) guidelines in place but on this occasion they were of no use as there was no build up of anxiety.

However there was a trigger that Dennis himself identified. Dennis explained that the member of staff had 'wound him up' and 'had taken a joke too far', when asked what the member of staff had done he said 'asked me not to bolt my food', this was confirmed by the member of staff who said 'Dennis was eating so fast he was choking'. I feel that this was a reasonable request made in a professional way, the only response Dennis made at the time was 'are you going to tell others not to eat their food?' to which the member of staff replied 'yes none of you should bolt your food', the incident took place about an hour after this comment was made. Dennis chased the member of staff round the ground shouting, swearing and saying that he was going to break her glasses and rip up her clothes.

Could we arrange a time to discuss the incident and possible changes in Dennis's care plan?

Harry:
Periods of confusion, frustration and agitation appear to happen at times when Harry cannot be given a 'firm' answer to his question, or if he is given an answer he does not like or agree with. For example (he) has heard two clients talking about a jumble sale, he will ask a member of staff about it, if the member of staff is unsure of what Harry is referring to; Harry may then verbally attack the staff member, calling them 'stupid' and say 'why don't you know?'
Harry exists very much in 'Harry's world'; he appears unaware of living in residential care, referring to it as a school and the staff as teachers.
There has also been notable increase in Harry talking under his breath. Although he has always done this it has changed from occasional and barely audible to loud and almost constant, you can hear Harry talking to himself in the third person.

Goffman and Foucault

Goffman, the interactionist sociologist, and Foucault, the philosopher, wrote about institutions where people who have been labelled live their lives. Goffman's *Asylums* (1968) explained how the 'total institution' sought to rehabilitate the individual by stripping him or her of his/her identity, while Foucault's *Discipline and Punish* (1977) explained how institutional systems sought to engage labelled people in disciplining themselves into docile bodies. Both refer to the surveillance and control of the person and the imposition of identity.

Goffman's insights allow us to look at the interactions between the people who are the subjects-objects of the referrals and the people who wrote the referrals. With Foucault it is possible to focus on the historical, social and cultural contexts that created these interactions, the group home and its practices. Foucault's concern with power directs us to consider how subject positions are produced in the texts of the referrals. Power and its relationship with knowledge generate the discourses that limit and define what is knowable. However while Goffman did not refer specifically to power, we consider power as creating the social practices, rules of interactions and discourse that he observed. 'For Goffman ... power and forms are intimately connected; power is a matter of a taken-for-granted, "normal" everyday order of interaction, which enables and constrains efficacy and capacity. Hence, the theoretical homology, such as it may be, with Foucault' (Jenkins, 2008: 164).

A short list of discursive practices of intellectual disabilities might include: surveillance, assessment, the clinical gaze, the psychological and pedagogical gazes, labelling and stigma, otherness, therapy, challenging behaviours, service workers, families, and so on. The identities of both the staff and the intellectually disabled men and women they support are constructed in the production-consumption of these discourses and associated 'technologies' that people have to learn. They have to be taught how to be intellectually disabled and how to be a worker in services for people with intellectual disabilities. Thus workers' interactions with the residents of the group home are sites where selves are created. These interactions and the locations where they take place are in effect what Foucault (1988a) termed 'technologies of the self', that is, the various ways by which one is subjectified, that is to say, one subjects one's self and is subjected to the rules that regulate what and who one can be (Tremain, 2005). Both the staff and the residents are subject to these technologies.

When group home staff write referrals, they select events/performances to demonstrate something. This something includes the idea that the subject of the referral is mentally suspect or bad, his/her reasoning is doubtful or that he or she is in need of surveillance-therapy-treatment. The person becomes subject to a referral when he or she is considered to disrupt the smooth running of the home. Like in Goffman's *Asylums*, we see in some of these narratives how the group home denies the humanity of the residents and describes resistance to this as 'challenging behaviour'. Both intellectual disability and challenging behaviour are socially constructed and thus subject to interpretative processes. When the person already labelled as intellectually disabled is singled out as exhibiting challenging behaviours, he or she carries a double load of stigma (Goffman, 1968a).

The interpretative process invoked here generates an ideological conception of the (ab)normal mind/body (Michalko, 2009) where challenging behaviour is made to appear as part of intellectual disabilities. Challenging behaviour can be both excess and absence. Challenging behaviour is often too much of something: too much anxiety, too much agitation, too much answering back, too much noise, too much aggression, too much seeking isolation, too much unwanted emotion, too much anger, too much love. Not enough obedience, not enough talk, not enough sociability are also challenging.

We all have troubles from time to time. The person with intellectual disability and challenging behaviour does not just have troubles; he or she is seen as trouble. Because he or she is trouble, he or she will be subjected via the discursive practices of the referral to the experts of the CLDT. In a study of staff discourse, Wilcox, Finlay and Edmonds (2006) showed how challenging behaviour is discoursed as a challenge to the control and power of the service organisation and its staff. The trouble with being a problem is the problem that other people have (Michalko, 2009).

The group home as producer of intellectual disability discourse

The group home and the referrals it creates are discourses about intellectual disabilities. For Foucault (1981), power produces dominant discourses. A discourse influences ideas-thought-actions-talk. Discourses influence realities. Discourse/power influences how those in the group home – staff and men and women with intellectual disabilities – should think, act, and talk. That is, dominant discourses position the person. Dominant discourse can be powerful, unknown or ambiguous and produce difficulties about how one is to position oneself. Resistance, however, is always a possibility.

The product of the group home might be the docile bodies of men and women with intellectually disabilities, the appropriate subjects of care. However, the stated purpose of these 'services' will be discoursed in other terms, for example, attending to 'quality of life'. Thus, to be eligible to experience quality of life, one must first of all be an object of self-surveillance, to keep one's nose clean so to speak and not to be troublesome to the workers and indeed to other people who live in the same building. Thus service goals might express, in Goffman's (1968) terms, the moral aspect of the group home as distinct from its instrumental aspect or how it sets about doing its business. That is, the business of keeping labelled people under surveillance, providing employment for workers, and business opportunities for entrepreneurs.

From *Asylum* we learn that the group home expects its residents and staff 'to be visibly engaged at the appropriate times in the activity of the organisation' (Goffman, 1968: 176). Furthermore, 'how individuals adapt to being identified and defined is the likely focus on how they deal with exhibiting engrossment in organisational activities (177).' The people who are subject to referral are in effect people who have not been engrossed in the activities of the group home. This also applies to staff; they have to show their engrossment in the identification of people who resist such engagement in the home activities. If the staff turn a blind eye to such acts of resistance, it might lead the managers of these organisations to think that they are not up to the job. Attending to such acts of resistance, and making a referral to the CLDT are simply what the organisation does. The production of referrals is part of the performance of staff. The writing of referrals as part of their surveillance work provides evidence of their vigilance.

The group home does not do its business in isolation. As an actor in the power-knowledge business of intellectual disabilities, it interacts with other symbolic actors in the business of health and social care. Its actions have consequences for these other actors and its legitimacy in the service ecology is sustained by producing the kind of intellectual disability trouble that we see in these referrals. Discursively, none of us ever does business in isolation. Our analysis of the referral texts show how they are built from the discursive resources of the wider culture such as the assumption of incompetence of the person and a professional gaze that describes anything outside the norm as 'deviant'.

The influence of the group home on the staff and residents

In the ecology of the group home, the interactions between the staff and residents are influenced by the assumptions that each group brings to their roles. Foucault's genealogy suggests that the institutional and punitive origins of residential services for men and women with the intellectual disability label still echo in the practices of the staff and residents. The symbolic interactionism of Goffman suggests that both the staff and the residents adjust their actions to complement their reciprocal roles. The problem is that staff have the power to re-adjust their roles, but when the resident does not act according to staff expectations she may be labelled 'challenging'. Defining the actions of the intellectually disabled person as 'challenging' legitimises his or her referral to the experts so that he or she can be disciplined into becoming a non-troublesome resident. The Goffmanesque take on this is that the 'inmate' is made to know her/his place and to cease to cause conflict by seeking to influence the more powerful staff. However, we understand that some members of the CLDT may focus on enabling the staff to change their perceptions and understanding of the resident's action (See Haydon-Laurelut and Nunkoosing, 2010).

It is possible that the positioning of carer and cared for itself undermines reciprocity between the person labelled and the employees of the group home. Rapport, negotiations and reconciliation – as indicator of equality and caring – are going to be difficult in a culture with its origin in confinement. In Goffman's *Asylum* (1968), the inmate of the total institution is subjected to 'mortification' characterised as obligations of deference and obedience to the staff. We see in Dennis's referral his questioning, *'are you going to tell others not to eat their food'*, is considered an act of resistance to his status as group home resident.

It is in their vocabulary, gestures, postures, glances and surveillance that we know how staff are engaging in staff work and residents doing intellectual disability work. It may not be inevitable that the actions of the staff of the group home have to continue in accordance with the model of the institution. In *Presentation of Self in Everyday Life* (Goffman, 1969) describes how the same person behaves differently in different situations. Sometimes as Goffman demonstrated, a waitress in the restaurant changes her behaviour in the kitchen; she behaves differently when she is at home and so on. Places, such as group homes, have significant effects on the behaviours of people who live and work in them. The staff member behaves 'staff' towards the 'residents', co-worker for his or her colleagues, employee to his or her managers and so on.

Power-knowledge and discursive practices of intellectual disability

Foucault and Goffman's theories complement each other. Foucault's (1977) work exposes the movement form 'Punishing Regimes' to 'Disciplinary Regimes'. The punishment society relies on the spectacular display of the power of a central authority. Disciplinary power relies on the visibility of people to one another; attention is drawn now towards those who are subjected to power, to those who are now controlled as they are gazed upon. For Goffman 'total institutions are places of coercion that change people' (Hacking, 2004: 294).

For both Goffman and Foucault, the institution was a discursive practice, made material, to show society's values about the people it considered either mentally unfit or genetically impure. The group home followed the closure of the institutions, but power is a relation, it is always present. It will be present in an institution and in a group home. Does the disciplinary regime of the group home of the early twenty-first century bear any relation to Goffman's total institutions they were created to replace? The geographical location of the institution at the margins of the city may have shifted to group homes scattered around the city, but we cannot be sure that the discursive practices of intellectual disability work have changed. We know that disciplinary power will still be operating. As Malacrida (2005: 528) points out, 'for Foucault the body is the critical site upon which discursive formations are practiced'.

Discursive practices are written on the surfaces of the body (Foucault, 1979). We venture to suggest that the discursive inscription on the body of the man or woman with intellectual disabilities influences how actions are perceived by staff. Thus at meal time in full view of everybody, staff and residents, the body and the person of Dennis is inscribed by the telling off as an inmate. How the body is responded to tells us about the working of power–knowledge of the particular place and time. In this episode, observation, surveillance and exposure continue the institutional practices. In *Asylums* (1968) Goffman referred to institutional practices that humiliate, deface and degrade the identity of the inmate. This process of stigmatisation as described by Goffman is seen to be going on here, in the referral, as an example of the power of the disciplinary regime. This dehumanisation ritual has the purpose of stripping Dennis of his identity and as an example of the authority of the staff to the other residents: '*none of you should bolt your food*' is not simply addressed at Dennis; it is for all to hear. This episode finds resonance with Foucault's notion of the creation of the docile body – a body, such as Dennis's to be 'subjected, used, transformed and improved' (Foucault, 1977: 136).

A central idea of Goffman's work in *Presentation of Self in Everyday Life* is the performance. A performance is an observable event, acts that take place in certain contexts, such as helping someone to eat, waiting to go to college and so on. Life in the group home is full of these acts. A performance is what one sees, such as gestures and postures, what one hears, such as the talk that accompany the acts, and of course how these are responded to. There is much to be gained in understanding how the performance of 'care' is conducted. It is in the understanding of these performances that we can decipher the nature of the relationships that populate the group home.

What was it about the relationship between Dennis and the carer that led to the carer commenting that Dennis should not 'bolt' his food? What is it about this act that Dennis took exception to and for him to point out that he was being singled out: *'Are you going to tell the others how to eat?'* The group home staff might point out that they were simply doing their job, engaging in their 'duty of care', however as Manning (2008: 681) points out: organisational guidance about how people do their jobs 'functions to reduce choice, not to guide it'. This trouble is simply an example of the unsaid agreement that the 'incompetent' group home residents should dutifully subject themselves to the scrutiny of the staff. Dennis broke this agreement by firstly refusing to be seen as incompetent and secondly by commenting on the unfairness of being singled out. This makes him a deviant.

Drawing on Foucault, Yates, Dyson and Hiles (2008: 249) commented that '[i]ndividuals are subjects of knowledge' who get positioned 'as potential subjects of power and tie them to particular identities which they are obliged to recognise in themselves'. This also happens when Goffman's inmate engages in self-debasement and mortification, that is in actions such as referring to oneself in derogatory terms in order to confirm one's low status. Intellectual disability emerges as an object of thought within specific systems of knowledge. Specific forms of knowledge render people subject to particular power–knowledge, which then makes them knowable in particular ways and specifically as aspects of power that can take hold over them (Yates et al., 2008). For example, people are created as mad, bad, asocial and so on so that these characteristics become sites for power to take hold, to be exercised. In the referrals 'challenging behaviour' is being created for the same purpose.

Power-knowledge produces the rationale for interventions into people's lives and defines how we are to relate to them and how we should act on their conduct. Foucault's (1982) power-knowledge axis creates categories of people, ascribes identities to these categories, formulates laws about who can and cannot be recognised as a member of this or that category. Thus a category of people with intellectual disabilities has been created; categories of people called staff and professionals are also products of this classification. That same power first created the institution, and now the group home, for the manufacture of intellectual disability. People are not just forced into a position; they also actively constitute and reconstitute themselves (Foucault, 1988). But where there is power, there is always resistance. Harry refuses to recognise and constitute himself as intellectually disabled and subject of residential care practices. He constitutes himself as a student and the staff as teachers. He rejects the identity of intellectually disabled resident. How he wants to live is not how the staff thinks he should live. However its purpose was to put Harry in his place and to get him to accept his place as inferior to the staff. The Foucauldian insight is the power of the intellectual disability organisation to either adjust itself to the wishes of Harry or to position him as one who will have to govern himself as 'patient-resident'. The latter path appears to be the preferred one for the organisation which can lead to further resistance from Harry.

'As Foucault showed us, these impairments and the "impaired individual" are emergent as object of thought only within the specific system of knowledge' we call intellectual disabilities (Yates et al., 2008: 250). Outside of this system of power-knowledge, there is nothing challenging about Harry and his response of *'why don't you know?'* The discourse 'challenging' is itself a product of the system of intellectual disability knowledge, although this discourse appears to have become part of everyday language.

Inside the disciplinary regime muttering under one's breath 'for all to hear' is sign of either resistance or madness. In the group home these acts of individuality confirm the person's status as intellectually unsound. It is the system of power–knowledge of intellectual disability that constructs these actions as problems of the mind or the body, when they are the products of relationships and of people who do not want to subject themselves, their identities, their bodies to the disciplinary regimes of care.

In these narratives of the group home 'intellectual disability' is itself being constructed and made real. Do the analyses of Goffman and Foucault deny us any hope that the state we call 'intellectual disability' might be valued in its own right as simply just another way of being a citizen? The simple answer is that these analyses call for a morality about how we should exist with each other and a tool for a reflexive engagement with our construction of knowledge-practice of the 'artificial' category of people labelled intellectually disabled.

Surveillance, governmentality and documentation: 'This turning of real lives into writing'

> Just as an article being processed through an industrial plant must be followed by a paper shadow showing what has been done by whom, what is to be done, and who last had responsibility for it, so a human object moving, say, through a mental-hospital system, must be followed by a chain of informative receipts detailing what has been done to and by the patient and who had most recent responsibility for him.
>
> (Goffman, 1968: 73)

Both Goffman and Foucault commented on the institutional practice of creating documents about people. The referral serves the same purpose described above by Goffman; it processes, brings the individual into the focus of surveillance, it 'situates them in a network of writing; it engages them in a whole mass of documents that capture and fix them' (Foucault, 1977: 189). The referral writers create narratives of intellectual disabilities and locate themselves in positions of power in the group home organisation. Such power 'presupposes a mechanism that coerces by means of observation; an apparatus in which the techniques that make it possible to see induce affects of power, and in which, conversely, the means of coercion make those on whom they are applied clearly visible' (Foucault, 1977: 170–1).

Referrals are documents that announce the arrival of the person into the service of the CLDT. In total institutions Goffman (1968: 32) found that '[d]uring admission, facts about the inmates social statuses and past behaviour – especially discreditable facts – are collected and recorded in a dossier available to staff'. The referrals become archives of individual lives and part of the documentation that the group home and the CLDT keep about the people in their care. Kitchen (1998) argues that the practices of dominant groups are presented as the norm to the extent that disabled people are portrayed as deviants who have to accept their exploitation in the places where exclusionary practices occur. One is being asked to see these practices as legitimate, acceptable and a necessary aspect of intellectual disability work. The experts of the CLDT are being asked to engage in biopower over the non-docile body, made troublesome by intellectual disability. Of course the CLDT may choose not to do so. However, that the CLDT exists informs us of the gaze that is permissible in an intellectual disability organisation, namely, the pathological gaze that constructs acts of resistance as challenging behaviour and is itself a performance of the authority of the staff to discipline those who are seen as incapable of self-surveillance. The resident has however the power to choose his identity and to engage in acts of resistance which may invoke referrals.

In the organisation of services for people with intellectual disabilities, the likelihood is that the CLDT and its process/procedures, such as referral forms, are part of the surveillance and governmentality project of organisations that provide care. By producing referrals the care providers show that they have a significant role in the project of maintaining a category of troublesome people. The staff who write the referrals also maintain the story that people with intellectual disabilities are in need of surveillance as they cannot be trusted to manage their bodies, behaviours and emotions and that these problems have their roots in the defective biology or/and mind of these people rather than in disabling social arrangements.

Discourses of intellectual disability are controlled by experts such as physicians, psychologists, therapists, nurses, social workers, educators and so on. In the institutional model of care, all of these experts exist in one place where they engage in the rituals of the application and promulgation of knowledge and power over what can be, and what cannot be, thought of as intellectual disability and the person to whom this label has been applied. The CLDT is made up of the same professionals who maintain the regime of power-knowledge we call intellectual disability. Members of the CLDT are deemed to be able to control such discourses by virtue of their formal education, professional certifications, the languages of their disciplines and the application of their technologies.

One of Goffman's insights about the perfomative or dramaturgical aspect of interaction is the idea of back-stage and front-stage performances. The referrals offer a glimpse back stage at the group home. The details and rationale given in the referrals tell us something about what and how the staff think about their work with people with intellectual disabilities and how they expect a group home resident to conduct herself. Dramaturgically speaking, these referrals were written for a specific audience, the professionals of the CLDT and the managers of the home. The referrals are dramaturgical in that they often describe the labelled person's actions as problems for both staff and the labelled person. For the drama to be successful as an indicator of challenging behaviour, the CLDT has to accept the authenticity of the performance as described by the referral writer. The CLDT is thus part of the performance.

Jenkins's (2008: 161) analysis of Goffman's theory of power identifies three ways that information might be controlled: 'revelation, blocking or withholding, and deception'. The referrals, like other human services documents, are clearly about revelation; however, they could also constitute 'withholding' of information – as a certain, truncated version of events is produced. The form itself and the information it seeks is implicated in this. It would be worth seeking to identify how such information is controlled in care organisations, including what level or degree of deception might be going on in the creation of these 'reports'. For example, in the referral about Dennis, we learn that there was a gap of about one hour between the 'food bolting' event and the 'incident' where Dennis is described as chasing the staff. The 'lost' hour leaves the reader free to fantasise concerning the inner life of Dennis during this time.

Interactions and trust

In an interaction between the resident and the staff, there has to be trust. In all interactions there is also the possibility for chaos and disorder and so effort is required on the part of all actors to manage interactions. This has not been the case in the interactions described in the referrals. It is in interactions that order is created and maintained. There are obligations that have not been acted upon and the intervention of the CLDT is to re-establish these obligations so that order can be maintained. Misztal (2001) argues that Goffman's notions of normality and trust are essential to our understanding of how interactions are predictable, reliable and orderly. The two referrals demonstrate that the group home resident does not have the authority to question the staff and their perceptions; these two men are unpredictable and unreliable. Harry asking the staff 'why don't you know' and Dennis asking 'are you going to tell the others (residents) how to eat?' have been identified as transgressions that merit treatment by the CLDT. Both of these events and the staff responses to them tell us that in the understanding of the people who wrote the referrals, these two men have transgressed one of the rules of their respective group homes by questioning the authority of the staff. While trust between the resident and the staff should have been the accepted position in the group home, we learn from Goffman's *Asylums*, that such trust has to be based on the resident knowing his/her place in the group home and accepting that the rules of interaction requires that he/she does not question the authority of the staff.

In interactions between equals, or in 'normal' interactions, conflict can be present, however, face saving and impression management can help with resolving such conflicts so that the relationship and normal order can be maintained (Goffman, 1983). The normal order between the staff and resident in the group home is not the same as normal order in everyday interactions. Both Goffman and Foucault demonstrate how the institution engages in normalising regimes to exert control on the lives of inmates (Misztal, 2001). Both also acknowledged that in such relationships of power, resistance is always an option. However there are also differences in their theorising. For Foucault, disciplinary power is everywhere, to either punish deviation from some prescribed norm or escape from such punishment by governing oneself. For Goffman, actors as 'merchants of morality' (1972: 115) have the option to manipulate their behaviour to put on a show of acquiescence and sham conformity to maintain order without subscribing to the norm. Some of the actors in the referrals could have chosen not to react in ways that question the authority of the staff. Why they chose to act as they did is difficult to know, but we can exclude that this has anything to do with 'their' disability. However, we note that the people in Yates et al. (2008) also sought to resist the control of the staff. In both the world of Goffman and the world of Foucault people have the option to engage in resistance, but they may do so in different ways and for different purposes.

In *The Interaction Order*, Goffman (1983: 6) asked why people seem to have 'a marked capacity for overtly accepting miserable interactional arrangements'. He explains this as a trade off between gains and losses as part of a tacit agreement that exists in the interactions – as a matter of acceptance of the existing consensus – in our case the care organisation. This explanation is similar to the idea of self-surveillance. The resident of the group home engages is self-surveillance as he or she knows how he or she should act to keep out of trouble (Levinson, 2005). However in *Frame Analysis* Goffman (1986) pointed out that once an interaction is framed, that is defined or agreed by the actors in the activity, there is always the possibility of disruptions just 'out of frame'. A frame refers to the events that are currently in focus, that is, what gets noticed among all the things going on in the group home. The implication of the likelihood of disruption just 'out of frame' is that staff in the group home may selectively focus on the actions of the residents that then get constructed as challenging behaviours. The concept of frame also implies that the same action by a resident can get framed, reported and referred to as challenging behaviour in one circumstance and not in another.

Goffman, Foucault and making up people

Goffman and Foucault were both involved in 'making up people' (Hacking, 2004: 287). That is people are classified-categorised and then find themselves living up to the classification which changes their behaviour and sustains the category. In this business of making up people, group homes are locations for the construction of intellectual disabilities. Without the label 'intellectual disability' most of the signs associated with intellectual disability are simply what differentiate one person from another. That is, what constitutes one's identity. So Dennis might be thought of a man who does not take criticism easily, who resents being singled out and humiliated in the presence of his co-residents.

'Looping' is one particular form of making up people in the total institution. Looping is explained thus: 'an agency that creates a defensive response on the part of the inmate takes this very response as the target of its next attack. The individual finds that his protective response to an assault upon self is collapsed into the situation; he cannot defend himself in the usual way by establishing distance between the mortifying situation and himself' (Goffman, 1968: 41). The loop is that the resident's attempt to resist mortification only leads to more mortification. Dennis's seeking to save face about how he eats attracts further blame and the event is 'looped' to the extent that the referral asked for a 'review' of Dennis's 'care plan'. The 'care plan' here is the institutional practice of reclassifying the status and treatment regime of Dennis. In the making up of people we find that Goffman allows us to understand how there is a 'disruption of the usual relationship between the individual actor and his acts' (Goffman, 1968: 41). In our example the looping is taken-for-granted as an appropriate response to a resident's defensive actions; the writer did not see it as odd to report such practice in the referral, indicating an ordinary practice of the group home for acts of resistance as justification for a referral.

Goffman's (1968) concept of stigma is also significant in explaining the situation of the resident. Discrimination, confirmation of negative expectancy, stereotypical expectation, threat to personal and social identity are likely consequences for the stigmatised person (Major and O'Brien, 2005). In the group home, the stigma of intellectual disability serves to demarcate the higher status of the staff vis-à-vis the resident. The connection between stigma and people making (and looping) is the way that the stigmatised person is affected by the negative expectance of the self-fulfilling prophesies (Jussim et al., 2000). What is significant here is the way in which a worker who harbours negative stereotypes – based on his or her perception of the stigma of intellectual disability – can behave towards the group home residents and how this has direct effects in the latter's feelings, thoughts and behaviours (Major and O'Brien, 2005).

Conclusion: Intellectual disability trouble

We have the choice to either join in the struggle of men and women with intellectual disabilities or to continue with our power-knowledge and its oppressive outcomes. For Foucault power and resistance go together. As one discourse becomes dominant it implies a contestation with another (Burr, 2003). We can see those with learning difficulties involved in a struggle for identity and suggest that a Foucauldian reading of the referrals in this chapter illustrates the response of a service to a threat to its power by a person engaged in resistance, for example, by positioning himself as one who will not be spoken to in a certain way. But there is, unfortunately, no resistance without power and the referrals draw on dominant discourses of madness and rationality, professionalism and clienthood in an attempt to neutralise the threat. For Goffman (1961) the situation is anything but hopeless, there is room for improvisation, the creation of an 'underlife' – of resistance – even in the confines of a total institution.

While Foucault tells us why, Goffman tells us how these things happen. Foucault's theory concerns the embodied aspect of social control, of the penetrating gaze of 'experts', while Goffman shows how the practices of this gaze seek to diminish the identity of the person with intellectual disabilities, as an object of care, by means of humiliation and degradation.

In the writing of both Goffman and Foucault, there is a degree of personal distance from those subjected to disciplinary and punishing regimes. By writing about Dennis and Harry we have attempted to make this writing closer to the lives of these two men. Although neither Goffman nor Foucault sought the accounts of the actors involved in social life, they do together create the possibility for analyses of how powerful social forces shape and impact the personal. We suggest the utility of these two theorists in stripping away the layers of the social making up of intellectual disability. There is a sense in which these analyses constitute an important glance away from the personal/psychological: we suggest that neither Dennis's nor Harry's attitudes need fixing. It is the organisation of the group home that has to consider how it does its work, for what purpose and to what ends. If for personal we can substitute 'individual' – 'discipline makes individuals' (Foucault, 1977: 170) – then it is the disciplinary techniques of intellectual-disability-making to which we must turn our attention, not without noting that individualism can be injurious to relationship building and that enabling men and women with intellectual disabilities to be socially connected remains a mostly unachieved goal (Clegg and Lansdall-Welfare, 2010). The work of the CLDT to restore order is also one of governmentality aimed at both the worker and the residents.

Power is in all relationships at all moments and this is what makes power changeable. We often associate power with domination, yet power can also be a source for good (Fraser, 1989). Since power is always there in the relationships and transactions of the staff and the residents of the group home, when the latter chooses to test out the power-knowledge of the regime, he or she engages in resistance which may be seen as troublesome by the staff. The referral is always an acknowledgement of the existence of trouble. The CLDT may practice from various theoretical perspectives; its task is always to restore order, to readjust relationships-behaviours-actions to reduce trouble.

It is striking that in just these two referrals we can read so much distance between the group home workers and the people who live there. We are left with the question: might the CLDT and others read referrals with the same critical rigour that has informed our writing here? There is neither a simple, nor a single answer to this. We are surrounded by texts and disability organisations are steeped in the production and consumption of problem-saturated texts about disability. If these organisations are serious about change, then it is important that they become more conscious of what they write and how they read what they write. We leave the last words for now to Titchkosky (2005: 664):

> The body does not appear outside of the social world within which it is made manifest. Just as the meaning of the text resides as much between its words and between reader and text, so too the meaning of the body resides between bodies, between those who live through them, in them, and those who bring them to mind.

Notes

People with intellectual disabilities are also referred to as 'people with learning disabilities' or 'people with developmental disabilities'. In the UK people with this label prefer to use the term 'people with learning difficulties'. Norman Fairclough (1992: 193) refers to the existence of several words with similar or near similar meanings as 'overwording'. Overwording indicates ideological concerns that seek to eclipse certain aspects, while illuminating certain other selective aspects of something. There is unfortunately no space to examine this aspect of the label 'people with intellectual disabilities' here.

1. To some extent what goes on in the group home is the product of the limits that such places impose on both the staff and the people with intellectual disabilities (Yates et al., 2008; Yates, 2005 and Levinson, 2005). The group home is simply not peoples' home. Such places for the intellectually disabled person are architecturally defined for surveillance and consequently the application of the medical gaze that seeks pathology in the actions and thoughts of the people who have to live there. Goffman's insight about stigma (1968) is pertinent here. The stigmatised individuals develop ways of interacting to manage their 'spoilt identities' and we could think of the label 'intellectually disabled' as one such stigma. Thus the man

who questions the staff about 'why they don't know' and the man who will not be told how he should eat are all engaged in managing to 'disguise' their intellectually disabled identities. There is a price to pay for these acts. The stigmatised individual who acts against the expectations of his or her stigma is considered a deviant and subject to acts to get him or her to accept his/her stigmatised status. That is to engage in self-government. We can see here how referrals are evoked when the person is seen to have failed to govern him or herself.

References

Burr, V. (2003). *Social Constructionism* (second edition). London: Routledge.
Clegg, J. and Lansdall-Welfare, R. (2010). 'From Autonomy to Relationships: Productive Engagement with Uncertainty'. *Journal of Intellectual Disability Research*, 54 (1), 66–72.
Fairclough, N. (1992). *Discourse and Social Change*. Cambridge: Polity Press.
Fairclough, N. (2001). 'The Discourse of New Labour: Critical Discourse Analysis'. In M. Wetherell, S. Taylor and S. J. Yates (eds), *Discourse as Data: A Guide for Analysis* (pp. 229–66). Milton Keynes/London: The Open University/Sage.
Foucault, M. (1972). *The Archaeology of Knowledge*. London: Tavistock Publications.
Foucault, M. (1977). *Discipline and Punish: The Birth of the Prison*. Allen Lane: Penguin Books.
Foucault, M. (1979). *The History of Sexuality, Volume 1, An Introduction*. London: Penguin Books.
Foucault, M. (1981). 'The Order of Discourse'. In R. Young (ed.), *Untying the Text: A Post-Structural Anthology* (pp. 48–78). London: Routledge & Kegan Paul.
Foucault, M. (1982). 'The Subject and Power'. In H. Dreyfus and P. Rabinow (eds), *Michel Foucault: Beyond Structuralism and Hermeneutics*. London: Harvester Wheatsheaft.
Foucault, M. (1988). 'An Aesthetics of Existence'. In L. Kritzman (ed.), *Politics, Philosophy and Culture: Interviews and Other Writings, 1977–1984*. London: Routledge.
Foucault, M. (1988a). In H. Martin, H. Gutman and P. H. Hutton (eds), *Technologies of the Self: A Seminar with Michel Foucault*. London: Tavistock Publications.
Foucualt, M. (1989). *Madness and Civilisation: A History of Insanity in the Age of Reason*. London: Routledge.
Fraser, N. (1989). *Unruly Practices: Power Discourse and Gender in Contemporary Social Theory*. Oxford: Blackwell.
Goodley, D. (1996). 'Tales of Hidden Lives: A Critical Examination of Life History Research with People Who Have Learning Difficulties'. *Disability & Society*, 11 (3), 333–48.
Goffman, E. (1968). *Asylums: Essays on the Social Situation of Mental Patients and Other Inmates*. Harmondsworth: Penguin (first published 1961).
Goffman, E. (1968a). *Stigma: Notes on the Management of Spoiled Identity*. Harmondsworth: Penguin (first published 1963).
Goffman, E. (1969). *The Presentation of Self in Everyday Life*. Harmondsworth: Pengiun.
Goffman, E. (1972). *Interaction Rituals: Essays on Face to Face Behaviour*. Harmondsworth: Penguin.
Goffman, E. (1983). 'The Interaction Order'. *American Sociological Review*, 48 (1), 1–53.
Goffman, E. (1986). *Frame Analysis: An Essay on the Organization of Experience*. Boston: Northeastern University Press.

Hacking, I. (2004). 'Between Michel Foucault and Erving Goffman: Between Discourse in the Abstract and Face-to-Face Interaction'. *Economy and Society*, 33 (3), 277–302.

Haydon-Laurelut, M. and Nunkoosing, K. (2010). '"I want to be listened to": Systemic Psychotherapy with a Man with Intellectual Disability and His Paid Supporters'. *Journal of Family Therapy*, 32 (1), 73–86.

Jenkins, R. (2008). 'Erving Goffman: A Major Theorist of Power?' *Journal of Power*, 1 (2), 157–68.

Jussim, L., Palumbo, P., Chatman, C., Madon, S. and Smith, A. (2000). 'Stigma and Self-Fulling Prophesies'. In T. F. Heatherton, R. E. Kleck, M. R. Hebl and J. G. Hull (eds), *The Social Psychology of Stigma* (pp. 374–418). New York: Guilford Press.

Kitchen, R. (1998). '"Out of place," "Knowing one's place": Space, Power and the Exclusion of Disabled People'. *Disability and Society*, 13 (3), 345–56.

Levinson, J. (2005). 'The Group Home Workplace and the Work of Know-How'. *Human Studies*, 28 (1), 57–85.

Major, B. and O'Brien, L. T. (2005). 'The Social Psychology of Stigma'. *Annual Review of Psychology*, 56, 393–412.

Malacrida, C. (2005). 'Discipline and Dehumanisation in a Total Institution: Institutional Survivors' Description of Time-Out'. *Disability and Society*, 20 (5), 523–37.

Manning, P. K. (2008). 'Goffman on Organisations'. *Organization Studies*, 29 (5), 677–99.

Michalko, R. (2009). 'The Excessive Appearance of Disability'. *International Journal of Qualitative Studies in Education*, 22 (1), 65–74.

Misztal, B. A. (2001). 'Normality and Trust in Goffman's Theory of Interaction Order'. *Sociological Theory*, 19 (3), 312–24.

Rapley, M. (2004). *The Social Construction of Intellectual Disability*. Cambridge: Cambridge University Press.

Reay, D. (2004). '"It's all becoming a habitus": Beyond the Habitual Use of Habitus in Educational Research'. *British Journal of the Sociology of Education*, 25 (4), 431–44.

Roets, G. (2009). 'Unravelling Mr President's Nomad Lands: Travelling to Interdisciplinary Frontiers of Knowledge in Disability Studies'. *Disability & Society*, 24 (6), 689–701.

Swain, J., French, S., Barnes, C. and Thomas, C. (eds) (2004). *Disabling Barriers – Enabling Environments* (second edition). London: Sage.

Titchkosky, T. (2005). 'Disability in the News: A Reconsideration of Reading'. *Disability and Society*, 20 (6), 655–68.

Tremain, S. (2005). 'Foucault, Governmentality, and Critical Disability Theory: An Introduction'. In S. Tremain (ed.), *Foucault and the Government of Disability*. Ann Arbor, MI: University of Michigan Press.

Wilcox, E., Finlay, W. M. and Edmonds, J. (2006). '"His brain is totally different": An Analysis of Care Staff Explanations of Aggressive Challenging Behaviours and the Impact of Gender Discourse'. *British Journal of Social Psychology*, 45 (1), 197–216.

Yates, S. (2005). 'Truth, Power and Ethics in Care Services for People with Learning Difficulties'. In S. Tremain (ed.), *Foucault and the Government of Disability*. Ann Arbor, MI: University of Michigan Press.

Yates, S., Dyson, S. and Hiles, D. (2008). 'Beyond Normalization and Impairment: Theorising Subjectivity in Learning Difficulties – Theory and Practice'. *Disability and Society*, 23 (3), 247–58.

13
Stalking Ableism: Using Disability to Expose 'Abled' Narcissism

Fiona Kumari Campbell

Introduction

One may wonder what museums and classification systems have in common. They share a feature of working with the systematisation and reification of relics and objects. For too long there has been an almost indecent preoccupation with measuring and quantifying the existence of disabled people with the grand and commendable objective to know 'us' more. Despite these obsessions with disability, the sociocultural relations of impairment and disabled people have remained an afterthought in civic consciousness and at best peripheral in sociologies of the body. The aberrant, the anomalous, the monster or the disabled have formed 'the background noise, as it were, the endless murmur of nature', where disability is nonetheless always present in its absence (Foucault, 1970: 155). An act of speaking otherwise, this chapter shifts to a focus on abled(ness) to think about the production of ableism. We all live and breathe ableist logic, our bodies and minds daily become aesthetic sculptures for the projection of how we wish to be known in our attempt to exercise competency, sexiness, wholeness and an atomistic existence. It is harder to find the language and space to examine the implications of a failure to meet the standard or any ambivalence we might have about the grounds of the perfectibility project. This chapter first will outline an approach to expressing ableism (its theoretical features and character) and secondly it will provide an example of how ableism works globally in the knowledge production of disability. Finally I will discuss the possibility of disabled people turning their backs on emulating abledness as a strategy for disengagement both ontological and theoretical.

Introducing the concept of ableism

I start our discussion by providing a brief sketch of the project of ableism (if you want more elaboration and complexity, see Campbell, 2009). A survey of the literature suggests that the term is often referred to in a fleeting way with limited definitional or conceptual specificity (Clear, 1999; Iwasaki and Mactavish, 2005). When there is commentary, ableism is described as denoting an attitude that devalues or differentiates disability through the valuation of able-bodiedness equated to normalcy (Ho, 2008). Or alternatively, ableism calls for a presumption of able-bodiedness and as Chounaird (1997: 380) puts it 'ableism entails a way of being'. For some, the term *ableism* is used interchangeably with the term *disablism*. In my book *Contours of Ableism* (2009) I note that *disablism* focuses on the negative treatment towards disabled people and social policy. I argue that while this approach is commendable, it still distorts research and policy responses. Why? *Disablism* is concerned with disabled people as Other (those people) – Other than 'us'. The 'us' is presumed to be able-bodied – an able-bodied perspective. There may be a tendency under this perspective to respond along the lines of what can 'we' do for them? There is little consensus as to what practices and behaviours constitute ableism. Paring it down, at its core ableism characterises impairment or disability (irrespective of 'type') as *inherently* negative and should the opportunity present itself, to be ameliorated, cured or indeed eliminated. Ableism refers to

> a network of beliefs, processes and practices that produces a particular kind of self and body (the corporeal standard) that is projected as the perfect, species-typical and therefore essential and fully human. Disability then is cast as a diminished state of being human.
>
> (Campbell, 2009: 5)

An ableist perspective might propose that in a democracy disabled people should be treated fairly on the basis of toleration. Such a stance does *not* however suggest that disability is considered a reasonable and an acceptable form of diversity, or indeed that disability can be celebrated. Ableist thinking is based on a premise where all disability, irrespective of type and degree is assumed to be unacceptable. Disability is harmful and *inter alia* a form of harm. In my work I conclude that disability is both *provisional and tentative* – it is always subject to being erased if a solution comes along (cure, correction, elimination). Ableism denotes the meaning of a healthy body, a normal mind, how quickly we should think and the kinds of emotions that are acceptable to express. The universal reach of reason gains potency when coupled to a self-assured individual autonomy. Reason as truth becomes discourse dependent and in turn generates notions of 'disability' and 'ability' (able-bodiedness). The human (adult) subject is assumed to be an independent centre of self-consciousness, who holds autonomy to be intrinsically valuable. Neo-liberalism's normative citizen in the words of C. B. Macpherson (1964: 3) is a nominal 'possessive individual':

> free in as much as he [sic] is proprietor of his person and capacities. *The human essence* is freedom from dependence *on the will of others,*

and freedom is a function of possession ... Society consists of relations of exchange *between proprietors* (emphasis added).

This imaging of the neo-liberal subject insists that all people fit Macpherson's regulatory ideal. Ableism involves a degree of mastery over the mind and body in particular ways where styles of comportment and habits are ranked. The tool of comparison, of normativity, is the 'benchmark man', the normative citizen who is 'who is invariably White, heterosexual, able-bodied, politically conservative, and middle class' (Thornton, 1996: 2). Of course these characteristics then are put out as aspirational markers. These beliefs do not take account of differences in the ways we express our emotions, use our thinking and bodies in different cultures and in different situations. There is pressure in modern societies, particularly in developing economies for us to show we are always productive (doing something 'useful') and contributing. Ableist belief values certain things as felicitous and particular sorts of contributions. Disabled people are often seen as a burden, a problem, a drain on the system, who make no civic contribution. According to this understanding of ableism, 'disability' refers to people who do not make the grade, are unfit in someway – and therefore are not properly human.

My first claim is that the notion of ableism is not just useful for thinking about disability but also other forms of difference that result in marginality or disadvantage. Theory far from being abstract can help each of us make sense of our lived experiences and provide the tools for considering what is 'going on', to help us ask the critical and vital questions of contemporary life. Interrogating ableism means thinking about what being *abled* means to us today in Britain, the US, Australia, South Africa or Sri Lanka. A focus on ableism can also unpack what is produced phenomenologically by the disability experience. The nuances of ableism are not static; they are transcategorical, having specific cultural alignments with other factors such as race, gender, sexuality and coloniality. Compulsory abledness and its conviction to and seduction of sameness as the basis to equality claims results in a resistance to consider peripheral lives as distinct ways of being human lest they produce marginalisation. Pointing to difference can be quite dangerous on a number of grounds. Differences can be reduced to the lowest common denominator, with attributable and immutable (pigeonholing) characteristics that can become signs of deviancy or delight. A call to sameness appears to be easier as these requests galvanise and *rearticulate the normative* even if such a norm is somewhat vacuous and elusive.

Often there is confusion about impairment and its relationship to social conditions that cause poverty, distress and difficulties. An ableist disposition makes it difficult to speak of imaginations of impairment as an animating, affirmative modality of subjectivity (see chapters by Goodley; Roets and Braidotti in this volume for counter ableist approaches). To speak about disability in this different, unfamiliar way constitutes a *disability offence* as disability *in and of itself* is offensive. Studies in ableism ('SiA') attempts to shift our gaze from a *disability pre-occupied minoritisation* towards *ableist normativity* and concentrate on what the study of disability tells us about the production, operation and continuation of ableism which has *all* the population implicated. Instead of looking directly at disability, 'SiA''' focuses on how the able, able-bodied, non-disabled identity is maintained. The direction is to examine elements of what is presented as 'normal' or aspirational. This approach not only rethinks disability, it provides a platform for reconsidering the way we think about *all* bodies and mentalities within the parameters of nature/culture. 'SiA' as a field of enquiry is concerned with the processes and effects of notions of normalcy and anomaly (disability).

The building blocks of ableism

The formation of an ableist epistemology occurs on the basis of relationships shaped by binaries that are mutually constitutive. For example I propose that it is not possible to have a fully inclusive notion of 'health' without a carefully contained understanding of not-health (we call this disability or sometimes chronic illness). Central to a system of ableism are two elements, namely, the notion of the *normative* (and normal individual) and the *enforcement* of a *divide* between a so-called perfected or developed humanity (how humans are supposedly meant to be) and the aberrant, the unthinkable, underdeveloped and therefore not really-human. The ableist divide can also capture asymmetrical relations based on differences of sex and (not white) race, which in different ways, in epistemology and social practices have been constituted as sites of aberrancy or disability. There are two features that produce ableism relations:

(1) The idea of *normal* (normative individual);
(2) A *constitutional divide* – a division enforced between the 'normal' = human and the aberrant (sometimes pathological) = subhuman.

What Normal? While it might be easy to speculate about the kinds of people that may be regarded as disabled and their interior life, when thinking about the essential aspects pertaining to able-bodiedness, this task becomes difficult and elusive. Being able-bodied is always relational to that which is considered its opposite, whereas disability involves assigning labels to bodies and mentalities outside the norm. With the development of enhancement technologies (cosmetic neurology and surgery for instance) the notion of the norm is constantly sliding, maybe creating a larger pool of 'abnormal' persons who because of 'choice' or limited resources cannot *improve* themselves and hence lapse into deficiency. Disabled people have not yet established their entitlement to exist unconditionally as disabled people. This ambivalent status means it is less certain whether we could regard disabled people's lives as grievable or merely dispensable, a form of collateral damage in the pursuit of progress (cf. Butler, 2009).

There are many people in the disability services field and working in universities who, if pushed, hold this view. It is assumed that disability always equals suffering. If disabled people suffer, people think it is related to impairment and not other issues like lack of support and belongingness. It is not surprising that we receive mixed messages about disability – 'be kind and nice to the disabled! ... but there is no real right to exist, and how dare you be happy *because* of your disability and not *in spite* of it'. In fact the catchcry of an ableist denotation of disability is captured in that famous song 'We shall overcome'! Impairment is the foreign invader, an injury or parasite that represses the authentic self – no wonder many seek non-envelopment and are encouraged to partition impairment from the rest of our *relevant* selves. A counter-ableist version of impairment might explore what the experience of impairment produces and ask how does disability *productively colour* our lives? I am getting ahead of myself, let us return to the key features of ableism.

The second feature is a *constitutional divide* between the normal and pathological. Many readers will know of this even if they have not up until now had a name for it or find the language of constitutions a bit bristly. Constitutions are related to the structure or attributes of an entity which shapes a characterisation. It is a division that requires people to identify with a category – 'are you disabled or not?' 'Oh, no I am not disabled, I am ill or depressed!', 'I am able-bodied as I can do things', please 'tick the box' say governments. For the ease of conversation we often feel the need to minimise any confusion. In traditional research design classes, students are encouraged to produce research that is coherent and has clarity about where people fit (participant sampling). I have a hunch that you as the reader already know that such a clear divide is blatant propaganda that supports the argument developed by the philosopher Bruno Latour (1993: 10–11) who states, 'these two independent practices of normalising and pathologising ... must remain distinct in order for them to work/function.' If the definitions of *abled-bodied* and *disabled* become unclear or slippery, the business of legal and governmental administration would have problems functioning. Alarm would arise due to uncertainty as to how to classify certain people and in which category. Clarification of this perceived 'uncertainty' is achieved through a division called *purification*, the marking of distinct archetypes. Ableism assists in the government of disability ensuring that populations that appear dis-ordered (maybe even causing social disorder) become ordered, mapped and distinct. Purification is essential to be able to count populations even if this counting and classifying does not reflect and in fact distorts reality (Altman, 2001). As impairment effects are relational, disability is not always present in the environment and within the realm of an individual's subjectivity. This division will be discussed later on in the chapter when I look at geodisability knowledge.

Turning to the realm of tacit knowledge gained from social relations, the second aspect to enforcing a constitutional divide is *translation*. Let us take a look at this. No human is self-contained and our lives are constantly changing and (trans)formed through the context in which we move. Humans are endowed by their relations with technologies (cars, clothing, implements, time, communications devices, prosthesis and drugs etc.). Relations between human and non-human entities (actors) are *already* hybridised and made up of changeable aspects. Our relationship to context (people, environments, mental and bodily changes) means that human typologies are endless and shifting (Goodley, 2007). The character of impairment can change through interfaces with behaviour modifying drugs and the use of apparatus (speech, hearing and mobility enhancing). Most of us rarely fit into the definitive classifications of *purification* – yet such confusion or 'grey zones' of daily life are neatened up into zones of distinction ~ he is 'this' and she is 'that'. Enshrined in ableism is a metaphysical system which feeds into an ethics of disability. A critical question to be asked is what is the nature of the ethics or ethos invoked by ableist practices? Does ableism produce a form of narcissism in the disabled person or are ableist practices themselves essentially narcissistic?

Ableism ~ a characterological narcissism?

Siebers (2008) and Davis (2002) furnish a discussion about the ways that psychosocial theories of narcissism have been used as a form of individualised victim-blaming of disabled people. Without rehashing their material, a psychology of narcissism asserts that disabled people are exemplary narcissists. In not being able to be cured, disabled people turn away from love of others towards themselves in a neurotic, disengaged form of self-gratification. Such a view reached its zenith in Australia in the professional indemnity insurance crisis of 2003–4, where 'high' disability compensation payouts were blamed for the collapse of a major insurer (Mendelson, 2008). This theory of narcissism would appear to conflict with emerging research around the experiences of disabled people and internalised ableism which suggests that there are extraordinary attempts at engagement with the abled 'Other' and high degrees of precariousness around self-approval (Campbell, 2008; Reeve, 2006). Critics of identity politics and disability studies argue that 'identity politics promotes a rage that threatens the social order' (Siebers, 2008: 44). Yet as I have argued, it is the processes of ableism that produce the reified category of disability and ontological difference! Indeed ableist narcissism can desubjectivise, by reducing the human to a mere organic state, functional, pliable and improvable (Hourigan, 2010). In this chapter I propose an inversion of that traditional understanding of disability's relationship to narcissism. Ableism as a mentality and as a practice is *inherently* narcissist. As a practice, ableism demands an unbridled form of individualism that is pre-occupied with self-improvement and corporeal enhancement. Ableist normativity (the view that assumes the preferability of abledness) demands entitlement to premium social and economic spaces and loud histories. 'SiA' I argue are a value-addition to the field of critical disability studies.

Reframing our study from disability to ableism prompts different preoccupations: what does the study of the politics of 'deafness' tell us about what it means to be 'hearing'? Indeed how is the very conceptualisation of 'hearing' framed in the light of discourses of 'deafness'? In law the juridical notion of sanity depends upon a delimitation of the 'insane', 'unfit' and 'incompetent'. A reframing of the question may expose underlying presuppositions about the grounds of pathology, reasonableness and mentality. By decentring abledness, it is possible to 'to look at the world from the inside out)' (Linton, 1998: 13) and unveil the 'non-disabled/ableist' stance. And in doing this act of inversion ableism 'loses its crucial position as a pre-condition of vision and becomes the object of scrutiny' (Haraway, 1989: 152). Developed from within the field of critical disability studies as well as broader insights drawn from gender studies and critical race theory, 'SiA' examines the ways that concepts of well-beingness and deficiency circulate throughout society and impact upon economic, social, legal and ethical choices.

SiA are *not* about the study of 'ability' which is held in a binary relationship with 'inability', rather we are concerned with the more productive nuance – *abledness as a constitutive centre*. This orientation foregrounds the limits of tolerance and hence the creation of objectionable lives that reside outside the bounds of society, becoming outlaw disabilities. Ultimately 'SiA' is also an attempt to build a new home, to make room by crafting a territory that is antithetical to ableist normativities. We could propose that the world extends the form of some bodies and mentalities more than others, and such bodies/mentalities in turn feel at home in the world. Before moving on this potential new reality, I want to show one of the ways that ableness operates more globally in the push for a *universal definition of disability* and disability coding – what I have termed *geodisability knowledge*. I will not be covering geohealth concepts in this chapter but refer the reader to Gregor Wolbring's (2006) piece. In the next section I move to discuss how ableism works in the global mapping of disability knowledge.

Geodisability knowledge

Geodisability knowledge acts a bit like the McDonalds™ strategy – just as there are documents, devices and drilled people all around the globe who know how to prepare and deliver a tasty BigMac™ hamburger, geodisability knowledge acts as the landscape for thinking about disability and shapes the flows of consciousness around vitality. With the ICD-10 (*International Classification of Disease* 10) and ICF (*International Classification of Functioning, Disability and Health*) – disability collectors can visit services and assess funding applications around the globe and believe that there is an operational clarity about the populations they are dealing with and the kinds of quality of life outcomes they can expect in *supra* culture and context. The argument of enumeratists and actuarialists is that systematisation will assist in social planning. This will only work however if disability is reduced to its lowest common denominator (Altman, 2001), resembling what I would call a 'skeletal model' where embodiment (flesh, memory, circumstances) are deflayed and peeled off to reveal a definitive cripped (disabled) essence. In terms of negative production, *purification* sharpens the divide of exclusion by forcing different bodies and mentalities to adopt emulative compartmentalisation and then to explain the reality of their daily experiences from within that categorical prism.

Foucault's early work on the panopticonal gaze whereby 'inspection functions ceaselessly [and ...] the gaze is alert everywhere' (1977: 195) is invoked in nodes of geodisability structures of systemisation and measurement. Without seeking to review the extensive studies of panopticism, it is important to summarise its key features. Jeremy Bentham's proposal for penal management in the form of a panopticon an architectural design for the surveillance and observation of prisoners has had long-ranging consequences for institutional monitoring at the local and global level. For Foucault the panopticon became a motif, a genealogical marker for ordering socio-material realities. The panopticon is a space not just of visibility through strategic gaze or scrutiny, but its space is ordered to produce norms and geoprofiles, for example hospital space, client areas, high security zones, silent spaces, international waters and airspace. The panopticon can be described as a type of socio-material assemblage for grouping and arranging social categories. Today the individual is compelled both individually and collectively, to attune and align themselves into observable, streamlineable and thus countable data. A good citizen is one that can be easily counted and their lives reducible to statistical aggregates and coded nuances. A more obtuse example is the French conceptualisation of disability as 'situation of disability' (*handicap de situation*). This idea bears witness to certain aspects of impairment that arise and then decline relationally and in situational contexts (Winance, Ville and Ravaud, 2007).

Geopolitical scrutiny does not need to be localised and is in effect transspatial. Governing from a distance (be it Geneva or New York) operates through two discursive modalities. One modality is *denotative* – a cartographical description of a particular spatial zone (our interest is in the mapping of ableist zones of 'health' and 'not-health'). The second modality forms an *authoritative atonement*, a discursive canon (such as international disability norms and conventions) which constructs and enacts foundational and thus sayable 'statements' (e.g 'who' is legally a 'disabled person') to guide policy formulation. United Nations (hereafter known as UN)-based international norm standard setting, in the form of geodisability knowledge production, is a form of panopticonism. The institutional strategic gaze, situated in the UN, is able to examine, normalise and condition nation states and cultures. International disability norm standard setting is represented as a system formulated by consensus, being transcultural (therefore detached) and objective. But knowledge formation by international consensus building is not a level playing field. As Connell (2007) argues non-Western approaches are not taken seriously enough to rupture the colonial experience.

The pre-eminent apparatus controlling the delimitation of disability originates with the UN. Without consensual international disability norms, it would not be possible to disclose and make visible the dynamics of disability at a country level and for the World Health Organization (hereafter known as 'WHO') to map disability globally. The 'seeing' of disability, it is argued, enables a surveillance both globally (of each country) and individually (everybody is surveilled for conformity). While it is beyond the confines of this chapter to have a thoroughgoing discussion of the government of disability globally, it is pertinent to outline a number of salient definitional instruments that are mandated for use by UN member nations.

UN formations of disability are deeply embedded with a broader nosology of disease (see ICD-10), which delimits disability in relation to a so-called objective comparator referred to as *health status* (i.e. a person without a health condition). The new ICF formulation, while being cognizant of the 'participatory' and 'contextual' dimensions of 'disability', continues to be constitutionally aligned with and thus becomes a sub-directory of the ICD-10. This is an instance of enframing as the partitioning of 'disability' and 'not-disability' can obscure cultural differences around health and aberrancy. In January 2001, the 54th World Health Assembly adopted the *International Classification of Functioning, Disability and Health* (ICF). The new system inaugurated four dimensions related to disability: impairment, activity, participation and context. The instrument's authors argue that the aim of the ICF was to develop a common language for speaking of 'health' and by default 'disability' (World Health Organization, 1992–4: 1–4). Moreover, the ICF provides the basis and tool for implementing various UN instruments by member states and enacting coherent national legislation. Without the ICF, the networked nodes of governance would have difficulty crossing borders and as such acts as a boundary object. The epistemological framework of the ICF has been adopted by a majority of the world's national governments and has shaped the domestic scene in terms of definitions and assessment instruments contained in legislation, social policy and the very semantics of disability (what is sayable and unsayable).

Advocates of global geodisability templates argue that universal systems can be used to bring 'into line' renegade nation states that do not appropriately plan for the needs of disabled people. We may ask what approaches to disablement are 'renegade'? What is the authoritative criterion and authoritative body? In the event of any contestations over the weighting of various elements, this framing within a disease paradigm most likely ensures that etiological factors remain pre-eminent and the social context eclipsed. In the mental health arena, mental health is described by WHO along the lines of coping with the 'normal stresses of life'. But as Fernandopulle, Thalagala and Barraclough (2002) point out, the notion of normalcy in the Sri Lankan context explodes given the almost normalised extra stress of living with 25 years of inter-ethnic conflict and war.

Among the major outcomes of the Decade of Disabled Persons was the adoption, by the General Assembly, of the *Standard Rules on the Equalization of Opportunities for Persons with Disabilities* in 1993. While the *Standard Rules* are not legally binding, they 'represent a *strong moral and political commitment* of Governments to take action to attain equalization of opportunities for persons with disabilities. The rules serve as an instrument for policy-making and as a basis for technical and economic cooperation' (UN, Division for Social Policy and Development, 2003–4, my emphasis). Member states are required to adopt legislative reforms in conformity with these rules. These instruments have come about through years of vigorous activism. A recent tool of governance is the 2006 *Convention on the Rights of Persons with Disabilities*. The strength of the Convention is that its formulation of disability transcends functional and medical orientation of traditional disability models. The *Preamble* states:

> Disability is an *evolving concept* and that disability *results from the interaction* between persons with impairments and attitudinal and environmental barriers that hinders their full and effective participation in society on an equal basis with others.
>
> (*Convention on the Rights of Persons with Disabilities*, 6 December 2006, at [e], my emphasis)

Article 1 of the Convention goes on to list the more usual type of functional and classificatory approaches to disability, yet there is room to even interpret these categories through the lens of an intercultural understanding as made possible through the emphasis of the Convention's *Preamble*. The impact of countries in the Global South in their disability affairs is uncertain. The Convention might stimulate debate and change around disability or alternatively impose little understood legal standards and obligations.

An alternate reading of international norms is to interpret geodisability knowledge as a mechanism to naturalise hegemonic ways of *seeing* (knowing), *citing* (summoning and hailing) and *situating* (localising) disability and thus an attempt to codify unruly forms of impairment differences. Of course increased geosurveillance can be associated with growing global concerns about risk and dangerousness. In Foucault's exposition of governmentality, there is recognition that the craft of welfare requires that individual identity concur and be formed within the matrix of administrative structures in society. This notion of governmentality moves beyond a liberal preoccupation with affairs of sovereignty at the level of nation states to focusing on the personal level of subjectivity and the formation of self. Geodisability knowledge in its attempt at universalisation moves away from the lived experiences of disability and becomes of meta-ascription of impairment, a cache of *disability anywhere.*

Escobar points out the erasure of 'place' and localised particularities have been foundational to Western epistemology since the time of Plato. The consequences are that space 'had to be dissociated from the bodies that occupy it and from the particularities that these bodies lent to the places they inhabit' (Escobar, 2001: 143). I argue that the move to enacting universalised geodisability knowledge production is a major modality for governing disability that places disability out-of-space, or *in* outer space, despite the implicit situation-specific creation and living of impairment. The *outer* space often has a similar aesthetic about it irrespective of geography – all hospital and care homes look alike right down to the uniforms and paint colour – in other words they could by *anyplace*, any where. The emptying of space means that disability can be anywhere; geopositioning does not really matter. The invention of disability occurs in the local and embodied notion of 'place' – in the distinctions made between health, not-health, disability, demonisation and so on. The following section of the chapter attempts to take disability and disabled beingness to another place away from the narcissism of ableism and the argy-bargy of the international scene.

Antisociality: Rupturing ableist hegemony

> [For liminal subjects] … style is both the sign of their exclusion and the mode by which they survive nonetheless.
>
> (Halberstam, 2005: 153)

Difference can be a vexed issue even within modern liberal societies. The tendency for many people is still to emulate or at least appear to refashion normative ways of being. Much of the intellectual traffic for the rethinking of disability in terms of anti-sociality has emerged through debates about the merits of social inclusion and liberal notions of equality and resilience strategies to break the abled stranglehold. Legal theorists like Ruth Colker who argues that anti-subordination rather than integration should be the measure of equality are the exception (Colker, 2006). There is limited work within disability studies, especially in approaches influenced by the social model of disability or social role valorisation theory, that take a trans-integration or post-normalisation perspective. *What if we turned our backs on 'fitting in' – what would be the opportunities, the consequences and maybe dangers*, to give 'attention to the lived intricacies of embodiment offer[ing] alternatives to normalization efforts aimed at homogenizing social outsiders (Snyder &

Mitchell, 2010, 113)'? For this imaginative undertaking it is necessary to turn to the theoretical work by other 'outsider' groups – queer theorists. Spearheading the critique of the 'different but same' stance of social justice formulations are 'anti-social' queer theorists (Bersani, 1986, 1996; Edelman, 2004; Halberstam, 2005, 2008; Muñoz, 2007). This section will outline some of the conceptual drivers of the anti-social argument and their adoption for developing an anti-sociality posture of disability.

Leo Bersani's seminal work (1986, 1996) formulated an anti-social, negative and anti-relational theory of sexuality. These works along with the writings of Edelman (2004), Halberstam (2005, 2008) and Muñoz (2007) set the stage for the decoupling of queer marginality from the liberal projects of tolerance and social inclusion. Before moving into a consideration of how certain conceptual renderings may be applied to the disability situation, it is useful to familiarise ourselves with how the neologism *queer* is understood by anti-social theorists. Lee Edelman's *No Future: Queer Theory and the Death Drive* does not indicate the parameters of *queer*, but concludes that 'queerness can never define an identity; it can only ever disturb one' (2004: 17). *Queer*, while originating from the purview of diverse sexualities, easily extends to other kindred forms of ontological and corporeal aberrancies and ambiguities (such as disability). So it is right for Halberstam (2005: 6) to embrace a more elastic connotation of queer which refers to 'non-normative logics and organizations of community, sexual identity, embodiment and activity in space and time'. From this reckoning, the disabled person is *already* queered. Queer, then is antitheoretical to the regime of ableist *translation*.

In a world that makes claims to integrity using the argument based on equality as sameness (we are normal, we are everyday people), it would seem a bit bold or offensive to suggest that people with disability are different from the run-of-mill ableist norm emulators. Ahmed (2006) points to an alternate prism, a 'migrant orientation' to capture a disorientation faced by queer folk which I extend to include disabled people. The disorientation, a form of radical estrangement propels a lived experience of facing at least two directions: towards a home that has been lost (the desire to emulate ableist norms), and to a place that is not yet home. Regimes of ableism have produced a depth of disability negation that reaches into the caverns of collective subjectivity to the extent that disability negativity is seen as a 'naturalized' reaction to an aberration. Not negating queerness or disability can cultivate alternate kinds of liberty that de-identify with the rhetoric of social inclusion.

A key marker of the anti-social turn is temporality – contemporarity and futurity – an explication of the current marginal stance and the vision for future. It is this orientation of predicament and utopianism that can speak to the disability realm. For disability, utopianism is a conflicted zone – there is no future existence, disability dreaming is expunged and the utopian drive is a device for promise (of curability), hence extinction of the impairment state. Jose Esteban Muñoz (2007: 453) in speculating about the absence of a queer imagination elicits a desire to engage in a *queer horizon*, a utopian hermeneutics where re-imagining futurity requires that 'the not quite conscious is the realm of potentiality that must be called upon'. The distance between imagination and potentiality means that 'queerness is not quite here'. Our imaginations are not yet exhausted. Muñoz explains:

> to argue that we are not quite queer yet, that queerness, what we will know as queerness, does not yet exist. I suggest that holding queerness, in a sort of ontologically humble state, under a conceptual grid wherein we do not claim to always already know queerness in the world, potentially staves off the ossifying effects of neoliberal ideology.
>
> (Muñoz, 2007: 454)

How does an alternative horizon for disabled people come to be formulated? Living in the now and not yet, as outsiders, not quite inside, requires a disposition or habit of contemporariness. Contemporariness signifies a relationship with the present but also a distance, a critical space from it. As Agamben explains:

> Those who are truly contemporary, who truly belong to their time, are those who neither perfectly coincide with it nor adjust themselves to its demands. They are in this sense irrelevant [*inattuale*]. But precisely because of this condition, precisely through this disconnection and this anachronism, they are more capable than others of perceiving and grasping their own time.
>
> (2009: 40)

Disabled people are called to live as contemporaries. The queering or cripping of contemporariness is the grasping and holding tight to ambivalence and obscurity so fundamental to the alternate lifestyle which is obtained through fixing the gaze not on our era's light but the underbelly, or in Agamben's language 'darkness' – which shines into the staree. In this sense, the contemporary queered and cripped person, in touching an elusive imaginary, sees the now and the emergent not as a death drive, but in terms of *unlivedness*:

> The present is nothing other than this unlived element in everything that is lived. That which impedes access to the present is precisely the mass of what for some reason ... we have not managed to live. The attention to this 'unlived' is the life of the contemporary.
>
> (Agamben, 2009: 51)

The matter of re-imagining a disability or cripped horizon, a future without the stain of ableism, although elusive and out of grasp, is nonetheless fundamental in order to move to hopefulness and capture that unlived possibility in the lives of many with disability. Can the so-called shadows of a disabled life be sites of invigoration? What is 'unlived' in our lives? Crippin' the human involves a differential gaze – where sometimes signs and gestures predominate, where there is a different mind style such as Tourette's syndrome or autism, or a centring on visuality or tactility. A grounded earthiness can be 'different' through echolocation and waist heightedness. Halberstam (2008) speaks of acts of unbecoming. Through what she describes as 'wilfully eccentric modes of being', it is worth conjuring and queering concepts of passivity held against disabled people, as a refusal to live up to ableist expectations of performativity:

> [I]n a performance of radical passivity, we witness the willingness of the subject to actually come undone, to dramatise unbecoming for the other so that the viewer does not have to witness unbecoming as a function of her own body.
>
> (Halberstam, 2008: 151)

This radical passivity, for disabled people, would indeed *have* to be radical, as disabled people already live under the enormous weight of being characterised as passive. It is a tough ask to claw back and produce a *cripped notion of passivity*. Sunny Taylor does this in her quest for the right *not* to work:

> I have a confession to make: I do not work. I am on SSI [social security benefit]. I have very little work value (if any), and I am a drain on our country's welfare system. I have another confession to make: I do not think this is wrong, and to be honest, I am very happy not working. Instead I spend the majority of my time doing the activity I find the most rewarding and valuable, painting.
>
> (Taylor, 2004: 30)

Such strange temporalities, imaginative life schedules present alternative temporalities which disability studies scholars have all along known, disrupt the parameters of the human (Halberstam, 2005; Campbell, 2009; McRuer, 2006). Having said this, it is all the more extraordinary that disabled people have not yielded to this repression but have resisted docility and engaged in transgressive ways of living disability. Ableism is founded on a utopian hermeneutics of the desirable and the disgusting and therefore it is, as Halberstam (2008: 153) puts it, necessary to inculcate alternative political imaginaries. McRuer (2008) drew my attention to the way Halberstam's perspective can incorporate disability as also outside the lifecycle:

> I try to use the concept of queer time to make clear how respectability, and notions of the normal on which it depends, may be upheld by

a middle-class logic of reproductive temporality. And so, in Western cultures, we chart the emergence of the adult from the dangerous and unruly period of adolescence as a desired process of maturation; and we create longevity as the most desirable future, applaud the pursuit of long life (under any circumstances), and pathologize modes of living that show little or no concern for longevity. Within the life cycle of the Western human subject, long periods of stability are considered to be desirable, and people who live in rapid bursts (drug addicts, for example) are characterized as immature and even dangerous.

(Halberstam, 2005: 4–5)

Cripped time can be staggered, frenzied, coded, meandering and be the distance between two events. Some of our time is shaped according to another's doing – *service time* – the segmenting and waiting on assistive agencies. Aside from service time, there is a *transient time* whereby our cripped selves rub up against biology, environmental barriers and relationality. Like queerness, the lifecycle refuses patterning – there is a different vision with localised goals. Instead of proposing argument based on normalisation and similarity to the heteronormative (and by extension ableist normativity), Edelman (2004) proposes a politics of negativity, on the basis that queers, as outsiders, are embodied differently having counter-intuitive, queered forms of negative knowing (Halberstam, 2008: 141). Edelman implores queers to be norm resisters, to come out from normative shadows and fess up to futurist 'inability': 'instead of fighting this characterization by dragging queerness into recognition, he proposes that we embrace the negativity' (Halberstam, 2008: 141). Relinquishing the norm as a lost cause enables an outlaw flowering of beingness that is anti-social.

Disability as perverse and anti-social

The disabled life puts out fear and possibility. This is a conflict over liminality that many disabled people experience. How does the person with a disability negotiate the expectations and compulsions of ableism? In other words, do they choose to conform to or hypermimic ableism or do they go it alone and explore alternative ways of being? People with impairments have impairment – mediated proprioceptive ways of experiencing being in the world. In contrast there is the unspeakability of communality and commonality where disabled people can, as Overboe does in his spasms 'give [him] great joy... [becoming] a life-affirming presence' (2007, 221). Elsewhere I have argued that disabled people 'are in effect strangers in ableist homelands – who because of their strangeness have the possibility of a new vision or orientation' (Campbell, 2009: 161).

Reading 'disability' in a positive (anti-social) light requires an *apriori* negotiation with what Foucault (1976) refers to as the effects of the 'implantation of perversions', the consolidation of erratic desiring. Foucault's' thinking about desire suggests that a desire towards emulation of the ableist subject mitigates against the development of an anti-social framing of disability *outside the realms* of the perverse. The challenge then is to take up these 'implantation of perversions', to develop as Foucault puts it 'the thought of the outside', a thought at the queer margins:

> A thought that stands outside subjectivity, setting its limits as though from within, articulating its end, making its dispersion shine forth, taking in only its invincible absence; and that, at the same time, stands at the threshold of all positivity, not in order to grasp its foundations or justification but in order to regain the space of its unfolding, the void serving as its site, the distance in which it is constituted and into which its immediate certainties slip the moment they are glimpsed.
>
> (1998, Orig 1966: 150)

Slippages in certainties do create precariousness but also the possibility to (re)imagine the circumstances of disability. It is in between these conflicted traces of subjectivity that the perverse inkling of anti-social disability, an outlaw ontology, lurks. For Foucault, 'the thought of the outside' contains a double imperative: (negative) desire reaches into our (disabled) interiority, the emptiness, and the state of be-ing outside: 'the fact that one is irremediably outside the outside ... infinitely unfold[ing] outside any enclosure' (Foucault, 1998: 154). Director Hara Kazuo's 1972 film *Goodbye CP*, a stark black and white portrayal of Green Lawn, a Japanese activist group of people with cerebral palsy, includes a scene where the central character Yokota Hiroshi who walks on his knees because it is faster than a wheelchair is followed, in handing out leaflets. Hiroshi remarks:

> I walk slow and look pathetic. What's wrong with that? ... We are outsiders. We really are. We can never be insiders. Those who think they are insiders may end up being outsiders. Why don't they realize that? That's the point we are trying to make.
>
> (Hiroshi, in Kazuo, 1972)

Foucault is correct that we can never really 'know' the outside, the liminal margins because its 'essence' remains inherently unknowable and ambiguous. To step outside the normative trajectories of negativity not only destabilises the conception of disability, but also confuses and disrupts the processes of subjectification by confronting the 'goodness' of disability. Hiroshi is emblematic of the anti-sociality stance of disability. Such an act is subversive as Hiroshi positions his impaired body as queered and perverse. He is perverse because Hiroshi in effect does not 'give a damn' about presumed appearances – he is his *own* man in his embrace of outsiderness.

I propose that at an ontological level the disabled body *as a* body is perverse; it is in effect anti-social in its departure from ableist normativity. A word of caution, in rejecting norm emulation the anti-social body still exists and lives under normative shadows. Anti-sociality can be about being on guard, reminding of, removing, resisting and rectifying the consequences of ableism.

Conclusion

SiA are an approach within disability studies that can provide a mechanism for interrogating the premises that underpin the notion of abledness. A focus on abledness can help expose the different kinds of beingness for more typical bodies and mentalities. In stalking ableism, it is possible to generate new kinds of research around ways people are enabled and prohibited in their internalisation of an ableist ethos. In this chapter I have introduced some of the core theoretical ideas underpinning the notion of and operation of ableist thought and practices. I have used as an example the emergence of geodisability knowledge, a system to systematise and stabilise not only disability figurings but ultimately a belief in a universal teleological system of species-typical functioning. In the final part of the chapter I present a sample counterpoint to ableism, namely anti-social or negative relational theory. Refuting an ableist narcissist preoccupation with perfection can pave the way for more work on natality, flourishing and beauty where the human continuum is more processional and relational.

References

Agamben, G. (2009). *What is an Apparatus? And Other Essays*. Stanford: Stanford University Press.

Ahmed, S. (2006). *Queer Phenomenology Orientations, Objects Others*. Durham: Duke University Press.

Altman, B. (2001). 'Disability Definitions, Models, Classification Schemes, and Applications'. In G. Albrecht, K. Seelman and M. Bury (eds) *Handbook of Disability Studies* (pp. 97–122). Thousand Oaks: Sage.

Bersani, L. (1986). *The Freudian Body: Psychoanalysis and Art*. New York: Columbia University Press.

Bersani, L. (1996). *Homos*. Cambridge: Harvard University Press.

Butler, J. (2009). *Frames of War: When is Life Grievable?* London: Verso.

Campbell, F. K. (2008). 'Exploring Internalised Ableism Using Critical Race Theory'. *Disability & Society*, 23 (2), 151–162.

Campbell, F. K. (2009). *Contours of Ableism: The Production of Disability and Abledness*. Basingstoke: Palgrave Macmillan.

Chounaird, V. (1997). 'Making Space for Disabling Differences: Changing Ableist Geographies'. Guest editorials, *Environment and Planning D: Society and Space*, 15, 379–90.

Clear, M. (1999). 'The "Normal" and the Monstrous in Disability Research'. *Disability & Society*, 14 (4), 435–48.

Colker, R. (2006). *Anti-Subordination Above all: A Disability Perspective*. Public Law & legal Theory Working Paper Series, No. 84, Moritz College of Law, The Ohio State University.

Connell, R. (2007). *Southern Theory: The Global Dynamics of Knowledge in Social Science.* Crows Nest (NSW): Allen & Unwin.

Davis, L. (2002). *Bending Over Backwards: Disability, Dismodernism, and Other Difficult Positions*. New York; New York University Press.

Edelman, L. (2004). *No Future: Queer Theory and the Death Drive*. Durham: Duke University Press.

Escobar, A. (2001). 'Culture Sits in Places: Reflections on Globalism and Subaltern Strategies of Globalization'. *Political Geography*, 20, 139–74.

Fernandopulle, S., Thalagala, N. and Barraclough, S. (2002). 'Mental Health in Sri Lanka: Challenges for Primacy Health Care'. *Australian Journal of Primary Health*, 8 (2), 31–8.

Foucault, M. (1970). *The Order of Things: An Archaeology of the Human Sciences.* New York: Random House.

Foucault, M. (1976). *The History of Sexuality: An Introduction, Vol 1*. Middlesex: Penguin.

Foucault, M. (1977). *Discipline & Punish: The Birth of the Prison*. New York: Vintage Books.

Foucault, M. (1980). 'Two Lectures'. In C. Gordon (ed.), *Foucault; Power Knowledge: Selected Interviews and Other Writings 1972–1977* (pp. 78–108). New York: Pantheon Press.

Foucault, M. (1998). (Orig 1966). 'The Thought of the Outside'. In J. Faubion (ed.), *Michel Foucault Aesthetics, Method, and Epistemology* (pp. 147–69). London: Allen Lane/The Penguin Press.

Goodley, D. (2007). 'Towards Socially Just Pedagogies: Deleuzoguattarian Critical Disability Studies'. *International Journal of Inclusive Education*, 11 (3), 317–34.

Halberstam, J. (2005). *In a Queer Time & Place: Transgender Bodies, Subcultural Lives.* New York: New York University Press.

Halberstam, J. (2008). 'The Anti-Social Turn in Queers Studies'. *Graduate Journal of Social Science*, 5 (2), 140–56.

Haraway, D. (1989). *Primate Visions: Gender, Race, and Nature in the World of Modern Science*. New York: New York University Press.

Hourigan, D. (2010). Personal Communication, by email 13/10/2010.

Ho, A. (2008). 'The Individualist's Model of Autonomy and the Challenge of Disability'. *Journal of Bioethic Inquiry*, 5, 193–207.

Iwasaki, Y. and Mactavish, J. (2005). 'Ubiquitous Yet Unique: Perspectives of People with Disabilities on Stress'. *Rehabilitation Counselling Bulletin*, 48 (4), 194–208.

Kazuo, H. (1972). *Goodbye CP*. Tidepoint Pictures, Facets Video [Film].

Latour, B. (1993). *We have Never Been Modern*. New York: Harvester Wheatsheaf.

Linton, S. (1998). *Claiming Disability: Knowledge and Identity*. New York: New York University Press.

MacPherson, C. B. (1964). *The Political Theory of Possessive Individualism*. Oxford: Oxford University Press.

McRuer, R. (2008). '"Bad Education": Crip Representation and the Limits of Tolerance', Audio Lecture & transcript, Temple University, http://www.temple.edu/instituteondisabilities/programs/ds/lecture20080917trans.shtml, accessed 29 March 2009.

Mendelson, D. (2008). *The New Law of Torts*. South Melbourne: Oxford University Press.

Muñoz, J. (2007). 'Queerness as Horizon: Utopian Hermeneutics in the Face of Gay Pragmatism'. In G. Haggerty and M. McGarry (eds), *A Companion to Lesbian, Gay, Bisexual, Transgender, and Queer Studies* (pp. 452–63). Oxford: Blackwell Publishing.

Overboe, J. (2007). 'Disability and Genetics: Affirming the Bare Life (the State of Exception)'. *The Canadian Review of Sociology and Anthropology*, 44, 219–35.

Reeve, D. (2006). 'Towards a Psychology of Disability: The Emotional Effects of Living in a Disabling Society'. In D. Goodley and R. Lawthom (eds), *Disability & Psychology: Critical Introductions & Reflections* (pp. 94–107). Basingstoke: Palgrave Macmillan.

Seibers, T. (2008). *Disability Theory*. Ann Arbor: Michigan University Press.

Snyder, S. and Mitchell, D. T. (2010). 'Introduction: Ablenationalism and the Geo-Politics of Disability'. *Journal of Literary & Cultural Disability Studies*, 4 (2), 113–26.

Taylor, S. (2004). 'The Right Not to Work: Power and Disability'. *The Monthly Review*, 55 (10), 30–44.

Thornton, M. (1996). *Dissonance and Distrust: Women in the Legal Profession*. Melbourne: Oxford University Press.

United Nations, Division for Social Policy and Development (2003–4). *The Standard Rules on the Equalization of Opportunities for Persons with Disabilities, Abstract*, http://www.un.org/esa/socdev/enable/dissre00.htm, accessed 02 November 2005.

Winance, M, Ville, I. and Ravaud, J. (2007). 'Disability Policies in France: Changes and Tensions between the Category-Based, Universalist and Personalized Approaches'. *Scandinavian Journal of Disability Research*, 9 (3–4), 160–81.

Wolbring, G. (2006). 'The Unenhanced Underclass'. In P. Miller James (ed.), *Better Humans: The Politics of Human Enhancement and Life Extension*, Demos Collection 21. London: Demos Institute.

World Health Organisation (1980). *International Classification of Impairment, Disability & Handicap*. Geneva: World Health Organisation.

World Health Organisation (1992–4). *International Statistical Classification of Disease and Related Health Problems*, 10th Revision, Vols 1–3. Geneva: World Health Organisation.

Part IV
Communities

Part 7.

14
Lave and Wenger, Communities of Practice and Disability Studies

Rebecca Lawthom (with Tsitsi Chataika)

Introduction

The focus of this book is social theories and we may ponder what makes a theory social? Is it about the ability to study and interpret social phenomenon utilising a particular school of thought? Harrington (2005), in discussing the etymology of social theory, locates the origins within ancient Greek culture, in enabling them to make sense of lives and question meanings. In this chapter, we hope to do just that by truly embracing 'the social' of disability theory through communities of practice. We have a number of aims; first we outline a particular theoretical framework – communities of practice, which has received scant attention within disability studies. We present the framework in terms of its historical origins, and then its contemporary usage focusing on the uniqueness of its approach. Second, we link this social theory to the landscape of disability, unpacking how this approach offers possibilities. Third, we outline how the theory can be utilised in a distinct disability employment project. Fourth, we evaluate its potential within this project and further afield. We ask questions about policy and practice and whether this approach can be linked to disability activism. What can a theoretical concept titled communities of practice offer to the disability studies field? This theoretical offering engages directly with processes of inclusion and exclusion – how is disability understood or counted out? There has been little prior work which links communities of practice idea to disability studies (cf. Tobbell and Lawthom, 2005), but we argue that applying these ideas gives rich insight. Identity ownership and contestation has been a key issue for the disabled people's movement and for those who stand inside and outside it. Unpacking how disabled people may come to understand and situate their own identity and that of others is key to this identity project (Giddens, 1991).

Unpacking and positioning communities of practice

The theoretical origins of this approach are located in ideas of cognition. A community of practice is a group of people who have in common a craft, an interest or a profession. The cognitive anthropologists Jean Lave and Etienne Wenger coined the term in the 1990s and the original work centred on ways in which individuals learnt skills through apprenticeship. While a work group such as tailors is a specific group with the explicit purpose of gaining relevant knowledge for that skill, other more emergent and newer groups can be conceptualised. Groups can evolve because of common interests in particular domains or areas. The crucial underpinning assumption here is around what this community of practice does. It is through sharing knowledge and experiences within the group that members learn from each other and hence individuals grow and develop, at the same time, shifting the group/community (Lave and Wenger, 1991). It is possible to see a community of practice in spaces as diverse as online communities, such as discussion boards, or in settings such as workplaces, training environments and leisure groups. The theoretical promise of this work seems both enticing for disability studies and everyday understandings of the dynamics of disability politics. The notion of learning from each other and sharing experiences has existed in disabled people's movements for many years now – so what new insights can this approach offer?

Communities of practice are aggregates of people who share communication, beliefs and values (known collectively as practices). Participants in these so-called communities of practice learn through *doing, becoming and belonging*. While social movements such as the disabled people's movement could be seen as a community of practice, the homogeneity of the identity is much more contested. Indeed, implicit in the term 'community' are processes of inclusion and exclusion – people are counted in or out of settings with potentially serious consequences. To understand inclusion/exclusion we need to theorise what form these communities may take and crucially how participation happens or is stymied.

Communities of practice offer much to our understandings of disability and impairment. In articulating the divergent models of disability – cultural, relational, social – the notion of communities of practice offers interpretative possibilities. When we frame the origins of disability studies to the disabled people's movement then we acknowledge these emancipatory foundations (Campbell and Oliver, 1996). Communities of practice can, however, be found in other models and paradigms of disability research. Following Goodley and Lawthom (2005), we argue that disability is therefore a sociopolitical category; a cultural artefact; a relational and psychological phenomenon; an exclusionary and discriminatory process; a positive identity and entity around which people can collectively and politically organise. Applying ideas from community of practice adds to the literature on disablement – the exclusion of people with impairments. From a macro perspective, the disability movement can be seen as a large global community of practice, with networks of meaning and contacts which are shifting and changing. These networks in different places shift ideas and discourses about disability, influencing and being shaped by policy. This wider disability community of practice is embedded with an ableist culture which treats and deals with disability on a daily basis (Campbell, 2009). Ableist communities of practice privilege 'normal' individuals who can participate fully. From a meso-perspective, disabled individuals or groups (supporters and activists) can intersect with service providers around issues such as access. From a more micro-perspective, having an individual label such as emotional and behavioural difficulties can entail wider social processes like marginalisation, treatment and participation in certain arenas (Tobbell and Lawthom, 2005; Goodley and Runswick-Cole, 2010). In this way, community of practice is seen as experience through which participation can potentially have a wide reach, and we will return to this later.

What is a community of practice?

A community of practice is a collection of people bound together by location, purpose, activity, values, desires or, perhaps, labels. The term first appeared in the seminal work of Jean Lave and Etienne Wenger, 'Situated Learning and Legitimate Peripheral Participation' (Lave and Wenger, 1991). Using the idea of 'legitimate peripheral participation', they described how novice apprentices developed expertise by engaging legitimately in practices of the community and how their trajectory typically involved moving gradually from simple, peripheral tasks to more involved activities that were central to the community. This theory of learning within its localised apprenticeships was then further extended by Wenger (1998) to develop a more generalised, socially situated theory of learning. In terms of understanding communities, communities of practice provide a flexible framework for exploring learning, participatory trajectories, identities and social change initiatives within group contexts. Its versatility and adaptability for exploring diverse communities is evidenced by its expansive adoption across a range of disciplines including, among many others, education (e.g. Bathmaker and Avis, 2006), community psychology (e.g. Lawthom, 2011), healthcare (e.g. Davis, 2006), women's studies and gender (e.g. Paechter, 2003) and sexuality (Whelan, 2009). The applications vary from work involving chosen identities, such as trained teachers through to its usage in how one negotiates identity around sexuality or gender. These more fluid ascriptions can be useful for disability politics around how to reconceptualise disabled identities and disability activism.

Wenger (1998) defined a community of practice as a group of people uniting to mutually engage in a joint enterprise, who together develop and share a common repertoire of resources. A community of practice therefore requires three key dimensions: mutual engagement, shared repertoire and a joint enterprise (Wenger, 1998). The notion of 'mutual engagement' describes the interpersonal relations that emerge from, and are negotiated through, the communal activities of the community. Wenger (1998) uses the term 'joint enterprise' to describe the negotiated processes that create relations of mutual accountability between community members, and to describe the shared activities that structure and lend coherence to the activities of the group. The final element of the tripartite definition, 'shared repertoire', incorporates the 'routines, words, tools, ways of doing things, stories, gestures, symbols, genres, actions, or concepts that the community has produced or adopted in the course of its existence, and which have become part of its practice' (Wenger, 1998: 83). The practice here is a concept, not about simply doing but sharing stories, implicit knowledge and symbols – in short, it is about culture. It encompasses both what is said and shared, and what is not said and assumed. A rich vein of disability theorising has articulated the importance of the tacit in ableist culture (Campbell, 2009) and maps of disability culture (Titchkosky, 2003, 2007).

Titchkosky (2003) uses maps as a representation of and guide to the world to describe the disability experience. While society normally maps disability through categories, interactions and statistics, she argues that rarely is disability seen to offer anything else beyond these details. These maps are commonly used by professionals from many disciplines to seek out spaces for intervention and to remedy deviance. Titchkosky emphasises the utility of a map where disability is located in a place of 'social significance'. The use of traditional cultural maps creates a state of 'between-ness' for disabled people. This state exists between the cultural ideal of 'normalcy' and the lived experience of marginality of disability. Titchkosky argues for the necessity of being receptive to those unique and unexpected lives disability offers and to the thoughts they provoke. Attending to what is privileged in culture is important – for example, whether psychological or physical access to participation in everyday life is allowed, enables particular practices and performances to emerge. An example may help make this more concrete.

Community of practice in a reception class

A child, Tom, begins primary school in a class of around 30 children all between the ages of 4 and 5 years. Tom does not yet have a 'label' although earlier childcare settings have reported problems with Tom's behaviour. The class teacher meets each parent before the start of school and discloses anonymously that a child with a 'problem' will be a class member. The teacher is alerting parents to this label and the consequent treatment. The child has a 'problem' which requires the class to follow a particular behaviour management programme and the information is simply transparently passed on. Some parents complain before school starts about the impact of this upon their children's learning. The teachers have been on a behaviour management course to learn how to manage behaviour according to some behaviourist guru. The treatment programme is communicated to other individuals who work with Tom (classroom assistants). The children in the classroom are all learning the community of practice of a reception class. This classroom is a clear community of practice where good pupils participate in a dominant community of practice, where problem behaviour is something to be managed. In visiting the classroom, the language, tools, documents and images, all reinforce the model of the good learner – a 'rule song' is learnt by heart which emphasises good sitting, good listening and good behaviour as being determinants of model classroom citizenship. In this arena, acting out, or whatever label Tom has, is not part of the dominant community of practice and not valued. The dominant practice of learning – achieved here through good sitting and good listening – marginalises other ways of classroom participation: moving around, talking spontaneously for example. In this setting, a particular kind of participation is valorised and while the behaviour management programme is applied to all in the classroom, Tom continues to learn and participate in his own way. The understanding of behaviour in this context is about curing or changing that which is not dominant – the problem behaviour. By ensuring that all children adhere to a homogeneous set of rules which are inherently linear, it is assumed that only good listening and sitting contributes to learning. Practices (rules, songs, behaviour programmes) and people (children, parents, teacher, behaviour management professionals) shape the experience of this reception classroom and while Tom's trajectory does not end well (he is removed from the setting), practices and people can, of course change communities of practice. The community of practice delineated here requires the mutual engagement of all, the development of shared repertoires and the joint enterprise of learning. It is a 'normal' and normative classroom setting where inclusion into a community of practice cannot happen for all.

While the above example takes place in a classroom, Wenger (1998) clarifies that a community of practice does not exist merely as a consequence of members sharing geographical proximity. The notion of 'community' within community of practice moves distinctly beyond the idea of community as merely concerned with members belonging to a shared space.

Indeed, a community of practice explicitly differentiates itself from definitions of community that are constructed purely in terms of interpersonal networks. It is expressly 'not defined merely by who knows whom or who talks with whom in a network of interpersonal relations through which information flows' (Wenger, 1998: 74). Rather, a community of practice 'exists because it produces a shared practice as members engage in a collective process of learning' (Wenger, 1998: 4). Wenger further unpacks and elaborates the notion of communities of practice:

> As we define enterprises and engage in their pursuit together, we interact with each other and with the world and we tune our relations with each other and with the world accordingly. Over time, this collective learning results in practices that reflect both the pursuit of our enterprises and the attendant social relations. These practices are thus the property of a kind of community created over time by the sustained pursuit of a shared enterprise. It makes sense, therefore, to call these kinds of communities, 'communities of practice'.
>
> (Wenger, 1998: 45)

This definition of engagement and pursuit resonates with the disability movement and the development of a disability community. The shared enterprise here centres on access, inclusion and rights for disabled people who engage with and relate to each other and those outside, thereby creating a community of belonging.[1] The collective learning undertaken by the global community and more localised versions seems to yield developments in social movements, legislation and access issues through sustained engagement. We will return to this point later when we locate the applicability of community of practice to disability activism.

The key concept of community of practice then is not about learning, but here, it is experience through participation. Lave and Wenger developed this concept further into legitimate peripheral participation. Here, the potential to learn, belong, do etc. is mediated by whether participation is allowed. Legitimate peripheral participation occurs when presence is allowed, and therefore members can peripherally participate in order to learn. A disabled individual may join an online network around disability and 'lurk' in the early stages without formally contributing. As times goes on, the lurking permits her/him to understand the debates being aired, see her/his own position differently, see how conflict is handled, and see how individuals respond to outbursts. Gradually, the legitimate peripheral participation afforded allows her/him a window in a community she/he had not previously experienced. Here online participation enables safe inclusion in the form of lurking. Peripheral participation can also be legitimated in 'real' settings where newcomers are given more leeway than core members. Membership in this account is about participation and experience, not learning or expertise. In the same way, participation in a given community is therefore not a given, is not automatic and is not a passive process. Wenger (1998) has suggested a number of sources for understanding individual participation and non-participation. These are:

1. How we locate ourselves in a social landscape
2. What we care about and what we neglect
3. What we attempt to know and understand and what we choose to ignore
4. With whom we seek connection and whom we avoid
5. How we engage and direct our activities
6. How we attempt to steer our trajectories

These sources can help in the context of disability to map how people, places and spaces are inclusive or excluding. For disability activist groups, a clear location in a social landscape may often be a starting point for staking claim to territory. Witness the spoof online group for the Institute for the Study of the Neurologically Typical (2010) (http:/isnt.autistics.org) which introduces the fake condition of neurological typicality. The website defines and derides the presumed normality of others:

> Neurotypical syndrome is a neurobiological disorder characterized by preoccupation with social concerns, delusions of superiority, and obsession with conformity. Neurotypical [NT] individuals often assume that their experience of the world is either the only one, or the only correct one. NTs find it difficult to be alone. NTs are often intolerant of seemingly minor differences in others. When in groups NTs are socially and behaviorally rigid, and frequently insist upon the performance of dysfunctional, destructive, and even impossible rituals as a way of maintaining group identity. NTs find it difficult to communicate directly, and have a much higher incidence of lying as compared to persons on the autistic spectrum. NT is believed to be genetic in origin. Autopsies have shown the brain of the neurotypical is typically smaller than that of an autistic individual and may have overdeveloped areas related to social behaviour.

Goodley (2011) notes that this process of writing back towards professionals and the wider community allows marginalised voices to re-enter the cultural and political critique. It is clear that participation is meaningful in this social theory and that experience in social relations can change people, practices and communities.

Before considering the potential of communities of practice to explore a distinct disability project, the ethical-political motivation driving the development of the framework needs to be outlined. The genesis of the communities of practice framework lies partly in the desire to avoid perpetuating processes of social exclusion:

> I began by arguing the importance of exploring a social rather than psychological theory of learning, motivated in part by a concern not to add blame for 'failure to learn in school' to other burdens of social marginality.
>
> (Lave, 1996: 161)

Rejecting traditional and normate psychological theories that situated learning within individuals, this approach explored learning and identity within its social context. As Lave describes the motivation behind this conceptual shift, her deliberate attempt to avoid the conceptual reproduction of social marginalities becomes apparent:

> It seems imperative to explore ways of understanding learning that do not naturalize and underwrite divisions of social inequality in our society.
>
> (Lave, 1996: 149)

The situated nature of learning described by the communities of practice framework also challenges the traditional supremacy attributed to academic learning and appreciates the knowledge of ordinary people in everyday contexts (Hammersley, 2005). Indeed, situated knowledge (the idea that knowledge cannot be solely an individual product) has a clear parallel in disability theory where marginality and liminality can often exclude or minimise access to traditional learning contexts. In this respect, a communities of practice approach clearly aligns with the principles of community psychology, recognising the expertise and value of people over their own experiences in their own contexts (Kagan et al., 2011).

The everyday experience and theorising of disability culture is a rich site from which to work. Moving away from classroom settings where traditional notions of learning are undertaken, a distinct communities of practice approach acknowledges experience, relating and being embedded occur within everyday settings. Indeed, community of practice thinking is useful in reading disability rather differently within everyday culture – exploring how limited representations of disability enable a particular understanding to emerge. In a similar vein, Paechter (2003) has utilised the community of practice framework to unpack ways in which children learn masculinities and femininities. She argues that gender is performative and through participation and legitimation in adult communities, children relate to issues of masculinity or femininity. The parallels here between gender and disability as itself a performative space are significant. It is in the moving *between* communities of practice which are largely ableist (Campbell, 2009) and potentially safer spaces such as disabled peoples' organisations that participation and belonging are key dimensions. Titchkosky (2007) notes that space (physical and psychological) and the organisation of space itself excludes disabled people. Deploying a community of practice approach allows us to look at the practices in and around disability in communities outside formal education and work contexts. This naturalisation of exclusion is paradoxically called to attention in the form of a call for access. Here, the relationships between the excluded and the included (those with power) can be seen as pivoting around participation and legitimation. Whether and how one participates in a community is as much about how one performs as whether access is enabled.

This original ethical-political motivation of community of practice is sometimes overlooked, or overshadowed by the extensive deployment of the communities of practice framework in explicitly commercial contexts (e.g. Wenger). However, there is also a considerable body of research that continues the tradition of employing communities of practice to explore and overcome the boundaries of social marginality. We argue here that community of practice has much to offer disability theorising.

The relationship between disability and the concept of communities of practice is multifaceted. It is possible to argue that disabled individuals are always trying to enter, participate in and belong to a wider community of practice – that is the non-disabled. Writers such as Campbell (2009) argue that the dominance of ableism needs radical rethinking. Michalko (2002, 1999) argues that disability is a difference needed by the collective other. While communities of practice theory would offer something to this argument, this is a wider philosophical and political debate which requires rather more space. Rather than theorising these wider macro relations of disabled people to non-disabled people using communities of practice, we will draw upon a distinct project. This project highlights and undergirds the problems faced by disabled people, but does so by exploring participation and non-participation in the labour market through a disabled people's organisation.

The jobs not charity project

The research aims of the project 'Jobs not charity' were to understand and challenge the continued exclusion of disabled people from the labour market (Goodley, 2005). In this part of the chapter, we analyse Goodley's report utilising the communities of practice analytical framework. 'Jobs not charity' was a partnership project funded by the European Social Fund, including academic partners at the University of Sheffield and disabled peoples' organisations (DPOs). This was a two-year project which started in

2004. One of the organisations, Greater Manchester Coalition of Disabled People (GMCDP) was established in 1985, and it is a leading organisation in the UK disabled people's movement. It has much experience in organising community-based responses to develop greater inclusion around service provision for disabled people. The other partner, Breakthrough UK Ltd is a community-based support network for disabled people to access employment. It provides mainstream community-based employment and training to disabled people who are aiming to overcome social exclusion in employment. Both partners are organisations for disabled people, run by disabled people who demonstrate a capacity to challenge discrimination and enable disabled people (see Campbell and Oliver, 1996).

The Disability Rights Commission estimates that disabled people in the UK are seven times more likely than non-disabled people to be out of work and claiming benefits. Recent figures from the Office for National Statistics (ONS, 2009) suggest that nearly one in five people of working age (7 million or 18.6%) have an impairment. In addition, only half of disabled people are in working age compared to 80 per cent of non disabled people. The research took place during 2005–6 when the economic climate was brighter and the legislative landscape different. While UK disability rights have been extended through the Disability Discrimination Act (1995) and the Special Educational Needs and Disability Act (2001), the more recent UK legislation is the Equality Act 2010, which provides a single legal framework to protect rights for all and equalise opportunity. Published data whether from ONS, Disability Rights or the Office for Disability Issues conveys a context where employment barriers remain (among other access issues). Against this backdrop, the 'Jobs not charity' project had four distinct aims:

1. To examine the position of disabled people in the labour market, including demographic details.
2. To qualitatively explore a number of disabled people's experiences of employment and to trace the impact of policy and practice on their life histories of work.
3. To critically account for the work of DPOs in promoting work opportunities of disabled people.
4. To disseminate findings in the context of legislation and policy related to disability and employment.

The aims were explored using methodologies appropriate for each focus and encompassed documentary analysis, narrative research with disabled people and ethnographic research with organisations of disabled people. Space here precludes in-depth analysis of each strand, but we interpret the data gathered using an explicit community of practice lens. We focus on aims 2 and 3, using aim 3 to contextualise the stories which follow.

Aim 3: Case study of Breakthrough UK as positive community of practice

Dorothy Smith (2005) earlier coined the phrase institutional ethnography as an approach which had a number of aims:

- To expose wider social relations that shape people's lives
- To view members of an institution as expert knowers
- To use lived experience of individuals to throw light onto systems that impact, describe and inform their lives
- To access the perspectives of those often excluded from dominant discussions of policy and society
- To unpick the philosophies that underpin an institution or organisation
- To look at how people's activities contribute to the maintenance of that organisation

In utilising this approach, the data revealed much of interest. Here, we apply a community of practice lens to this institutional ethnography. The key organisation, Breakthrough UK is a social enterprise. Social enterprises are businesses with primarily social objectives whose surpluses are principally reinvested for that purpose in the business or in the community, rather than being driven by the need to maximise profit for shareholders and owners. Here, the enterprise is around supporting disabled people into employment. The social enterprise is managed and run by disabled people, engaged in training and employment support. Advisors are key participants in this process, and they receive referrals from agencies or individuals who self-refer, and conduct interviews to profile each individual. Tailor-made training, goal setting and skill development are key components of the role. This encompasses both practical tasks such as updating CVs, application forms and enhancing interview and presentation performance. Individuals looking for work may undergo mock interviews and deliver mock presentations in order to realistically prepare for 'real world' settings. In addition to working within the organisation, advisors also market clients to employers (focusing on strength) and provide follow up support. Here, advisors are boundary spanners, scanning the employment environment and enabling clients into work.

What is really going on in this enterprise, and can this kind of supportive environment be read as a community of practice? We shall leave larger questions behind, such as ideas around work, productivity and citizenship; but clearly, these could be interpreted as moral discourses of communities of practice – the notion of work itself as gainful. In exploring what Breakthrough UK does, it acts as an-employment community of practice replicating and transmitting the dominant employment practices of the day and a broker for employment outside. In employing paid workers and enabling volunteers, it allows for standard employment contracts and provides

244 Communities of Practice

a gaze in the form of a realistic job preview for volunteers. Participation in this enterprise is legitimated from core members (who may identify themselves as disabled) and enable opportunities to participate in a work setting through volunteering opportunites. The advisors act as brokers both to the immediate community of practice, Breakthrough UK, but also the wider employment community of practice. The voluntary work experience allows individuals to experience the culture of organisations and work as an active member rather than as a client in a professional setting. Participation in this environment enables more than individual growth and expertise – in working alongside disabled people, the organisation consistently morphs and shapes to accommodate novelty. The general social exclusion of disabled people is not a valued practice in this organisation, and thus the vision of enabling practice is very much part of the culture – a 'can do' philosophy. Mock interviews serve to induct the newcomer into the everyday practices of employment related organisations and also provide a window of peripheral participation into how organisations out there do recruitment and selection. Individual clients in belonging to Breakthrough can see how disability can be dealt with positively and in working alongside disabled people within the community can see how other disabled people thrive and survive at work.

This community of practice lens allows us to gaze upon employment spaces as contexts in which disabled and non-disabled individuals are embedded in systems which shape actions, reactions and interactions. This gaze allows experience to be prioritised over learning per se. Titchkosky (2003), in centring disability, shows that experiencing the world through a disability-centred lens provides insight. 'To put it bluntly, it is often not pragmatic for a disabled person to move, live and work in some environments but it is valuable.'

In positioning its clients, Breakthrough UK seems to allow individuals to possibly transcend the between-ness of being disabled and the accompanying marginality. The space afforded them allows disabled individuals to navigate employment trajectories with support and to utilise different ways of participating.

The community of practice lens employed here builds on a body of work which has emphasised jobs over charity (McQuaid and Lindsay, 2005); advocated in/formal means of supporting disabled people into and through work (Roulstone et al, 2003); positioned employment as one route out of a more general social exclusion (Barnes and Mercer, 2003); and developed enabling practice built on the social model (Gibbs, 2005). A distinct communities of practice approach offers insight into how these processes (advocacy, inclusion, enabling practices etc.) may occur.

Aim 2: Exploring disabled people through life history

This strand of work explored the ways in which the life stories of individuals were entwined with disabled people's organisations – Breakthrough UK and the GMCDP (Goodley, 2005). Rich narratives from 30 diverse participants were collected, representing each organisation, a mix of ethnic backgrounds and ranging in ages, gender and type of impairment. Interviews were transcribed, written into stories and checked by informants. In this chapter we refer below to extracts from these stories presented in Goodley (2005). The anonymisation process removed names from individuals and organisations. While storytelling is a feature of everyday life, it also enables individuals to make sense of their life through story. There is insufficient space to rehearse arguments around the merits of analysis and stories (see Goodley et al. (2004) for fuller discussion of this). Here, we take the position that stories are in need of analysis to interrogate the reciprocal relationships between individuals, groups and social structures. We refute the ubiquity of the overcoming disability story (Titchkosky, 2008), rather locating disability within structures and experiences which serve Western culture (Titchkosky, 2008). The stories, in line with Dorothy Smith, allowed access to institutional practices and the wider social world. Stories are related to time and space:

> We are connected to our histories .... [t]hrough our experience of participation as our identities are formed, inherited, rejected, interlocked and transformed through mutual engagement in practice from generation to generation.
>
> (Wenger, 1998: 89)

A number of overlapping themes emerged from the 30 stories. These included the importance and meaning of work, the continuing existence of barriers, how knowledge of legislation and human rights impacted on life stories, and how DPOs they belonged to promoted the interdependence of disabled people and the significance of the social model to understanding. Here, we explore this latter theme only. Shakespeare (2000) and others have noted the importance of interdependence around being supported back into work. Reindall (1999) critiques employment initiatives which locate problems within disabled individuals, and prioritise achievements and targets at the individual level rather than within workplace culture. Participants spoke of appropriate support (financial and otherwise) towards employment. While interdependence (Morris, 1996; Goodley, 2001) is a normative way of life for all, disabled people are exhorted to achieve independence. A participant notes:

> I think there are ways to get round whatever impairment you've got so that you have got control to do things yourself. For me, I just wanted to pay people to do what I want them to do ... It's getting very hard for me now to do the audits (around direct payments) because of my memory and I am going to let an accountant do it who is employed by Direct Payments.

Here, options are increased by appropriate support. Informants narrated ways in which the DPO elevated interdependence through shared values of commonality, respect, recognition, a sense of worth and understanding the social model. Across the interviews individuals self-identified as disabled and the commonality allowed a relational identity to emerge.

> My involvement with GMCDP made me aware of my rights as a disabled person, something I wasn't aware of before. It made me feel that although I was a disabled person, I was an equal, I am a person, and I am just the same as anybody else. When you are outside of that loop, you feel as if you are alienated, as if you are different to everybody else, as if you should be seen and not heard. This was completely different, and this really appealed to me. I learnt so much in a short space of time about my rights about myself as a person, my confidence grew immensely.

Here, we see ways in which disability can be a community of practice, or communities of practice. While 'out of the loop' the informant feels alienated and different, utilising an old Victorian phrase reserved for children – 'seen and not heard'. For this individual, the legitimate peripheral participation afforded by the DPO is a lens on how other disabled people do identity. In this context, an awareness of rights and equal status begins to emerge. Here, the disabled individual learns to perform identity rather differently – in community of practice language terms – this process allows a different participation in a social space. While participating in the radical space (here the DPO), they are also simultaneously participating in other communities of practice outside. Belonging to the DPO is seen through practices which are represented (formal channels of support, finance, accessible buildings, etc.) but also assumed. An informant notes:

> People out there have no respect for people like ourselves. People in Breakthrough UK Ltd, just respect each other. It feels like a second home to me. Respect is everything isn't it?

The respect and recognition inherent in the DPOs here is shared across proximal and distal contexts. A refugee project within one of the DPOs provided support and education to disabled refugees. One of the refugees expressed shock at being taught by other disabled people – this had, however, inspired him. Here, a disabled refugee is learning to be a full member in a number of competing communities of practice – the new host country, the local community, the DPO and the world of employment. In this way, the disabled refugee group is learning/doing a different positive disabled identity *and* shifting practices through renegotiating the disability focus of the DPO around refugee concerns. The negotiation and renegotiation of meaning is a distinct dimension of practice for Wenger (1998). The localised understanding given by the DPO around being disabled intersects with a larger community of practice (society) and other communities of practice such as being a refugee. At times, individuals will share full membership of the community (a shared marginal refugee status), while at other peripheral membership is more likely (access to DPO through a disabled refugee group). We are arguing here that practices shift and flex, through reciprocal interaction. The community of practice lens allows social configurations to be just that as fluid configurations rather than intersections. Titchkosky (2008) notes that the processes of inclusion are 'part of that which structures the continued manifestation of disabled people as a non-viable type' (2008: 5). She argues for the need to think about how we notice and not notice these forms of inclusion and exclusion. Disability is both excluded and included simultaneously in ways that we notice and not notice otherness. The contradictions in this belonging and not belonging are potentially glimpsed through a communities of practice analysis. A participant talks of recognition and belonging:

> It is about not overcoming my impairment but recognising my impairment: it's a part of me. More importantly it's about recognising that I have the right to be equal in society

In accessing DPOs, participants articulated a sense of local service coherence. At times, this was very much about their own individual gain; but crucially, a glimpse of wider more complex relationships was often voiced. The shared history of the social model serves community membership – the memory of earlier struggles encourages a sense of belonging:

> The social model, independent living, the acceptance of the right of disabled people to have reasonable adjustments, these are all cultured into the organization, our policies and our practice.
>
> (DPO employee)

This 'radical' advocacy of rights of disabled people contrasts sharply with the implicit kinds of organisations referred to here. Paechter's usage of pollution and purity are useful here. Powerful communities of practice – here the dominant work community for non-disabled people – police their boundaries to retain 'purity'. Claims to penetrate the community can blur the boundaries and in many ways Breakthrough UK is doing just this – aiming to 'pollute' and therefore transform the community. Informants who were embedded firmly within the DPO articulated a rich sense of identity, community and belonging:

> Non-disabled people have been duped by these ideas of what is normal. They have been disempowered by this concept of normality as much as I have.

The concepts within communities of practice open up a space for disability activism. We may theorise that politicisation is mobilised by legitimate peripheral participation within explicit disability related spaces; this is in opposition to illegitimate peripheral participation in non-disabled spaces. However, as Campbell (2009) argues, disability studies needs to engage more with an ableist landscape – the very spaces where participation is contested. The non-recognition or pitying recognition bestowed upon disabled people by others is heightened through rich recognition within safe, disability friendly spaces – the DPOs in this study. In this context, DPOs are investing in normalcy (Titchkosky, 2008) to advocate for individuals, sustain and extend employment opportunities and recognise the disabled individual as a person:

> This personhood can be found if others possess the right attitude and can see past disability to the inner core of an essential self – the economic and social contributor.
>
> (Titchkosky, 2007: 69)

The approach of community of practice has allowed fresh insight into processes of inclusion, exclusion and participation. Humphreys (2000) notes the folly of complete pre-determination of a model prior to gathering data. Using a lens retrospectively allows a different world-view to emerge. Critics have argued that a communities of practice approach does not explicitly attend to power. We have little time to redress this but following Paechter (2003), we note the relationship between localised communities of practice and wider configurations. This imports a Foucauldian notion of power relations as within and between local communities of practice contributing to and underpinning power relations within and between wider practices. We would argue that the project drawn upon in this chapter provides an analysis of power. For example, a disabled refugee engaging with a DPO explicitly engages with power everyday – through healthcare, legal and housing battles. Questions of access and status are individually experienced differently across communities of practice (the DPO, healthcare settings, education) but are part of a wider surveillance individuals are subjected to. We see many of these processes at play in a recent project exploring local and global constructions of disability (www.mmu.ac.uk.rihsc/malaysiauk/), where complex issues arise around the simple exporting of Global North ideas into other contexts. The ways in which power and knowledge are connected to constructions of disability raises important research questions. To understand more about the different communities of practice inhabited by non-disabled and disabled people, or exporting those in Global North contexts to those in Global South, we need to unpack the relationship between power/knowledge, legitimation and the learning of non-disabled and disabled identities within communities of practice.

Elsewhere, one of us has argued (Lawthom and Goodley, 2005) that enabling psychological practices (around understanding disability) demands that impairment be rethought of as more than an individual variable and move towards transformational change in organisations. We need to move towards a future espoused by Michalko (2002) where disability is conceived of as a difference that does not make a difference. 'An ethics of alterity holds that, through reflective analysis, the notion that disability is only a problem in need of a solution can itself be dis-solved' (Titchkosky, 2007).

A communities of practice approach gazes at the designations of disabled and non-disabled, the lived and the living with – to imagine how 'we', disability and non-disability community members, might tell a story differently (Titchkosky, 2007). Through seeing and reading disability and otherness as related to ability, a community of practice approach configures alterity rather differently. It is possible to see the discursive space as one in which practices of inclusion and exclusion coexist and jar.

Conclusion

In this chapter, we explored the community/communities of practice theoretical framework, and its relevance within the disability studies discourse. We further unpacked this social theory through the 'Jobs not charity' project, which explored experiences of disabled people in the labour market. What is clear is that this theoretical offering engages directly with processes of inclusion and exclusion and how disability is conceptualised. We therefore argue that although there has been little prior work which links communities of practice idea to disability studies, applying these ideas gives rich insight and offers possibilities. This approach can also be linked to disability activism. We therefore strongly feel that through sharing knowledge and experiences within diverse communities (communities of practice), members can learn from each other, and promote both individual and community growth and development. In this way, there is a possibility of fostering common understanding within groups/communities, and eventually building communities of trust where respect, tolerance, trust and diversity are embraced. We need to reach a space where disability is theorised in rich ways, acknowledging that we are all to varying extents engaged with notions of ability and disability. Recent interdisciplinary work (e.g. Goodley, 2011) advocates for dialogue across disciplines and approaches.

Web resources

Breakthrough UK Ltd – http://www.breakthrough-uk.co.uk/, accessed 13 June 2010.
'Jobs not charity' research project – http://www.shef.ac.uk/jobsnotcharity/, accessed 13 June 2010.

Greater Manchester Coalition of disabled people – http://www.gmcdp.com/, accessed 13 June 2010.

Notes

1. For a brilliant account of how touch through dusting relates to belonging, see Michalko's (2010) work on Dusting: Blindness, Touch and Belonging. In this account, place is practice which affords touching and belonging. Dusting invites looking.

References

Barnes, C. and Mercer, G. (2003). *Disability: Key Concepts*. Cambridge: Policy Press.

Bathmaker, A. and Avis, J. (2006). 'Becoming a Lecturer in Further Education in England: The Construction of Professional Identity and the Role of Communities of Practice'. *Journal of Education for Teaching*, 31 (1), 47–62.

Campbell, F. K. (2009). *Contours of Ableism: The Production of Disability and Abledness*. London: Palgrave Macmillan.

Campbell, J. and Oliver, M. (1996). *Disability Politics: Understanding Our Past, Changing Our Future*. London: Routledge.

Davis, J. (2006). 'The Importance of the Community of Practice in Identity Development'. *Internet Journal of Allied Health Sciences and Practice*, 4 (3), 1–8.

Gibbs, D. (2005). 'Employment Policy and Practice: A Perspective from the Disabled People's Movement'. In A. Roulstone and C. Barnes (eds), *Working Futures Disabled People, Policy and Social Inclusion*. Bristol: Policy Press.

Giddens, A. (1991). *Modernity and Self-Identity: Self and Society in Late Modern Age*. London: Polity Press.

Goodley, D. (2011). *Disability Studies: An Interdisciplinary Introduction*. London: Sage.

Goodley, D. (2005). 'Jobs not charity' project report, http://www.shef.ac.uk/jobsnotcharity/, accessed 3 September 2010.

Goodley, D. (2001). '"Learning Difficulties", the Social Model of Disability and Impairment: Challenging Epistemologies'. *Disability and Society*, 16 (2), 207–31.

Goodley, D., Lawthom, R., Clough, P. and Moore, M. (2004). *Researching Life Stories: Method, Theory and Analyses in a Biographical Age*. London: Routledge Falmer Press.

Goodley, D. and Lawthom, R. (eds) (2005). *Psychology and Disability*. London: Palgrave Macmillan.

Goodley, D. and Runswick-Cole, K. (2010). 'Emancipating Play: Dis/abled Children, Development and Deconstruction'. *Disability & Society*, 25 (4), 499–512.

Hammersley, M. (2005). 'What can the Literature on Communities of Practice Tell Us about Educational Research? Reflections on Some Recent Proposals'. *International Journal of Research & Method in Education*, 28 (1), 5–21.

Harrington, A. (2005). *Modern Social Theory: An Introduction*. Oxford, UK: Oxford University Press.

Humphreys, C. (2000). 'Researching Disability Politics, Or, Some Problems with the Social Model in Practice'. *Disability & Society*, 15 (1), 63–86.

Institute for the Study of the Neurologically Typical (2010). (http:/isnt.autistics.org), accessed 10 October 2010.

Kagan, C., Burton, M., Duckett, P., Lawthom, R. and Siddiquee, A. (2011). *Critical Community Psychology: Critical Action and Social Change*. London: Blackwell.

Lave, J. (1996). 'Teaching, as Learning, in Practice'. *Mind, Culture and Activity*, 3 (3), 149–64.

Lave, J. and Wenger, E. (1991). *Situated Learning: Legitimate Peripheral Participation*. Cambridge: Cambridge University Press.

Lawthom, R. (2011). 'Developing Learning Communities: Using Communities of Practice within Community Psychology'. *International Journal of Inclusive Education*, 15 (1), 153–65.

McQuaid, R. W. and Lindsay, C. (2005). 'The Concept of Employability'. *Urban Studies*, 42 (2), 197–219.

Michalko, R. (1999). *The Two in One. Walking with Smokie, Walking with Blindness*. Philadelphia: Temple University Press.

Michalko, R. (2002). *The Difference that Disability Makes*. Philadelphia: Temple University Press.

Morris, J. (ed.) (1996). *Encounters with Strangers: Feminism and Disability*. London: The Women's Press.

Paechter, C. (2003). 'Masculinities and Femininities as Communities of Practice'. *Women's Studies International Journal*, 26 (1), 69–77.

Reindal, S. M. (1999). 'Independence, Dependence, Interdependence: Some Reflections on the Subject and Personal Autonomy'. *Disability & Society*, 14 (3), 353–67.

Roulstone, A., Child, L. and Price, J. (2003). *Thriving and Surviving in the Workplace: Disabled Peoples' Employment Strategies*. Bristol: Policy Press.

Shakespeare, T. (2000). *Help*. London: Venture Press.

Smith, D. E. (2005). *Institutional Ethnography: A Sociology for People*. Toronto: Alta Mira Press.

Titchkosky, T. (2003). *Disability, Self and Society*. Toronto: University of Toronto Press.

Titchkosky, T. (2007). *Reading and Writing Disability Differently: The Textured Life of Embodiment*. Toronto: University of Toronto Press.

Tobbell, J. and Lawthom, R. (2005). 'Dispensing with Labels: Enabling Children and Professionals to Share a Community of Practice'. *Journal of Child and Educational Psychology*, 22 (3), 89–97.

Wenger, L. (1998). *Communities of Practice: Learning, Meaning and Identity*. Cambridge: Cambridge University Press.

Whelan, P. (2009). 'Using a Communities of Practice Approach within LGBT Communities'. Unpublished MSc Thesis, Manchester Metropolitan University.

15
Disability, Development and Postcolonialism

Tsitsi Chataika

Introduction

The core of this book is to draw from a body of interdisciplinary analyses for the development of disability studies. In line with the object of this text, this chapter unpacks the political struggle in the disability, development and postcolonial discourses. The struggle is about challenging oppression, voice-lessness, stereotyping, undermining, neo-colonisation, postcolonisation, 'them and us' and bridging the gap between Global North and Global South spaces in the disability and development research agenda. This chapter adopts terms Global North and Global South to refer to the broad division of countries in relation to resources and power. Global North states are usu-ally known as 'developed, high in-come, thriving, or first world countries'. Global South nations are located in Africa, Central and Latin America, and most of Asia, and are usually referred to as 'developing, low-income, failing, majority world, or third world countries' (Stubbs, 1999).

Disability, development and postcolonialism are critical tripartite inter-twined discourses in the social construction of any country. Unfortunately, these discourses have always been approached as independent from each other, thus missing the critical analysis that informs critical disability studies research (Goodley, 2011; Barker and Murray, 2010; Sherry, 2010). Goodley (2011) points out that disability studies takes into account the social, cul-tural and political phenomena. Consequently, this chapter brings together debates around disability and development and how they intertwine with postcolonialism. It further explores possible pathways of bridging the gap between the Global South and Global North's power relations, informed by a critical analysis of disability research understanding (Goodley, 2011; Barker and Murray, 2010).

The chapter concludes with a call for a critical disability and development agenda that promotes genuine collaboration between the Global North and the Global South, with the view of engaging in a 'marriage of commitment'. The intention is to create an echelon platform that is accessible to the usually marginalised Global South research communities by enabling them to make use of indigenous knowledge, which in many cases, is neglected or misrepresented. The ultimate goal is to build communities of trust that can enrich both spaces using a critical postcolonial disability studies research agenda.

Disability, development and postcolonialism

Disability researchers, development workers and postcolonial theorists have, for a long time, worked independently, and they have made little effort to ensure that their work complement each other. Sherry (2010), Barker and Murray (2010) and Meekosha (2008) are among the very few writers to acknowledge the interconnectedness of the three discourses. Barker and Murray (2010) in their article explore the intersections of disability and postcolonialism, and propose not to hold them at a distance from one another because of the arbitrary lines that divide the two disciplines. This chapter interrogates the critical interface between disability and postcolonial studies, the argument being that disability potentially stresses the material and located nature of postcolonial cultures (Barker and Murray, 2010). It further emphasises the embodied nature of agency and community that have a direct impact on any country's development initiatives (Meekosha, 2008). Regrettably, disability issues still struggle to infiltrate into the development agenda and postcolonial theory work, marking a significant exclusion of a critical disability studies analysis that examines the social, cultural, economic and political relational dimensions (Goodley, 2011; Barker and Murray, 2010; Meekosha and Dowse, 2007).

This chapter has no intention of defining disability, but to acknowledge that it manifests itself through the interaction of individuals with their functional limitations (impairment) and the social, attitudinal and physical environment in which they live (Masala and Petretto, 2008). Disability is also a complex notion, whose debate is often partial and fragmented, often bypassing the power relations and cultural dynamics defining it. The major purpose of the emerging critical disability studies is directed towards challenging power relations (Meekosha and Dowse, 2007), questioning the overriding epistemologies and exploring the themes frequently bypassed, ignored or rejected by the dominant Global North disability studies (Grech, 2010; Meekosha, 2008).

The chapter further acknowledges that development is a complex concept, with diverse and sometimes, debatable definitions. However, I draw upon Comhlámh's Volunteering Options' (2008) perspective of development, which is about freeing people from obstacles that affect their ability to develop their own lives and communities. The emphasis here is on empowerment whereby local people take control of their own lives, expressing their own demands and seeking their own solutions to their problems. Although many funders are now demanding that disabled people be included as a condition for awarding disability and development project funds, Albert and Harrison (2010) argue that in most cases, Global North organisations with the resources and 'knowledge' to bid for such grants have always developed the research proposals. Later, they hunt for Global South organisations of disabled people willing to become 'partners'. This downstream partnership might end up having a preset research agenda, with unequal and unchallenged power relations between the researchers and the researched and with real control lying in the hands of the former. Meaningful research meant to support sustainable development demands that local people take a leading role, and not merely be 'included' or 'consulted' (Albert and Harrison, 2010).

Postcolonial theory looks at literature and society in two ways: how the writer, artist, cultural worker, and his or her context reflects a colonial past, and how they survive and discover a new way of creating and understanding the world (Said, 2004; Ashcroft et al., 1995). It may also deal with literature written by former colonial nations who take their colonies as the subject matter. The theory is based upon the concepts of otherness and resistance (Said, 2004).

I prefer not to hyphenate 'postcolonialism', since 'post-colonialism' might imply that colonialism and its effects disappear as soon as the occupying country has vacated and rule is returned to the indigenous people. To believe that colonialism can just come to a sudden end upon attainment of political independence is certainly naive. Colonialism, which brings with it 'new values, new beliefs, foreign languages, and alien traditions; cannot be shed like the skin of a snake and then tossed away and forgotten' (Ashcroft et al., 1995: 2). It will always leave some colonial remnants. Nelson Mandela's experiences in his book *Long Walk to Freedom* sums up typical apartheid indoctrination, which regrettably still shape the thinking of some Global South occupants, including those from the Global North:

> We were taught and 'believed' that the best ideas were English ideas, the best government was English government, and the best men were English men.
>
> (Mandela, 2002: 53)

Disability and development intersecting with postcolonialism

The articulation of intersecting identities is a significant though ignored area within the designated disability, development or postcolonial studies. In cases where there are intersections, most of the time, they are defined by the Global North and its epistemologies (Parekh, 2007). For instance, disability and development in Africa has largely been spearheaded by the Global North development agencies and researchers. Caught in the torrent of upheavals that characterised the victory over colonialism, it can be easy for the Global North (colonial masters) to become romantic and blinkered by their own enthusiasm of 'bringing development to the [Global South] people' (Manji and O'Coill, 2002: 7). In many cases, the challenge is that the dominant discourse of development is framed not in the language of emancipation or justice, but in the vocabulary of charity, technical expertise, and a deep paternalism as its syntax. The disability and development agenda, in some sense, turns out to be like the Welfare discourse where professionals such as social workers come in to 'fix' the individual or the situation. What comes to mind here is the tendency of many Global North research institutions and agencies who enter into a 'relationship' as consultants with the 'expertise' (and of course the budget); instead of developing collaborative relationships where parties are equal, and where differences are used as learning moments to benefit both parties. The Global North development partners such as the Department for International Development (DFID) have now acknowledged the need to develop disabled people's capacity in order to shift power to the Global South stakeholders. The Southern African Federation of the Disabled (SAFOD) challenged the DFID's way of conducting disability research, which in turn agreed to fund the SAFOD Research Programme (SRP). This programme started in 2009, with the intention of seeing disabled people in the research driving seat (Fumulani, 2010). The objective of the SRP is to build capacity (among DPOs) to design, drive, own and use research to influence policy and practice that responds to the particular needs and interests of disabled people in Southern Africa. SAFOD's argument was that disability research has to be socialised and claimed back by the people concerned, and '[find] its way from the academic shelves to the centre of society in order to provide evidence to action' (Fumulani, 2010: 3). This setting vindicates SAFOD and member organisations' assertion that currently there is a huge gap in research on the link between disability and poverty (Fumulani, 2010; Phiri, 2010). This is evidenced by very minimal (if at all) involvement of disabled people in many Global South Poverty Reduction Strategy Papers (PRSPs), initiated by the World Bank and IMF (Mwendwa, Murangira and Lang, 2009). While there is a comprehensible link between disability and poverty, the lack of resolute studies, has not only prevented the creation of a sound understanding of the specific causal links, this regrettably has also provided the basis for a discourse that denies the agency of disabled people, and continues to portray them as dependent on the good will of the 'significant' others. Here, a critical disability studies discourse becomes inevitable if the current situation of disabled people is to change.

While the vision of development appears to offer a more inclusive path to 'progress' than had previously been the case, the discourse is little more than a superficial reformulation of old colonial prejudices (Crush, 1995). The question now is: 'What baggage do the Global North stakeholders bring along (beliefs and values) into the Global South space when engaging in disability and development initiatives?' Prejudice is abhorrent and should not have any space in the twenty-first century. Unfortunately, such deplorable issues still exist, particularly in Africa; and they should be addressed in order to have sustainable Global South/Global North research collaboration. As with the racist ideologies of the past, the discourse of development continues to define the Global South in terms of their perceived divergence from the cultural standards of the Global North (Manji and O'Coill, 2002). Sadly, this definition reproduces the social hierarchies that have always prevailed between the Global South and Global North under colonialism.

Africa faces the greatest challenge of establishing and making use of its own research for effective decision-making in development programmes and policymaking. Budgets for research and development are not as adequate as for those of our colleagues in the Global North, hence research personnel to support the research evidence, which is so critical in policy development and implementation in the Global South is very limited. There have been numerous international research grants meant to gather empirical evidence in Africa, without developing practical solutions to address the way in which Africa may become more responsive to, and more inclusive of disabled people (Chataika, 2007; Mpofu, 2002). In many cases, these expeditions have undermined the indigenous knowledge and cultural dynamics of the African continent (Mji et al., 2009). It is this scarcity of indigenous voices in disability research that saw the establishment of the African Network on Evidence-to-Action on Disability (AfriNEAD) (www.afrinead.org). AfriNEAD is a flagship project of the Centre for Rehabilitation Studies at Stellenbosch University in South Africa. The African Decade of Persons with Disabilities and the Centre for Global Health at Trinity College in Dublin are early partners in this initiative (Mji et al., 2009). This fluid network facilitates networking among researchers, disabled people, government representatives, business, civil society and international partners who hold a similar vision. The vision is to facilitate a comprehensive, inter-sectoral, interactive forum for debate around evidence-to-action on disability with a view to ensuring that disability is part of the national development agenda in Africa (Mji et al., 2009). It further seeks to build communities of trust with partners from the Global North.

The first AfriNEAD symposium was held in Cape Town in November 2007, and it attracted delegates from 14 African countries, and a few from the Global North. Since the UNCRPD had just been passed, the theme of the symposium was 'Realising the Rights of People with Disabilities in Africa'. Following the success of the first symposium, and to follow up on critical issues that were raised, delegates unanimously agreed to make the symposium a bi-annual event. The theme of the 2009 AfriNEAD symposium was: 'The ABC for Research Evidence-to-Action: Putting the UNCRPD Principles into Action for Rights-Based Change'. The third AfriNEAD symposium took place in Victoria Falls (Zimbabwe) in November, 2011 under the theme: 'Building Communities of Trust: Evidence-to-Action on Disability Research', which fits very well with the deliberations of this book chapter.

As highlighted before, disability and development conversations between the Global North and the Global South, particularly Africa, have tended to be unequal and in favour of the former. They have been unequal in the sense that models, technologies and practices for instance in disability are adopted from the Global North, and applied to African communities without any cultural adaptations (Mpofu, 2002). These include the contested medical model of disability and the social model of disability. These two conceptualisations of disability have been treated as competitors where one has to triumph over and abolish the other in thinking about who disabled people are, and what should be said and done to them (Silvers, 2010). However, Silvers ascertains that both models (Western) see disability as the nucleus of the difficulties faced by disabled people:

> Whilst the medical model treats disability to be a problem requiring medical intervention as both the prerogative and responsibility of medical professionals to fix, the social model understands disability as a political problem calling for corrective action by citizen activists who alter people's attitudes and reform the practices of the state.
>
> (Silvers, 2010: 19)

The social model has been enjoying some solid support from disability activists, disability studies scholars and development agencies because of its ability to challenge the physical and social dynamics of society in relations to disability. However, critics of the social model have emerged from both camps. They claim that the social model should be revised into a disability theory that accurately reflects disabled people's experiences, priorities and needs (Silvers, 2010; Grech, 2010; Scully, 2008). Silvers indicates that

> The social model stands accused in some quarters of misrepresenting disabled people by abridging who they are, or even malignant distortions such as promoting values that exclude people with certain kinds of physical or cognitive limitations. These complaints are connected in that the former criticizes the social model for suppressing rather than showcasing disabled people's differences, especially dysfunctional ones, while the latter objects to advancing an idea of independence what some disabled people's dysfunctions make unrealizable for them.
>
> (Silvers, 2010: 19)

Silvers further points out that the above charges also echo issues that the medical model bring

> that to ignore experiences of being weak, enervated, in pain and vulnerable in modelling disability is deceptive because these are the most salient experiences in most, or at least, in many disabled people's lives.
>
> (Silvers, 2010: 19)

Grech (2010) argues that the social model seems to be unequipped and even reluctant to engage with contextual, historical, economic and many other critical aspects that differentiate the Global South in its intricate heterogeneity. These include the colonial legacy, lack of access to social services such as health services, chronic poverty and civil wars that characterise most Global South nations, further fuelling the magnitude of disability prevalence. Scully (2008) fears that the social model artificially splits the personal and the political apart, and fails to recognise that embodied perception and cognition distances disabled people's experiences from those people with non-disabled bodies.

Ironically, at the same time as some disability studies scholars are distancing themselves from the social model, some medical professionals are drawing closer to it. Silvers (2010) cites recent Institute of Medicine's (2007) report, which pointed out the social dimension of disability by highlighting that disability is not inherent in individuals, but rather it is the result of interaction between people and their physical and social environments. This is a clear paradigm shift for some of the medical professionals from the medical model towards the social model. With the above mixed perceptions, Grech (2010) calls for a critical global disability studies, informed by both the Global North and Global South, which cuts across disciplines and is transparent, questioning and eager to learn, and to challenge its own ideas at the centre.

The above contested models from the Global North, in many cases, are transplanted into the Global South arena without taking into cognisance cultural, political, economic and social dimensions. Anita Ghai critiques the Western universalising discourse by arguing that it 'ignores the harsh realities of disabled people who live in countries such as India, which are caught in social and economic marginalization' (Ghai, 2002: 96). She further argues that 'postcolonialism can destabilize the totalizing tendencies of imported western discourse' (2002: 96). On the other hand, welcoming new influences should not mean a rejection of positive traditional culture. Neither should it mean an acceptance of the view that African culture is inferior to new culture from foreign countries. If foreign ideologies bring positive elements into a culture, those positive elements should be accepted if they serve a useful purpose or fill in a gap in the traditional culture (Chung and Ngara, 1985). Similarly, negative aspects of traditional culture should be discarded. These include viewing disability as a form of punishment from God, angry ancestral spirits or a result of witchcraft (Chataika, 2007). It is critical to recognise postcolonial commentators' view that we need to be wary of colonising the Global South in the name of globalisation without striking a balance between the two spaces (Chataika, 2007). By implication, any bi-lateral links should avoid undermining local expertise and local cultural values. In this way, knowledge exchange can be promoted in a more impartial way.

In the twenty-first century, globalising disability and the development agenda have often become inseparable from the 'scramble for Africa' era where the Global North was determined to occupy the 'most fertile land'. However, the flipside of the coin now is that the Global North is armed with 'research funds' to execute disability and development projects. The intention of these 'expeditions' is to 'bring light' to the Global South through redressing its 'social ills', which, to a larger extent, are manifestations of the colonial legacy. Here, the culture of 'development' seems to focus on the 'crucial role' of the Global North 'developing' the Global South. Unfortunately, very little has been examined about the role of the Global South as equal partners or as agents, as opposed to receivers or 'victims' of the Global North agendas (Boshoff, 2009; Meekosha, 2008). As indicated earlier, meaningful research should be informed by local needs and driven by the intended beneficiaries. Like postcolonial scholarship, critical disability studies research might have the potential of addressing these 'them' and 'us' master narratives, and hence challenging the disabling relationships, and any forms of discrimination or oppression (Sherry, 2010). The core of critical disability studies contains both structural critique and frameworks for emancipatory practice and social change. This new paradigm can provide the basis upon which to develop strategies, which may overcome entrenched stereotypical and demeaning approaches, to the Global South stakeholders.

Stubbs's (1999: 257) sums up the power relations debate, which is still a huge issue between the North and the South:

> In my travels, I had been inspired by examples of integrated and inclusive education in the poorest countries with the fewest resources. Many seemed to be much nearer the ideals of inclusion than the so called 'model programmes' of the North. Yet all the writing, research, discussion, experience-sharing was based on examples from the Global North. Worse still, these examples and ideas were being exported to the South, transplanted into alien cultures and contexts, frequently propped up by funding from the North (which did not last forever), and totally unaffordable in the local context.

Consequently, the notion of authorship becomes central as it is by no accident that the terms 'authority' and 'authenticity' come from the term 'author'. It is from this basis that the monthly Global South to North Disability Research e-Network (http://www.breakthrough-uk.co.uk/Resources/drn) is aiming to situate disability in a global context by bridging the knowledge power relations between the two spaces. Through the newsletter, we also bring out from the Global South and encourage both disabled and non-disabled people to share activities taking place in their own spaces. We also encourage contributors to come forth and establish strong and genuine links between continents.

Building communities of trust in disability research

Panting (1992) emphasises the need to assume that we know nothing about a community rather than running the risk of displaying cultural arrogance. For instance, when the United Convention on Rights of Persons with Disabilities was being developed, defining disability became a contentious issue. Eventually delegates came back without agreeing on any definition, but to say that different countries can define disability according to their own situations. This illustrates the complexities surrounding the disability concept; and until now, no definition of disability has achieved international consensus (Vladu and Bullot, 2010). Therefore, not acknowledging such complexities in any collaborative work would be like 'microwaving' each other's sociocultural dynamics without critiquing the self. For example, although food microwaving is very convenient, very little thought is put on its health-related consequences. Similarly, this is an epistemic setback that disregards the significance of indigenous knowledge and imposes upon communities, representations and practices that may be detrimental to their development (Smith, 1999).

Alexander Phiri, a disability activist and director of SAFOD shared a story he read in an in-flight magazine (Phiri, 2010). The story was about three people (white, black and Indian Muslim) who shared a seat on a flight to Johannesburg in 2003. The three got talking and laughing, and seriously engaging with each other until they arrived; they exchanged business cards and made promises to make further contacts before saying their 'good byes'. This type of engagement was obviously not possible during the apartheid era when whites and blacks would not sit next to each other. This story reminded Phiri of their own struggle as disabled people, where discrimination they experience from time to time on the grounds of disability is similar to apartheid. This situation makes it difficult to build communities of trust. It is this level of political consciousness among the three men that geographical location, race, colour, or other form of differences (including disability) should be used to enrich, rather than to impoverish relationships. A critical disability studies analysis seems to fulfil that. Within the different cultures and contexts of the Global North and Global South, there is diverse knowledge and experience relating to disability and development; and such diversity should be used to unite rather than separate the two spaces.

There is a notion which Stubbs (1999) refers to as 'building towers on quicksand', where there is a tendency for the same small number of Northern academic writers to be cited in all writings, with no critical examination of the facts and perceptions originally presented. These authors are assumed to have solid foundations on which to build a literature regardless of geographical location, which calls for understanding of cultures and circumstances which might be unfamiliar to the writers (Stubbs, 1999). Most writers from the Global South seem to be fearful of being challenged about the relevance of their studies by the Global North writers (Meekosha, 2008).

As indicated earlier, what constitutes a disability in the Global South might not necessarily be the same as in the Global North. Therefore, it is critical to fight the 'What can we learn from Zimbabwe, India, Sierra Leone, and Burundi syndrome', and rather to have an open mind on the Global South indigenous knowledge systems. For instance, the Zimbabwean *Shona* concept of *'kubatana'* (oneness) places inclusiveness at the core of humanness (Chataika, 2007: 38). Again, the Zimbabwean philosophy of *'unhu'* (Shona), *'ubuntu'* (Ndebele) or 'beingness' is defined by qualities of the individual's participation in family and community activities – *'kubatana'* (Mbiti, 1992, cited in Chataika, 2007: 38). This communal participation is valued more than individual differences or other human attributes because it brings people together despite their differences. These indigenous knowledge systems can be a strong basis for any collaborative efforts. The same also applies to the Global North indigenous knowledge systems, which can be adopted and contextualised to suit the Global South. Therefore, it is possible for the two spaces to learn from each other, as long as the social, cultural, political and economic factors are taken into account. Here, it is essential to challenge the Global South stakeholders to shake off the 'Cinderella syndrome' by being assertive, proactive and being able to read the 'small print' (formal or informal) in any bi-lateral links prior to entering into any disability research agreements, to ensure that there is equal power relations.

The power in global research (including agendas and resources) is usually located in the North; and in disability research, this power is largely held by non-disabled researchers and agencies (Bradley, 2007). This is not to discredit those who have worked in these areas and have proved to be incredible practitioners and facilitators for social change. However, there is need to support and utilise local research capacity to address local research agendas. The SRF provides a practical example of how local disabled people can be empowered to conduct research. Training in generic research commenced with 20 DPO leaders from SAFOD member organisations. Later, the training included 20 young disabled people where two people (a male and a female) were drawn from each member country. Already, these trained researchers are engaging in some conventional disability research currently going on in the region (Fumulani, 2010). As part of unpacking the Millennium Development Goals, already four trainees from the team of 20 are part of the research groups that won tenders to carry-out research projects for SAFOD (Fumulani, 2010). Three of the 20 trainees made their first ever presentation at an international research conference – the AfriNEAD Symposium in Cape Town in 2009. It is this political consciousness, which is needed to ensure that the Global South stakeholders take centre stage in solving their own challenges.

What we need to realise is that the Global North researchers' capacity is also enhanced through these partnerships, as they learn from their Southern colleagues how to navigate different cultural contexts, and how to adapt research methodologies to suit local conditions when engaging in any disability related research (Grech, 2010; Silvers, 2010; Chataika, 2007). What is crucial in any partnership is having practical Global North–Global South strategies that address processes and dynamics affecting such research partnerships, that are able to identify real collaborative concerns. These include power relations, capacity building, funding, research processes (e.g. research agendas, research bids, research methods, ethical considerations), publications, the use of data, responsibility to the local research context, benefits and possible disadvantages of international collaboration (both formal and informal), and issues of reciprocity (Grech, 2010; Boshoff, 2009; Meekosha, 2008; Dufour, 2006). Such structural and historical obstacles should be identified and be able to suggest practical arrangements that enable both parties to move away from the typical roles of the Global North as a 'giver' and the Global South as a 'receiver' (Jentsch and Pilley, 2003). To be genuinely cooperative, Dufour (2006) emphasises that it is essential that the research questions subsequently posed should equally address the theoretical and applied interests of both partners. Dufour further asserts that both sites should recognise the potential significance of the findings to their respective national settings and to their indigenous knowledge theory building.

Tijssen (2007) acknowledged that African countries are increasingly co-authoring with foreign authors in international journals, which is a leap of faith towards building communities of trust. In South Africa, for example, the percentage of international research co-authorship increased from 41 per cent in 2000 to 53 per cent in 2005 (Sooryamoorthy, 2009). However, the study also reveals that only about 1 per cent of South Africa's publications are co-authored with researchers from other African countries. This figure is supported by Jacobs and Pichappan (2006) (cited by Boshoff, 2009) who analysed the publications of the five most research-orientated universities in South Africa and found that only 3 per cent of the universities' publications involved co-authorship with other African countries. Such insignificant figures have implications in promoting South–South collaboration, particularly in Africa. The AfriNEAD could be a useful platform to promote such collaborations when it comes to research and publishing issues around disability and development in an African context.

Why South–South research partnership?

Relative to the North–South collaboration, South–South research collaboration is considered more responsive to the challenges and needs of most Global South countries (Ohiorhenuan and Rath, 2000). This collaboration is also better suited to finding appropriate solutions to common challenges experienced by low-income nations. The Global South partners, particularly those within the same region, share similar environmental conditions and social burdens such as chronic poverty, food insecurity and tropical diseases, high incidence of disabilities, and have an almost intuitive sense of the research actions required to address national and regional development priorities (Boshoff, 2009). In Africa, the AfriNEAD network can be a starting point to forge such partnerships.

In this chapter, there has been growing concern regarding research output being led by the Global North researchers. For instance, most researchers in Africa collaborate internationally, they tend to participate in projects that have been conceptualised and designed by the Global North partners. By implication, African-based researchers become part of the implementation strategy. North–South relationships, therefore, tend to be highly unequal; and it is not uncommon for Southern collaborators to play a secondary role, or even to be completely ignored as co-authors in the eventual publication (Dahdouh-Guebas et al., 2003). One classic example was a call for a research bid for UK/Africa research collaboration on health-related issues in Africa sometime in June 2010. The agency categorically indicated that the principal investigator should be a UK citizen, while the co-principal investigator should be from an African country. Instinctively, issues of power relations, trust and neo-colonialism came to my mind. Is Africa not ripe enough to produce a principal investigator to lead a study taking place her own backyard?

A recent study on South–South research collaboration of countries in the Southern African Development Community (SADC) (including disability) established that a mere 5 per cent of SADC papers were jointly authored with researchers from African countries outside the SADC. In contrast, 47 per cent of SADC papers were co-authored with writers from the Global North. Where papers were co-authored with others within and outside SADC countries, it was mainly due to existing North–South collaboration. Authors from the Global North are included in 60 per cent of intra-regional co-authored papers and in 59 per cent of continental co-authored papers (Boshoff, 2009). The study also reported that between 2005 and 2008, South Africa produced 81 per cent of all SADC papers and 78 per cent of all intra-regional co-authored papers. This implies that there is an extremely unbalanced partnership, which seems to reflect the flipside of the Global North–Global South collaboration with the African Global South giant of Africa (South Africa) 'taking on the role of the political North' (Boshoff, 2009: 481). Certainly, the need to extend the guiding principles for genuine North–South partnerships to the currently unbalanced South–South collaborations cannot be overemphasised.

The combined effort of the best of Global South disability research could increase the international visibility of research and publication outputs, and strengthen the Global South's participation in the global research arena (Ohiorhenuan and Rath, 2000). Again, the credence of a unified Global South could be used as ammunition to effectively negotiate with Global North partners.

South–South research collaboration too has the potential to contribute to the best possible and cost effective use of scarce resources (particularly disability, which happens to compete with other topical issues like HIV and AIDS) since research work requires considerable human, material and financial resources to effectively yield positive results. Critical to developing a strong research base in the Global South is to ensure that all stakeholders concentrate more on capacity development, particularly in Africa, who spent a great deal of time teaching huge classes, which is not the case in many Global North higher education institutions. The counter-argument for South Africa could be 'what lessons can the rest of Africa learn from the processes followed in order to strengthen the research base across the continent?' By creating a unified resource base, the Global South countries may avoid or reduce duplication of efforts in many areas (Ohiorhenuan and Rath, 2000).

Towards a critical postcolonial disability studies research

The motivation and concern giving rise to this chapter is the quest for commitment to social justice by bringing together the disability, development and postcolonialism debates. Disability studies has the potential to make a more urgent intervention into the development and contemporary postcolonial studies, since disability is both a development and a political issue (Meekosha, 2008). Disability is now being considered as a development issue by planners and policymakers in an increasing number of countries across the world (Coleridge, 2000). Disability and development are closely linked in a cycle of cause and consequence, and both are regarded as political issues because the way they are defined by society will influence the measures taken to deal with them. While disability studies has critically begun looking towards the important work of globalising its outlook, disability is almost absent from the postcolonial theory discourse (Barker and Murray, 2010). Regrettably, this situation creates a short circuit when it comes to tacking issues of marginalisation, voicelessness and representation.

In moving towards a critical disability postcolonial studies, it is important to challenge the common assumption about the location of knowledge and to recognise this undertaking as central to those who are concerned with the colonial legacy of 'them and us', which leads to exclusion and oppression (Lavia, 2010; Said, 2004). With his emphasis on power differential between communities in postcolonial contexts, Said's writings offer a useful guide for all manner of academic fields involved in similar endeavours. He stresses on 'humanism', whose intention is to make things more available to critical scrutiny. Said expands this idea further and clarifies his positionality about the 'humanism' concept:

> In my understanding of its relevance today, humanism is not a way of consolidating and affirming what 'we' have always known and felt, but

rather a means of questioning, upsetting, and reformulating so much of what is presented to us as a commodified, packaged, uncontroversial, and uncritical codified certainties.

(Said, 2004: 28)

Said's humanism concept seems to fit well into the critical postcolonial disability studies framework. Colonialism does not cease to have salience simply because a nation attains political independence. It also affects other aspects of life in one way or another (Rizvi, 2009). Again, the 'nothing about us without us' slogan coined by the disability movement informs my positionality in adopting a critical postcolonial disability studies research agenda. It is therefore imperative to engage in a decolonisation process, and reclaim the academic, intellectual and cultural spaces, which ultimately lead to the re-emergence and upholding of indigenous knowledge. Decolonisation seeks to come to terms with the ways in which hegemonic forces of colonisation insidiously pervade the Global South knowledge systems (Appadurai, 2001). Such forces seek to categorise and consolidate hierarchical systems and in the process, 're-arrange, represent, redistribute materially and discursively, indigenous systems of knowing and being' (Appadurai, 2001: 4). Apparently, the challenge is on designing collaborative research agendas that press forward mutual interests, but are firmly rooted in the Global South's needs and priorities. The majority of the disability and development literature is produced by the Northern scholars and institutions, while the Global South plays the second fiddle (Meekosha, 2008). The implication here is that

Disability Studies problematically transports theories and methodologies developed within the Western academy to other global locations, paying nominal attention to local formations and understandings of disability.

(Barker and Murray, 2010: 219)

The overall aim here should be to deliberately promote 'productive exchange and cross-fertilizations' (Barker and Murray, 2010: 219) between the two spaces, while addressing the inequalities and silences that have been in existence for too long. Thus, more in-depth North/South reflections on the questions and challenges surrounding partnerships would be an invaluable to a critical postcolonial disability studies. In doing so, it is imperative to push for the unification of the three fields (disability, development, postcolonialism) by articulating precisely how a critical postcolonial disability studies research agenda should incorporate and respond to the development and postcolonial locations of disability. Barker and Murray (2010: 220) identify some key terms and approaches that can have the capacity to undo the over-rigid models and vocabularies. A personal analysis that could be useful to the critical postcolonial disability studies is provided below:

Situation analysis – defining and interpreting the state of the environment in order to have full knowledge about the context and knowledge for planning. It also describes the environment's socio-economic and political circumstances.

Cultural difference – stakeholders involved need to realise that cultures provide messages that shape our perceptions, attributions, judgements and ideas of self and other. Critical to relationship is the ability to understand that when working with people from other cultures, there is no 'right' or 'superior' culture. Instead of drawing stakeholders apart, cultural differences should enable to strengthen relationships through understanding each other's way life.

Environments of disability – The *International Classification of Functioning, Disability and Health* (ICF) specifies five environmental domains: products and technology; natural environment and human-made changes; support and relationships; attitudes; and services, systems, and policies.

Representational practices – who is involved? What is the inclusion or exclusion criterion? For instance, if disability and development studies are focusing on the Global South, to what extent are the key stakeholders involved (e.g. disabled people and local researchers).

The above processes, according to Barker and Murray (2010), give greater detail to understanding ways in which postcolonial cultural presentation works by adopting a critical method that is sensitive to the particularities of disability as it is experienced in postcolonial societies.

Conclusion

In conclusion, both the Northern and Southern stakeholders need to promote a critical postcolonial disability studies agenda that is useful and solves daily challenges and making a positive impact on people's lives, rather than focusing on advancing their academic profiles. A critical postcolonial disability studies aims to reject the idea of researchers turning into 'academic tourists' who move between projects, and from country to country, camouflaging behind the disability and development agenda, with the core motive to advance personal interests. Research 'decolonisation' means that the processes and outputs should be communicated to and used to benefit the researched communities. The thrust of any partnership should be about building authentic relationships based on the values of equality, mutual respect and regardand mutual understanding of contexts and cultures. Again, a critical postcolonial disability studies research could assist in bridging the gap between the Northern and Southern spaces. Barker and Murray's (2010) approaches could also be useful strategies in building genuine partnerships between the Global North and Global South. South–South collaborations should also be enhanced. Finally, Global North/South agenda should ensure that disabled people are in the driving seat if it is meant to change their lives. It implies having disabled people, who are among the poorest of the poor, as part of any national development plans.

Acknowledgements

I would like to express my gratitude to the two referees who engaged with this chapter, and provided insightful comments. I also thank the 2010 Lancaster Disability Studies Conference delegates who attended the session where I presented the earlier version of this chapter and whose comments were useful. To Judith Mckenzie, Fortune Chikateka and Viola Zimunya, thank you for commenting on earlier drafts.

References

Albert, A. and Harrison, M. (2010). 'Disabled People at the Heart of Research: A Retrospective Appreciation of the Disability Knowledge and Research Programme'. *Disability Dialogue*, 6, 9–10.

Appadurai, A. (2001). 'Grassroots Globalisation and the Research Imagination'. In A. Appadurai (ed.), *Globalization* (pp. 1–20). Durham, NC: Duke University Press.

Ashcroft, B., Griffiths, G. and Tiffin, H. (1995). *Post-Colonial Studies Reader*. London: Routledge.

Barker, C. and Murray, S. (2010). 'Disabling Postcolonialism: Global Disability Cultures and Democratic Criticism'. *Journal of Literary and Cultural Disability Studies*, 4 (3), 219–36.

Boshoff, N. (2009). 'South–South Research Collaboration of Countries in the Southern African Development Community (SADC)'. *Scientometrics*, 84, 481–503.

Bradley, M. (2007). 'North-South Research Partnerships: Challenges, Responses and Trends – A Literature Review and Annotated Bibliography'. Working Paper 1, IDRC *Canadian Partnerships Working Paper Series*. Ottawa: International Development Research Centre).

Chataika, T. (2007). 'Inclusion of Disabled Students in Higher Education in Zimbabwe: From Idealism to Reality – A Social Ecosystem Perspective'. Unpublished Ph.D. Thesis, University of Sheffield.

Coleridge, P. (2000). 'Disability and Culture'. In M. Thomas and M. J. Thomas (eds), *Selected Readings in Community Based Rehabilitation Series 1: CBR in Transition* (pp. 21–38). Bangalore: National Printing Press.

Comhlámh's Volunteering Options (2008). *What is Development?*, http://www.volunteeringoptions.org/, accessed 17 September 2010.

Crech, S. (2010). 'Intersections in Disability, Poverty and Development: A Global Disability Studies?' A Paper Presented at the Disability and the Majority

World: Challenging Dominant Epistemologies Manchester Metropolitan University Conference, Manchester: UK, 2 July 2010.

Chung, F. and Ngara, E. (1985). *Socialism, Education and Development: A Challenge to Zimbabwe*. Harare: Zimbabwe Publishing House.

Crush, J. (1995). *Power of Development*. London: Routledge.

Dahdouh-Guebas, F., Ahimbisibwe, J.,Van Moll, R. and Koedam, N. (2003). 'Neo-Colonial Science by the Most Industrialised upon the Least Developed Countries in Peer-Reviewed Publishing'. *Scientometrics*, 56 (3), 329–43.

Dufour, P. (2006). 'The Emerging Contextual Space for Priority Setting in Development Research'. In L. Box and R. Engelhard (eds), *Science and Technology Policy for Development: Dialogues at the Interface* (pp. 227–46). London: Anthem Press.

Fumulani, A. (2010). 'Radical and Evolutionary: SAFOD Research Programme (SRP) to Prevent Past Mistakes'. *Disability Dialogue*, 6, 3–5.

Ghai, A. (2002). 'Disability in the Indian Context: Post-Colonial Perspectives'. In M. Corker and T. Shakespeare (eds), *Disability/Postmodernity* (pp. 88–100). London: Continuum.

Goodley, D. (2011). *Disability Studies: An Interdisciplinary Introduction*. London: Sage.

Jentsch, J. and Pilley, C. (2003). 'Research Relationships between the South and the North: Cinderella and the Ugly Sisters?' *Social Science and Medicine*, 57, 1957–67.

Lavia, J. (2010). 'Caribbean Thoughts and the Practice of Community'. In J. Lavia and M. Moore (eds), *Cross Cultural Perspectives on Policy and Practice: Decolonizing Community Contexts* (pp. 28–42). London: Routledge.

Mandela, N. (2002). *Long Walk to Freedom: The Autobiography of Nelson Mandela, Volume 1, 1918–1962*. London: Abacus.

Manji, F. and O'Coill, C. (2002). 'The Missionary Position: NGOs and Development in Africa'. *International Affairs*, 78 (3), 567–83.

Masala, C. and Petretto, D. R. (2008). 'From Disablement to Enablement: Conceptual Models of Disability in the 20th Century'. *Disability and Rehabilitation*, 30 (17), 1233–44.

Meekosha, H. (2008). 'Contextualizing Disability: Developing Southern/Global Theory'. *Keynote paper to the 4th Biennial Disability Studies Conference*, Lancaster University (UK), 4 September 2008.

Meekosha, H. and Dowse, L. (2007). 'Integrating Critical Disability Studies into Social Work Education and Practice: An Australian Perspective'. *Practice*, 19 (3), 169–83.

Mji, G., MacLachlan, M., Melling-Williams, N. and Gcaza, S. (2009). 'Realising the Rights of Disabled People in Africa: An Introduction to the Special Issue'. *Disability and Rehabilitation*, 31 (1), 7–13.

Mpofu, E. (2002). 'Psychology in Africa: Challenges and Prospects'. *International Journal of Psychology*, 37, 179–86.

Mwendwa, T. N., Murangira, A. and Lang, R. (2009). 'Mainstreaming the Rights of Persons with Disabilities in National Development Frameworks'. *Journal of International Development*, 21, 662–72.

Ohiorhenuan, J. F. E. and Rath, A. (2000). 'The History and Urgency of South-South Cooperation in Science and Technology – Cooperation South'. *Special Unit for Technical Cooperation among Developing Countries (TCDC)*. New York: United Nations Development Programme, 1, 6–28.

Parekh, P. N. (2007). 'Intersecting Gender and Disability Perspectives in Rethinking Postcolonial Identities'. *Wagadu*, 4, 42–161.

Pantin, G. (1992). *SERVOL through the Years – 1970–1993 Report*. Port of Spain: SERVOL Ltd.

Phiri, A. (2010). Editorial. *Disability Frontline*, 31, 3.
Rizvi, F. (2009). 'Mobile Minds'. In J. Kenway and J. Fahey (eds), *Globalizing the Research Imagination* (pp. 101–14). New York: Routledge.
Said, E. W. (2004). *Humanism and Democratic Criticism*. New York: Columbia University Press.
Scully, J. L. (2008). *Disability Bioethics: Moral Bodies, More Difference*. Lanham, MD: Rowman and Littlefield.
Sherry, M. (2010). '(Post) colonizing Disability'. In E. J. Davis (ed.), *The Disability Studies Reader* (third editionn) (pp. 94–106). London: Routledge.
Silvers, A. (2010). 'An Essay on Modelling: The Social Model of Disability'. In D. C. Ralston and J. Ho (eds), *Philosophical Reflections on Disability* (pp. 19–36). London: Springer.
Smith, L. T. (1999). *Decolonizing Methodologies: Research and Indigenous Peoples*. London: Zed Books.
Sooryamoorthy, R. (2009). 'Collaboration and Publication: How Collaborative are Scientists in South Africa?' *Scientometrics*, 80 (2), 419–39.
Stubbs, S. (1999). 'Engaging with Difference: Soul-Searching for a Methodology in Disability and Development Research'. In E. Stone (ed.), *Disability and Development: Learning from Action and Research on Disability in the Majority World* (pp. 257–79). Leeds: The Disability Press.
Tijssen, R. J. W. (2007). 'Africa's Contribution to the Worldwide Research Literature: New Analytical Perspectives, Trends, and Performance Indicators'. *Scientometrics*, 71 (2), 303–27.
Vladu, C. and Bullot, C. (2010). *A Regions' Handbook to Understanding and Implementing the United Nations Convention of the Rights of Persons with Disabilities*, http://www.aer.eu/fileadmin/user_upload/Commissions/HealthSocial/EventsAndMeetings/2010/Working_Group_Disabilities_Barcelona/UN_Convention_H, accessed 20 November 2010.

16
Engaging with Disability with Postcolonial Theory

Anita Ghai

Introduction

Following a brief introduction about disability in India, I underscore disability (and gender) in postcolonial theory and practice. I discuss some of the postcolonial scholars – such as Albert Memmi, Edward Said, Homi Bhabha and Chandra Mohanty – with the hope that an assimilation of postcolonial thinking would enrich the disability studies perspective. Briefly, I examine the social framing and ideological work of disabled characters in a recent film *Black*. Using this film I underscore the dialectic between coloniser (read 'able subject') and colonised (read 'disabled subject'). Although cinema resists simple 'answers' to the question of how gender intersects with disability in the postcolonial world, films also offer stimulating instances of the transgressive potential of 'different' bodies.

Understanding disability in India

Within the Indian cultural ethos, a disabled person is considered an incomplete entity. The deterministic framework of destiny/fate allows very few to escape the erosion of agency, thus creating a situation where a person with disability is not accorded expert status either on his/her own life, or that of the dominant group. While the medical framing of disability is well known, the cultural understanding of disability has several interesting features. The theoretical understanding is that if a human being has committed misdeeds in previous births, s/he has to inevitably bear the consequences. Suffering the wrath of God, the notion of a 'just world' is firmly ingrained in the Hindu mind and is frequently invoked to explain whatever happens in one's life (Ghai, 2002a, 2003; Singh and Ghai, 2009). Disability, therefore, is a punishment for the sins of previous births. The theory is paradoxical as one understanding is that 'karma' (action) has very often led to a ready acceptance of physical disability, with little effort in the direction of improving life conditions. Accepting pain and suffering as a learned helplessness, the internalised oppression can be quite difficult to overcome. Since culture denies access to social, political and economic opportunities, disabled people and their families cannot help but respond to their life situations in a resigned manner. It is presumed to be a deterrent to collective efforts put in by persons with disabilities to assert their right of equal access to social opportunities.

The other belief is that the religious doctrine of 'karma' (action) does not allow passive resignation. The potentiality of change is embedded within these religious beliefs. It is possible to repay the debts and work for a better rebirth. This induces an attitude of tacit acceptance (Ghai, 2001). Belief in karma, in this sense, helps people in understanding their own and others' angst. A sense of desolation and hope are thus entertained together. Paranjpe (1986) indicates that karma can keep the faith of a 'just world' intact and convince people that good deeds will ultimately result in good outcomes. Another belief is that suffering was inflicted on good people to test their resilience and inner strength so that people did not cease to make efforts to cure the disease. There are instances where disabled people were considered as the children of God. This positioning provided spaces, in spheres of religion and knowledge, where the ability to transcend the body was and remains a distinct possibility. Even though the implicit meaning of such possibilities may be disturbing within our present understanding of disability, it does indicate a dignified negotiation of difference. Thus, the renowned scholar Ashtvakra, who had eight deformities, and the great poet Surdas, who was visually impaired, are illustrations of strength and the ability to fight oppression.

Psychologically, there is evidence that people with disabilities are pragmatic in their causal attributions. When they see the possibility of medical intervention, they approach it while keeping their faith in traditional healing methodologies alive. The patients intuitively learn to keep these two aspects of the disease separate. Kleinman (1988) in his extensive work in the South Asian context found that in all these places, traditional healing and biomedical treatment coexist and are not perceived as contradictory.

However within the dominant Indian cultural ethos, labels such as 'disability', 'handicap', 'crippled', 'blind' and 'deaf' are used synonymously. The assumption of the label's naturalness is unquestioned. As I have written elsewhere (Ghai, 2002b: 6) in the popular media, disability is often portrayed as a 'lack' or 'deficit'. These assumptions are rooted in the dominant Hindu mythology where the two most popular epics *Mahabharata* and *Ramayana* carry the deprivation as well as negative images associated with disability. In the former, King Dhritrashtra is deprived of the throne because of his visual impairment. Another set of images associates disability with evil and as something to fear and as an expectation to be submissive. Within the stories of both the epics *Mahabharata* and *Ramayana*, the central turn comes with the interventions of an orthopaedically impaired man

Shakuni and a dwarf woman Manthra, respectively, both being presented as evil. The popular images in mythology attest to extreme negativity associated with disability in India (Ghai 2002a). In a culture in which there is widespread female infanticide, killing imperfect children will not even count as a crime. Historically, treatment of those who have survived was sought mostly from shamans and mystics. The general response of the non-disabled world ranges from pity and charity to hostility, anger, banter and ridicule. Very rarely has the public response been positive.

Miles (2002), while tracing the historical and cultural roots and heritage of disability services over the past millennium in South Asia, begins with a dream that was recorded in Zoroastrian scriptures. This dream visualises a 'perfect world' in which there were no disabled people. The dream fits in with the hegemony of 'normality' that characterises societies at large in which any kind of difference is marginalised. A dominant theme which has been articulated in the writings of various scholars (See Dalal, 2002; Ghai, 2002a, 2003; Miles 2002; Sen, 1988) concerns the impact of disability constructions.

Within Indian culture, disability is also often conceived as eternal childhood, where survival is contingent upon constant care and protection by families. Here, the emphasis is on images of dependency, thereby reinforcing the charity/pity model. Carrying a sense of shame, 'the disabled' find that their voices are silenced as they are always looked upon as the 'Other'. The dominant ideologies in Indian culture have continued to operate paradoxically in characterising the binaries that define social realities. While in principle they might be postulated as complementary, their actual meaning/working is oppositional. Thus there is a strong cultural belief that while the female is opposed to male, she is at the same time encompassed in the male. This is symbolised in the manifestation of lord Shiva titled *Ardh Nareshewar*, where the left side is depicted as the feminine or *Shakti* and the right side as male. Similarly, *Purusha* (man)/*Prakriti* (nature), touchable/untouchable represent the same paradox. In contrast, the binary of disability/ability is understood more as a medical issue. To my mind the idea that there are commonalities in all disabled lives raises significant questions in a country like India. In the fight for rights, whose ideology and whose agenda it is are more important questions. Just as who will determine the dominant cultural ethos and what kind of social systems will be sanctioned? The meaning attributed to disability is different for those who speak the language of rights when compared to the language of those who look at disability as a curse. From my vantage point, the categories of disabled and the able-bodied as fixed, permanent, internally homogeneous and as oppositional are problematic. At this juncture within the Indian milieu, I would not want to argue that 'a specific' theory of disability would comprehensively explain disability. Though these are complex questions, I am attracted to postcolonial theories for a way out.

Why postcolonial theory?

Postcolonial theory, to my mind, looks at literature and culture from two perspectives. The postcolonial writings reflect a colonial past, and etch out a new way of creating and understanding the world. I look at the theory with the hope that oppressed identities and representation of disability can be understood in the domain of postcolonial theory. To me, postcolonial theory has a number of connotations, but the one which is close to my heart is the understanding of the Other, historically and symbolically. For Robert Young (2003), postcolonialism is a dislocating discourse that raises uncomfortable questions regarding how overbearing and sweeping theories 'have themselves been implicated in the long history of European colonialism – and, above all, the extent to which [they] continue to determine both the institutional conditions of knowledge as well as the terms of contemporary institutional practices – practices which extend beyond the limits of the academic institution' (2003: viii). As a disability scholar, I have always been uncertain about the merging or separation of 'us' (read 'disabled') and 'them' (read 'able'). In many instances, disability theorists have addressed political issues through the construction of binary oppositions that not only contain prejudice and bias but also fall into the trap of naively reversing the old colonial legacy and problematic of oppressed vs. oppressor. Disability in India has not been studied in terms of power and suppression as well as the possibilities of resistance. Taking a note from Arthur Frank (1995) we could read all narratives of illness as postcolonial since they contest and revise the master narratives of medicine and culture that define 'the ill/disabled subject' (1995: 10). Thus 'the Other' or 'them' is always colonised, dominated and violated. Following scholars such as Lyotard (1984) and Corker (1998: 232), an 'incredulity towards grand narratives' is imperative. I am aware of the danger in a postcolonial perspective as it can have the impact of denying the realness or materiality of the impaired body. Notwithstanding the danger of discursive essentialism, postcolonialism can be instrumental in setting the tone for engaging in the idea of disability as 'difference' rather than as an oppositional lack or inability. Despite the impressions created, especially in the aftermath of colonial rule, about the multicultural nature of Indian society, in reality there is hegemony and hierarchy that prevails in the construction of social reality.

For me, the work of Albert Memmi *The Colonizer and the Colonized* (1967) serves as a useful benchmark in understanding the process of Othering. My reading of Memmi tells me that those of 'us' who have been marginalised by our respective disabilities enter the life space of the more complete 'Other' from the position corresponding to that which the colonised holds in relation to the coloniser. Most fundamentally, my contention is that the creation of a devalued 'Other' is a necessary precondition for the creation of the able-bodied rational subject who is the all-pervasive agency that sets the terms of the dialogue. Taking over from the portrait that he draws of the 'Other' as it means to the coloniser, the colonised emerges as the image of everything that the coloniser is not. Every negative quality is projected onto her/him.

In fact, to understand disability, many significant aspects need to be noticed in Memmi's description. First, the Other is always seen as 'not', as 'lack', as 'void', as someone lacking in the valued qualities of the society, whatever those qualities may be. Second, the humanity of the other becomes 'indistinguishable' from the able-bodied humanity. Third, the Others are not seen as belonging to the human community, but rather as part of a muddled, confused and nameless collectivity. They carry, according to Memmi, 'the mark of the plural'. In other words, they all look alike. This is indicative of the cultural hegemony that strives to posit an autonomous, rational and competent able-bodied subject as representative of a 'normal existence'.

It is with this assumption that the disabled, as Memmi's colonised others, have heard on more than one occasion that they are 'lacking'. This internalised oppression is affirmed by society, which continues to accept them as wanting and deficient. Further, the message of non-comprehension of their feelings and thoughts gets communicated. Whether the Other thinks or not is doubtful. It is quite strange that the colonised (in this case the disabled) must indeed be very odd, if she/he remains mysterious and opaque after years of living with the coloniser/able-bodied society. This results in the Other being dehumanised to such a great extent that all that s/he can become is an object. Finally, in the world of the coloniser/non-disabled the ultimate desire is that s/he should exist only as a function of the needs of the coloniser, that is, to be transformed into a pure colonised. The colonised loses its entity as a subject in its own right and remains only what the coloniser is not. It is thus an erasure both out of history and all significant aspects of development. Though Memmi's work has not been very frequently used in understanding the disabled identity, in my view it can contribute substantially in understanding how there is always a distance between the coloniser and the colonised and by extrapolation, the non-disabled and the disabled. While Memmi helps us in highlighting the far-reaching understanding of disability and repression, there is a need to look beyond the hierarchies to the negotiation of power dynamics.

Edward Said (1978) is another postcolonial scholar who recognises this process of alterity in his examination of the account of the European construction of the Orient. In emphasising the political dimensions of this ideological move, Said understands the construction of the Orient as an outcome of a yearning for power. Said (1984: 4) states:

> Thus the status of colonized people has been fixed in zones of dependency and peripherality, stigmatized in the designation of underdeveloped, less-developed, developing states, ruled by a superior, developed,

or metropolitan colonizer who was theoretically posited as a categorically antithetical overlord. In other words, the world was still divided into betters and lessers, and if the category of lesser beings had widened to include a lot of new people as well as a new era, then so much the worse for them.

I think the description is pertinent for disabled people. Said (1978: 3) argued that 'European culture gained in strength and identity by setting itself off against the Orient as a sort of surrogate and even underground self'. Thus the disabled are framed as an opposition to the category of the able-bodied. The way Orientalism is part of the European identity that defines 'us' versus 'them' (non-Europeans), the normal hegemony defines the disabled as the Other within the Indian context.

A significant issue for me is that though binaries reflect the opposition against normative hegemony, I do believe that binary constructions served a political purpose. The lived reality of the disabled offer a far more complex picture. I do understand that a binary and essentialist approach to identity is conceptually flawed, inconsistent and has undesirable moral and political consequences (see Sherry, 2007; Ghai, 2002b). In one sense, the disabled/non-disabled divide is also extremely knotty and theoretically limited. For instance, the division between black/white is ineffective for conceptualizing disability, ethnicity or caste. As Sherry (2007: 19) says, 'people often position themselves somewhere in-between or outside these binary categories, and this positioning is fluid and contextually dependent'. My submission is that it is important to read disability not in terms of a monolithic 'third world woman', at once 'homogenised' and 'systematised' under oppression, but instead with attention to the contradictions and conflicts that can arise from their distinct historical and material relationships to class, religion, culture and patriarchy (Chandra Talpade Mohanty, 1991: 214).

In this light, it will not be out of context if we were to ask 'whether the Subaltern (read disabled) can Speak?' Historically the very infamous question was a result of the subaltern studies group, a project led by Ranajit Guha. Having borrowed Gramsci's term 'subaltern', the objective was to locate and reinstate the marginalised by giving them a 'voice' or shared locus of agency in postcolonial India. What is significant is that Spivak (1988a) recognises the 'epistemic violence' done upon Indian subalterns. She says, 'Subalternity is the name I borrow for the space out of any serious touch with the logic of capitalism or socialism. Please do not confuse it with unorganised labour, women as such, the proletarian, the colonized ... migrant labour, political refugees etc. Nothing useful comes out of this confusion' (Spivak, 1995: 115). Thus to Spivak the very definition of the subaltern is entailing 'stillness', whereby the cultural space of subalternity is cut off from the lines of mobility producing the class- and gender-differentiated colonial subject. However, the quandary is whether the subaltern has no agency or is fated to silence. Spivak's argument is that elite or hegemonic discourses are 'deaf' to the subaltern, even when s/he does speak or resist (1996: 289; 1999: 308). To me it seems that if the subaltern (i.e. disabled) could speak in a way that really counted for us, that we would feel obligated to listen to, it would not be subaltern. As Moore-Gilbert (1997: 106) puts it, 'While Spivak is excellent on "the itinerary of silencing" endured by the subaltern, particularly historically, there is little attention to the process by which the subaltern's "coming to voice" might be achieved' (1997: 106). Spivak, however, believes that she 'question[s] the authority of the investigating subject without paralyzing[sic] him' and that deconstruction can lead 'to much better practice' (1988b: 201; 1990: 122).

Perhaps it would help to understand Homi Bhabha (1994) who has highlighted the notion of ambivalence and irony to move away from what often appear to be overly simple binary oppositions. Bhabha's influential work *The Location of Culture* (1994) is helpful in extending the models of unilateral 'oppression' located in many disability studies texts. Bhabha sees the binary relationship as slippery and illusory such that the fixed identities of the parts in the binary division cannot hold during the process of colonial discourse. Notwithstanding the significance of evident signs of protest and conflict around issues of 'oppression', Bhabha's understanding of understated forms of resistance, such as the displacement, distortion, dislocation and ambivalence generated by the process of colonial domination is far more complex. Says Bhabha (1994: 1–2):

> The move away from the singularities of 'class' or 'gender' as primary conceptual and organizational categories, has resulted in an awareness of the subject positions – of race, gender, generation, institutional location, geopolitical locale, sexual orientation – that inhabit any claim to identity in the modern world. What is theoretically innovative, and politically crucial, is the need to think beyond narratives of originary and initial subjectivities and to focus on those moments or processes that are produced in the articulation of cultural differences. These 'in-between' spaces provide the terrain for elaborating strategies of selfhood – singular or communal – that initiate new signs of identity, and innovative sites of collaboration, and contestation, in the act of defining the idea of society itself.

The understanding is that within the process of cultural discourse, two ostensibly trouble-free, opposing groups collide and express their differences from each other. The periphery where the two groups clash, the 'in-between spaces' in the above quote, is where and when 'new signs of identity', that is, culture or societal meaning, are created, a culture which is a hybrid of the two opposing cultures. Though Bhabha did not directly write on disability, what is intriguing is that the postcolonial subject whether disabled or able fits into neither of the 'traditions in the discourse of identity'. In fact postcolonial identity lies *between* the frames of these mirrors of identity. Consequently, Bhabha sees the postcolonial subject as 'displaced', 'dislocated', 'hybrid' (in the sense of combining several different cultural traces into a new formation): the postcolonial subject is 'an incalculable object, quite literally difficult to place' and 'the demands of authority cannot unify its message nor simply identify its subjects' (Bhabha, 1986: xxi).

Bhabha's understanding makes it clear that any national culture can never be holistic and uncorrupted, the coloniser's (read 'able-bodied') culture, far from being the simple, oppressive force upon the colonised (disabled) culture, is open to ambivalence. Elaborates Bhabha (1994: 36):

> The reason a cultural text or system of meaning cannot be sufficient unto itself is that the act of cultural enunciation – the place of utterance – is crossed by the *difference* of writing. ... It is this difference in the process of language that is crucial to the production of meaning and ensures, at the same time, that meaning is never simply mimetic and transparent.

Further Bhabha uses the concept of 'hybridity' as a new lens of reading world literature in general. He maintains that 'If cultural diversity is a category of comparative ethics, aesthetics or ethnology, cultural difference is a process of signification through which statements *of* culture or *on* culture differentiate, discriminate and authorize the production of fields of force, reference, applicability and capacity' (1994: 50). In the introduction itself, Bhabha describes the liminal space. Says Bhabha,

> The stairwell as liminal space, in-between the designations of identity, becomes the process of symbolic interaction, the connective tissue that constructs the difference between upper and lower, black and white. The hither and thither of the stairwell, the temporal movement and passage that it allows, prevents identities at either end of it from settling into primordial polarities. This *interstitial* passage between fixed identifications opens up the possibility of a cultural hybridity that entertains difference without an assumed or imposed hierarchy.
>
> (1994: 50)

This powerful way of depicting resistance resonates in my mind. My anxiety, however, is about the choice of stairway as a metaphor for political mobility and rebellion. In a literal sense, this would keep out disabled subjects. Notwithstanding the inopportune choice of the stairwell, Bhabha clearly indicates that in the moment of recognition, the Self cannot be wholly contained within a Self/Other binary, a binary dependent upon fixed and static boundaries. In other words, as soon as we recognise that the rift which divides 'us' from 'them' as artificial and reductionist, we move into a place

where identity is ambivalent and mutable. As Bhabha notes, the very struggle to maintain that Self/Other binary articulates the possibility of slippage
between the two categories and reminds us that 'identity is never an a priori,
nor a finished product; it is only ever the problematic process of access to
an image of totality' (1994: 51). As I write elsewhere, 'disability is not really
a fixed category most clearly signified by the white cane user or a crutch
user. Rather it denotes a fluid and shifting set of conditions' (2003: 32). As
Mairian Corker (1999: 3) points out, 'disability, like most dimensions of
experience is polysemic – that is ambiguous and unstable in meaning – as well
as a mixture of truth and fiction that depends on *who says what, to whom,
when and where*' (the emphasis is mine). The process of creating the hybrid
culture does not destroy the disabled and the able bodied for any unified
narrative resulting in some grand amalgamation. What the hybrid does is to
make both the disabled and the able aware that culture is never static or in
terms of T. S Eliot 'mummified'. Culture is alive, as seen in the hybrid, with
the result that no essential and a-historical conceptions of disabled identity
are possible. As Bhabha (1994: 208) argues,

> the intervention of the Third Space, which makes the structure of mean-
> ing and reference an ambivalent process, destroys this mirror of repre-
> sentation in which cultural knowledge is continuously revealed as an
> integrated, open expanding code. Such an intervention quite properly
> challenges our sense of historical identity of culture as a homogenis-
> ing unifying force, authenticated by the originary past kept alive in the
> national tradition of the past.

However, my concern is that while power can be understood as 'discursive'
formation, it is devoid of its material underpinnings. Though in reflecting
moments of impending slippage between identity categories, Bhahba brings
in the notion of the 'evil eye', that figure which reminds us of what is absent
or invisible in a text, those figures whose gaze 'alienates both the narrato-
rial I of the slave and the surveillant eye of the master' (1994: 53). The evil
eye is the exterior, the margin, that 'structure of difference' which blurs the
gap between slave and master by making both objects of observation and
judgement. The evil eye therefore has power, as it unnerves the simplistic
polarities of Self/Other or to extrapolate disabled/able.

The implications for India to engage with its multiple realities seem pertinent. I am reminded of Corker (1999: 635) who argued that 'real differences
are based on the socially constructed categories of disability, gender, race,
sexuality and class which precisely because they are constructed, embrace a
fluidity that cannot mark a collective identity'. The assumption that people
with impairments would view the experience of impairment and oppression as identical and subscribe to a general category of disability does not
hold water. In India, cross impairment distinctions are still commonplace.

A presumed logic or unity of impairment requires a stable oppositional category of normality. This institutionalised 'normality' both requires and produces the communality of each 'voice' of impairment that represents the limits of possibilities within an oppositional binary disabled/nondisabled system (Corker, 2000: 635). In the Indian context, individual aspects of disability matter, and their clubbing together as one creates tensions. For instance, though mental illness has been one of the categories which are included in the 1995 legislation, not much work has been done in order to alleviate the problems of mentally ill people. Similarly, after much effort, a national trust has been constituted which will look after autism, cerebral palsy, mental retardation and multiple disabilities. It is in this context that homogenising experiences prevent the recognition of cross disability distinctions, and their specific realities and necessary responses to them. In effect, legitimisation of certain differences have been instrumental in increasing the vicious cycles of marginalisation. This is what we need to do, what Susan Suleiman (1986: 24) recommends for contemporary feminism: to attempt 'to get beyond, not only the number one – the number that determines unity of body or of self – but also to get beyond the number two, which determines difference, antagonism, and exchange'. 'The number one' clearly represents for Suleiman the fictions of unity, stability and identity characteristic of a phallocentric world-view. 'The number two' represents the grid of gender, which exposes the hierarchical, oppositional structure of the world-view. Beyond the number two is nothing but endless complication and a dizzying accumulation of narratives. Suleiman refers to Derrida, in which he speaks of a dream of the innumerable 'a desire to escape the combinatory ... to invent incalcuable choreographies' (1986: 76). Suleiman presents Derrida's idea as offering an epistemological or narrative ideal for theory, practice and politics.

Bollywood and disability in India

Being disabled in India does have a context and a certain meaning. In our attempts to change the meaning, we must recognise the multiple political, social, economic and cultural realities. For instance, the depiction of disability in Bollywood cinema captures the postcolonial discourse by weaving a tapestry composed of threads of many different hues rather than one that is woven in a single colour. In order to acquire a social front of disability advocacy, Bollywood has been keen to include marginal identities. However, images in films and television rarely, if ever, inform the viewer about the everyday lived experience of being disabled. Cinema relies on invoking emotional reactions such as pity, horror or a sense of tragedy: a fleeting moment where a 'crippled' beggar is shown extending his/her begging bowl into the window of a car, or the good-hearted protagonist is shown helping a visually impaired person cross the busy city road and receiving heartfelt blessings for the abled-bodied person's assistance. To contextualise the multiple nuances of disabled identity in postcolonial cinema, I discuss the movie *Black*.

Black

Bollywood projects itself as a fantasy of a homogeneous culture, that masks the hierarchy of subject positions and belonging divided along the lines of gender, class, rural/urban divide, caste and to my mind disability. Disability in most Indian films is used as a meta-narrative, thus allocating the viewer to create meaning within the larger, scattered, melodramatic filmic space. In the movie *Black*, I explore the ambivalent role of characters with disabilities, both as sites of transgression and as repositories for cultural tensions in a postcolonial world. Based on the life of Helen Keller, the film traces the tensions of a Christian family, where the protagonist Michelle McNally (Rani Mukerji), a blind and deaf woman reflects on her life. She is in search of her lost teacher Debraj Sahai (Amitabh Bachhan) who was the 'perfect' teacher. Her quest to find him takes 20 years. The story reveals how, over the years, the teacher has lost his memory and ability to recognise. Michelle's search is rewarded with her discovery of her tutor seated at the fountain near her house, his back turned towards the camera. Interestingly, this is the exact place where Debraj, though in an unorthodox manner, led Michelle's first tryst with the joy of a spoken word, when she utters 'water'!

Similarly, we first see the baby Michelle, with her back towards us, being cajoled by her mother Catherine. Thus in turning away from life, they face each other. Michelle as a little girl is totally confused and angry because of her disabilities. Her parents do not know how to deal with the little girl as she becomes more and more destructive and wild – she topples a candle and starts a fire at home and hurts her little baby sister. The father (Dhritiman Chatterjee) decides to put her in an institution. Her mother (Shernaz Patel) fights to find solutions so that she is not institutionalised. The mother manages to find a teacher, Debraj, from a deaf and blind school. Though eccentric, the teacher is dedicated to his profession. Though the teacher's meeting with his ward is not pleasant, he slowly reaches a truce with her. He gradually changes the wild persona into a presentable young lady. Though the father was at first against his rough handling of the girl, he later accepts him when he sees the positive progress in Michelle. Debraj slowly introduces Michelle to the world of light and sound. With his help she tries to make sense of the pitch dark world around her – hence the title of the film *Black*. She learns her first words. The teacher becomes her constant companion and he has big ambitions for her. He helps her to get into a regular college and sits with her during class interpreting the lessons to her through hand contact to fulfill their dream to make her a graduate.

I am not sure whether the director has been able to capture the pain of a sibling who is frustrated with her parents for not giving her adequate attention. Consequently, the sister (Sara) is ambivalent and it is very late when Michelle learns of this antagonism when Sara confesses her dislike towards her older sibling. She is hostile towards her sister and is made the object of the audience's fury. As Bhabha suggests, 'the work of hegemony is itself the process of iteration and differentiation [which] depends on the production of alternative or antagonistic images that are always produced side by side and in competition with each other', then we can understand 'a politics of struggle as the struggle of identifications and the war of positions' (1994: 29). After attending Sara's wedding, Michelle begins to wonder about love. An inexperienced and curious Michelle wants to kiss Debraj. He reluctantly does so but decides to leave Michelle on her own because of this demand and the position she has put him in. Twenty years after enrollment, Michelle does manage to gain her Bachelors of Arts, and with her proud parents looking on her, she even gives a speech to the graduating class. Wearing no black graduation robe, she thanks her parents and her teacher and she announces that she will only wear the robe so that her teacher may see her. Within the Indian scenario, overcoming is the thesis that is played in innumerable movies. Consequently the failures in college do not tend to overcompensate. What is worrying is that the only way that Debraj can deal with Michelle is by use of aggression and therein lies the pedagogical problem with this powerful film. Michelle is not like the other students, so ordinary methods do not apply to her. Incessantly yelling through the entire first half of the film at a child who he knows cannot hear and see, the narration of taming of a troubled and disabled child is so loud, noisy and over-expressive that it somewhere kills a sensitivity that comes from being subtle. Any educator would be able to tell the director that a child, who has the mother as the sole support, would not get along with the teacher immediately. Though the teacher, unlike others, does not assume that the child is cognitively impaired, his reactions are problematic. It is almost as if Michelle's silence places her outside the normative and ultimately, she serves as an Other, an abject outside.

The movie touchingly creates a fusion between the vulnerabilities of both the teacher and the student. It is through the encounter with these that they become aware of both their disabling and their ablest parts. For instance, Michelle and Debraj's first meeting is complemented by the rattling sounds of tin cans tied to Michelle's waist, so that her whereabouts are known and years later Michelle finds Debraj tied to chains after getting an Alzheimer attack. Water is symbolic for both Debraj and Michelle as the latter's first breakthrough is when she learns the world for 'water' through an understanding of 'touch' The key word at the end is also 'water', as Michelle creates a new world for Debraj impressions into words.

In one sense *Black* and other films on disability break the pattern of fantasy. Cinema has moved away from escapism and makes the viewers understand other people's realities. Many disabled people in India loved

282 Engaging with Disability with Postcolonial Theory

the movie as they identified with the characters in *Black*, perhaps coping with similar problems, anxieties and relationships. The cathartic aspect of Bombay cinema can be understood as a resolution in some way. Real problems in life such as disability are more complicated and difficult to resolve. The critical question is whether the reality allows the viewers to overcome feelings of alienation and marginality. The film endorses patriarchal structures, specifically those of family, 'expectations' from mothers, gender roles in society. Debraj's masculinity stands out as he takes over Michelle's life as he seems to be managing everything including translation, instruction, organisation and support. I think the director contributes to disability as being firmly rendered as pathological and asexual. I wonder what would be the reason for changing the teacher Anne Sullivan in *Miracle Worker*, an American version (1962), from woman to man? Intuitively, if I presupposed Michelle to be a boy, and make the teacher into an aging woman, I wonder whether the same masculinity issues would work out. Is it because the director knows for sure that heteronormative rendering is part and parcel of Bollywood? The fact that an older man's character is introduced, the plot is then set to construct sexual tension. Had the director been genuinely addressing disability in the context of sexuality, there would have been discursive spaces where a dialogic possibility could be created. However here there is no space for the narrative to develop further. Notwithstanding the morality issues of the teacher and his deep investment in her, the abandonment of the student who is sexually becoming alive seems distinctly ableist. There is the issue of subjugation for those who have been disabled (read colonised) and how the fantasies of inferiority and subordination have been internalised and have become a part of the self. Her sexual desires, however, have to be sublimated and possibly displaced. In this sense, images of masculinity in the movie reflect the silence of the disabled woman, thus perpetuating dominant social ideas about sexuality in the context of disability. The image of disabled woman, thus dialectically read, reveals that it is not simply the able male, who is always already the oppressor, as is the common assumption, but rather that woman as an abject signifier can be merchandised even by enlightened, able women. Even the feminist voices have implicitly, and sometimes explicitly, undermined disabled women's rights to sexuality, motherhood and intimate personal relationships. Such an unwelcoming image of woman remains, therefore, a fixed trope in the hands of Bollywood, negotiating coloniality and postcoloniality, and crossing over able-bodied parts to disabling parts, with little chance of emancipation. A disabled woman could be read as an abject figure, in Julia Kristeva's (1980) terms. The abject is not defined by its 'lack of cleanliness or health', but by its capacity for 'disturb[ing] identity, system, order'. It is that which 'does not respect borders, positions, rules. The in-between, the ambiguous, the composite' (1980: 4). Although Kristeva has not disconnected the abject from ill health, my understanding is that ill health and the 'in-between' that troubles order inform one another. The disabled body (or mind) exists in a realm of ambiguity, lingering somewhere between life and death – a constant reminder of the *other* side of normative life. If the abject is what one must 'thrust aside in order to live' (1980: 3), then the ill or disabled subject, especially she who resists cure and containment, is by definition abject. One strategy to grant woman full agency requires the contemporary feminist viewer to take responsibility. Though Bollywood cinema has increasingly begun to include 'queer representations', disability seems to be complex and fleeting exploration of sexuality reifies the ableist discourse. What is critical is that Bollywood continues to glorify disability through and strengthening dependency and vulnerability.

In their attempt the films tend to problematise the 'naturalness' of disability and normalcy, while allowing audiences a false defensive ideology of ability. Such a rendering allows viewers to perpetuate their wish to pass for normal, and able-bodied. The 'desire' remains out of the ambit of the film. Taking a cue from Gayatri Spivak (1999: 304), the figure of the woman disappears, not into a pristine nothingness, but into a violent shuttling that is the displaced figuration of the 'third-world' woman caught between tradition and modernisation, culturalism and development. As Amrita Chhachhi puts it, 'the symbols and repositories of communal/group/ national identity... [so] threats to or the loss of control over their women . ...are seen as direct threats to manhood/community/ family. It therefore becomes essential to ensure patriarchal controls over the labour, fertility, and sexuality of women' (1991: 163–5). *Black* therefore does not seem to articulate the transformative potential of disability, as the physical and gender-based representations resonate with cultural and political implications. *Black* returns repeatedly to Michelle but does not go ahead to accept the figure of the sexualised woman. Though it does create space for disability and values Michelle's personhood, the difficulty is to prompt the audience to read Michelle's disability as a political message. If it happens then cinema itself becomes an alternative form of political participation.

Conclusion

Black creates and maintains a status quo where the 'disabled' body is incorporated with the existing social patterns, while arbitrating the normative hegemony. In this sense the representation of disability is trapped in a subordinate relationship to able-bodiedness and patriarchy. One wishes that the disabled character would exist in a binary that excludes them even as it depends upon them to develop a status quo. Postcolonial theorists have problematised the issues of disability, though in a metaphorical understanding. However caution needs to be exercised when we use disability and postcolonial as reciprocal metaphors. As a feminist I do feel that postcolonial becomes alive to the issues of embodiment. My wish is that both disability theory as well as postcolonial theory adopt a contrapuntal reading, which means reading a text

> with an understanding of what is involved when an author shows, for instance, that a colonial sugar plantation is seen as important to the process of maintaining a particular style of life in England ... the point is that contrapuntal reading must take account of both processes, that of imperialism and that of resistance to it, which can be done by extending our reading of the texts to include what was once forcibly excluded.
>
> (Said, 1994: 66–7)

Thus the understanding is that a colonial sugar plantation is seen as important to the process of maintaining a particular style of life in England. Extrapolating from Said, my submission is that disability should not be concerned with *what* to read but *how* to read it. Thus 'contrapuntal' reading is critical not only for its aesthetic merit but also for an awareness of the historical, cultural, and political associations, which he calls structures of attitude and reference. Thus, the wish is to evolve a meaningful conversation between disability studies and those scholars who can help us attend to the social act of interpretation in new ways. My submission is that disability theory's understanding of disabled bodies as 'problems' can restore the social model underpinnings of the body-as-impaired. A *contrapuntal reading* will assist so that disability studies and cultural studies can be in resonance with each other. Such a reading suggests that more is at stake than a problematising discourse (Spivak, 1990: 42). For instance we need to be engaged in the unlearning of one's own privilege. So that, not only does one become able to listen to that other constituency, but one learns to speak in such a way that one will be taken seriously by that other constituency. Also the hope is that both the discourses of postcolonialism and disability studies rewrite the relationship between the margin and the centre by deconstructing the colonialist and imperialist ideologies as well as ableist hegemony. The attempt is to make obvious how disability would be deeply implicated in ableism. It is not enough that disability and Otherness relate not as binarisms in postcolonial discourse but in ways in which both are complicit and resistant, victim and collaborator and oppressed and oppressor. As bell hooks (1995) reminds us, achievement of colonialism does not require the assumption of power in someone else's country. Rather colonialism can be accomplished by dominant and normative hegemonies through social apartheid. The postcolonial discourse reminds us that the apartheid is always subject to constant revision. Perhaps the greatest challenge is to comprehend that we have consciously or unconsciously oppressed each other. It is only when we create intersections that we attack social apartheid which places limits on human beings, both disabled and non-disabled.

References

hooks, bell (1995). *Killing Rage: Ending Racism*. New York: Henry Holt and Co.

Bhabha, Homi K. (1986). 'Foreword: Remembering Fanon: Self, Psyche, and the Colonial Condition'. In Frantz Fanon, *Black Skin, White Masks*. London: Pluto.

Bhabha, Homi K. (1994). *The Location of Culture*. New York: Routledge.

Chhachhi, Amrita (1991). 'Forced Identities: The State, Communalism, Fundamentalism and Women in India'. In Deniz Kandiyoti (ed.), *Women, Islam and the State* (pp. 144–75). Philadelphia: Temple University Press.

Corker, M. (1998). 'Disability Discourse in a Postmodern World'. In T. Shakespeare (ed.), *The Disability Reader*. London, New York: Cassell.

Corker, M. (1999). 'Differences, Conflations and Foundations: The Limits to "Accurate" Theoretical Representation of Disabled People's Experience?' *Disability and Society*, 14 (5), 627–42.

Frank, A. (1995). *The Wounded Storyteller: Body, Illness and Ethics*. Chicago: University of Chicago Press.

Ghai, A. (2001). 'Marginalization and Disability: Experiences from the Third World'. In Mark Priestley (ed.), *Disability and the Life Course: Global Perspectives* (pp. 26–37). Cambridge: Cambridge University Press.

Ghai, Anita (2002a). 'How Indian Mythology Portrays Disability'. *Kaleidoscope*, 45, 6–10.

Ghai, Anita (2002b). 'Disability in the Indian Context: Post-Colonial Perspectives'. In M. Corker and T. Shakespeare (eds), *Disability and Postmodernity: Embodying Disability Theory* (pp. 88–100). London and New York: Continuum.

Ghai, Anita (2003). *(Dis) Embodied Form: Issues of Disabled Women*. New Delhi: Shakti Books, Haranand Publications.

Guha, R. (1988). Preface. In R Guha and G. Spivak (eds), *Selected Subaltern Studies* (pp. 35–6). New York: Oxford University Press.

Kleinman, A. (1988). *The Illness Narrative. Suffering, Healing & the Human Condition*. New York: Basic Books.

Kristeva, J. (1980). *Pouvoirs de l'horreur: essai sur l'abjection*. Paris: Seuil.

Miles, M. (2002). 'Community and Individual Responses to Disablement in South Asian Histories: Old Tradition, New Myths?' In M. Thomas and M. J. Thomas (eds), *Selected Readings in Community Based Rehabilitation, Series 2, Asia Pacific Disability Rehabilitation Journal*, 1–16.

Moore-Gilbert, B. (1997). *Postcolonial Theory*. London: Verso.

Paranjpe, A. C. (1986). *Theoretical Psychology: Meeting of East and West*. New York: Plenum Press.

Said, W. Edward (1989). 'Representing the Colonized: Anthropology's Interlocutors'. *Critical Inquiry*, 15 (2, Winter), 205–25.

Said, Edward (1994). *Culture and Imperialism*. New York: Knopf.

Singh, Vanessa and Ghai, Anita (2009). 'Notions of Self: Lived Realities of Children with Disabilities'. *Disability & Society*, 24 (2), 129–45.

Sen, Anima (1988). *Psychosocial Integration of the Handicapped: A Challenge to the Society*. Delhi: Mittal Publications.

Sherry, M. (2007). '(Post) Colonising Disability'. Special issue of *Wagadu, Journal of Transnational Women's and Gender Studies*, Volume 4, Summer, 10–22.

Spivak, G. (1988a). 'Can the Subaltern Speak?' In C. Nelson and L. Grossberg (eds), *Marxism and Interpretation of Culture* (pp. 271–313). Chicago, IL: University of Illinois Press.

Spivak, G. (1988b). *In Other Worlds: Essays in Cultural Politics.* New York: Routledge.

Spivak, G. (1990). *The Post-Colonial Critic: Interviews, Strategies, Dialogues* (edited by S. Harasym). New York: Routledge.

Spivak, G. (1995). 'Teaching for the Times'. In J. Nederveen Pieterse and B. Parekh (eds), *The Decolonization of Imagination: Culture, Knowledge and Power* (pp. 177–202). London: Zed.

Spivak, G. (1996). 'Scattered Speculations on the Question of Value'. In D. Landery and G. MacLean (eds), *The Spivak Reader.* New York: Routledge.

Spivak, Gayatri Chakravorty (1999). *A Critique of Postcolonial Reason: Toward a History of the Vanishing Present.* Cambridge, MA: Cambridge University Press.

Young, R. (2003). *Postcolonialism: A Very Short Introduction.* Oxford: Oxford University Press.

17
Recognition, Respect and Rights: Women with Disabilities in a Globalised World

Carolyn Frohmader and Helen Meekosha

Introduction

We are very aware of the inequalities between men and women. Men own most wealth, most institutions are run by men. Women are given less respect and their skills are less recognised than those of men. Even where women have made inroads into education and professional employment, many barriers remain (Walby, 1997; Broderick, 2010). But in the twentieth century struggles by women, especially in rich countries in the Global North, have led to reforms and improvements such as the right to vote, the right to own property and services such as refuges for victims of domestic violence, women's health centres, equal employment programmes and educational initiatives. Women are no longer seen as victims, but as agents in their own right (Walby, 1997; Wollack, 2010). As agents they have a gender identity 'as a lived set of embodied potentialities, rather than as an externally imposed set of constraining norms' (McNay, 2000: 31).

Women with disabilities, on the other hand, have not achieved the same level of social, economic, cultural and political equality. In this chapter, we will argue that a precondition of women with disabilities achieving these equalities is recognition and respect by wider society. Lack of recognition constitutes a form of harm. Following Honneth, we argue that denial of recognition is a form of disrespect that can be injurious to women with disabilities' 'positive understandings of themselves' (Honneth, 1995: 131). Honneth argues that lack of recognition affects individuals first at the level of physical integrity, secondly at the level of moral self-respect where they are denied certain rights, and finally where the individual or group's way of life is seen as inferior or deficient.

In this chapter, we examine the intersection between disability and gender and attempt to provide a global overview, while being mindful of the inadequacy of the data available and the major disparities between women with disabilities in the Global North and the Global South (Meekosha, 2011). We will demonstrate how women with disabilities experience all forms of disrespect in their daily lives by examining three issues: violence, sterilisation and the denial and shame attached to their perceived inability to parent. Disrespect of women is historically a product of patriarchal societies where men hold power over women who are seen as inferior. According to Honneth,

> [M]oral injustice is at hand whenever ... human subjects are denied the recognition they feel they deserve. I would like to refer to such moral experiences as feelings of social disrespect.
>
> (2007: 71)

Using our own organisation, Women with Disabilities Australia (WWDA), as a case study, we look at the challenges and successes over the past two decades that have confronted the organisation and its members in trying to bring about change for women with disabilities. The lives and experiences of women with disabilities have been hidden from history, and we are only just emerging as political actors in the struggle for human rights.

In the twenty-first century increasing numbers of women with disabilities' groups are organising for their rights in their own localities and national organisations, but also networking at international forums and via social media. Women with disabilities are active not just in the privileged countries of the Global North such as in Europe and the US, but also in the poorer countries of Africa, and Asia. Women with disabilities provided strong input into the writing of the United Nations Convention on the Rights of Persons with Disabilities, which was adopted on 13 December 2006, by the General Assembly. Pressure by women's groups succeeded in getting a separate clause in the text of the convention as well as several references to girls, women and gender issues.

How do we think about disability and gender?

Disability and gender come together in a set of social relations in which individuals and groups act. Both disability and gender involve relationships with physical bodies. But it is not simply a matter of physicality. Sometimes women's bodies are objects of social practice, sometimes agents in social practice (Connell, 2009). Social practices construct our understanding of disability and gender. Social embodiment is the process by which women with disabilities live in the world as agents and objects (Connell, 2009). Some writers have argued that a 'double handicap' (Schur, 2004) still exists as gender and disability exacerbate women with disabilities' unequal status. This concept is limited in describing the multi-dimensional experience of women with disabilities. Gender and disability are not like layers of a cloak that can be taken off or put on at will depending upon the circumstances. Improving the lives of women with disabilities is an immensely complicated affair.

There are no easy solutions. Sometimes disability can be acknowledged and embraced with pride (for example, women who are deaf); sometimes it is merely tolerated as part of life's experience and some women with disabilities are desperate to seek a cure for their condition.

Societies may impose the disabled identity against the subject's will for the purposes of containment in institutions. Disability is also a reason for violence and brutality. The presence of disability legitimises abuses such as forced sterilisation. On the other hand, women with disabilities who need special services may not be recognised – such as when they have mobility impairments and require appropriately sized examination tables in hospitals (Salthouse, 2005).

One important perspective for understanding disability has been through the social model. This model was developed in Britain in the late 1960s/ early 1970s by a group of disabled activists. They argued that the disability was primarily located in the social organisation of society and 'disability as oppression' would not be removed until disabling barriers to participation were removed (Barnes, 1998). While this model enabled disabled people to gain personal and political power, a number of feminists have argued that the social model is inadequate to understand the position of women with disabilities especially as they considered that the impaired body had been neglected (Crow, 1996; Meekosha, 1998; Thomas, 2004). From the work of pioneering women with disabilities, feminist disability studies arrived and feminists began to examine issues outside the social model such as

> representation and difference ... [and] issues of identity, subjectivity, the body, sexuality and language. For example stereotypical representation of disabled women in public imagery and the media contributes to their second-class status. Moreover the social relations of disability are often experienced as endangering the psycho-emotional well being of the individual.
> (Meekosha and Shuttleworth, 2009: 59)

When we talk of women with disabilities, we need to take into account the historical and contextual dimensions. Women with disabilities who live in cities have different experiences from their rural counterparts and women who live in the Global South experience more hardship than those in the mainly rich nations of the Global North (Mobility International US, 2003; World Bank, 2009). Even the concept of disability is not agreed upon (Shuttleworth and Kasnitz, 2005; Meekosha, 2011). Many traditional and indigenous communities do not use the concept. This is the case for Australian Aborigines. However, women with disabilities share one thing in common – there are very few women with disabilities with power, position and influence in the world. They also share the need for equal recognition of our lived experiences and equal respect for our differing impairments, which may be physical, sensory, cognitive or mental. While acknowledging the great difference that exists between women with disabilities, the picture at a global level shows that the situation for women in the Global South and poorer countries is most acute (World Bank, 2009).

Women with disabilities and girls: An overview

It is roughly estimated that over 650 million people, or approximately 10 per cent of the world's population, experience a disability (United Nations, 2009; International Labour Office, 2007). Around one in five are born with a disability, while most acquire their disability after the age of 16, mainly during their working lives (ibid.). The vast majority (80%) live in developing countries (Thomas, 2005) with two-thirds in the Asia-Pacific region (McMullan, 2008). We can estimate from existing figures that there are now 325 million women with disabilities and girls in the world, most of whom live in rural areas of developing or resource-poor countries (World Bank, 2009). However, a detailed global picture on how gender and disability intersect is not yet possible as data collection and research has been extremely limited and often clouded by factors that are quantification challenges, such as the feminisation of poverty, cultural concepts of gender roles and sexual and reproductive rights, violence, abuse and other types of exploitation, such as child labour (ibid.).

Regardless of country, the employment rates of women with disabilities are significantly lower than those of their male peers, and the activity gap between them is greater than that between persons with and without disabilities (International Labour Office, 2007). Worldwide, less than 25 per cent of women with disabilities are in the workforce (United States Agency for International Development, n.d.). Women with disabilities earn less than their male counterparts.

In developing countries, many women with disabilities have no income at all and are totally dependent on others for their very existence (Sheikha Hessa, 2005); the wage gap between men and women with disabilities is as high as 39 per cent (International Labour Office, 2007) and while unionisation helps bridge the gap between people with disabilities and people without disabilities, it is not as effective in helping women with disabilities obtain a higher level of wages compared to their male peers (ibid.). The literacy rate for women with disabilities worldwide is estimated at 1 per cent. Statistics from individual countries and regions, while often higher, nonetheless, confirm the gender inequalities (Nagata, 2003; United Nations Educational, Scientific and Cultural Organisation, 2003). In developing countries boys with disabilities attend school more frequently than do girls (ibid.).

Neglect, lack of medical care and less access to food or related resources have resulted in a higher mortality rate for girls with disabilities (United States Agency for International Development, n.d.). In the face of limited resources, girls are more likely than their male counterparts to be deprived of basic necessities such as food and medicine (Groce, 1997). For example, a UNICEF study in Nepal found that the survival rate for male children several years after they have had polio is twice that for female children, despite the fact that polio itself affects equal numbers of males and females (United States Agency for International Development, n.d.).

Women and girls are at an increased risk of becoming disabled during their lives due to neglect in healthcare, poor workforce conditions, gender-based violence and harmful traditional practices (ibid.). Their access to reproductive health care is minimal and as a result they suffer greater vulnerability to reproductive health problems (Department for International Development, 2000). For example, 20 million women a year are disabled as a consequence of pregnancy and childbirth. In the developing world, where cultural practices and poverty lead to forced and/or early marriages and early pregnancies, at least two million girls are disabled by the consequences of obstetric fistula (United Nations Children's Fund, 2006).

Worldwide, an estimated 130 million women have experienced the disabling consequences of female genital mutilation (FGM) and an additional two million girls and women are being subjected to it each year (United Nations Development Fund for Women, 2005). The physical and psychological consequences of these practices range from mobility difficulties, impaired sexual function and infertility because of infection to an increased risk of HIV infection (Department for International Development, 2000). Approximately half of the 40 million people living with HIV are women, and are now being infected at a higher rate than men. Seventy-seven per cent of all HIV-positive women in the world are African (United Nations Population Fund, 2005).

Eighty per cent of all people trafficked worldwide are women and girls (United Nations High Commissioner for Refugees, 2008). Victims are tricked or coerced into various exploitative situations, including prostitution, other forms of sexual exploitation, forced labour, begging and slavery. Traffickers target women and girls because of their ethnicity, race, disability or poverty (ibid.). Human trafficking studies have found that the proportion of child prostitutes who have mild developmental disabilities is six times greater than what might be expected in the incidence in the general population (United States Agency for International Development, n.d.).

Thus, the situation for women with disabilities, particularly those who live in the Global South is often dire. With globalisation, the human rights movement has been adopted almost universally, which begs the question as to why such inequalities remain?

Women with disabilities in a globalised world

Despite the fact that many countries have embraced and ratified a number of international human rights treaties and instruments affirming their commitment to protect and promote the human rights of women and girls (including women with disabilities and girls), in practice, they have had little bearing on improving their human rights. These rights include:

- the right to freedom from exploitation, violence and abuse
- the right to bodily integrity, and
- the right to found a family and to reproductive freedom

Women with disabilities continue to experience serious violations of their human rights, and these experiences need to be understood on a local level but also require analysis on a global scale. While we need to be culturally sensitive, significant similarities exist. Some writers (Mutua, 2002), for example, have argued that the human rights movement is hostile to diversity and difference as it emerges from Western liberal democracies with an agenda of cultural imperialism. It is not within the scope of this chapter to debate the politics of human rights or to propose a more sensitive framework, although this is research that needs to be undertaken especially with regards to women in the Global South.

The following sections of this chapter examine human rights violations in the context of violence, sterilisation, motherhood and parenting.

Violence

Women with disabilities are two to three times more likely to be victims of physical and sexual violence (Brownridge, 2006; WWDA, 2007b). They tend to be subjected to violence for significantly longer periods of time; violence takes many forms and there is a wider range of perpetrators. Fewer pathways to safety exist and they are, therefore, less likely to report experiences of violence (Dowse, Frohmader and Meekosha, 2010). Violence kills and disables as many women between the ages of 15 and 44 as cancer (Krug et al., 2002). Its toll on women's health surpasses that of traffic accidents and malaria combined (United Nations Development Fund for Women, 2005). Systematic rape, used as a weapon of war, has left millions of women and girls traumatised, forcibly impregnated or infected with HIV (Watts and Zimmerman, 2002).

Violation of women with disabilities comes with legal, social, cultural, economic and psychological dimensions and costs. Despite increasing recognition of and attention to gender-based violence as the 'most widespread human rights abuse in the world' (Krug et al., 2002); worldwide violence continues in a culture of silence, denial and apathy (Raye, 1999; Nosek et al., 2003). The lack of international research and data collection on violence against women with disabilities remains one of the reasons for the lack of community intervention and specific programmes and services. Worldwide, women and girls with disabilities are at great risk of violence due to many factors, in particular their entrenched social exclusion. Poverty can also make them more vulnerable to violence (WWDA, 2009c), as well as their impairment (such as inability to communicate using conventional means), dependence on others, fear of disclosure and lack of knowledge of their rights, services and support. They may also experience low self-esteem and lack assertiveness (Dowse, Frohmader and Meekosha, 2010). Violence against women and girls with disabilities can occur in the home, the community, institutional settings and in the workplace.

Although the forms of violence against women with disabilities are similar to those for women generally, women with disabilities often experience different dimensions of physical, psychological and sexual violence. For example, both involuntary sterilisation, which permanently removes a woman's ability to reproduce, and the use of Depo-Provera to suppress menstruation constitute a form of sexual violence. Women with disabilities who rely on personal care assistance may be subject to frequent violence and abuse, ranging from neglect, poor care and rough treatment to verbal, physical and sexual abuse (WWDA, 2009b).

Some babies experience violence from birth. The practice of 'infanticide' (also known as 'mercy killing') still occurs in some societies, where disabled children may be killed either immediately at birth or at some point after birth, and sometimes years after birth. Disabled female infants and children are much more likely to die through 'mercy killings' than are male children of the same age with comparable disabling conditions (United Nations Children's Fund, 2005).

In a number of countries, girls with disabilities are regularly used to generate income through begging. Some are placed on the streets to beg by their own families, some are sold by their families to others who keep stables of disabled children in organised rings of beggars (United Nations Children's Fund, 2005; International Labour Organization, 2009). In some cases, girls with disabilities used as beggars are deliberately mutilated in order to make them appear more pathetic and worthy of charity (Wonacott, 2004; International Labour Organization, 2009). In many parts of the world, girls with disabilities are sold into prostitution by poor families to raise money to meet basic needs or to simply rid them of the burden of caring for a disabled girl child (Rousso, 2003; Nepalese Youth Opportunity Foundation, 2004). Girls with disabilities may also be considered 'good catches' by prostitution rings as their disabilities can prevent them from escaping (Rousso, 2003).

Across the world, state authorities attempt to respond to violence through the legal and judicial systems, on the one hand, and through service systems, which provide protection, support, treatment and education, on the other hand (Roeher Institute, 1994). Women with disabilities are not only marginalised and ignored in many of these responses, but paradoxically, experience violence within and by the very systems and settings which should be affording them care, sanctuary and protection (WWDA, 2007c).

The lack of inclusive services and programmes for women with disabilities experiencing or at risk of experiencing violence is well documented (ibid.). There are limited support options for those who do escape violence. Recovering from the trauma of victimisation and rebuilding their lives as independent, active, valued members of society is a difficult challenge (Frantz et al., 2006). Where services do exist (such as refuges, shelters, crisis services, emergency housing, legal services, health and medical services, and other violence prevention services) a number of specific issues have been identified which make access for women with disabilities particularly problematic:

- while violence is a significant presence in the lives of large numbers of women with disabilities, many do not recognise it as a crime, are unaware of the services and options available to them, and/or lack the confidence to seek help and support.
- experience in community support services suggests that accessible information and communication is very limited in terms of both content and format of information available.
- the physical means of fleeing a violent situation (such as accessible transportation) are often unavailable. Crisis services do not necessarily have accessible transport nor are they able to assist a woman to physically leave the violent situation.
- the low likelihood of being referred to a refuge because it is assumed that such agencies do not or are unable to cater to their needs.

Although many countries today have some type of legislation concerning violence against women, it is often outdated (United Nations Population Fund, 2003) and is limited in recognising the range of forms of violence against women. This is critical for women with disabilities who experience forms of violence that are not traditionally included in existing legislation. Both general provisions and specific laws also frequently fail to take into account the context in which violence occurs, a major factor for women with disabilities experiencing violence (WWDA, 2007c). For example, in Australia, legislation, policy and services that focus on the broader issue of violence against women ignore the complexity of issues facing women with disabilities. Many of the current laws do not contain definitions that specifically encompass the range of settings in which women with disabilities may live, such as group or nursing homes. Whether these experiences fit traditional or contemporary definitions, it remains uncontestable that violence against women with disabilities often goes unidentified or unaddressed.

Sterilisation

Forced sterilisation has been acknowledged as a critical human rights issue facing women and girls with disabilities in a variety of international contexts, including the United Nations and within international disability and women's rights forums. 'Forced sterilisation' refers to the performance of a procedure that results in sterilisation in the absence of the consent of the individual who undergoes the procedure. This is considered to have occurred if the procedure is carried out in circumstances other than where there is a serious threat to health or life. This approach to naming sterilisation is underpinned by a human rights perspective, which holds that all individuals have the right to bodily integrity and the right to reproductive choice (Dowse, 2004).

There is a historical precedent in several countries, including for example the US (until the 1950s), in Canada and Sweden (until the 1970s) and Japan (until 1996), indicating that abuse of women with disabilities by sterilisation occurred on a large scale – that is, mass forced sterilisation. This policy was rationalised by a pseudo-scientific theory called eugenics – the aim being the eradication of a wide range of social problems by preventing those with 'physical, mental or social problems' from reproducing. Although eugenic policies have now been erased from legal statutes in most countries, vestiges still remain within the attitudes of some sectors of the community, and in some areas of the legal and medical establishments (Dowse and Frohmader, 2001). In the twenty-first century throughout the world, there are a number of women and girls with disabilities who have been and continue to be denied their right to bodily integrity through the ongoing practice of forced sterilisation.

Sterilisation is a procedure that is notorious for having been performed on young women with disabilities for various purposes ranging from eugenics, through menstrual management and personal care to the prevention of pregnancy, including pregnancy as a result of sexual abuse. In Australia, for example, the overwhelming majority of sterilisations and certainly all the cases heard by relevant Australian courts and tribunals involve girls with intellectual impairments (Brady, Briton and Grover, 2001). In the Australian context, gender and disability are not mutually exclusive where sterilisation in family law is examined (Steele, 2008).

Activists and advocates have continued to maintain that 'non-therapeutic' sterilisation[1] is a question for adulthood not childhood, and constitutes an irreversible medical procedure with profound physical and psychological effects (WWDA, 2007b). WWDA, for example, has insisted that the Australian government take all necessary steps to stop the forced sterilisation of women and girls with disabilities. This work[2] has included calls for the Australian governments to:

- develop universal legislation, which prohibits sterilisation of any child unless there is a serious threat to heath or life;
- address the cultural, social and economic factors which drive the sterilisation agenda;

- commit resources to assist women and girls with disabilities and their families and caregivers to access appropriate reproductive health care; and,
- create the social context in which all women and girls are valued and respected.

Despite strong condemnation of forced sterilisation from many sources, including women's organisations, disability rights organisations and international and national human rights bodies,[3] women and girls with disabilities in Australia still experience and face a serious threat of forced sterilisation. The United Nations Committee on the Rights of the Child has criticised the Australian Federal Government for its regulation of the practice of sterilisation in light of its status as a breach of children's human rights (Committee on the Rights of the Child, 2005). Despite this, Australian legislation still fails to prohibit non-therapeutic sterilisation of minors.

With WWDA's support, other women with disabilities' groups around the world are demanding action from their governments on the ongoing practice of forced sterilisation. Most recently, for example, the European Disability Forum (EDF) released its 'Declaration Against Forced Sterilisation of Girls and Women with Disabilities'. This Declaration, released on International Day for the Elimination of Violence against Women, recognises that forced sterilisation is a form of violence that violates the rights of women and girls with disabilities to form a family, decide on the number of children they wish to have, gain access to information on family planning and reproduction, and retain their fertility on an equal basis with others. The Declaration calls on governments to act immediately to revise the legal framework to prohibit the forced sterilisation of women and girls with disabilities; undertake research and data collection; and provide appropriate supports for women and girls with disabilities.

In this section, we have shown that reproductive choices for women with disabilities, far from remaining in the realm of the personal and private, are intensely political and ideological. Significantly state authorities, the medical profession as well as families and caregivers are involved in these unjust practices. If women with disabilities are to retain their autonomy around reproductive issues, then we need to work collectively across national borders.

Motherhood and parenting

For many women with disabilities around the world, the right to parent remains unrealisable. Women with disabilities have traditionally been discouraged from or denied the opportunity of bearing and raising children. They are perceived as being asexual/overly sexual, dependent, recipients of care rather than caregivers, and generally incapable of looking after children

(McKay-Moffat, 2007; Prilleltensky, 2003; Radcliffe, 2008; WWDA, 2009b). The denial of the right to have and maintain a family is a critical issue for women with disabilities, yet in many countries, it remains largely ignored in legislation, policy, research and services.

In addition to sterilisation, the denial of the right to become a parent takes many forms for women with disabilities, including coerced abortions, lack of appropriate reproductive health care and sexual health screening, limited contraceptive choices, a focus on menstrual control, denial of access to assisted reproductive technologies, and poorly managed pregnancies and births (Dowse and Frohmader, 2001). Women with disabilities also face economic, social and environmental barriers to their parenting role. Policies that fail to serve families adequately, along with the widely held belief that women with disabilities are 'naturally' unsuited for parenthood, all comprise an ableist culture for women with disabilities who are parents, or seeking to become parents (Malacredia, 2009).

Although there has been little research on any aspect of parenting and women with disabilities, anecdotal evidence suggests discriminatory attitudes and widely held prejudicial assumptions that question women's ability and, indeed, their right to experience parenthood (WWDA, 2009a). They experience significant difficulty in accessing appropriate parenting information, services and support in a host of areas – including preconception, pregnancy, birth, postpartum and the varying stages of child rearing (e.g., infancy; early childhood; adolescence), as well as in areas such as adoption, assisted reproduction and broader sexuality and reproductive health issues and care.

The lack of financial support, coupled with the higher cost of parenting with a disability, is a substantial barrier. In countries where there are income support systems, the extra costs incurred by disabled parents are not recognised. The lack of appropriate, adapted equipment to help women with disabilities in their parenting, especially of babies and young children, is another significant obstacle. For many, parenthood is not a viable option when social and financial supports are not available and some women have reported undergoing termination of much wanted pregnancies solely on the grounds of lack of such supports (WWDA, 2007a).

In some countries, families discourage their sons from marrying a woman with a disability. A lack of awareness means they believe that a woman with a disability either will not be able to have children or that any child born will inherit her disability. If a woman becomes pregnant, she is likely to be abandoned – facing the added stigma of being an unmarried mother (Johnston, 2008).

In many countries, including Australia, the denial of women with disabilities' right to have and maintain a family finds clear expression in the ongoing practice of the removal of babies/children from women with intellectual impairments. More than six decades of research has demonstrated that intellectual impairment is an unreliable predictor of parenting performance (Stenfert Kroese et al., 2002; Aunos et al., 2003; Llewellyn et al., 2008). Notwithstanding this, such parents (particularly mothers) are more likely than any other group of parents to have their children permanently removed (International Association for the Scientific Study of Intellectual Disabilities, 2008; Llewellyn et al., 2003). In many cases, child removal is ordered without evidence of abuse, neglect and/or parental incapacity, and occurs at the time, or within days, of a child's birth.

The removal or threat of removal of babies/children is also an issue for other women with disabilities, most notably women with psychiatric or intellectual impairments. Another dimension to this issue is in family court decisions where women are denied contact with, or lose custody of, their child/ren solely on the basis of the mother's disability (Sobsey and Sobon, 2006).

Women with Disabilities Australia (WWDA)

We have demonstrated how women with disabilities suffer disrespect at the level of physical integrity, moral self-respect, and as devalued human beings. WWDA has been involved primarily in the politics of recognition and representation, in particular where the private sphere crosses over into the public sphere (Meekosha, 2002). Secondly, WWDA has been fighting for women with disabilities to be recognised as legal persons and morally responsible agents deserving of respect. WWDA has a strong and growing international presence. WWDA's innovative programmes have been critically acclaimed at national and international levels, and the organisation has been rewarded with a number of prestigious awards.[4]

In 1995, WWDA was incorporated as an independent organisation run by women with disabilities for women with disabilities. In its embryonic state, WWDA was considered by its founders as 'an opportunity to work together as women with disabilities to build confidence, self-esteem and positive expectations about life's goals'. For the first few years, WWDA was required by government to re-apply for its funding every six months. This uncertainty of its future was a major challenge for WWDA, however, the organisation forged ahead with its strategies to improve the status of women with disabilities in Australia. In 1998 after much negotiation, the Australian government agreed to provide WWDA's operational funding on an annual basis. The organisation has grown and matured considerably in the past decade. It has moved from being a small group of women with disabilities concerned primarily with building individual confidence and self-esteem to an international and virtual organisation, harnessing the new social media and enabling and representing the collective interests of women with disabilities.

The politics of representation has been central to the disability rights movement (Charlton, 1998, Meekosha, 2001) and to ensure that WWDA maintains its integrity to its mission, there have been a number of strategies initiated to ensure that the 'voices' of women with disabilities are maintained at all levels throughout the organisation. These include legal organisational structures, such as the constitutional framework embedding restrictions upon able-bodied women's participation within the governing management committee through to ensuring that membership is open to all women with disabilities. This has been a central issue for the disabled women's movement in Australia as the majority of Australian women with disabilities live on a disability pension with little and, in most instances, no additional resources to spare for membership. Further, maintaining minimal fee, and in some cases, providing free membership, ensures that the membership is reflective of the majority of women with disabilities WWDA purports to represent rather than a minority of elite women (see Young, 2000 for full discussion on this issue). This has ensured that during the 'hard times' of government reform, WWDA has maintained its commitment to the rights of women with disabilities in line with its mandate, while other organisations have moved away from this agenda (see Soldatic and Chapman, 2010).

Challenges and successes

Dealing with authorities

A major challenge for non-government organisations (NGOs) remains one of relationships with government. Can we have meaningful relationships with governments when we are challenging their authority? States do not always act in a democratic way or in the interests of the people. Women with disabilities have to understand the nature of power, both within and outside government. As the majority of our funding comes from government, tension exists when we challenge the government policy. At what point do we accept limited success on one issue and move onto another one? There are both ethical and strategic questions at stake here.

In Australia, under the government of Prime Minister John Howard, WWDA had to sign a funding contract whereby we agreed not to speak to the media unless we had cleared our statements with the Minister of Family and Community Services. On the occasions we decided to speak out without permission the Minister reprimanded us, but no further actions were taken against the organisation. Speaking out was a difficult decision and the Management Board, made up of members, was fearful of losing funding. But we considered it important to disseminate our message to as wide as possible a constituency – in other words gaining support of women with disabilities and their allies in Australia. Regardless of the substantive issue, gaining public *recognition* of the rights of women with disabilities is always high on the agenda. Not only governments hold power, the medical profession has exercised much power over women's lives with disabilities and their members continue to be insensitive and disrespectful to women with disabilities and their needs.

Negotiating the local, the national and the global contexts

Before WWDA was established, we were a minority group within the Australian disability movement. The birth of WWDA was a result of marginalisation within the movement and the domination of positions of power by disabled men. The initial group of women saw themselves as being disaffected by the women's movement and the disability movement. In order to inform the broader community of the needs of women with disabilities, we had to reach out on a national level. Initially, with only one part time worker, the task was immense. There were times when the key players in the organisation felt powerless to sustain connections with women at the local level in such a large country. Australia is the sixth largest country in the world, 50 per cent larger than Europe, with the lowest population density in the world – only two people per square kilometre. An even greater challenge as social movements have gone global is to keep a balance between working at the local, the national and the international levels. This entails maintaining a balance between being part of a broader national and international disability movement and remaining true to our mission as an NGO for women with disabilities in Australia. Advances in communication technologies have accelerated our international engagement and we have both sought support for our own causes and campaigns and also lent support to other groups of women with disabilities worldwide. An NGO is fundamentally different from an activist group. As an NGO, we are a formalised organisation with a membership and governance structure. As part of both a feminist and a disability social movement, we are dealing with a much more fluid and changing phenomena where there is no particular person or organisation with whom to make alliances.

Communication technologies

New communication technologies have been a vital part of WWDA's success as well as an essential part of maintaining contact with women with disabilities around Australia. As a national body with very few resources, it is unlikely we would have been able to continue without the advent and widespread use of the Internet. The globalisation of communication has thrown up the means to contest, resist and oppose stigmatising and demeaning representations of women with disabilities. We act at multiple levels of the local, national and international context in our political practice. Our website is a major source of information for women in Australia and around the globe (see www.wwda.org.au). Through using new media we have been able to network with women with disabilities from all over the world and engage in mutual learning.

Women with disabilities who do not see themselves as political actors have been able to participate in online mobilisation for change. Yet, at the same time, these new technologies are expensive and not available in remote and rural areas. It is clear that the rapid dissemination of blogs, online videos and artwork can be helpful for women with disabilities, but a challenge for small organisations such as WWDA is to keep abreast of new developments and also to ensure that women with disabilities have access to new forms of interactivity. We also need to instil in women the confidence to speak out, especially in the social media. Social media does not automatically engender confidence in marginalised groups. Many women with disabilities do not have access to the Internet. There are issues of affordability, capacity and 'gatekeepers' to technology.

Forming strategic alliances

Access to new communication technologies has brought us more possibilities for forming coalitions and alliances than ever before. Yet we need to be careful not to compromise our values and ideals. WWDA has successfully made alliances with the women's health movement in Australia so that at the five yearly conferences there has always been a prominent woman with a disability keynote speaker. We also need to form alliances with workers, usually women, within the existing power structures of the bureaucracy, as although governments may change, the bureaucrats often remain the same. There are inevitably dangers in this type of pragmatic opportunity, but within a liberal democracy some gains can be made for women with disabilities.

Women with disabilities moving forward

Recognition of the personhood and rights of women and girls with disabilities is long overdue. Lack of recognition of their needs and experiences constitutes a serious form of disrespect, which compounds their lack of self-esteem and self-worth. This lack of recognition also contributes to the ongoing neglect and pervasive denial of their rights and fundamental freedoms.

That women with disabilities are now specifically recognised in an international human rights convention, as the result of an international, and largely virtual, movement of women with disabilities is a major achievement. Yet, despite the adoption of the United Nations Convention on the Rights of Persons with Disabilities, our goals remain substantially the same. We see the new convention providing a minimum framework for change and leverage at national and international levels, but not as providing all the answers. Our goals remain to have our needs recognised and seek an end to exclusion, inequality and violence. We need to be able to participate in education, employment and political, civil, social and cultural organisations. We need to have our safety guaranteed whether we live in the community or in institutions. Recognition and respect by governments and by broader society are fundamental to our identity and to achieving our goals.

Broader gender politics needs to recognise the harm done to women with disabilities but also recognise the value of our political work. Women with disabilities have and are contributing much to the world. The creativity and many talents of women with disabilities need to be recognised. There are now many groups of women organising locally, nationally and internationally on the many issues that affect their lives. We are campaigning and lobbying for our rights as women and as persons with disabilities. We are also learning to be comfortable with our differing embodiments. The global nature of gendered disability means we also have to work at an international level with feminist movements and human rights groups, including groups of men supporting gender equality.

Women with disabilities argue that one of the best ways to challenge oppressive practices, cultures and structures is to join with other women with disabilities – to share experiences, to gain strength from one another and to work together on issues that affect them. They have researched and recorded their issues and experiences, developed programmes to address these issues, and worked to influence legislative, policy and service development. These collectives enable women to recognise their own needs for personal autonomy, and perhaps more importantly, develop a sense of personal worth. At the broader level, it enables the formation of a collective identity, where women with disabilities are able to speak out about their experiences *together* and take action to realise their rights and improve their lives as a group.

The *International Network of Women With Disabilities* (INWWD) is one such example of an international initiative developed by women with disabilities to promote the human rights of disabled women and girls. The INWWD was established at a Global Summit for Women With Disabilities, conducted as an adjunct to the 21st Rehabilitation International World Congress in Canada in August 2008. As an outcome of the Summit, participants adopted the following Resolution:

> *Women with disabilities have been the world's forgotten sisters. There are over 300 million women with disabilities around the world, representing a huge and important part of society. We face multiple forms of discrimination. We, the participants in a global Summit on the Rights of Women with Disabilities, held in Quebec, Canada, in August 2008, have come together to claim our rights, through the Convention on the Rights of Persons with Disabilities (CRPD), Convention on the Elimination of Discrimination Against Women (CEDAW) and the human rights framework. Today, we take the first, historic step by creating a global network of women with disabilities, which must include women with ALL types of disabilities from ALL over the world. We will use this network to share our knowledge and experiences, speak up for our rights, bring about change and inclusion in our communities, and empower women with disabilities to be leaders of today and tomorrow. We invite ALL women with disabilities to join us and we will achieve these goals TOGETHER.*

(Adopted on 27 August 2008, Quebec, Canada)

From this, the INWWD was established. The network is currently e-mail based, and has more than 200 members from all over the world.[5] As a virtual community, the INWWD is working collaboratively to develop and publish position statements (e.g., on issues such as Violence Against Women With Disabilities) and establishing a presence within the United Nations treaty reporting system and processes.

However, like many activist networks, the INWWD relies on the volunteerism and goodwill of its members. What *is* needed is the support (including funding support) of governments and indeed the broader community to enable the establishment and strengthening of organisations, networks and groups run and controlled by women with disabilities in the pursuit of their collective interests.

The obligation to respect, protect and fulfil women with disabilities' human rights, clearly requires governments to do much more than merely abstain from taking measures which might have a negative impact on women with disabilities. The obligation in the case of women with disabilities is to take positive action to reduce structural disadvantages and to give appropriate preferential treatment to women with disabilities in order to ensure that they enjoy all human rights. This invariably means that additional resources will need to be made available for this purpose and that a wide range of specially tailored measures will be required (WWDA, 2010).

Notes

1. *'Non-therapeutic sterilisation' is sterilisation for a purpose other than to 'treat some malfunction or disease'*: Secretary, Department of Health and Community Services v JWB and SMB, 1992, 175 CLR 218; 106 ALR 385.
2. For an overview of WWDA's work on sterilisation, see: Sterilisation of Women and Girls with Disabilities at www.wwda.org.au/sterilise.htm.
3. See for example: Committee on the Rights of the Child, General Comment No 9 (2006): *The Rights of Children with Disabilities*, UN Doc CRC/C/GC/9 (2007); Committee on the Rights of the Child, *Concluding Observations: Australia*, UN Doc CRC/C/15/Add.268 (2005) [46(e)]; Committee on Economic, Social and Cultural Rights (1994) *Persons with Disabilities: CESCR General Comment*, 5 (31). Eleventh session, 1994.
4. National Human Rights Award 2001; National Violence Prevention Award 1999; Tasmanian Women's Safety Award 2008; Australian Crime & Violence Prevention Awards 2008; French Republic's Human Rights Prize 2003 (Nominee); UN Millennium Peace Prize for Women 2000 (Nominee).
5. To learn more about the inwwd group, go to:http://groups.yahoo.com/group/ inwwd.

References

Aunos, M., Goupil, G. and Feldman, M. (2003). 'Mothers with Intellectual Disabilities Who Do or Do Not Have Custody of Their Children'. *Journal on Developmental Disabilities*, 10 (2), 65–79.

Barnes, C. (1998). 'The Social Model of Disability: A Sociological Phenomenon Ignored by Sociologists?' In T. Shakespeare (ed.), *The Disability Reader: Social Science Perspectives*. London: Cassell.

Brady, S., Briton, J. and Grover, S. (2001). 'The Sterilisation of Girls and Young Women in Australia: Issues and Progress'. A report commissioned by the Federal Sex Discrimination Commissioner and the Disability Discrimination Commissioner; Human Rights and Equal Opportunity Commission, Sydney, Australia, http://wwda.org.au/brady2.htm, accessed October 2010.

Broderick, E. (2010). *Gender Equality Blueprint 2010*. Sydney: Australian Human Rights Commission.

Brownridge, D. A. (2006). 'Partner Violence Against Women with Disabilities: Prevalence, Risk and Explanations'. *Violence Against Women*, 12 (9), 805–22.

Charlton, J. (1998). *Nothing About Us Without Us: Disability, Oppression and Empowerment*. Berkeley: University of California Press.

Connell, R. (2009). *Gender in World Perspective*. Cambridge: Polity.

Crow, L. (1996). 'Including All of Our Lives: Renewing the Social Model of Disability'. In C. Barnes and G. Mercer (eds), *Exploring the Divide: Illness and Disability* (pp. 55–73). Leeds: Disability Press.

Department for International Development (DFID) (2000). *Disability, Poverty and Development*. London: DFID.

Dowse, L. and Frohmader, C. (2001). *Moving Forward: Sterilisation and Reproductive Health of Women and Girls with Disabilities*. Tasmania, Australia: Women With Disabilities Australia (WWDA).

Dowse, L. (2004) 'Moving Forward or Losing Ground? The Sterilisation of Women and Girls with Disabilities in Australia'. Paper presented to the Disabled Peoples' International (DPI) World Summit, Canada, http://wwda.org.au/steril3.htm, accessed October 2010.

Dowse, L., Frohmader, C. and Meekosha, H. (2010). *Intersectionality: Disabled Women*. In P. Easteal (ed.) *Women and the Law in Australia*. Australia: Reed International Books.

Frantz, B., Carey, A. and Nelson Bryen, D. (2006). 'Accessibility of Pennsylvania's Victim Assistance Programs'. *Journal of Disability Policy Studies*, 16 (4), 209–19.

Groce, N. (1997). 'Girls and Women with Disability: A Global Challenge'. *One in Ten*, 14 (2), 2–5.

Honneth, A. (1995). *The Struggle for Recognition: The Moral Grammar of Social Conflicts*. Cambridge: Polity.

Honneth, A. (2007). *Disrespect: The Normative Foundations of Critical Theory*. Cambridge: Polity.

International Association for the Scientific Study of Intellectual Disabilities (IASSID) (2008). 'Parents Labelled with Intellectual Disability: Position of the IASSID Special Interest Research Group (SIRG) on Parents and Parenting with Intellectual Disabilities'. *Journal of Applied Research in Intellectual Disabilities*, 21, 296–307.

International Labour Office (ILO) (2007). 'Equality at Work: Tackling the Challenges'. Global Report under the follow-up to the ILO Declaration on Fundamental Principles and Rights at Work. International Labour Office, Geneva.

International Labour Organization (2009). *Training Manual to Fight Trafficking in Children for Labour, Sexual and Other Forms of Exploitation*. International Labour Office, International Programme on the Elimination of Child Labour (IPEC), Geneva.

Johnston, G. (2008). 'Disability and Development'. *Disability, Pregnancy & Parenthood International*. 62, Summer, http://dppi.org.uk/journal/62/goodpractice.php, accessed November 2009.

Krug, E., Dahlberg, L., Mercy, J., Zwi, A. and Lozano, R. (eds) (2002). *World Report on Violence and Health*. Geneva: World Health Organisation.

Llewellyn, G., Mayes, R. and McConnell, D. (2008). 'Towards Acceptance and Inclusion of People with Intellectual Disability as Parents'. *Journal of Applied Research in Intellectual Disability*, 21 (4), 293–5.

Llewellyn, G., McConnell, D. and Ferronato, L. (2003). 'Prevalence and Outcomes for Parents with Disabilities and Their Children in an Australian Court Sample'. *Child Abuse and Neglect*, 27, 235–51.

Malacredia, C. (2009). 'Performing Motherhood in a Disablist World: Dilemmas of Motherhood, Femininity and Disability'. *International Journal of Qualitative Studies in Education*, 22 (1), 99–117.

McKay-Moffat, S. (2007). *Disability in Pregnancy and Childbirth*. Edinburgh: Churchill Livingstone.

McNay, L. (2000). *Gender and Agency: Reconfiguring the Subject in Feminist and Social Theory*. Cambridge: Polity.

McMullan, B. (2008). 'Disability, Disadvantage and Development in Asia and the Pacific'. Transcript of speech given at the Australian Disability and Development Consortium Conference 2008, Canberra, http://ausaid.gov.au/media/release.cfm?BC=Speech&ID=6598_4444_4031_1552_4691, accessed October 2009.

Meekosha, H. (1998) 'Body Battles: Bodies, Gender and Disability'. In T. Shakespeare (ed.), *The Disability Reader: Social Science Perspectives*. London: Cassell.

Meekosha, H. (2001). 'The Politics of Recognition or the Politics of Presence: The Challenge of Disability'. In M. Sawer and G. Zappalà (eds), *Speaking for the People*. Melbourne: Melbourne University Press.

Meekosha, H. (2002). 'Virtual Activists? Women and the Making of Identities of Disability'. *Hypatia*, 17 (3), 67–88.

Meekosha, H. and Shuttleworth, R. (2009). 'What's so "Critical" about Critical Disability Studies?' *Australian Journal of Human Rights*, 15 (1), 47–75.

Meekosha, H. (2011). 'Decolonising Disability: Thinking and Acting Globally'. *Disability and Society*, 26 (6), 667–82, http://www.tandfonline.com/doi/abs/10.1080/09687599.2011.602860.

Mobility International USA (2003). 'Loud, Proud and Passionate: Including Women with Disabilities in International Development Programmes'. In A. Hans and A. Patri (eds), *Women, Disability and Identity*. London: Sage.

Mutua, M. (2002). *Human Rights: A Political and Cultural Critique*. Philadelphia: University of Pennsylvania Press.

Nagata, K. (2003) 'Gender and Disability in the Arab Region: The Challenges in the New Millennium'. *Asia Pacific Disability Rehabilitation Journal*, 14, (1), 10–17.

Nepalese Youth Opportunity Foundation (NYOF) (2004), http://nyof.org/aboutNepal.html, accessed August 2006.

Nosek, M., Hughes, R., Taylor, H. and Howland, C. (2003). 'Violence against Women with Disabilities'. In D. Marge (ed.), *A Call to Action: Ending Crimes of Violence Against Children and Adults with Disabilities: A Report to the Nation*. State University of New York, Upstate Medical University; Department of Physical Medicine and Rehabilitation, Syracuse, New York.

Prilleltensky, O. (2003). 'A Ramp to Motherhood: The Experiences of Mothers with Physical Disabilities'. *Sexuality and Disability*, 21 (1), 21–47.

Radcliffe, V. (2008). 'Being Brave: Disabled Women and Motherhood'. Dissertation for the Degree of Master's of Arts in Disability and Gender, School of Sociology and Social Policy, The University of Leeds, UK.

Raye, K. (1999). *Violence, Women and Mental Disability*. Women's Rights Advocacy Initiative, Mental Disability Rights International (MDRI), Washington DC.

Roeher Institute (1994). *Violence and People with Disabilities: A Review of the Literature*. Prepared by Miriam Ticoll of the Roeher Institute for the National Clearinghouse on Family Violence, Health Canada, Ontario.

Rousso, H. (2003). *Education for All: A Gender and Disability Perspective*. A report prepared by Harilyn Rousso, CSW, Disabilities Unlimited, for the World Bank.

Salthouse, S. (2005). 'The Sick State of Health for Women with Disabilities'. Paper presented to the 5th Australian Women's Health Conference, Melbourne, http://wwda.org.au/health1.htm, accessed October 2010.

Schur, L. (2004). *Is There Still a 'Double Handicap'?* In *Gendering Disability*, edited by B. G. Smith and B. Hutchison. New Brunswick: Rutgers University Press.

Sheikha Hessa, Khalifa A. Al Thani (2005). *Statement by the United Nations Special Rapporteur on Disability on the occasion of International Women's Day, March 2005*. United Nations Program on Disability, http://un.org/esa/socdev/enable/womenday05.htm, accessed October 2010.

Shuttleworth, R., and Kasnitz, D. (2005). 'The Cultural Context of Disability'. In G. Albrecht (ed.), *Encyclopedia of Disability* (Vol. 1, 330–6). Thousand Oaks: Sage.

Sobsey, R. and Sobon, S. (2006). 'Violence, Protection and Empowerment in the Lives of Children and Adults with Disabilities'. In C. Vine and R. Alaggia, *Cruel but Not Unusual: Violence in Canadian Families*. Waterloo: Wilfrid Laurier Univ. Press.

Soldatic, K. and Chapman, A. (2010). 'Surviving the Assault? The Australian Disability Movement and the Neoliberal Workfare State'. *Social Movement Studies*, 9 (2), 139–54.

Steele, L. (2008). 'Making Sense of the Family Court's Decisions on the Non-Therapeutic Sterilisation of Girls with Intellectual Disability'. *Australian Journal of Family Law*, 22 (1).

Stenfert Kroese, B., Hussein, H., Clifford, C. and Ahmed, N. (2002). 'Social Support Networks and Psychological Well-Being of Mothers with Intellectual Disabilities'. *Journal of Applied Research in Intellectual Disabilities*, 15, 324–40.

Thomas, C. (2004). 'How is Disability Understood: An Examination of Sociological Processes'. *Disability & Society*, 19 (6), 569–83.

Thomas, P. (2005). *Disability, Poverty and the Millennium Development Goals: Relevance, Challenges and Opportunities for DFID*. Final Report of the DFID Disability Knowledge and Research (KaR) Programme, http://disabilitykar.net/, accessed October 2009.

United Nations Committee on the Rights of the Child (CRC), UN Committee on the Rights of the Child: *Concluding Observations, Australia*, 20 October 2005, CRC/C/15/Add.268, at para. [46(e)], http://www.unhcr.org/refworld/docid/45377eac0.html, accessed June 2009.

United Nations Children's Fund (UNICEF) (2005). *Violence against Disabled Children: Summary Report*. UN Secretary Generals Report on Violence against Children: Thematic Group on Violence against Disabled Children, Findings and Recommendations. Convened by UNICEF, New York, 28 July.

United Nations Children's Fund (UNICEF) (2006). *The State of the World's Children 2006: Excluded and Invisible*. New York: UNICEF.

United Nations Development Fund for Women (UNIFEM) (2005). *Violence against Women: Facts & Figures*. New York: UNIFEM.

United Nations Educational, Scientific and Cultural Organisation (UNESCO) (2003). *Gender and Education for All: The Leap to Equality*. Paris: UNESCO Publishing.

United Nations High Commissioner for Refugees (UNHCR) (2008). *UNHCR Handbook for the Protection of Women and Girls.* Geneva, Switzerland: Office of the United Nations High Commissioner for Refugees.

United Nations Population Fund (UNFPA) (2003). *Addressing Violence against Women: Piloting and Programming.* New York: UNFPA.

United Nations Population Fund (UNFPA) (2005). *State of World Population 2005: The Promise of Equality – Gender Equity, Reproductive Health and the Millennium Development Goals.* New York: UNFPA.

United Nations, *Some Facts about Persons with Disabilities,* http://un.org/disabilities/ convention/facts.shtml, accessed October 2009.

United States Agency for International Development (USAID) (n.d.). *Women with Disabilities and International Development,* http://www.usaid.gov/our_work/cross-cutting_programs/wid/gender/wwd_statistics.html, accessed March 2012.

Walby, S. (1997). *Gender Transformations.* London: Routledge.

Watts, C. and Zimmerman, C. (2002). 'Violence against Women: Global Scope and Magnitude'. *The Lancet,* 359, 1232–7.

Wollack, K. (2010). *Women as Agents of Change: Advancing the Role of Women in Politics and Civil Society.* Statement to the House Committee on Foreign Affairs Subcommittee on International Organizations, Human Rights and Oversight, 9 June 2010, http://www.ndi.org/Congress_Looks_to_Women, accessed October 2010.

Women with Disabilities Australia (WWDA) (2007a). E-mail correspondence to WWDA from members regarding parenting support for women with disabilities in Australia [unpublished].

Women with Disabilities Australia (WWDA) (2007b). *Policy and Position Paper: The Development of Legislation to Authorise Procedures for the Sterilisation of Children with Intellectual Disabilities,* http://www.wwda.org.au/polpapster07.htm, accessed October 2010.

Women with Disabilities Australia (WWDA) (2007c). *Forgotten Sisters – A Global Review of Violence against Women with Disabilities.* WWDA Resource Manual on Violence Against Women With Disabilities. Tasmania, Australia, WWDA.

Women with Disabilities Australia (WWDA) (2009a). *Parenting Issues for Women with Disabilities in Australia: A Policy Paper.* Rosny Park, Tasmania, WWDA, http://www. wwda.org.au/subs2006.htm, accessed October 2010.

Women with Disabilities Australia (WWDA) (2009b). *Submission to Inform the Development of the Framework for the National Women's Health Policy.* Tasmania: WWDA, http://www.wwda.org.au/subs2006.htm, accessed October 2010.

Women with Disabilities Australia (WWDA) (2009c). *Submission to the National Human Rights Consultation.* Tasmania: WWDA, http://www.wwda.org.au/subs2006.htm, accessed October 2010.

Women with Disabilities Australia (WWDA) (2010). *Submission to the Australian Government's Draft National Disability Advocacy Framework,* http://www.wwda.org. au/subs2006.htm, accessed November 2010.

Wonacott, P. (2004). 'QuanQian's Tale: In Beggars' Village, Disabled Girl Fell Into Con Man's Net'. *Wall Street Journal.* New York, 7 December, Easter edition: A.1.

World Bank (2009). *Gender and Disability,* http://go.worldbank.org/O14DRFLK90, accessed October 2009.

Young, I. M. (2000). *Inclusion and Democracy.* Oxford: Oxford University Press.

18
Conclusion: Disability and Social Theory

Bill Hughes, Dan Goodley and Lennard Davis

Why theory for disability?

Why theory? It is a question the Greeks would probably not have asked. *Theoria* for our classical cousins was about 'contemplation', reflecting on observation and experience, in other words, ways of making sense of the world, reaching out through reason to the juicy fruit of truth. It was built in to what they did and how they approached the world. A gymnasium was both a place for getting naked and for philosophical speculation, a combination of the intellectual and the physical, incongruous in the modern academy where thinking is wrapped in robes and gowns. Nietzsche, in marked contrast to his fellow philosophers down the ages, taught that while our ideas did not serve the untouchable tribunal of truth, theory was a psychological necessity, an outcome of the need for human actors to impose intellectual order on a chaotic world. 'The categories are "truths"', he wrote, 'only in the sense that they are conditions of life for us' (Nietzsche, 1968: 516). Foucault summed up this insight with his aphorism, 'the will to truth'. We do not discover truth; we work it up into an *episteme* – a collection of ideas that makes most of us nod with approval. Theory has a reputation for being esoteric but as it settles into everyday discourse, into habit, it transforms into common sense. Nietzsche's perspectivism might debunk truth, but it does not question the need for theory.

No matter which philosophical perspective we take on the history and generation of ideas and the relationship between theory and practice, we can probably claim that where one finds curiosity, theory will be in close proximity. Reason – the faculty that supposedly separates us from the animals – makes theory both necessary and probably desirable. Antonio Gramsci (1971) made it absolutely plain that we are all intellectuals; we are all philosophers; we all do theory! It is a universal practice, not simply a game for intellectuals. In Gramsci's view the theoretical and the quotidian are bedfellows. We may mock the public house philosopher for his or her inebriated wit, but he or she is still a philosopher. So why do we sometimes reach apologetically for justifications at the mere mention of the word theory? Why would we need to make a puzzle of, or even interrogate for a moment, the value of such a basic activity? If it lies at the heart of the human condition, why do so many people have a problem with it?

If one examines the position of disability studies in the UK, the question might be answered – in the first instance – in two words: British empiricism! This tradition developed in philosophy in the eighteenth century. It germinated in the work of Francis Bacon and grew through the deliberations of Hume, Locke and J. S. Mill. It had a powerful influence on British social science in the nineteenth and twentieth centuries. At a cultural level it can manifest itself as anti-intellectualism, a practical approach to the world in which the danger of too much thought and analysis leads to paralysis and inaction. One does not build an empire of world historic proportions on the back of contemplation. Universities are ivory towers and one needs to escape them in order to live in the 'real world'. The continent – particularly the philosophical heartlands of France and Germany – is largely immune from these 'Anglo-Saxon' tendencies. Empiricism's focus on the search for facts and how these might be oriented and understood by hypotheses and laws of social life left an indelible impression on British intellectual culture. Suspicion of concepts and theory – not *per se* a facet of empiricism which offers clear advice on building and doing theory – is a legacy of this tradition. The tradition runs deep and one can see it manifest in disability studies in the UK. The epistemological foundation for disability studies on the Eastern side of the pond was a 'model' rather than a theory, a practical political credo rather than a critical praxis and it held this kind of ground from the 1970s through to the 1990s.

However, this is not the whole story. The social model of disability is, in fact, far from atheoretical. Its theoretical debt to historical materialism is considerable and evidence for this leaps from nearly every page of the most seminal account of the social model. The homage to Marx and Gramsci in Mike Oliver's book *The Politics of Disablement* (1990) is deep and meaningful. The social model is unthinkable without historical materialism, but it has melted into the background, become a foundation, a premise that does not need to be restated. The tendency in British empiricist culture to play down theory – as a bit of an embarrassment like teenagers who are affronted by their parent's lack of cool – may account, in part, for the social model's reluctance to engage, a great deal, with its theoretical foundation. However, one can utilise this foundation to say a little bit about the relationship between theory and practice in UK disability studies.

The relationship between theory and practice in disability studies in the UK could be described during the last three decades of the twentieth century as a balanced Hegelian Marxist style dialectic in which the social model acted as the intellectual and theoretical expression of the disability movement. However, as the movement became more complex and differences within disability developed around social and impairment factors, the social model remained wedded, pretty implacably, to its original insight and, more importantly, to its practical mission which was to dismantle the barriers that blocked disabled people's participation in society. The movement marched on but the theory stayed still; a critique that Karl Korsch (1923/1970) made of Marxism itself in the early 1920s. The accent on activism drove forward the imperative to transform disabled people into citizens, to pull down the walls of the custodial existence that had marked and marred the modern disability experience and replace it with freedom and opportunity. In the UK context, theory did not evolve alongside practice in a meaningful dialectic and the main tenets of the social model became more or less axiomatic. The social model embodied a paradigm shift in thinking about disability and became a clear and unequivocal intellectual point of entry into the struggle for disability rights but it did not become a focal point for theoretical debate and development. Its proponents were largely unconvinced of the value of such a journey partly because they were more concerned with forms of knowledge production that fed directly and unequivocally into palpable political gains. Practice was more important than theory (Oliver, 1996) and epistemologically it was the relationship between research and politics, academy and movement that mattered most (Barnes, Oliver and Barton, 2002). Theory was not on this agenda.

The atheoretical disposition of the social model probably played some part in inscribing a tendency towards orthodoxy and revisionism rather than heterodoxy and debate. The gain, nonetheless, was enormous and the benefits to disabled people impossible to quantify. We should re-iterate that the social model has its origin in the key source of *Critical Theory* and this is evidenced, clearly in, *inter alia*, its aspiration to promote emancipatory research (see, for example, Mercer, 2002), to produce knowledge that is built in the name of the progressive overcoming of oppression. At the heart of this book is the suggestion that emancipatory research has need of emancipatory theory and that one can find this necessary ingredient of social movement in diverse – even unpromising – depositories.

The singular approach to disability studies in the UK, despite the powerful presence of the social model well beyond the borders of the land of its inception has, however, largely, both continued and imploded. The globalisation of disability studies has been marked by the proliferation of perspectives with polychrome contributions from the Global South and North meeting to make a new epistemological soup. Nordic preferences for social role valorisation form a melting pot with the minority status and cultural models that have energised the US scene and the bio-psychosocial models that inform the work of medical sociologist and social model revisionists form a lifeline for rehabilitation scientists and health professionals to re-enter – with legitimacy more or less – the great disability debate. Australian disability studies has given us the theoretically rich concept of 'ableism' (Kumari Campbell,

2010) and US scholarship – housed mostly in the humanities rather than the social sciences – has produced, recently, a significant number of contributions to disability studies that are immersed in the theoretical (see for example – to reference but a few – Siebers, 2008, 2011; Stoddard Holmes, 2004; Deutch and Nussbaum, 2000; Davidson, 2008; Rose, 2003; Wheatley, 2010). Canada too has a production line of fine disability scholars who mark out their intellectual territory in a way that draws heavily on social theory (see for example: Tremain, 2005; Titchkosky and Michalko, 2009; Michalko, 2002). Contributions from Marxists, feminists, phenomenologists, post-structuralists, cultural analysts and critical realists and from a multiplicity of humanities and social science disciplines have introduced layers of theory to the well-founded empirical claim that disabled people are excluded, marginalised and oppressed (for an overview of the developing eclecticism of disability studies, see Goodley 2011). The arrival of theory received impetus also from the development of social science perspectives on the body, presaged by the collapse of the categorical distinctions between nature and culture, the body and society that had stood at the centre of Cartesianised modernity (Hughes and Paterson, 1997). Culture, body, postmodernity: these categories became the icons upon which debate in the humanities and social sciences *turned* as the twentieth century slipped, sluggishly, brutally towards its wayward end. The repository of knowledge that it carried with it, once – so the myth of progress contended – ordered, objective, scientific had the look of a pile of debris. The turn to theory was an attempt to clear it up.

Turn, turn, turn

The UK disability movement was well blessed with 'organic intellectuals': disabled academics deeply involved in the struggle for disability emancipation. The social model was the intellectual tool that organic intellectuals armed themselves with and it proved most effective in breaching the walls of the ableist *weltanshaaung*. The social model turned on externalising and de-personalising the problem of disability, transforming it 'from pathology to politics' (Goodley, 2011: 5). Disability was re-modelled into a disembodied social phenomenon. In its new social model shape disability was completely redefined. Once the influence of the medical model was swept to one side, disability became equivalent to the forms of social organisation that produced discrimination against and exclusion of disabled people. If disability was a form of social oppression, then the medical conception of it as a faulty body was erroneous and the long established medicalised and hypostatised link between disability and biology was shelved *tout court*. Ironically, however, impairment fell from the agenda of British disability studies just as the body was becoming a key launch-pad for social theory. 'Second wave' disability intellectuals were well schooled in the turn to the body and in the kind of social science that had become fed up with the dead weight of all the dualisms that had hung around since Descartes' day. In the last 30 years of the last century, there were turns at every turn: postmodern, cultural, somatic, emotional and each and everyone was happy to embrace theory, to engage with new ways of thinking that would problematise or defend the project of modernity, an unconscious extended review of the long march from enlightenment to puzzlement, from certainty to chaos, objectivity to disenchantment. Where once reason, the mind and Kant had reigned supreme, as the new millennium approached, passion, the body and Nietzsche started to look a lot more attractive.

In the US, disability studies, given its stronger grounding in the humanities, was better placed than the UK to embrace successive turns and the theoretical predilections that each embodied. The liberal arts approach to disability is clearly manifest in the series published by the University of Michigan Press, titled *Corporealities: Discourses of Disability*. The series editors, David Mitchell and Sharon Snyder, have this to say about the project which, at last count, boasts 20 titles:

> *Corporealities: Discourses of Disability* promotes a broad range of scholarly work analyzing the cultural and representational meanings of disability. Definitions of disability underpin fundamental concepts such as normalcy, health, bodily integrity, individuality, citizenship, and morality – all terms that define the very essence of what it means to be human. Yet, disabilities have been traditionally treated as conditions in need of medical intervention and correction. Rarely has disability been approached as a constructed category forwarded by social institutions seeking to legislate the slippery line that exists between normative biology and deviant bodies. In addition to identifying the social phantasms that have been projected upon disabled subjects in history, the series aims to theorize the shifting coordinates of disabled identities.
>
> (University of Michigan Press, 2011)

In this project, bodies loom large. The idea – to which the social model became wedded – that impairment constituted a pre-social domain outside the ambit of the social model is, clearly, rejected. The idea that impairment and disability represent respectively the biological and the social appears as yet another example of the Cartesian way, a paradigm that had broken down. There was a strong feeling that this modernist approach to knowledge was struggling for legitimacy and should be confined to the epistemological graveyard. The distinction between impairment and disability looked a little ghostly from birth, but it had become impossible to sustain. Second wave disability scholars were not only keen to theorise disability but inclined to give impairment the same treatment. In the collapse of the distinction between impairment and disability, one can detect the origins of critical disability studies (Goodley 2011: 157–75). However, the social model can still claim parental rights to critical disability studies as a wayward eclectic offspring, mired in the myriad *fin de millennium* turns that have changed the landscape of disability. Social model DNA is evident in the emancipatory thrust of critical disability studies but the latter is much more inclined to interrogate the emancipatory potential of social theory.

Mining the seams of social theory: An example

The use of Nietzsche in disability studies is rare (notable exceptions include Mitchell and Snyder, 2000 and Smith, 2005) yet – *despite Nazi appropriations of his ideas that draw him into association with genocide against disabled people* – there is much useful material to bend to the emancipatory cause. We offer up a short exegesis of Nietzsche which draws on some of the ways that he might be pressed into the service of the emancipatory manifesto of critical disability studies. We do so in a final attempt to reiterate the aim of this book: to make theory go to work in the name of the global movement of disabled people.

The critique of modernity that we find in the nineteenth century philosophers such as Soren Kierkegaard and especially Nietzsche pivots on the psychological view that modern persons are in denial when it comes to facing up to their own vulnerability. We fail to recognise, let alone celebrate pain, loss and death. In these powerful critiques of modernity, we hear tell of a culture that is being emptied of passion, on the one hand, and stoked-up with objectivity and scientific essentialism on the other. The blight of objectivity is such that it empties lives of meaning and purpose and replaces the candour that honest reflexivity inspires with denial and fear, particularly in relation to our carnal frailties. This outline of Nietzsche's ideas might double as a critique of medicine from a disability perspective, and it takes our thinking down a track that owes nothing to a fixed view of the moral superiority of the healthy, wholesome subject. For Nietzsche, it is difficult to love life if we do not cherish death or to celebrate health if we live in constant fear of infirmity. If 'we' turn these intrinsic carnal dimensions of living and being into ontological negatives in our own lives, then 'we' will not want others to remind us of what 'we' might become. This attitude of modernity and the moderns is the attitude of the 'we' described in the preceding sentences, and it is also the perspective of normality and non-disablement as it cheats itself out of the very qualities that help humanity deal with what it is and must be. Smith (2005: 564) argues that Nietzsche's, '"yes to life" ... empowers a disabled person's capacity to live life to the full, unrestricted by norms and standards defined and imposed by non-disabled people'.

These processes of self denial – embedded in the ableist constitution of modernity – not only disfigure the non-disabled imaginary but also have negative social consequences for disabled people. Those who are singled out to represent loss, pain and suffering become objects of fear and disgust. In this argument, we encounter notification of the historical conditions in which the stigma and exclusion of disabled people is fostered. Nietzsche, however, cuts through this with one of his singular aphorisms. He notes that '[w]herever progress is to ensue, deviating natures are of greatest importance' (Nietzsche, 2004: 224). His specific scientific and theoretical target, in this respect, is Darwin's doctrine of natural selection and its sociological companion, social Darwinism. He develops the critique in a way that explicitly valorises the outsider and challenges what, today, we would call ableism:

> In a warlike and restless clan, for example, the sicklier man may have occasion to be alone, and may therefore become quieter and wiser; the one-eyed man will have one eye the stronger; the blind man will see deeper inwardly, and certainly hear better. To this extent, the famous theory of the survival of the fittest does not seem to me to be the only viewpoint from which to explain the progress of strengthening of a man or of a race.
>
> (Nietzsche, 2004: 224)

This is testimony to Nietzsche's 'embrace of the value of outsiderness' and it 'points to the possibility of a transgressive narrative space for disability' (Mitchell and Snyder, 2000: 35).The ontological insecurities of modernity become projected on to disabled people and, therefore, the positivity, wisdom and strength that Nietzsche can recognise in the so called unfit become obscured. In practice these positive ideas about outsiders and difference disappear into obscurity in much the same way as disabled people in modernity disappear into institutional confinement. 'The inversionary tactics in Nietzsche ... involve an open embrace – even a stalwart declaration – of those who are most debased by cultures of the normal' (Mitchell and Snyder, 2000: 34). Unfortunately, the modernity, on which Nietzsche vented so much spleen, had embraced the normal as an article of faith, paving the way for eugenics and the characterisation of disability as a social contaminant.

Disability studies can find much of value in Nietzsche's critique and restoration of reason. For him reason is not the ultimate organising principle for knowledge and life, because in the standard form that it has been bequeathed to us from antiquity to modernity, it is unreasonable. The passions, he argues, are at the root of reason and, while he is no irrationalist, he believes that irrationality is a condition of existence. The Apollonian without the Dionysian is a bland and broken basis for vital culture. He disrupts the standard distinction between reason and emotion, rescuing unreason from the pure negativity that became its philosophical home. 'Madness', he argues (1973: 85), 'is something rare in individuals – but in groups, parties, peoples and ages it is the rule'. This stands in stark contrast to the Western discourse of reason and its powerful condemnation of individual insanity. The disability scholar Tim Stainton (2001: 453) notes that 'for both Plato and Aristotle, it was reason that separated men from beasts. To be wanting in respect of reason – to be what today we would call intellectually disabled – was to be less than human, to lack value, to stand apart from and deserve to be cast out of the polity.' The social consequences of madness, for those so labelled, have been, almost invariably, invalidation and exile, but if our thinking about reason is wrong headed, then we must begin to articulate – as Michel Foucault (1988) has done – the connections between the history of insanity and the history of injustice.

A final word on Nietzsche will rest with the way he destabilises the relationship between beauty, virtue and reason, through his 'stormy' relationship with Socrates.

> *Twilight of the Idols*, his work on Socrates' well known deformities, claims that the philosopher's body disrupted the Athenian faith in the correlation between bodily beauty and moral goodness. Yet despite Socrates' physical nonconformity, Nietzsche critiques him for championing the supremacy of rationality and ignoring the power of his own aberrant corporeality. According to Nietzsche, much of the Greek philosopher's appeal for the ancient Athenians was based on the freak show like spectacle of a thinker who championed rationality as beauty in spite of physical evidence to the contrary. Arguing that Socrates' visible presence introduced the destabilising power of physical difference into philosophical discourse, Nietzsche berates Socrates and his followers for sacrificing the power of 'the ugliest man' to the more banal superiority of abstract Reason.
>
> (Mitchell and Snyder, 2000: 34)

In *Twilight of the Idols*, Nietzsche argues that Socrates is a decadent because he represents the authority of the idea, the virtue of argument and the power of logic. He establishes icons that encourage in us a certain servility, universal codes that are dogmatic traps. Nietzsche warns against Socrates' will to control, his will to tyranny. We must never accept the authority expected of us be it manifest in the man of reason or the creative genius: 'No price is too high for the privilege of owning oneself'. One might be forgiven for thinking that this Nietzschean aphorism was written as a slogan for the disability movement.

Plunder as method

One might take the view that the approach to Nietzsche manifest in the preceding section is nothing short of intellectual plunder, a form of piracy. This would be a fair conclusion. A significant variety of theories have been read from a disability standpoint and appropriated for their efficacy in relation to that particular perspective. The view we have taken is that any intellectual system or social theory is fair game when it comes to building a case for emancipation or for sharpening the tools that are of value in opposing discrimination, exclusion and oppression. Throughout this book we have treated theory as a resource, as a means to furnish critical disability studies with the wherewithal to advance the cause of disabled people. A significant range of theoretical perspectives have been rolled out and stripped of any tasty morsel that can be devoured. The remains have been returned to the pantry. We make no apologies for employing plunder as method.

References

Barnes, C., Oliver, M. and Barton, L. (2002). 'Disability, the Academy and the Inclusive Society' (pp. 250–60). In C. Barnes, M. Oliver and L. Barton (eds), *Disability Studies Today*. Oxford: Polity Press.

Deutch, H. and Nussbaum, F. (2000). *Defects: Engendering the Modern Body*. Ann Arbor: Michigan University Press.

Foucault, M. (1988). *Madness and Civilization: A History of Insanity in the Age of Reason*. New York: Vintage Books.

Goodley, D. (2011). *Disability Studies: An Interdisciplinary Introduction*. London: Sage.

Gramsci, A. (1971). *The Prison Notebooks*. London: Lawrence and Wishart.

Davidson, M. (2008). *Concerto for the Left Hand: Disability and the Defamiliar Body*. Ann Arbor: University of Michigan Press.

Hughes, B. and Paterson, K. (1997). 'The Social Model of Disability and the Disappearing Body: Towards a Sociology of Impairment'. *Disability & Society*, 12 (3), 325-40.

Kumari Campbell, F. (2010). *Contours of Ableism: The Production of Disability and Abledness*. Basingstoke: Palgrave Macmillan.

Korsch, K. (1923/1970). *Marxism and Philosophy*. London: New Left Books.

Mercer, G. (2002). 'Emancipatory Disability Research' (pp. 228–49). In C. Barnes, M. Oliver and L. Barton (eds), *Disability Studies Today*. Oxford: Polity Press.

Michalko, R. (2002). *The Difference that Disability Makes*. Philadelphia: Temple University Press.

Mitchell, D. and Snyder, S. (2000). *Narrative Prosthesis: Disability and the Dependencies of Discourse*. Ann Arbor: Michigan University Press.

Nietzsche, F. (1968a). *The Will to Power*. New York: Vintage.

Nietzsche, F. (1968b). *Beyond Good and Evil*. Harmondsworth: Penguin.

Nietzsche, F. (2004). *Human: All too Human*. Harmondsworth: Penguin.

Oliver, M. (1990). *The Politics of Disablement*. Basingstoke: Palgrave Macmillan.

Oliver, M. (1996). *Understanding Disability: From Theory to Practice*. London: Macmillan.

Rose, M. L. (2003). *The Staff of Oedipus: Transforming Disability in Ancient Greece*. Ann Arbor: University of Michigan Press.

Siebers, T. (2008). *Disability Theory*. Ann Arbor: University of Michigan Press.

Siebers, T. (2010). *Disability Aesthetics*. Ann Arbor: University of Michigan Press.

Smith, S. (2005). 'Equality, Identity and the Disability Rights Movement: From Policy and Practice and from Kant to Nietzsche in More Than One Easy Move'. *Critical Social Policy*, 25 (4), 554–76.

Stainton, T. (2001). 'The Roots of Exclusion: The Thought of Aristotle and Plato and the Construction of Intellectual Disability'. *Mental Retardation*, 39 (6), 452–60.

Stoddard Holmes, M. (2004). *Fictions of Affliction: Physical Disability in Victorian Culture*. Ann Arbor: University of Michigan Press.

Titchkosky, T. and Michalko, R. (2009). *Rethinking Normalcy: A Disability Studies Reader*. Toronto: Canadian Scholars/Women's Press.

Tremain, S. (ed.) (2005). *Foucault and the Government of Disability*. Ann Arbor: University of Michigan Press.

University of Michigan Press (2011), http://www.press.umich.edu/series.do?id=UM117, accessed 25 March 2011.

Wheatley, E. (2010). *Stumbling Blocks before the Blind: Medieval Constructions of a Disability*. Ann Arbor: University of Michigan Press.

Glossary

We have reproduced a number of theoretical concepts that are used in this text. The works cited in this glossary can be found in the reference lists of the chapters. In some cases we have offered a number of definitions of the same concept in order to reflect different contributors' takes on these concepts.

Ableism: Campbell (2008: 153 and 2009: 5) defines ableism as, 'a network of beliefs, processes and practices that produces a particular kind of self and body (the corporeal standard) that is projected as perfect, species-typical and therefore essential and fully human'. Ableism is a concept that expresses the ways in which society privileges physical and mental wholeness as a normative ideal, promotes an unobtainable corporeal aesthetic and encourages bodily projects towards that end. It embodies a moral grammar that leaves disabled people at or beyond the very margins of society refusing to recognise their value or esteem their differences and competencies.

Alienation: In general terms this refers to the estrangement of individuals to one another; however, this idea has been applied in many different ways. In a Marxist sense it refers to a state of being where individuals are unable to recognise the products of their own labour as products of their own labour, instead they feel distanced (alienated) from those products and consider them to belong to their employers. The maintenance of alienated labour is said to be fundamental to the growth of capitalism.

Anthropoemic: Bauman argues that societies can develop anthropoemic strategies for dealing with 'strangers', people who fail to embody the values and norms of a given community. The strategy involves 'vomiting the strangers, banishing them from the limits of the orderly world and barring them from all communication with those inside' (Bauman 1997: 18). There are many examples in history of the implementation of anthropoemic strategies by ableist cultures, for example the 'great confinement' of the nineteenth century during which the vast majority of disabled people were 'buried' in 'total institutions'. Exile, exclusion and even the physical annihilation of disabled people are associated with this response to disability.

Anthropophagic: An anthropophagic approach to disability focuses on the elimination of difference through measures that attempt to make it identical to non-disability, that is, to transform the other into the same. The use of prostheses is an example, and the doctrine of rehabilitation embodies the same logic and ethic since it proposes the correction of disability based on the assumption that it is a flawed or deficit identity.

Antisociality: Sometimes referred to as negative theory within queer studies (Halberstam, 2005; Edelman, 2004). Antisociality is a queer critique that aims to decentre positivity, productivity, redemptive politics of affirmation and narratives of success, and politics that are founded on hope for an imagined future. Antisociality aims to disorientate the quest for normalisation and assimilation by siding with the aberrant and celebrating outsiderness and difference.

Ardh Nareshewar: In Hinduism there is the concept of *ardhnarishwar* which means half male, half female.

Autism: It is widely understood as a developmental disorder. People labelled as having autism are considered to share three main areas of difficulty, otherwise known as the 'triad of impairments' (Wing, 1991); these are difficulty with social communication, social interaction and social imagination. In this volume autism is conceptualised as cultural category and as a 'product' with exchange value.

Benchmark man: Coined by Margaret Thornton, legal scholar, the benchmark man is the normative citizen 'who is invariably White, heterosexual, able-bodied, politically conservative, and middle class' (Thornton, 1996: 2). Typically in law there is always a comparator to measure 'reasonableness', or the 'ordinary common' perspective.

Biological essentialism: The essential qualities attributed to disabled people, as analogous to those attributed to women, often turn out to be interpreted as biological in a reductionist way. The branch of post-structuralism as introduced in the chapter takes the risk of essentialism that is an anti-essentialist essentialism, displacing the dichotomy between essentialism and anti-essentialism, unsettling the Cartesian split of body/mind, and challenging essentialism as well as deterministic social constructivism. In this frame of reference, the impaired body implies social, embodied and non-dualistic potential rather than pre-social, inert matter and individual pathology based on binary mind–body interaction.

Biopower: The manner in which persons and problems (e.g. people with intellectual disabilities and challenging behaviour) come to be made in institutional contexts. Biopower focuses on the measurement and management of populations. Techniques of biopower include behavioural and IQ assessments, typologies such as severity of 'challenge' or disability, institutionally defined 'pathways' of mental health problems such as 'psychosis', 'anxiety' and 'dual diagnosis' and so on.

Capital: For Bourdieu, the social world is accumulated history. He states that if the social world is not to be reduced to a discontinuous series of instantaneous mechanical equilibria between agents who are treated as interchangeable particles, one must reintroduce into it the notion of capital (Bourdieu, 1983: 242). And this means capital in all its forms, and not solely in the one form recognised by economic theory. All forms of capital can be accumulated, or lost, from one moment to the next.

Capitalism: It is a type of economic and social system whose underlying principle is the cooperative production of commodities for exchange and profit rather than the immediate subsistence needs of the producers.

Cartesian dualism: It refers to the split made between the mind and the body originating in the neo-classical seventeenth century philosophical works of Rene Descartes. Human subjectivity was deemed to be fundamentally different from the objective world of matter and bodies. The mind was an individual human freedom to be celebrated in contrast to the unruly body and the wild natural world.

Civilising process: Norbert Elias (2000) presents the journey of history from the late medieval period to and through modernity as a 'civilising process', a de-barbarisation of European manners that begins with court society and is taken up, successively by the bourgeoisie and the other 'lower' classes, who in embracing the practices of civil social behaviour, simultaneously circumscribe their own desires and regulate their impulses. Civilisation, therefore, is the process of the strengthening of subjective self-control including the 'proper' comportment of the body. The civilising process creates social distance between the disabled and non-disabled body, constituting the former as an object of repulsion.

Clean and proper body: A term used by Julia Kristeva to indicate a body – ideally masculine – that perceives of itself as orderly, invulnerable and self-contained, failing thus to recognise the mess and abjection that is an integral part of its being. In this volume the 'clean and proper body' refers to the ableist body of modernity and to the 'civilized body' that has been produced by the long march of the 'civilising process'. The 'clean and proper body' is the normative opposite of the disabled body which is marked by mess and abjection and therefore becomes an object of fear, pity and disgust. The 'clean and proper body' lives with the fear that the polluting leakiness of the disabled body might become a source of contamination.

Clinical gaze: In Foucault's *Birth of the Clinic* (1975) he identified the beginning of the clinical gaze towards the end of the eighteenth century and the beginning of the nineteenth century, when physicians started to change their practices of diagnosis from listening to patients stories about their illness to looking-gazing-staring-peering at their bodies for signs of lesions, deformity, abnormality and deviations from the norm. The shift from listening to observing began a process that developed some of the instruments that we associate with the practice of medicine from the stethoscope (a word of Greek origin that means examining the chest) to Magnetic Resonance Imaging (MRI) scan. These technologies of medicine discerned and inscribed on bodies the signs marking out the normal and the abnormal and in doing so objectified bodies (and mind). The clinical gaze and its objectification of the disabled body functions to divert attention-gaze from the socially created disablement of people. Under the clinical gaze people become the sum of their distance from the norm.

Colonialism: It is the process of settling and forming a community in a new locality while simultaneously subjugating or eliminating through negotiation, warfare or genocide the populations that had previously existed in that locality.

Commodification: It is the process by which 'things' are produced, exchanged and consumed through the market for profit rather than for the immediate use by the producer.

Commodity fetishism: A concept Marx appropriated from the study of religion to mean the human capacity to ignore the fact that we create our own material culture and instead treat commodities as though they are 'things' independent of how we think about them.

Community of practice: A group of people who have in common a craft, an interest or a profession. The cognitive anthropologists Jean Lave and Etienne Wenger coined the term in the 1990s and the original work centred on ways in which individuals learnt skills through apprenticeship. Communities of practice are aggregates of people who share communication, beliefs and values. Wenger (1998) defined a community of practice as a group of people uniting to mutually engage in a joint enterprise, who together develop and share a common repertoire of resources.

Constitutional divide: Based on the ideas of Bruno Latour in his book *We Have Never Been Modern* (1993) and adapted by Campbell (2009), this divide picks up on the false division between nature and anti-nature (culture), the normal and that which is an 'unnatural' deviation. The term 'constitutional' points to the inference that such a divide is fixed and of the natural order of things, rather than shifting and context bound.

Contact improvisation: It is an 'improvised movement system based on the communication between two moving bodies and their combined relationship to the physical laws that govern their motion: gravity: momentum: friction and inertia' (Koegler, 1982: 103). The introduction of contact improvisation is generally attributed to Steve Paxton in 1972, a member of the Judson group, New York.

Continental materialism: Deleuze and Guattari represent a strand of continental materialism, a theoretical perspective perceiving inert matter in a vitalist mode. In this frame of reference, matter is taken as intelligent, vital and self-organising. Deleuze and Guattari adopt Foucault's theory, introducing the notion of *biopower* as a binary logic that reduces 'difference' to a disqualified and essentialist phenomenon. Here Deleuze and Guattari's nomadic philosophy inspires a politics of *bio-diversity*, 'a practice of pragmatics where ontology is overthrown, foundations are done away with and endings and beginnings are nullified' (Deleuze and Guattari, 1980: 28).

Critical disability studies: An emerging area of research and practice which revisits many of the traditional tenets of disability studies and draws upon a host of theoretical approaches ranging from phenomenology to poststructuralism. One area of focus is that of impairment. Critical disability studies takes up the challenge of impaired bodies to highlight the limits of the straight body, calling into question 'the "givenness" of the "natural body" ... conceptualized as as bodies of interconnection and production ... Disabled bodies expand and envelope in exciting ways ... offering us critical languages for denaturalising impairment' (Goodley, 2011: 159).

Cultural imperialism: It is a term used across a range of disciplines and discourses but broadly refers to a pattern of inherited colonial practices and attitudes that continues to support the economic domination of the Global South by the Global North.

Cultural model of disability: It was employed by Garland-Thomson (2002: 2), who posits that disability is a cultural trope and historical community that raises questions about the materiality of the body and the social formulations that are used to interpret bodily and cognitive differences. This approach emerged particularly in North America and Canada from the 1970s onwards.

Cyborg: The word comes from the joining of cyb[ernetic] + org[anism] and was first coined during the US space research programme in the 1960s to describe the integration of cybernetic mechanisms into living beings. Science fiction and literature was quick to use the figure of the cyborg and to widen its definition; at the start of the twenty-first century many of us are 'cyborg' given the proliferation of technology within everyday life whether it be using an iPod or mobile phone, as well as those who live more intimately with technology in the form of replacement joints or insulin pumps.

Defetishisation: It is the process by which we acknowledge our denial of our role in the creation of material culture and work through the consequences of that acknowledgement.

Depo-Provera: It is a contraceptive that is administered by injection. There are serious risks and effects including loss of bone density, weight gain and depression. Disabled women, particularly women with intellectual disabilities, are given this drug, often without their informed consent.

Disability I: It is 'the disadvantage or restriction of activity caused by a contemporary social organisation which takes no account of people who have physical impairments *and or learning difficulties* and thus excludes them from mainstream social activities' (italics added, UPIAS, 1976: 3–4).

Disability II: For Garland-Thomson (2002: 5) dis/ability is best understood as a sign system that, by differentiating and marking bodies and minds, produces dis/abled-bodies and maintains the ideal of the inherently stable non-disabled body or mind.

Disability III: It speaks of society: being disabled is not simply a descriptor of an object – a person with a cane – but 'a social process that intimately involves everyone who has a body and lives in the world of senses' (Davis, 1995: 2).

Disability IV: For Ghai (2006: 147) disability refers to bodies that have become dis-embodied because of constructions around them that create a total invisibility of the disabled individual. Society discriminates against disabled people when it becomes disablist. Disablism occurs when disabled people experience or are subjected to discrimination.

Disability studies: For Garland-Thomson (2002) disability studies is a matrix of theories, pedagogies and practices.

Disablism: A concept defined by Thomas (2007: 73) as 'a form of social oppression involving the social imposition of restrictions of activity on people with impairments and the socially engendered undermining of their psycho-emotional well being'. *Disablement* captures the consequences of disablism (Oliver, 1990).

Disabled Peoples' Organisations (DPOs): They are organisations with a majority of disabled people in their membership and managing board whose objectives are to further the rights and equality of disabled people. DPOs subscribe to the social model of disability and are committed to the human rights of disabled people. DPOs work for the empowerment of disabled people either implicitly or explicitly and provide a range of activities. These are typically community based such as advice, advocacy, representation, research, policy development, campaigning, inclusive design and other initiatives.

Disavowal: The simultaneous contradictory act of staring at something while staring through. Disabled people often experience cultural disavowal by ableist society. That is to say, they are stared at and stared through, loved and hated and prompt reactions of fear and fascination. These contradictory processes have been theorised specifically through psychoanalytic theories.

Discipline: It is a Foucauldian concept that captures the regulation of subjects by power. Discipline operates by means of shaping the subjects actions employing, for example, hierarchies, physical spaces, routines and timetables and operating 'internally' by encouraging persons to subject themselves to normalising judgements – to engage in self surveillance.

Discourse I: It is a system of representation and signifiers, where rules and practices apply to set the tone and detail of what, and how topics and concepts, can be constructed. This includes the written and spoken words, but also other signs, forms and mediums of expression, such as the body or a map. However, language is not to be taken as value neutral, nor merely a linguistic concept, but rather considered as a form of social action and knowledge practice (Foucault, 1972). Discourse provides a way of speaking and knowing things through language. For Foucault power and knowledge are expressed through discourse.

Discourse II: Discourses are sets of statements, images, meanings, practices, metaphors, technical terms and so on that produce versions of the world and its objects (such as 'intellectual disabilities', 'challenging behaviour', 'IQ', 'adaptive behaviour' and so on). Discourses regulate what can be known and by whom. Foucault was particularly interested in the discourses of professional and technical communities and the ways in which these versions of the world come to be dominant in the shaping of subjectivities.

Docile bodies: These are bodies to be 'subjected, used, transformed and improved' (Foucault, 1977: 136). These are the bodies that have been 'successfully' disciplined and will not cause trouble for others in a hierarchy.

Dramaturgical approach: It is the metaphor employed by Goffman to describe the situation of persons in social life in his book *The Presentation of Self Everyday Life* (1959). Social life is viewed as possessing actors, audiences, front and back stage areas and so on. Life is always lived in the co-presence of others who must be managed.

Emancipatory disability research: It is an approach to research which emphasises the role of disabled people and their representative organisations as *co-researchers* producing knowledge that is built in the name of the progressive overcoming of oppression.

Embodiment: The recognition that the body is not simply a fleshy object but instead exists as a thinking/sensing subject at the intersection of the corporeal, social and cultural. Within disability studies this concept is used to explore the ways in which impairment is socially and historically mediated (see, for example, the discussion about a sociology of impairment advocated by Paterson and Hughes, 1999).

Empathic attunement: It is the capacity to recognise, understand and be responsive to another's emotional state.

Empiricism: It is a tradition developed in philosophy in the eighteenth century that emphasises a focus on evidence in the formation of ideas. It germinated in the work of Francis Bacon and grew through the deliberations of Hume, Locke and J. S. Mill. It had a powerful influence on British social science in the nineteenth and twentieth centuries. At a cultural level it can manifest itself as anti-intellectualism, a practical approach to the world in which the danger of too much thought and analysis leads to paralysis and inaction.

Enfreakment: The abrogation of a person's humanity by identifying them solely with their 'deformity' and exploiting that 'deformity' as a spectacle or entertainment for the pleasure and repulsion of others whose humanity is vindicated by the social distance created between them as observers and the dehumanised and tarnished objects of their gaze.

Facticity: Martin Heidegger used this term to describe a feature that is ascribed to all things in the world, including people. It is this feature of facticity that allows us to recognise all things as existing in actuality. For example, someone may write a book and, after being written, the book takes on its own integrity, it becomes a thing in itself, separate even from its author.

The family: It is for Fanon (1993: 149) the 'nation's workshop in which one is trained'. The family provides the context for the development of the child and their encounters with others.

Feminisation of poverty: It refers to the global situation whereby women are more likely to be in poverty than men. Women are more likely to experience not only income and material poverty, but also time poverty, overwork and broader unequal gender relations.

Field: Bourdieu represents the objective world as field. Field is defined as, 'a network, or a configuration, of objective relations between positions objectively defined' (Bourdieu and Wacquant, 1992: 72–3).

Frame/framework: This term derives from the work of Erving Goffman on frame analysis. Our knowledge and opinions about the world and the ways in which we experience it are possible only because we see the world within particular frames. If sunshine and warm weather frames our understanding of a beautiful day, for example, we will then judge a day to be beautiful or not within this frame. By examining the frameworks through which we experience the world, we can come to a better understanding of how it is that we come to know what we know, and to experience what we experience.

The game: Bourdieu conceptualises the accumulation, or loss, of power and influence in the language of the game (Bourdieu, 1979). This reflects his belief that the location of power and influence within human activity is relational, and in a constant state of flux and change.

Gender: It is not simply about biology and sexuality. It is socially reproduced in daily activities where we learn our gender identity. The sexual order of gender has generally meant that men are more powerful and seen as superior to women. There is societal pressure to conform to our assigned gender, but not all human beings are comfortable with their assigned gender or sex and sometimes seek to change. The concept of transgender or transsexuality has come into common usage for such individuals.

Gender roles: The behaviours, attributes and mannerisms that are associated with being a man or a woman. These are learnt through the socialisation process and are central in all societies. Examples of traditional roles for women are caregiving and nurturing.

Genealogy: The creation of discourses (science, intellectual disabilities) via the operations of power. When traced these – Foucault demonstrated – will show a history of accident and circumstance rather than progress via ordered rationality.

Geodisability knowledge: A concept developed by (Campbell, 2011) to denote mobile knowledge systems of disablement that can traverse cultures and national borders. Reductionist definitions and schemas of impairment result in a global push for a *universal definition of disability* and disability coding.

Global South: The term clearly delineates a divide with the Global North, and hence with rich and powerful countries, where wealth is largely concentrated and controlled, and which exert influence and power over the South, a power that is a function of and manifest in history (e.g. in colonial appropriations), ideologies, economics and politics among others. The term does not refer only to geography, but economic, political and social disadvantage and disparities, with the implication that the existence of a poor Global South is reflected in and maintained by the existence of the rich North and vice-versa. The South, like the majority world, is denoted here as a space that exists not only physically but also ontologically as something separate to the Global North or the minority world. This is space where the bulk of the world's population resides, and where poverty is largely concentrated.

Governmentality: Activities that attempt to shape the actions of persons. Power produces discourses that are internalised by subjects who learn how to govern themselves. For example, the discourse 'vulnerable' guides those in human services to engage in surveillance of those with the label of intellectual disability who are then likely to be incapable of self-surveillance/governmentality.

Habitus: This is a description of the individual entity's internal make up, what Bourdieu calls their savoir faire. This can include several aspects of an entity, including its internal workings, and how and what it does and its public face.

Haeccity: Thisness, an occurrence or happening as noted by Phillip Goodchild.

Hierarchies of impairment: These are the culturally informed rankings of different impairments by status: for example, people with acquired impairments are seen as being higher up the list than those born with impairments, those with cognitive impairments are ranked beneath those with a spinal cord injury. These hierarchies can have a direct influence on the treatment of disabled people by others; for example an employer might be more willing to employ someone with a missing limb than someone with a learning difficulty, people with mental health problems experience more disablist hate crime than those with mobility impairments.

Human trafficking: A phenomenon that exists across the globe where people are abducted and transferred to other countries often for the purpose of sexual or other exploitation, such as begging. Children and women are most at risk and they are often powerless to seek help.

Hybridity I: Offers a way out of essentialist thinking (either/or) and instead allows for the possibility of mixing or blurring boundaries. While most commonly associated with postcolonial theory, this term is often linked to discussions of subjectivity which better represent the fluid ways in which people move between different subject positions (see also Goodley, 2011: 167–71).

Hybridity II: Bhabha's notion of hybridity stems from his interpretation of the colonial situation, in which colonisers and colonised stand not in a separate, oppositional relationship, but in a more complex, mutually influential and deformative relationship.

*i*Crip: This concept invented by Donna Reeve is derived from the reclaimed Crip word (McRuer, 2006) which describes the ways in which impaired bodies and minds exceed the bounds of compulsory able-bodiedness, allowing for hitherto unimagined ways of being and doing. The prefix 'i' in *i*Crip is a shorthand notation for technology (as in iPod and iLimb) and is used in conjunction with Crip as a metaphor for the twenty-first century impaired cyborg which has the potential to destabilise the disabled/non-disabled binary. See also **cyborg**.

The imaginary phase: Lacanian perspective on child development between six and 18 months, where the child starts the process of seeing herself as a separate entity, a self that is distinct from others around her. The child sees her self in the mirror and becomes captivated by it. As well as seeing herself, she notices significant distinct others (often the mother). The child recognises an image of herself as fixed, frozen, whole and unitary. This is an image of her body that contrasts markedly with the body she is living with in the real (see real phase). The child therefore commits a misrecognition: they are transfixed by an image that is no more than a fantasy of wholeness. Ableist society upholds this fantasy of the *imaginary* autonomous, self-sufficient, whole-functioning citizen.

Impairment: According to the Union of the Physically Impaired Against Segregation (UPIAS, 1976: 3–4): Impairment – lacking part of or all of a limb, or having a defective limb organism or mechanism of the body.

Impairment effects: Thomas defines this as the 'restrictions of bodily activity and behaviour that are *directly attributable* to bodily variations designated "impairments" rather than to those *imposed upon* people *because* they have designated impairments (disablism)' (Thomas, 2007: 136, emphasis in original). This allows for recognition of the direct impact that impairment can have on daily life, without detracting from discussions about the realities of living with disablism.

Impersonal or pre-individual singularities: The essence of life. They provide the materiality for the self. But within the constitution of the self, the vagueness of life is sacrificed in the name of certitude and identity. By shifting the focus from the self or person to that of pre-individual or impersonal singularities in their vagueness, it is hoped to open new possibilities for life.

Institutional ethnography: Defined by Dorothy Smith (2005) as an approach to research which had a number of aims: to expose wider social relations that shape people's lives; to view members of an institution as expert knowers; to use lived experience of individuals to throw light onto systems that impact, describe and inform their lives; to access the perspectives of those often excluded from dominant discussions of policy and society; to unpick the philosophies that underpin an institution or organisation; to look at how people's activities contribute to the maintenance of that organisation.

Interactionist/symbolic interactionism: A sociological theory focusing on the meaning making activities of interactants.

Integrated dance: A dance genre that comprises dancers with and without disabilities performing together. The movement system most frequently utilised by such companies is contact improvisation. *Axis* in San Francisco and London-based *Candoco* are both internationally recognised companies that comprise dancers with and without physical disabilities.

Interpersonal synchrony: When two people simultaneously adjust their attention and stimulation in response to their partner's signals. In infancy, the primary caregiver and child interact in this way in a pattern of attention/inattention, as each adjusts to the other's signals. This process of communication happens in milliseconds and is the basis of social interaction. The concept is widely used within psychotherapy, especially when discussing the development of attachment between infant/primary caregiver.

Interstitial: Comes from the Latin 'interstitium' which was derived from 'inter' meaning 'between' and 'sistere' meaning 'to stand' = to stand between.

Life stories: An approach to research which assumes that storytelling is a feature of everyday life, thus enabling individuals to make sense of their life through story. Life stories therefore have a personal quality (they say something of an individual life) but also public quality (they reveal social, cultural, political, economic and historical backgrounds that frame individual lives).

Lifeworld/Lebenswelt: Lifeworld is the way in which Edmund Husserl describes the everyday world in which we live. We live in the world, but in order to do so, we must assume that there is a world in which to live. The world we assume to undoubtedly exist is the lifeworld.

Looping I: '[A]n agency that creates a defensive response on the part of the inmate takes this very response as the target of its next attack. The individual finds that his protective response to an assault upon self is collapsed into the situation; he cannot defend himself in the usual way by establishing distance between the mortifying situation and himself' (Goffman, 1968: 41).

Looping II: Human kinds for Hacking are interactive kinds that involve looping. Human sciences produce or constitute individuals – their identities – as they engage in discovering them.

Mahabharata: The world's longest epic poem (110,00 verses) about the Mahabharata (Great Indian) War that took place about three thousand years ago. The *Mahabharata* also includes the Bhagavad Gita, the most popular sacred text of Hinduism.

Maps: Titchkosky (2003) uses maps, as a representation of and guide to the world, to describe the disability experience. While society normally maps disability through categories, interactions and statistics, she argues that rarely is disability seen to offer anything else beyond these details. These maps are commonly used by professionals from many disciplines to seek out spaces for intervention and to remedy deviance.

Minority model of disability: The view that the sociocultural formations of disability place disabled people in minority positions akin to the experiences of women, people of colour, and the gay, lesbian, bi- and trans-community. This approached emerged in North America in the 1970s.

Modernism: Typically traced to the period in which culture moved from the so-called Dark Ages of medievalism (characterised by an unquestioning adherence to totalitarian royal or religious decree) to the Enlightenment (promising the bounded and sacred sanctuary of the mind, autonomous capacities and the beginnings of systematic human science) (see Gergen, 2001: 803–4).

Mortification: For Goffman, the process of stripping the individual of his non-institutional self and the creation of a new institutionally determined self. A variety of techniques are employed in the total institution to achieve this effect.

Narcissism: Put simply, selfish or self-preoccupation with one's own importance or predicament. A psychology of narcissism asserts that disabled people are exemplary narcissists. In not being able to be cured, disabled people turn away from love of others towards themselves in a neurotic, disengaged form of self-gratification. Alternatively one could argue that capitalist relations are essentially a narcissistic obsession with continual self-enhancement.

Natural attitude: Alfred Schutz invokes the natural attitude as a way to show how people approach, orient to, the world. We approach the world as if it is naturally there and we do so with an attitude that seems just as natural as is the world. The natural attitude allows us to approach the world without questioning its existence.

Neo-colonial: The term neo-colonial, perhaps to a much greater degree than postcolonial, stresses that colonialism has not ended; many of the 'old' mechanisms of domination and subjugation not only remain, but are perpetuated and recreated through contemporary forms of discursive and material imperialism, and which critically serve to maintain the neo-colonising relationship between the metropole and the periphery. In this chapter, the term is used in line with and supporting the critique by Latin American theorists (see for example Coronil, 2000, 2008) insisting that postcolonial theory, while focused on the experience of colonialism, remains substantially disengaged from the continuing aftermath of the colonial encounter, contemporary or post 'independence' imperialism and associated political, cultural and economic domination, the neo-colonial. As Coronil (2008: 415) emphasises, this may be triggered by the postcolonial studies' obsession with recollecting colonialism 'rather than its eventualities'.

Nordic relational model of disability: It approaches the study of disability with three main assumptions: (i) disability is a person-environment mis/match; (ii) disability is situational or contextual and (iii) disability is relative. This approach has emerged in the Nordic countries over the last three decades and has been influential on recent global reports on disability including the World Health Organisation's 2011 *World Report on Disability*.

Nomadic subjectivity: What is at stake in Deleuze and Guattari's theory is the subject as becoming, perceiving the raw materials of existence as a nomadic distribution of being, as a social and political process ontology. Here, the 'real', the 'body' and 'materiality' are terms opened up to their becomings, to the temporal forces of endless change (Grosz, 2005). Rosi Braidotti provides a theoretical elimination of the materiality of the body by cross-reading Deleuze and Guattari's nomadism with the late psychoanalytic work of Luce Irigaray. She suggests a new figuration of layered, embodied subjectivity as a set of differences.

Nomadic theory: For Gilles Deleuze, nomadic thought represents a form of critical consciousness that resists settled, hegemonic patterns of thought. Nomadism is central to contemporary post-structuralist and feminist theories. Rosi Braidotti, adopting Deleuze's nomadic epistemology, employs this to describe the nomadic character of feminist theory. Nomadism can be used as a metaphor of travel in disability theory as well, as the concept affords opportunities to go beyond monologic modes of thought, disrupting linearity, fixity and biological essentialism.

Normative shadows: They, like all shadows, travel among us. They are seductive as norms we are supposed to achieve. And yet the brass ring of normality is forever beyond our grasp. Ableness perpetuates this myth of normality. Simultaneously, these normative shadows perpetuate disablism by constantly reminding disabled people of what they 'lack' due to impairments. The reason I use the concept of shadows is that in a material sense they are not real but still leave us with a sense of uneasiness when startled by them. Like all shadows, you cannot grasp them nor can you separate yourself from them. They are simultaneously everywhere and nowhere.

Ontological invalidation: To undermine the humanity of a person, specifically the social, cultural, economic and emotional processes that create the view that a disabled life is not worth living and that a disabled existence is what not to be. Invalidation refers to the social processes of othering that 'spoil' the identity of disabled people by undermining their credibility and worth and to the processes that constitute the misrecognition of disabled people as flawed, abject, anomalous and lacking moral virtue to the point that their very humanity is questioned.

Organic intellectuals: Antonio Gramsci's view that intellectual thought can be found not simply in the academy but in the acts and words of everyone, particularly those involved in revolutionary or subversive activities. We are all intellectuals; we are all philosophers; we all do theory.

Other/otherness: The non-normate, the marginalised characterised by negatively valued differences from acceptable characteristics such being 'white', able to walk unaided, male and so on. Those made other may have their voices silenced and experience disempowerment. In an oppositional construction of identities, 'Other' becomes a way of designating the identity which is not the dominant one nor the one doing the designating.

Othering: This is one process by which binary divisions between people are created and maintained. Originally the term came from postcolonial theory to show how imperialism was founded on the 'natural' distinction between the civilised coloniser and the savage colonised. Within disability studies 'Othering' is used to describe the process which separates 'the disabled' from an imaginary non-disabled population, the 'abnormal' from the 'normal'. In order to maintain the illusion of the invulnerable autonomous subject, unwanted fears about mortality, dying and physicality are projected onto disabled people (the Other) who are seen as being in need of cure/rehabilitation to become 'normal' or otherwise banished (see Shakespeare, 1994).

Pedestrian Movement: This style of dancing is based on everyday movement and does not require technical skill. It emerged in the early 1970s within the postmodern dance movement, through the work of choreographers such as Yvonne Rainer and Anna Halprin.

Panopticonal gaze: A theoretical lens based on the work of Michel Foucault (1977) and the penal system. The panopticon gaze, based on Jeremy Bentham's architectural designs for a new prison, promotes the idea of a silent, unknown overseer that subconsciously controlled all aspects of life. Furthermore, as the Watched do not know whether they are being observed or scrutinised, they in turn modify their behaviour (become their own overseers) just in case they are being monitored.

Phallus: The phallus denotes codes of behaviour and social laws, originally played out in the cultural microcosm of the family, that reflect wider demands of patriarchal societies. Moral status is conferred through entrance into the symbolic, in similar ways to the emergence of the superego in Freudian theory, in which psychical inventions of the phallus attempt to deny the threat posed to the subject by the jouissance of the other. The phallus lays the foundations for other ideologies including the heteronormative, occidental, capitalist and the able.

Phenomenology: A descriptive methodology to study the grounds of the appearance of any phenomenon. A way to interrogate how what appears, appears; how experience is experienced, by revealing the natural attitude that takes-for-granted our participation in the achievement of social reality. Maurice Merleau-Ponty suggests that this is a radical form of reflection on the sensibility of the world, that it is not a new philosophy but a method of encountering the unbreakable intertwining of self/world, subject/object, sense/sensibility.

Politics of representation: It is tied to both speaking for and about representing others. For disabled people this is problematic and troublesome. 'Nothing about us, without us' has been the rallying cry of the disability movement and thus both what is known about disability and who has power over disabled people has been an ethical, moral and political issue.

Postcolonialism: The term that points out a range of practices in social and literary criticism that address the Third World, its relationship to the West, and the results and consequences of modern colonialism.

Post-structuralism and psychoanalysis: This branch of post-structuralism is associated with the work of Michel Foucault and Gilles Deleuze. Besides, it is post-Lacanian psychoanalysis mediated by French feminism and associated with the work of Irigaray which is influential as a key actor in the making of post-structuralism. Rosi Braidotti has made innovative use of these theories to provide a feminist account of subjectivities in society, arguing for the possibilities of the symbolic and the imaginary.

Poverty: Poverty is extremely hard to define in particular because it involves numerous value judgements, for example around 'deprivation' or 'well being'. It is also the subject of and can be analysed through a range of epistemological standpoints and disciplines, for example, development, philosophy, economics along others. As Riddell (2004) highlights, apart from the agreement that poverty is a problem and needs to be dealt with, a number of disagreements persist: what constitutes poverty; the unit of focus (individuals, families or households); the importance of different dimensions (e.g. material, social or psychological aspects); the causes; who should decide what poverty consists of; and how it should be understood temporally. Amidst the disagreements, though, there seems to be sufficient consensus in particular around the notion that no single dimension can account for the comprehensive aspects of poverty. Poverty is therefore said to be multidimensional (see for example, Lister, 2004) and is not simply about lack of income and consumption, but incorporates a range of social, political, psychological and a myriad of other dimensions that importantly allow for and differ according to subjective understandings.

Power: For Foucault, power is a productive and shared resource, operating across the realm of social life, ever persistent in the transmission of knowledge forms and regimes of truth. Neither is it only negative, seeking to control, but can be reformative, generating pleasurable alternatives. Foucault further asserted certain types of power, such as biopower and disciplinary power (see Foucault, 1972, 1975, 1976). Biopower is a technology, emerging in the late eighteenth century, for managing populations, by the surveillance and record keeping of our births, deaths, reproduction and dysfunction. Disciplinary power is the mechanism or training of the actions of bodies to produce and regulate desired behaviours, through the construction of particular space, time and structure.

Power/knowledge: Foucault's (1982) power/knowledge axis creates categories of people, ascribes identities to these categories and formulates laws about who can and cannot be recognised as a member of this or that category. Power produces these relations via the recruitment and complicity of all – those in dominant and subjugated positions – and it is this complicity that creates the conflict-resistance. That is why resistance is always a possibility.

Psychoanalysis: A method of therapy which explores the unconscious; a theory of personality and, for our purposes, a set of concepts, theories and stories which allow us to make sense of society and its major institutions. Psychoanalysis is engaged with subjectivity: who we are, where we came from and where we might go. For Butler (1993) psychoanalysis allows one to rearticulate symbolic legitimacy: to seek dis-identification with the regulated, normed and secured schemas of normative society to revise the world.

Psychoanalytic concepts: Concepts such as the unconscious, the ego, repression, Oedipus complex, projection, denial are a common part of everyday parlance, while the practices of psychoanalysis – confession, dreamwork, sublimation, therapy and the couch – are to be found in cultural practices across the globe.

The psyche: A cultural artefact of contemporary society that individualises social problems. Individual, medical, bio-psychological, traditional, charity and moral models of disability locate social problems in the heads and bodies – the psyches – of (disabled) people. This leads to the commonly held view that disabling society is not the problem: the disabled individual is. In contrast, the psyche can be acknowledged as a complex tightened knot of the person and the social word, the self and other people, the individual and society. At the heart of this is the internalised experience of disablism: oppression is felt both psychically, subjectively and emotionally but is always socially, cultural, politically and economically produced. Questions are raised, then, not simply about 'the disabled psyche' but, more importantly, about 'the non-disabled psyche'.

Psycho-emotional disablism: This refers to the forms of social oppression which undermine the psycho-emotional well-being of people with impairments (Thomas, 2007: 73) and are barriers to *being* rather than *doing* (structural disablism), for example, the experience of being stared at or made the butt of jokes, being treated like a child rather than an adult, being treated as a lesser being simply because of the presence of impairment. Another important form of psycho-emotional disablism is that of internalised oppression when someone internalises the negative images and low expectations of disabled people that exist in society; for example, a disabled person may assume they cannot become a parent because of the image of disabled people as asexual and in need of care by others. These are the more 'private' forms of oppression experienced by people with impairments and while not excluded from a social model analysis of disability, are nonetheless often overlooked.

Psychogenesis: It refers to the processes of social change that impact on personality structure and to how these are shaped by and intertwine with wider social processes (sociogenesis). In other words Elias traces the process of modern state formation from medieval times to the present (sociogenesis) and links it to the growth of forms of emotional control (psychogenesis). As our social world becomes more rational, we become less spontaneous, less emotionally volatile and develop a greater sense of self-control. The modern self is formed as a consequence of its role in the process of internalising norms of control in the form of manners, rules of hygiene and other behavioural codes related to ways of dressing, eating, sleeping and other practices of the body. In modernity, the physical self becomes a shameful thing, a source of embarrassment that requires constant vigilance. Shame and embarrassment provide the emotional basis for distance between people, for what Elias calls 'individualisation'. Selfhood is the product of the affects (or emotions) being directed at the development of inhibitions, of making our-selves separate from one another. The prohibitions that surround bodily self-management become important in sustaining the boundaries of self and other. In fact, they provide the 'wall of affect' that legitimates the aloof, self-contained personality that has become the legitimate form of self presentation in the contemporary West.

Purification: Following Latour (1993), it refers to a categorical process that creates the fiction of distinct differences between things and bodies. I like the notion of purifying because it points to getting rid of the blemishes, cleaning up and creating clarity about categories. Purification is fundamental to the government of disability which relies on clear distinctions between wellness and disability.

Prakriti: From Sanskrit language, means 'nature'.

Purusha: In some lineages of Hinduism, *Purusha* (Sanskrit 'puruṣa') is 'Cosmic man'. In Sutra literature also called *puṃs* ('man') it is the 'Self' which pervades the universe.

Queer: Often conceived of as anti-identity. Queer, while originating from theory about gay, lesbian and transgendered people, is used to designate blurring, fluidity and gender ambivalence. Hence, queer easily extends to other kindred forms of ontological and corporeal aberrancies and ambiguities (such as disability).Queering disability enables an examination of disability as an affirmative and leaky state of being and incorporates cultural notions of disability.

Ramayana: It is the shorter of Hinduism's two great epics and is traditionally attributed to Valmiki, but scholars have shown that it is the result of multiple authors. Consisting of about 20,000 stanzas, it is the story about the exile of Prince Rama from his kingdom, the abduction of his wife, Sita, by a demon, her eventual rescue, and finally Rama's eventual restoration to the throne.

The real phase: A Lacanian view of the first six months of a child's life where they are at one with their primary caregiver which is more often than not the mother. There is no sense of separation of the child's world from that of others. The child is a psychic scrambled egg: anarchically and chaotically organised (Grosz, 1999: 268). They are a mass of turbulent movements, of sprawling limbs or desiring entity; gazing and being gazed at, touching and being touched. What they see is simply themselves and what they want is what they desire. This is a time filled with fulfilling desires, a times of pure jouissance.

Reciprocity of perspectives: Alfred Schutz coined this term in order to demonstrate how we take the perspectives of others into account within our own perspectives. We assume that people will share the same perspective we do if they were in our position and that we would assume their perspective if we were in their position. Moreover, we assume that everyone assumes this, and this is one of the ways that people are able to communicate with one another.

Resistance I: Power can be subverted and reclaimed into positions of resistance that rework oppression and create everyday opportunities for equality and liberation to emerge. Contrary to the nihilist criticism Foucault receives, this suggests that no matter how powerful or oppressive a system maybe, it can be resisted.

Resistance II: For Foucault, power is ubiquitous and produces social reality – through competing discourses there is an ongoing struggle and resistance is always possible.

Signs: As the basic unit of language the sign is made up of a signifier (word or symbol) and signified (meaning). The signified (meaning) of a sign is understood 'only because of the relationship between two or more signifiers (words or symbols)' (Eagleton, 1983: 127). Hence, we could say that the sign 'disabled' gathers meaning through its contrasting meaning with the sign 'abled'.

Situated knowledge: The situated nature of learning described by the communities of practice framework (see above) challenges the traditional supremacy attributed to academic learning and appreciates the knowledge of ordinary people in everyday contexts. Indeed, situated knowledge (the idea that knowledge cannot be solely an individual product) has a clear parallel in disability theory where marginality and liminality can often exclude or minimise access to traditional learning contexts.

Social constructionism: The meta-theoretical position that knowledge is socially constructed, that is, it is tied to cultural and historical social processes. It is an anti-essentialist position in that knowledge of the world is not to be found in the supposed essences of things or people but rather in the social processes of knowledge construction. To seek understanding of intellectual disabilities and challenging behaviour, this approach points towards the contexts of construction of these categories of human life and not 'inside' persons themselves.

Social model of disability: An approach developed in British disability studies which focuses attention on the material barriers of everyday life that oppress and marginalise people with impairments and thus deny them opportunities to participate in mainstream life.

Social theory: Harrington (2005), in discussing the etymology of social theory, locates the origins within ancient Greek culture, in enabling them to make sense of lives and question meanings. Social theory is also aimed at praxis. *Theoria* for the Greeks was about 'contemplation', reflecting on observation and experience, in other words, ways of making sense of the world, reaching out through reason to the juicy fruit of 'truth'.

Sociogenesis: 'Civilization' is the process of change that simultaneously transforms the social and the emotional. Sociogenesis refers to the macro processes of change that occur at the level of culture and state formation. Elias is fascinated by the link between sociogenesis and psychogenesis or the way in which culture and personality develop such that they collude and become enmeshed. Indeed, one of the central messages of the 'civilising process' is contained in the thesis that personality structure (psychogenesis) and sociopolitical structure (sociogenesis) develop through mutual intertwinement and the rationalisation of the state and individual emotional restraint go hand in hand.

Stigma: For Goffman, a stigma refers to a visible or invisible personal attribute that brings moral discredit to the bearer. In this sense a stigma is a relational process, the stigma is an attribute of the bearer, but he or she is stigmatised by others. The bearer does not have to accept the stigma; however there may be a social cost to such resistance.

Structural disablism: This refers to the forms of social oppression which restrict the *activities* of people with impairments (Thomas, 2007: 73): for example, exclusion from the built environment, lack of employment opportunities, segregation in special schools and other acts of discrimination. These reflect the traditional barriers identified by a social model of disability approach and are the more 'public' forms of oppression experienced by people with impairments.

Subaltern I: Spivak insists this is not 'just a classy word for oppressed, for the Other, for somebody who's not getting a piece of the pie'. She points out that in Gramsci's original usage, it signified 'proletarian', whose voice could not be heard, being structurally written out of the capitalist bourgeois narrative.

Subaltern II: Meaning 'of inferior rank', it is a term adopted by Antonio Gramsci to refer to those groups in society who are subject to the hegemony of the ruling classes. Subaltern classes may include peasants, workers and other groups denied access to 'hegemonic' power. 'The history of the capitalist ruling class is realised in the state and history is the story of dominant groups'.

Subject: The use of the term allows the intimation of the subjective sense of self as well as pointing towards the ways in which the self is also subject to discourses of which it is constituted.

Subject position: Discourses provide locations to speak and act from. These subject positions have rights and obligations associated with them – for example, 'man', 'woman', 'child', 'staff', 'therapist', 'service user', person 'with challenging behaviour' and so on. We will occupy multiple positions and we can – but may fail – to resist and occupy positions and their associated affordances and constraints.

Subjectivity: Within the realm of philosophy and psychology, it is a much-debated concept. However it can refer to judgements based on individual senses, interpretations, personal impressions and opinions rather than external phenomena. Subjectivity is always associated with the self.

Surveillance: Michel Foucault described the ways in which modern societies use forms of disciplinary power to classify and documents individuals, placing them under continuous forms of surveillance. As well as surveillance by a host of professionals, such as doctors, teachers and employers, people also undergo self-surveillance, changing their behaviour to match expectations and norms.

The symbolic phase: According to Lacan, it appears between a year and a half and four years of life (Parker, 1997: 215). The child is thrown into the disorientating world of words where they are expected to speak of themselves and others as human subjects. The symbolic includes spoken, written and visual discourses. Where the imaginary permitted a distinction of one's self from an other, the symbolic phase allows the child to speak of this separation – of 'I', 'you' and 'them' – in an order outside the child. This phase is where the child begins the process of enculturation. The symbolic recognises the cultural, linguistic and discursive shaping and alienation of the self.

Taken-for-granted: This term was introduced into the scholarly literature by Harold Garfinkel. He used this term to depict the activity that members of society employ to ensure that they share a sense of the world in common with one another. This shared sense of world between us, or the facticity of a reality, is reliant upon not noticing the achieved sense of social reality.

Temporal/temporality: Denotes ways of talking about and conceptualising 'time'. Time can be linear, cyclical or involve the past, present and future merging into one. Temporality in the West is often viewed teleologically (the idea that history is progressively improving and moving forward). Anti-social queer theory points out that much of societal thinking is based on the notion of futurity.

Tentative or provisional disability: Unlike sexed or raced positionalities, disability is never permanently validated within ableist relations. Firstly, disability involves an evaluative ranking between and within impairment categories and such ranking often determines access to goods and services, legal protections and (medical) technologies. Second, social inclusion is provisional to the extent that an impairment might be nullified or evacuated once a cure or 'preventative' technology is developed. Disability *ipso facto* is seen as harm.

Threshold of repugnance: A term used by Elias to indicate that the march of the civilising process entails a narrowing of norms of bodily comportment and emotional display. The impact of the process on disabled people is negative and demeaning since those who do not appear to have control over their affects or their bodies must of necessity become the flotsam and jetsam of the civilising process. In other words the civilising process cannot be separated from the 'cultivation' of incivility towards disabled people. Psychogenic processes of affect and bodily management transform disabled people into objects of repulsion creating emotional, moral and social distance between disabled and non-disabled people.

Total institution: For Goffman, a place where the separation of various aspects of a person's life, for example, work and social and/or familial life, are collapsed into an all encompassing, dominating social space. Goffman describes the characteristics of the total institution as concerning such spaces where all the activities of daily life are carried out, where the activities of 'inmates' are timetabled, where inmates are placed alongside others assigned to the same or similar categories: all of this having the purpose of realising the goals of the institution.

Transgression: The crossing or violation of perceived boundaries or dichotomies. This is a key aspect of the cyborg figure which arises from the crossing of boundaries such as human/animal, animate/inanimate, human/machine. See also **hybridity**.

Transvalutive turn: Nietzschean concept: simply a re-evaluation. For example, within the binary of good and evil Nietzsche analysed the negative aspects of the concept of good and the positive aspects of the concept of evil to eventually get beyond the dialectic of good and evil. In the same manner, I analyse the negative aspects of the concept of being a person with its personal registry and consider the positive aspects of 'impairments' within an impersonal registry.

Index

Page numbers followed by 'n' denotes notes.

CPI Antony Rowe
Chippenham, UK
2018-11-07 10:12